Bobby Fischer Rediscovered

New updated, expanded and re-analyzed edition

Andrew Soltis

First published in 2003
Second revised edition published in the United Kingdom in 2020 by
Batsford
43 Great Ormond Street
London
WC1N 3HZ

An imprint of Pavilion Books Company Ltd.

ISBN 9781849946063

A CIP catalogue record for this book is available from the
British Library.

25 24 23 22 21 20
10 9 8 7 6 5 4 3 2 1

Printed by CPI Group (UK) Ltd

This book can be ordered direct from the publisher at the website:
www.pavilionbooks.com, or try your local bookshop.

Contents

Author's Note

Nearly a decade after Bobby Fischer won the world chess championship – and then disappeared – he was living secretly in San Francisco. For months in 1981 he was the house guest of Grandmaster Peter Biyiasas and his wife Ruth Haring a few blocks north of Golden Gate Park. Fischer felt he was living underground, freed from the public attention he said he hated. Fischer had developed a deep interest in all things Indian. He convinced Biyiasas to go with him to see a motion picture made in India. It was playing at a movie theatre some distance away so they decided to take a city bus. Fischer insisted they sit at the back of the bus so he wouldn't be recognized. All went well until a young man got on at the front of bus and, after finding a seat, looked back and stared. Biyiasas realized he was a regular member of the busy Bay Area chess community.

Fischer became upset. I hate it when they recognize me, he told Biyiasas.

What do you mean recognize *you*? Biyiasas replied. Chessplayers haven't seen you in years. You don't even look the same. He recognized *me* said Biyiasas, who had won several major California tournaments.

For the rest of the bus ride, until the starer got off, Fischer and Biyiasas argued about who was the real target of the starer's attention.

This was one of the many contradictions in the life of Fischer. He craved fame and fiercely disdained it. He lived most of his life like a miser but demanded huge (for his time) amounts of money. He said all he ever wanted to do was play chess – then virtually gave up the game at age 29. He was deeply religious but kept changing religions. He was a fanatic about his health yet refused the common medical treatment that would have prolonged his life for many years.

Why was Bobby the way he was? I suspect that many of his quirks came from his upbringing. I got a clue to this during my early days as a newspaper reporter.

In October 1972 I was sitting at my typewriter at the *New York Post* when my desk phone rang. The caller identified herself as Regina Pustan. I recognized the name. She didn't have to add – but she did – "I am Bobby Fischer's mother."

She said she had been living in Great Britain for years but had come to America to be interviewed by newspapers. I couldn't believe my good luck. This was just a month after the Fischer – Spassky match ended and he was a media phenomenon. He didn't have to be identified by surname in headlines. When he won the final match game in Iceland, my paper's front page read simply "Bobby's The Champ."

We quickly agreed on logistics: Yes, I could interview her at her hotel. No, I would not need more than an hour. Yes, I could bring a *Post* photographer. We were winding this up when she casually added that she could not say anything about her son.

I knew that she and Fischer had had a strained relationship. But I was still dumbfounded. What would we be talking about, if not Bobby, I asked?

Why, the election, of course, she said. She had come to the United States to explain to American voters how they must vote. Something simply had to be done to prevent President Richard Nixon from being re-elected the following month.

I understand how you feel, I replied. There are many people who live in America and feel that way. But they would also like to see their opinions given prominent display in the pages of a newspaper with one million readers. Why should we be giving space to someone who had left the United States several years before?

She was shocked by the question. To her, the answer was obvious: "Because I am Bobby Fischer's mother," she said.

Like her son she expected the respect and attention of a celebrity. But, like her son, she saw no reason to pay the price of publicity. I politely declined to interview her.

I had been fascinated by Fischer for more than ten years. I first saw Bobby one night in late 1961. This was well before my first clocked game – in fact, it was not long after I'd learned that chess was played with clocks. The occasion, oddly enough, was my grandmother's first and only visit to New York from Newton, Iowa. My mother decided to shock her by taking a stroll through the bohemian streets of Greenwich Village. Walking ahead of them along Thompson Street I spotted a dilapidated storefront that was labeled "Rossolimo's Chess Studio" and convinced my mother and grandmother to drop in for a minute or two. While the three of us stood a few steps inside the doorway to admire the exotic sets for sale, Fischer walked in. Or, rather, lurched in. He never seemed to move in a routine manner, but as a burst of energy.

He was 18, four years older than me, and his oversized suit made him look taller and more rumpled than his 6-foot-2 and 180 or so pounds. He had come to see Nick Rossolimo, the proprietor of the studio, who, I had heard, was some kind of master. I had never actually seen a master but was well aware of Fischer. He explained to Rossolimo that he had just returned from a tournament at a place called Bled and seemed eager to talk about it. I realized that he wanted – no, he needed – to talk about it to an audience that understood him. He was relaxed, natural and not at all the prima donna I'd read about. He was just Bobby. There were four skittles games going on in the cramped studio, but none of the players, who were paying the outrageous sum of 25 cents an hour to play one another, looked up. It struck me that chess was very strange indeed if one of the best players in the world didn't even get a flicker of recognition when sitting a few feet away and talking about his latest success.

The next time I saw Fischer he was playing chess. Not in the same 1600-rated tournaments I was, of course. He was in the U.S. Championship, which had become an annual event, thanks in large part to interest in Fischer. The tournament was held each Christmastime in a Manhattan hotel ballroom. Before each round Hans Kmoch, the tournament director, or one of his assistants would choose which of us young myrmidons would be allowed to operate demonstration boards on the stage. (My friend Russ Garber had learned how the pieces moved only a few months before he handled Fischer's 1963 game with Benko, a.k.a. the 19 ♖f6!! game.)

Everyone, of course, wanted to work Bobby's board. If you were lucky, he might send you on an errand, in between moves, to bring him back a container of milk – always milk – and some food. I never got the chance. Usually I was assigned to a Sherwin-vs.-Mednis or, if I was lucky, a Byrne-vs.-Benko. But seated at the demo board, you were usually only a few feet from the players, so I got a chance to watch Fischer first hand.

He had quick, large eyes that darted about the board as he concentrated, and distinctive eyebrows that always gave away his surprise when he saw something new in his calculations. And he had extraordinarily long fingers. They cradled his head when he went into a deep think – which for him meant

only ten minutes. Fischer seemed awkward at everything else, even when signing his name in block letters (he apparently never learned script). But when moving the pieces, he exuded a kind of strange, athletic grace. Moving the pieces may have been his most comfortable form of communication. Years later Angela Julian Day told me of her one meeting with Fischer. She was helping to run the Grandmaster Association office in Brussels in 1990. The great promotional hope of the GMA was their World Cup tournaments, and what was supposed to save the Cup from going the way of all previous chess promotions was getting Fischer to play in it. One night Angie went to what she thought was a social get-together with various GMA dignitaries when she discovered the man seated across from her was Bobby Fischer. But Fischer seemed mute. After several clumsy moments of silence, he pulled out of his pocket a well-worn version of the hand-held game in which you move 15 numbered tiles around a plastic grid that has spaces for 16. Fischer indicated that she should mix up the tiles, and then time him with her wristwatch. She did. Fischer unscrambled the tiles in a fraction of a minute. His long, nimble fingers worked remarkably fast. In fact he regarded himself as the world champion at this. "And all I could think was what a waste," Angie Day recalled.

In September 1963 I got a closer look at Fischer when I played at the New York State Open in Poughkeepsie. It turned out to

9

be Fischer's last Swiss System tournament and he won all his seven games. I started out rated around number 40 in the field of 57 players but by the final round had worked up to board three where I had White against James T. Sherwin. When I resigned around move 60, there didn't seem like much to say, and besides there was no time to post-mortem if I was going to catch my car ride back to New York. But on the following night there was some event at the Marshall Chess Club that attracted a throng.

Sherwin showed up and asked if I wanted to look over the game. I was shocked. After all, he outrated me by more than 500 points and had just proven it. We headed to the back room, to the "Capablanca table," to analyze. My second surprise came when Fischer materialized and sat down on my side of the board. Several other masters looked on, peering over one another's shoulders, at the position. Sherwin had been working on this opening (1 e4 c5 2 ♘f3 ♘f6 3 e5 ♘d5) for months and had spent more than 20 hours on it. But no one had allowed him to show over the board what he'd found until I had the previous day. Even Fischer avoided the issue, playing 3 ♘c3 against Sherwin in the previous year's U.S. Championship.

Sherwin presented the moves with a flourish, particularly 15...♗g1, his TN. (As far as I know, it remains virtually unknown.) He really did make moves he was proud of by pushing the piece with his pinky, as Fischer described in the first pages of *My 60 Memorable Games*. But when matters got interesting, around

move 17, Fischer stopped the show by asking, "Whadya got on this?" and moved a white piece. Sherwin had an answer but it was demolished by a few quick Fischer follow-ups. This happened again a move later in the game, and then again. After the fourth time that he'd refuted a Sherwin move, Fischer asked, "You spent 20 hours on *this*?"

I witnessed Fischer in action several more times over the next few years. For example:

- Shortly after his great 11-0 triumph in the U.S. Championship, when he demonstrated his win over Robert Byrne in the front room of the Marshall, next to the bust of Frank Marshall, and joked about how the Soviets would try to ridicule his play.

- When he returned to the "Capablanca table" in 1965, playing opponents long-distance because the U.S. State Department wouldn't let him play them face-to-face in Havana. Despite the bizarre setting, he remained approachable, willing to chat about his last game, about what went wrong and what went right.

- When he would show up, usually late at night, at the Manhattan Chess Club, or at the Times Square dive called The New York Chess and Checker Club – but known among games players as "The Fleahouse" – Fischer would give outrageous time odds in blitz games to masters. Or just chat about chess. When that was the subject he was always just Bobby.

It seems incredible now, but no one in New York's small chess community seemed to think it the slightest bit odd that perhaps the greatest player in history was among us, periodically disappearing and then reappearing again when he was ready to play chess. Once, when he had vanished for several months, it was passed through the grapevine with matter-of-factness that Fischer had confined himself to a Midtown hotel room from which he wasn't going to leave until he perfected his play in rook endgames.

How Fischer earned a living was a mystery. He had asked for – and gotten – the astronomical sum of $250 for each simultaneous exhibition he gave. But after 1965 he rarely gave simuls. Al Horowitz, who began the *New York Times* chess column in 1962, told me that the *Times* had offered Fischer $15,000-plus a year for a regular column, even a ghostwritten column. Whether that was true was unclear, to use the traditional annotator's hedge, because Horowitz was somewhat unreliable. Fischer told other people that he was paid $300 a month for his monthly column in *Boy's Life,* the Boy Scout magazine.

And there were always rumors about a book. I knew his first book, *Bobby Fischer's Games of Chess,* a gossamer collection of his games from his first U.S. Championship and Interzonal. He also contributed some ideas, but chiefly his name, to *Bobby Fischer Teaches Chess,* which earned more than twice as much for him as any of his other books. But Fischer had been working for years on his magnum opus, which was supposed to be called *Bobby Fischer's Best Games of Chess.* He first said it would

appear after "my match with Botvinnik." When that didn't come to pass, he added more games and it was retitled *My 50 Memorable Games.* But by 1966 there was still no sign of it.

Accounts of its fate percolated through New York chess circles but the only thing that was certain was that Fischer decided against publishing after the manuscript was already set in metal type. The Fischer hangers-on I knew said he didn't want to give up his openings secrets or be caught in an analytical error so he bought his way out of the contract. Larry Evans, whose role in the book is surely more than anyone admitted, said Fischer reversed himself in 1968 and decided to go ahead with the now *60 Memorable Games.* "The world's coming to an end anyway," Bobby explained.

When the book appeared in 1969, Fischer had been invisible for months. By that time I was a 2400 player and even got to play a few boards away from him in a Manhattan Chess Club – Marshall Chess Club team match in November 1968. The closest contact I had with him in the next year was odd and quite indirect, at the World Student Olympiad in Dresden. Just before one round I had to borrow a pair of shoes from teammate Bernard Zuckerman. They fit my size 12 feet nearly perfectly. "They're Bobby's," Zuckerman explained. "He gives me some of his old clothes." (That afternoon I played Fischer's favorite 6 ♗c4 against the Najdorf Variation and won the prettiest game I ever played.)

The only time I faced Fischer over the board was in August 1971. This was in between Fischer's 6-0 Candidates match victories over Mark Taimanov and Bent Larsen. The Manhattan Chess Club had just moved to new quarters – they made three more forced moves before going out of business in 2002 – and a speed tournament was arranged to mark the occasion. This was during one of Fischer's press-friendly periods, and the organizers allowed photographers a short period to work the room. I was paired with Fischer in the first round. The result was a huge photo in the next day's *Times:* We're playing a 6 &c4 Najdorf, of course, and he's waiting for my 11th move. About thirty fans are watching, some standing on chairs to get a better view. Around move 30 Fischer blundered away his queen for a rook and pawn. It was an easy win but I knew I'd never win it. Fischer's presence paralyzed me. Instead of trying to promote a pawn, I tried to blockade his, and lost miserably. I put up no resistance in the second game.

The last time I saw him was Sept. 21, 1972, "Bobby Fischer Day" in New York, a celebration at City Hall three weeks after the match ended. There were the usual speeches, including brief (scripted) remarks by Bobby. Later there was a reception in the Blue Room, a ceremonial hall usually reserved for special occasions. Fischer and I chatted about the news coverage of the match in New York. He seemed relaxed, natural – still just Bobby.

Thirty years later, I looked at Fischer's games for the first time since they were played. What struck me is that they fell into two categories. Some were, in fact, overrated. But many more were underrated – if known at all. And his originality, so striking at the time, had been lost with time. It seemed to me Fischer deserved an entirely new look.

The more I played over the moves again, the more it occurred to me that Fischer's chess was shaped by a single goal – to beat the Soviets. I guess that shouldn't be surprising, strategy in chess – as in war, business, election campaigns and sports – evolves for a practical reason: Great innovations aren't created for the sake of science. They're created for the specific aim of defeating the strategy that made other guys successful. Alexander the Great and his father didn't invent the Macedonian battle phalanx because of some lofty desire to improve battlefield theory. They did it to crush the Persians.

The Soviet style that Fischer faced had come about in much the same way. The Russians, Ukrainians, *et al* wanted to defeat the dominant style of the 1930s – the material-driven endgame-oriented strategies that had served Capablanca, Flohr and Fine so well. They developed a sharply different set of priorities, beginning with the initiative. Black was entitled to it as much as White and he could start the struggle for it as early as the opening, even if he has to give up material – such as in the celebrated "Soviet Exchange sacrifice" – or incur positional weaknesses, such as backward pawns or giving up bishop for knight.

Fischer, it struck me, was a reaction to this reaction. He adopted many of the Soviets' weapons, like the King's Indian and the Najdorf Sicilian, but with the eyes of a Classical player. And he liked to grab material. "I don't know who is better, Bobby, but I offer a draw," Vlastimil Hort said after 44 moves at Siegen 1970. "I don't know who is better either but I have an extra pawn," Fischer said in refusing. He was, in the words of one Russian admirer, the perfect harmony of position and material. If the Soviets were the antithesis of the 1930s' thesis, Fischer was the new synthesis. It's a dialectic that would have pleased Marx.

I found certain recurring themes in Fischer's games. Among them:

- *"To get squares, you gotta give squares,"* as he put it. He understood that in order to win you had to control certain crucial points of the board and that often meant you had to concede others. This is particularly evident in Games 2, 56, 57, 60, 61, 86, and 92.

- *Ugly moves aren't bad.*

Although he could be as dogmatic as Steinitz, Fischer had an instinct for moves that few other grandmasters would consider. For example, 19 ♘xe7+ in Game 2, 13 ♕e2 in Game 11, 13...♘g4 in Game 27, 5 ♕e2 in Game 30, 13 a3 in Game 66, 11...♘h5 in Game 96 and giving up a fianchettoed bishop for a knight on d4 in Games 40 and 79.

- *Material matters.* Fischer played great sacrificial games but almost all of them occurred before he was 21.

He was basically a materialist, a materialist who had a deeper understanding of the exchange value of pieces than almost any other player. His handling of a bishop-versus-knight middlegame or queen-versus-two-rook endgame was remarkable, as was his appreciation of how great the winning chances are in rook-and bishops-of-opposite-color endings. I had always felt uncomfortable giving up two rooks for my opponent's queen. Then I realized Fischer's discovery: The more minor pieces there are on the board, the greater the queen's chances against the rooks.

- *Technique has many faces.* Few players are equally good at obtaining and realizing an advantage – they are quite different skills – but as Mark Dvoretsky pointed out, Fischer was the exception. His trademark was the timely conversion of one kind of advantage to another, as in Games 6, 7, 25, 28, 35, 40, 50, 55, 57 and 95.

What would have happened if Fischer had continued to play? What would we have learned from his games with Karpov and Kasparov – if not Carlsen? (Carlsen was a strong grandmaster during the last years of Fischer's life.) How would he have countered new weapons such as the Kalashnikov Sicilian, the Trompowsky Attack, and the many anti-Sicilian attacks that became popular from 1975 on? Would he have been the one to figure out how to beat the Berlin Defense? How would he have coped with faster time controls? He was, after all, the world's best blitz player. Would he have been able to compete alone in an era of entourages and teams of seconds? How would he have fared against computers like Deep Blue? How different would chess be today if he had stayed?

We will never know. All we have left is the games.

Since the first edition of this book, Fischer games have been re-analyzed by many others, including Garry Kasparov, with the help of computers. Everyone finds something new – hidden resources, nuances and errors in earlier annotations. This is almost certain to go on with each new generation of stronger analytic engines. I have made extensive revisions since I tackled these games in 2003. But I suspect Fischer's moves, like his life, will remain a source of fascination – if not mystery – well into this century.

Andrew Soltis
New York, 2019

1

A one-paragraph snippet of news under the headline "New York's New Prodigy" appeared in the November 9, 1956 issue of the British magazine *Chess*. It reported that Samuel Reshevsky had won the 3rd Rosenwald tournament, a prestigious event which was marked by a controversial double forfeit, and a remarkable game: "Donald Byrne was beaten by a 13-year-old boy named Fischer who totaled 4½ points, in a game of great depth and brilliancy..."

Donald Byrne – Fischer
Rosenwald Tournament,
New York 1956
Grünfeld Defense (D96)

1	♘f3	♘f6
2	c4	g6
3	♘c3	♗g7
4	d4	0-0
5	♗f4	d5
6	♕b3	

Before 1956 White usually combined ♗f4 with e3 before ♕b3. The difference is that 6...c5 can be met by 7 dxc5 ♕a5 and then 8 ♗d2! favors White.

6	...	dxc4
7	♕xc4	c6
8	e4	

Most opening books of the day cited one example of this position, from a 1943 game that continued 8...b5 9 ♕b3 ♕a5 10 ♗d3 ♗e6 with advantage to White after 11 ♕d1 ♗g4 12 0-0 ♖d8 13 e5!.

| 8 | ... | ♘bd7 |

| 9 | ♖d1 | ♘b6 |
| 10 | ♕c5! | ♗g4 |

Black prepares 11...♘fd7 12 ♕a3 e5! 13 dxe5 ♕e8 and ...♘xe5 with good play.

| 11 | ♗g5? | |

This way of stopping 11...♘fd7 is the source of White's troubles. Preferable was 11 ♗e2 ♘fd7 12 ♕a3 ♗xf3. Then 13 ♗xf3 e5 14 dxe5 ♕e8 15 ♗e2 ♘xe5 16 0-0 and ♖fe1 leaves White a tiny edge. But 13 gxf3!, a common theme in the Grünfeld, gives him more: 13...e5 14 dxe5 ♕e8 15 ♗e3 ♕xe5 16 f4 and 17 e5.

"The next seven moves provide one of the most remarkable passages in the whole of recorded chess," W.H. Cozens wrote in *The King Hunt*.

| 11 | ... | ♘a4!! |

Now 12 ♘xa4 ♘xe4 13 ♕xe7 ♕a5+ 14 ♘c3 ♖fe8 or 14 b4 ♕xa4 15 ♕xe4 ♖fe8 16 ♗e7 ♗xf3 17 gxf3 ♗f6 are lost. Better but still poor is 13 ♕c1 ♕a5+ 14 ♘c3 ♗xf3 15 gxf3 ♘xg5.

| 12 | ♕a3 | ♘xc3 |
| 13 | bxc3 | ♘xe4! |

Without this move, exploiting the absence of the c3-knight, Black's

11th move might have been remembered as a positional error that only strengthened White's center. Now 14 ♕xe7? ♘xg5 or 14...♕xe7 15 ♗xe7 ♖fe8 lose quickly.

14 ♗xe7

Byrne expected 14...♕e8, after which 15 ♖d3! is seemingly powerful. But 15...c5 is a strong Exchange sacrifice (16 ♗xf8 ♗xf8 17 ♕b2 cxd4 18 cxd4 ♕a4).

14 ... ♕b6!

The second stage of the combination is founded on 15 ♗xf8 ♗xf8 16 ♕b3 ♘xc3 17 ♕xc3?? ♗b4 or 17 ♕xb6 axb6 with a winning ending.

15 ♗c4

Now 15...♖fe8 16 0-0 ♗xf3 17 gxf3 ♘xc3 fails to 18 ♗c5 ♘b5 19 ♗xf7+!, a trick we'll see again.

15 ... ♘xc3!

Based on 16 ♕xc3 ♖fe8 17 ♕e3 ♗f6.

16 ♗c5 ♖fe8+

17 ♔f1

Paul Keres, profiling Fischer on the eve of Curaçao 1962, imagined the scene: "Byrne apparently gloated silently at his opponent." Black loses

on 17...♕c7 18 ♕xc3 and gets insufficient compensation for the queen after 17...♘xd1 18 ♗xb6 axb6 19 ♕b3. The *desperado* 17...♘b5 again fails to 18 ♗xf7+! (18...♔h8 19 ♗xb6 ♘xa3 20 ♗xe8 or 18...♔xf7 19 ♕b3+ ♗e6 20 ♘g5+).

17 ... ♗e6!!

"But White's joy was suddenly destroyed by Bobby's move," Keres wrote in *Ogonyok*. Byrne must take the queen since 18 ♗xe6 allows smothered mate (18...♕b5+ 19 ♔g1 ♘e2+ 20 ♔f1 ♘g3+ and ...♕f1+) and 18 ♕xc3 ♕xc5! 19 dxc5 ♗xc3 is a lost ending. Also, 18 ♗d3 allows the *desperado* to work (18...♘b5! 19 ♕b4 ♕c7 20 a4 a5! and wins).

18 ♗xb6 ♗xc4+

19 ♔g1 ♘e2+

20 ♔f1 ♘xd4+

Black's level of risk is minimal since he can draw by perpetual check at several points and White has few choices (21 ♖d3?? axb6 22 ♕c3 ♘xf3 23 ♕xc4 ♖e1 mate).

21 ♔g1 ♘e2+

22 ♔f1 ♘c3+

23 ♔g1 axb6

Now 24 ♕c1?? ♘e2+ or 24 ♕d6 ♖ad8 25 ♕xd8 ♘e2+ 26 ♔f1 ♘d4+! and 27...♖xd8.

24 ♕b4

24 ...   ♖a4

Black decides to bank his material edge rather than preserve the discovered check mechanism with 24...♘e2+ 25 ♔f1 ♗b5. The latter is stronger – but if Black had chosen it and gone on to win mundanely (26 ♖d2 ♗c3! 27 ♕xb5 cxb5 28 ♖xe2 ♖xe2 29 ♔xe2 ♖xa2+) would this game be remembered more than half a century later?

25 ♕xb6

Or 25 ♕d6 ♘xd1 26 ♕xd1 ♖xa2 and wins.

25 ...   ♘xd1

26 h3?

With 26 ♕xb7! Black would have been forced to prove he has a mating attack – which he probably does after 26...♗d5 27 ♕d7 ♖ea8.

26 ...   ♖xa2

27 ♔h2   ♘xf2

28 ♖e1   ♖xe1

29 ♕d8+   ♗f8

30 ♘xe1   ♗d5

"It was quite an experience to watch him during the critical stage of the game," Hans Kmoch wrote of Fischer. "There he sat like a little

Buddha, showing his moves with the calm regularity of an automaton."

31 ♘f3   ♘e4

32 ♕b8

32 ...   b5

Black handles the final stage carefully. Here 32...♔g7! and ...♗d6+ was also strong, particularly since 33 ♕xb7? ♗d6+ 34 ♔h1 ♖a1+ ends the game.

33 h4   h5

34 ♘e5   ♔g7

35 ♔g1   ♗c5+

36 ♔f1

This allows mate but so does 36 ♔h1 ♘g3+ 37 ♔h2 ♘f1+ 38 ♔h3 ♗xg2 (and 36 ♔h2 ♗d6 37 ♕e8 ♘f6 was hopeless).

36 ...   ♘g3+

Faster was 36...♖f2+! 37 ♔e1 (37 ♔g1 ♖f4+) ♗b4+ 38 ♔d1 ♗b3+ 39 ♔c1 ♗a3+.

37 ♔e1   ♗b4+

Another quicker mate was 37...♖e2+ 38 ♔d1 ♗b3+ but it hardly matters.

38 ♔d1   ♗b3+

39 ♔c1   ♘e2+

40 ♔b1   ♘c3+

41 ♕c1   ♜c2 mate

More than a decade later Fischer said this was one of the few games of his that he had committed to memory.

2

Fischer's first nickname was the "Corduroy Killer" because he would show up, day after day, at the Brooklyn Chess Club in the same pants, sneakers and sweater to play hours of chess. His progress to "killer" status was extraordinarily quick, even compared with more recent prodigies such as Carlsen, Caruana and Karjakin. Fischer received a U.S. Chess Federation rating of 1830 after his first tournament outside Brooklyn. But within two and a half years he was U.S. Champion. "I just got good," he explained. The following, played against one of his mentors, was much more typical of his style at the time than the Byrne brilliancy.

Fischer – Attilio Di Camillo
Eastern Open,
Washington, D.C. 1956
Ruy Lopez (C78)

1	e4	e5
2	♘f3	♘c6
3	♗b5	a6
4	♗a4	♘f6
5	0-0	b5
6	♗b3	d6

An old variation whose chief virtue is that it may lure White into the 7 ♘g5 d5 8 exd5 ♘d4! gambit – and whose chief liability is that it tempts Black into a premature ...♗g4.

7	c3	♗g4?

Black could get back into a main Lopez line with 7...♘a5 8 ♗c2 c5 9 d4 ♕c7. This was a topical move order because of a Bronstein – Evans game from the 1954 U.S.S.R. – U.S. match that went 10 ♘bd2 g6? 11 b4!.

8	h3	♗h5

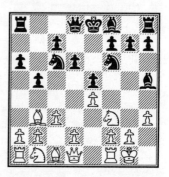

9   d3!

White can obtain an edge by attacking Black's bishop with ♘d2-f1-g3. But pushing the pawn to d4 would vindicate Black's seventh move by granting him ...exd4 pressure.

9	...	♗e7
10	♘bd2	0-0

Black should try to justify his previous play with 10...♕d7 and ...g5-g4 (since 11 g4? allows 11...♘xg4 12 hxg4 ♕xg4+ and 13...♗g5!).

11	♜e1	♕d7
12	♘f1	♘a5
13	♗c2	h6

To ease Black's congestion by ...♘h7-g5 or ...♗g5.

14 g4!   ♗g6

Now the sacrifice 14...♘xg4 15 hxg4 ♕xg4+ is refuted by 16 ♘g3 ♕xf3 17 ♘xh5.

15 ♘g3   ♘h7

16 ♘f5   ♘b7?

The knight is headed for e6 via c5 or d8. But better was 16...♗g5, and if 17 d4, then 17...♕e6.

17 d4!

Well timed since 17...♗f6 or 17...♖fd8 cost a pawn to 18 dxe5, and 17...f6 18 dxe5 ♗xf5 19 gxf5 fxe5 drops a piece after 20 ♕d5+. Finally, 17...♕e6 is bad because of 18 dxe5 dxe5 19 ♘xe7+ ♕xe7 20 ♕d5!.

17 ...   exd4

18 cxd4   ♘d8

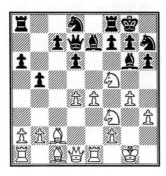

19 ♘xe7+!

White exchanges a knight that took four moves to reach f5 for a bishop that didn't seem to be doing much. (Much like 22 ♘xd7+ in Game 95.) But this is a necessary prelude to closing the center, since 19 d5? ♗xf5 20 gxf5 ♗f6 gives Black better chances than the game.

19 ...   ♕xe7

20 d5   c5

Otherwise 21 ♘d4.

21 ♗f4!

Not 21 dxc6 ♘xc6 22 ♗f4 ♘e5.

21 ...   ♘b7

22 ♗g3

Remarkable caution. White is playing for e4-e5 but there is no obvious way to make progress after 22 e5 ♗xc2 23 ♕xc2 ♖ae8. Instead, Fischer will probe the queenside before e4-e5 and for that reason he anticipates distractions such as ...♕f6.

22 ...   ♖fe8

23 a4!   ♕f6

On 23...♘g5 White avoids 24 ♘xg5 hxg5! and ...f6 and plays 24 ♘d2.

24 axb5   axb5

25 ♔g2   ♘g5

White is closing in after 25...♕xb2 26 ♖b1 ♕f6 27 ♖xb5, e.g. 27...♘a5 28 e5! or 27...♖e7 28 ♖b6 or 28 ♕b1.

26 ♘xg5   hxg5

27 ♖xa8   ♖xa8

28 e5!   ♗xc2

29 ♕xc2   dxe5

White pockets a pawn after 29...♕e7 30 ♕d2.

30 ♗xe5   ♕d8

31 d6!   c4

More active is 31...♘xd6 32 ♕xc5 ♘c4. But 32 ♖d1! ♖a6 33 ♔g1 avoids ...♕a8+ and would have left Black's queen in a bad pin.

32 ♕e4   ♘c5

33 ♕c6

White could shorten matters with 33 ♕d5!.

33 ...   ♘d3

34 ♖e3   ♖c8

Not 34...♘xe5 35 ♖xe5 ♖c8 36 ♕d5, e.g. 36...♕d7 37 ♖e7 ♕c6 38 ♕xc6 followed by ♖e8+ and d6-d7. The text sets a trap: 35 ♕xb5?? ♖c5.

35 ♕b7   ♖b8
36 ♕d5   ♘b4

At some point Black should blockade on d7 but 36...♕d7 37 ♗g3 loses to ♕xg5 or ♖e7. Also, 36...♘xe5 37 ♖xe5 and d6-d7.

37 ♕c5   ♘d3
38 ♕d4   ♖b6

Now was the time for 38...♕d7! (but not 38...♘xe5 39 ♖xe5 ♖b7 40 ♕e4! ♖b8 41 ♕d5 and wins).

39 d7!   ♖b7

40 ♗c7!   ♘f4+!

Hoping for 41 ♗xf4 ♖xd7 or 41 ♕xf4 ♕xd7!.

41 ♔f1!   Resigns

3

Fischer's rise occurred during a chess drought in the United States, and his first national championship tournament, at the end of 1957, was a major event. Since 1951 there had been only one U.S. Championship and one international tournament (Dallas 1957, which was deeply reduced in stature when the Soviet invitee, David Bronstein, couldn't get visa clearance).

Sidney Bernstein – Fischer
U.S. Championship
New York 1957-58
Sicilian Defense,
Najdorf Variation (B99)

1	e4	c5
2	♘f3	d6
3	d4	cxd4
4	♘xd4	♘f6
5	♘c3	a6
6	♗g5	e6
7	f4	♗e7
8	♕f3	♘bd7

A short time later it was discovered that 8...♕c7 9 0-0-0 ♘bd7 is the right move order because the text allows 9 ♗c4, threatening ♗xe6!.

9	0-0-0	♕c7
10	g4	b5
11	♗g2	

This natural move all but disappeared from practice soon after this game.

11 ...   ♗b7

There was no time for 11...b4 because of 12 e5!, e.g. 12...dxe5 13 ♘dxb5 axb5 14 ♘xb5 ♕b7 15 ♕xb7, with advantage to White.

12 ♖he1   b4!

A later Korchnoi game showed that 12...♘b6, safeguarding against sacrifices on d5, grants White a reasonable attack with 13 ♗xf6 ♗xf6 14 g5 ♗e7 15 h4.

13 ♘d5?

Plainly more palatable than 13 ♘b1 ♛a5. Fischer had faced a similar ♘d5 sacrifice two rounds before against Bernstein's good friend, Herbert Seidman, and drew.

13 ... exd5!

A case when it's safer to accept a piece than a pawn: On 13...♘xd5 14 exd5 ♗xd5 White has 15 ♛xd5! exd5 16 ♖xe7+ ♔f8 17 ♗xd5 or 16...♔d8 17 ♗xd5 with a crushing attack. Black does better with 14...♗xg5 15 fxg5 0-0 but he would be worse after 16 ♛g3.

14 exd5

White's threats are immediate (15 ♘f5) and intermediate (doubling rooks on the e-file).

14 ... ♔f8!

Black prepares to demilitarize the e-file with ...♖e8 and ...♗d8. On

14...♔d8 15 ♘f5 ♖c8 16 ♛e2 or 15...♖e8? 16 ♛e3 ♘c5 17 ♘xg7 ♖g8 18 ♘f5 ♖e8 19 ♘xe7 White wins.

But 15...♗f8! was better since 16 ♛e4 ♔c8 17 ♛e8+! ♛d8 18 ♛xf7 favors White but 16...♛a5! 17 ♛e8+ (17 ♔b1 h6) ♔c7 18 ♛xf7 ♛xa2 is unclear.

15 ♘f5

Nothing comes of 15 ♘c6? ♗xc6 16 dxc6 ♘c5 and ...♖e8.

15 ... ♖e8
16 ♛e3

Now 16...♛d8 allows White to fuel his initiative with 17 ♛d4 followed by doubling rooks or ♗h4 and g4-g5.

16 ... ♗d8
17 ♛d4

17 ... ♗c8!

The engine of White's attack is the f5-knight. Simply swapping pieces (17...♖xe1 18 ♖xe1 ♘c5) permits White to improve his chances considerably with 19 ♗xf6!, e.g. 19...♗xf6 20 ♛e3 ♛d7 21 g5! ♗d8 22 ♘xd6. But 18...♛a5 19 ♛d2 h6 was good.

18 ♗h4

With 18 ♛xb4 White admits his initiative is dead, e.g. 18...♖xe1

21

19 ♖xe1 ♘c5 20 ♗xf6 ♗xf6!
followed by ...♘d3+ or ...♗xf5 and
wins.

Now, however, he is threatening
19 g5.

18 ...   ♘c5!

Also good is 18...♖xe1 19 ♖xe1
g6. Less accurate is 18...♕c5?
19 ♖xe8+ or 18...♖xe1 19 ♖xe1 ♕c5
20 ♕xc5 dxc5 21 ♘d6!.

Also tempting is 18...b3 19 axb3
♘c5, which threatens 20...♘xb3+ as
well as ...♗xf5. However, White can
ignore that with 20 ♗xf6! since
20...♘xb3+ 21 ♔b1 ♘xd4 22 ♗xg7+
and a mate. He has some chances
even on 20...gxf6! 21 ♖xe8+ ♔xe8
22 ♕e3+ ♔f8 23 b4.

19 ♘xg7

White's last bullet. On 19 ♗xf6
♗xf6? 20 ♖xe8+ ♔xe8 21 ♘xg7+
he could turn the tables – but
19...gxf6! wins for Black.

19 ...   ♔xg7

20 g5   ♗f5!

Another point of Black's 17th
move: he threatens 21...♘b3+! and
mate next.

21 gxf6+   ♔h6!

22 ♕c4   ♘d7

23 ♕xc7   ♗xc7

24 ♗f3   ♗d8!

White continued through the
inertia of time pressure:

**25 ♗g5+ ♔g6 26 ♖g1 ♗xf6
27 ♗h4+ ♔h6 28 ♗xf6 ♘xf6
29 ♖g5 ♗e4 30 ♖f1 ♗g6 31 ♖fg1
♖e3 32 ♗d1 ♘e4 33 ♖5g2 f5
34 ♗e2 a5 35 h4 ♖h3 36 h5 ♗xh5
37 ♗d3 ♗g6 38 ♖f1 ♖f8 39 ♔d1
♘f6 40 ♖e1 ♘xd5 41 ♖f2 ♖e3
42 ♖g1 ♖e7 43 ♔d2 ♔g7 44 ♖f3
(sealed) and White resigned.**

4

Fischer started the 1957-8 U.S.
Championship with a modest 2-1
score then went on a 8½-1½ spree
that won the tournament. Some of
his games were marred by shocking
tactical lapses, including double-
question-mark moves by both
players. But his slips were offset by
this game, which won the second
brilliancy prize:

Fischer – James T. Sherwin
U.S. Championship,
New York 1957-58
*Sicilian Defense,
Najdorf Variation (B87)*

1   e4   c5

2   ♘f3   d6

3	d4	cxd4
4	♘xd4	♘f6
5	♘c3	a6
6	♗c4	e6
7	0-0	b5
8	♗b3	b4
9	♘b1!?	

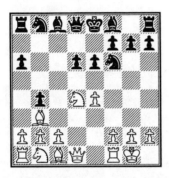

For a brief time in the 1950s this retreat, with ♘d2-c4 in mind, was a major alternative to 9 ♘a4, which can expose the knight to attack from ...♗d7/...♕a5.

9	...	♗d7

In his first book, Fischer said he didn't believe Soviet analysis that claimed White had enough compensation after 9...♘xe4 10 ♕f3 ♗b7 and he gave 11 ♗a4+ ♘d7 12 ♗c6 ♗xc6 13 ♘xc6 ♕b6 14 ♕xe4 d5 as evidence. But the Russians suggested 12 ♘d2 was better, but there haven't been enough practical tests to tell.

10	♗e3	♘c6

Taking the pawn now is too dangerous (10...♘xe4 11 ♕f3 d5 12 c4).

11	f3	♗e7?

Black misses his best equalizing chance of the opening (11...♘a5).

12 c3!

White now obtains the upper hand on the queenside (12...a5 13 ♘b5! ♕b8 14 a4).

12	...	bxc3
13	♘xc6	

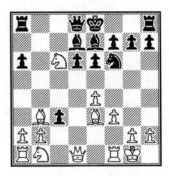

13	...	♗xc6

Black loses two queens in three moves after 13...cxb2? 14 ♘xd8 bxa1(♕) 15 ♗d4!.

14	♘xc3	0-0
15	♖c1	♕b8

Overlooking – or underestimating – White's combination. Better was 15...♗b7 after which 16 ♕d3 ♖c8 17 ♖fd1 and ♘a4-b6, or the immediate 16 ♘a4, offers White a slight pull.

16 ♘d5! exd5?

Black might have tried to hold the extra pawn after 16...♗xd5 17 exd5 ♘xd5 18 ♗xd5 exd5 19 b3 ♕b5. But he apparently didn't trust positions such as 20 ♕d2 ♖fe8 21 ♖fd1 ♗f6.

However, after the text Black has long-term problems on the light squares, as he would also have after 16...♗xd5 17 exd5 e5 18 ♖c6! ♕b5 19 ♖b6 ♕a5 20 ♖b7 or 18...a5 19 ♕e2 ♕b4 20 ♖fc1.

The same goes for 16...♘xd5 17 exd5 ♗b5?, which invites a terrific Exchange offer, 18 dxe6 ♗xf1 19 exf7+ ♔h8 20 ♕xf1 followed by ♗d5, ♖c6 and ♕c4.

17 ♖xc6   dxe4

18 fxe4

If Black had counted on 18...♘xe4 when he chose his 16th move, he would have been disappointed now to see how strong 19 ♗d5 ♘f6 20 ♖b6 would be.

18 ...   ♕b5

19 ♖b6   ♕e5

20 ♗d4!   ♕g5

Not 20...♕xe4? 21 ♖e1.

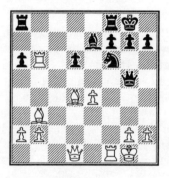

21 ♕f3?

Fischer has two flaws, Larry Evans wrote in 1963: Overconfidence "which causes him sometimes to forget that his opponents are also capable of finding good moves" and "impetuosity in winning positions." Here he allows an excellent maneuver that nearly equalizes. With 21 ♖b7! Black's straits are dire because 21...♘xe4 22 ♖e1 costs material (22...d5 23 ♖xe7! ♕xe7 24 ♗xd5 or 22...♖ac8 23 ♖xe4 ♖c1 24 ♖bxe7 ♖xd1+ 25 ♗xd1).

21 ...   ♘d7!

Now 22 ♗xf7+ ♔h8 23 ♖b7 ♘e5 is fine for Black.

22 ♖b7   ♘e5

23 ♕e2   ♗f6

Black threatens 24...♘f3+ 25 ♕xf3 ♗xd4+, with good drawing chances due to the bishops of opposite color.

24 ♔h1!

Now Black's best is 24...♕g4! and then 25 ♗c4 a5.

24 ...   a5

25 ♗d5   ♖ac8

White had threatened 26 ♗xe5 dxe5 27 ♖xf7 or 26...♕xe5 27 ♖b5.

26 ♗c3   a4

Black would love to drum up kingside play with 26...♘g4. But he has nothing to show for a pawn after 27 ♗d2 ♕h4 28 h3 ♘e5 29 ♗xa5.

27 ♖a7   ♘g4

28 ♖xa4

Fischer took barely a minute to reject 28 ♗xf6 ♘xf6 29 ♖xa4 ♘xd5 30 exd5 ♕xd5 (31 ♖a7 ♖ce8). But 28 ♗d2 was a worthy alternative, especially since 28...♖c2? allows 29 ♖xf7! ♖xf7 30 ♕b5! and wins.

28 ...   ♗xc3

29 bxc3   ♖xc3?

30 ♖xf7!!

Why two exclamation points? Isn't 30...♖xf7 31 ♖a8+ obvious? Yes, but White's combination is much deeper. He saw that 30...♕xd5, which ends discovered checks and threatens 31...♖c1+, is refuted by 31 ♖xf8+ ♔xf8 32 ♕f1+! ♕f7 33 ♖a8+ ♔e7 34 ♖a7+.

30	...	♖c1+?

But White's main point is revealed after 30...h5!, which seems to win:

(a) 31 ♖f1+ ♔h7 32 ♖xf8 ♖c1+ 33 ♖f1? ♕f4! or

(b) 31 ♕b2! ♔h7! 32 ♕xc3 ♖xf7 33 ♗xf7 ♕f4 34 ♗g8+ ♔h8! or

(c) 31 ♕f1 ♔h7! 32 ♖xf8 ♖c1 33 ♗g8+ ♔h6 34 ♗c4 ♘e3!, or

(d) 31 ♖f3+ ♔h7 32 ♖xc3 and Black passes up the 32...♘f2+ 33 ♔g1 ♘h3+ draw for 32...♕e5 or 32...♕d2! and wins.

Nevertheless, there is a likely White win in a queen-and-minor piece endgame after 31 ♖c4! ♖xc4 32 ♖xf8+ ♔xf8 33 ♕xc4.

31	♕f1!!

This retreat is the difference between winning and losing (31 ♖f1+? ♔h8 32 ♖a8? ♖xa8 33 ♗xa8 ♕f4!).

31	...	h5

Now this move lacks bite. But on 31...♖xf1+ 32 ♖xf1+ ♖f7 33 ♖a8+ Black has no *luft* and is mated.

32	♕xc1!	♕h4

Equally hopeless was 32...♕xc1+ 33 ♖f1+.

33	♖xf8+	♔h7
34	h3	♕g3
35	hxg4	h4
36	♗e6	Resigns

5

Fischer's mother, Regina, drew a revealing picture of him in a letter to the Yugoslav Chess Federation in early 1958. She asked the Yugoslavs to find room and board for her 15-year-old son while he adjusted to the Balkan climate in the weeks before the Interzonal at Portorož. But she indicated Bobby had certain conditions that must be met: He would not give simultaneous exhibitions or interviews – and didn't like journalists "who ask non-chess questions" about his private life. She volunteered to the Yugoslavs that Fischer didn't smoke, drink or date girls and "doesn't know how to dance." But, she added, "He likes to swim, play tennis, ski, skate, etc."

By the time of the Interzonal in August, Fischer had settled into other lifetime habits. Dimitrije Bjelica, a Yugoslav chess journalist who established an early rapport with the young American, recalled how Bobby would analyze in his hotel room until the early a.m., sleep until noon – and rarely leave the room except to play.

Fischer's start at Portorož was decidedly unimpressive – a first-round draw with White in 16 moves followed by a swindle that turned a loss to the tournament tailender into a win. He had only an even score when he met Bent Larsen in round eight:

Fischer – Bent Larsen
Interzonal, Portorož 1958
Sicilian Defense,
Dragon Variation (B77)

1	e4	c5
2	♘f3	d6

3	d4	cxd4
4	♘xd4	♘f6
5	♘c3	g6
6	♗e3	

Anti-Dragon weapons were in their infancy. One of the few books then available that considered 6 ♗e3 – Reuben Fine's *Practical Chess Openings* – gave only 6...♗g7 7 f3 a6 8 ♕d2 ♘c6 9 ♘b3 h6 10 a4 ♘a5 11 ♖a3 and concluded White had the advantage because of his queenside attack(!).

6	...	♗g7
7	f3	0-0
8	♕d2	♘c6
9	♗c4	

This Dragon-bashing system could be called the "Fischer Attack." In *My 60 Memorable Games* Fischer said it was so simple to play that "weak players" could beat grandmasters with it.

9	...	♘xd4

Larsen adopts the ...♕a5, ...♖fc8 and ...b5 setup that remained the main line until the late 1960s.

10	♗xd4	♗e6
11	♗b3	♕a5
12	0-0-0	b5

This move was awarded an exclamation point in the tournament book by Gligorić and Matanović because the chief alternative, 12...♗xb3 13 cxb3! followed by ♔b1, leaves Black scant counterplay (13...♖fd8 14 ♔b1 ♖d7 15 g4 ♖ad8 16 ♕e2).

13	♔b1	b4
14	♘d5	♗xd5

15 ♗xd5?

Fischer didn't fully understand the finesses of this line yet. A year later Tal demonstrated White's positional superiority after 15 exd5!, e.g. 15...♕b5 (threatening ...a5-a4) 16 ♕d3 ♕xd3 17 ♖xd3 and ♖e1.

15	...	♖ac8?

Larsen explained that he saw 15...♘xd5 16 ♗xg7 ♘c3+! 17 bxc3 ♖ab8! 18 cxb4 (or 18 c4 ♔xg7 and ...♖fc8) ♕xb4+ 19 ♕xb4 ♖xb4+ 20 ♗b2 ♖fb8. But he rejected it because 17 ♗xc3 bxc3 18 ♕xc3 ♕xc3 19 bxc3 ♖fc8 was drawish.

Fischer indicated he would have played for a win after 15...♘xd5 with 16 exd5, and if 16...♕xd5 then 17 ♕xb4.

16 ♗b3!

Fischer believed the game was already won for him: Thanks to his bishop, Black's heavy pieces can't pierce the defenses of a2 or c2, and the ...a5-a4 plan is too slow. White has a free hand to advance his h-pawn and, he wrote, It's "sac, sac...mate!"

16	...	♖c7

Black opts for ...a5 but the immediate 16...♕b5 allows 17 ♗xa7!.

17	h4	♕b5

More than 10 years later the Dragon began another of its revivals, thanks to the defensive resource ...h5 (that is 12...h5 after 9...♗d7 10 0-0-0 ♖c8 11 ♗b3 ♘e5 12 h4). But here the ...h5 idea fails to "sac, sac...mate!" For example, 17...h5 18 g4 hxg4 19 h5! ♘xh5 20 ♗xg7 ♔xg7 21 fxg4 ♘f6 22 ♕h6+.

18 h5!   ♖fc8

White's attack is proven faster by 18...gxh5 19 g4! hxg4 20 fxg4 ♘xe4 21 ♕h2, e.g. 21...♘g5 22 ♗xg7 ♔xg7 23 ♖d5! and wins.

19 hxg6   hxg6

It's time to begin looking for a winning plan and there are three candidates. But the first one, 20 ♗xf6 ♗xf6 21 ♕h6, fails to 21...e6! followed by ...♕e5.

20 g4   a5

A second try – 20 g4 followed by tripling on the h-file (21 ♖h3, 22 ♖dh1 and 23 ♕h2 followed by ♖h8+) – is too slow because of 21...a4.

21 g5!

But this one works. After 21 g5 a4 White's attack arrives one step ahead of Black's – 22 gxf6 axb3 23 fxg7! bxc2+ 24 ♕xc2 ♖xc2 25 ♖h8 mate or 24...e5 25 ♕h2.

A better defense is 21...♘e8 22 ♗xg7 ♘xg7. But Fischer showed White is winning with 23 ♖h6! a4 24 ♕h2 ♘h5 25 ♖xg6+ or 23...e6 24 ♕h2 ♘h5 25 ♗xe6! fxe6 (25...♕xg5 26 ♖xg6+! ♕xg6 27 ♗xc8 and ♖g1) 26 ♖xg6+ ♘g7 27 ♖h1.

21 ...   ♘h5

Now 22 ♗xg7? ♘xg7? 23 ♖h6 transposes into the previous note. But 22...♔xg7! is hard to crack.

22 ♖xh5!   gxh5

Or 22...♗xd4 23 ♕xd4 gxh5 24 g6 and White wins following 24...e6 25 ♕d6! or in the endgame of 24...♕e5 25 gxf7+ ♔f8 (not 25...♔h7 26 ♕d3! and 27 f4 followed by discovered check) 26 ♕xe5! dxe5 27 ♖g1 e6 28 ♗xe6 ♔e7 29 ♗xc8 ♖xc8 30 ♖g5.

23 g6   e5!

This, preparing his 25th move, is the only way to place obstacles in White's path. Black is quite lost after 23...e6 24 gxf7+ ♔xf7 25 ♗xg7 ♔xg7 26 ♖g1+ ♔h7 27 ♗xe6!.

24 gxf7+   ♔f8

25 ♗e3

Threatening 26 ♗h6 or 26 ♕xd6+. A pretty finish would be 25...a4 26 ♕xd6+ ♖e7 27 ♕d8+! ♖xd8 28 ♖xd8+ ♖e8 29 ♗c5+!.

25 ...   d5!

Based on 26 ♗xd5 ♖xc2.

26 exd5

The d-pawn becomes a factor (26...a4 27 d6!).

26 ...   ♖xf7

27 d6   ♖f6

White had two ways to beat 27...♖d7 (28 ♗e6 and 28 ♗h6).

28 &g5! ♕b7

Another nice finish would have been 28...♕d7 29 ♕d5 ♖f7 30 &e7+!.

29 &xf6   &xf6

30 d7   ♖d8

31 ♕d6+   Resigns

The tournament book incorrectly credits Fischer with playing the faster win, 31 ♕h6+!.

6

Fischer's second U.S. Championship title wasn't certain until the penultimate round when Arthur Bisguier botched a favourable middlegame against him and then blundered away a drawn rook-and-pawn endgame. Jack Collins, another of Fischer's mentors, cited this game in *My Seven Chess Prodigies* as an example of Bobby's "versatility." But it's a better testament to his will to win – and over-optimism.

Fischer – Charles Kalme
U.S. Championship,
New York 1958-59
Ruy Lopez (C98)

1 e4   e5

2 ♘f3   ♘c6

3 &b5   a6

4 &a4   ♘f6

5 0-0   &e7

6 ♖e1   b5

7 &b3   d6

8 c3   0-0

9 h3   ♘a5

10 &c2   c5

11 d4   ♕c7

12 ♘bd2   ♘c6

13 dxc5   dxc5

14 ♘f1   &e6

Kalme, who gave up chess for mathematics a few years later, heads into what was a main line of the Lopez in 1959.

15 ♘e3   ♖ad8

16 ♕e2   g6

Better may be 16...c4 17 ♘f5 (not 17 ♘g5 h6 18 ♘xe6 fxe6 19 b4? ♘d4! and Black had the upper hand in Fischer – Kholmov, Havana 1965) 17...&xf5 18 exf5 ♖fe8.

17 ♘g5   &c8

The loosening of Black's king position after 16...g6 makes 17...c4 18 ♘xe6 much better than in the previous note (18...fxe6 19 ♘g4!).

18 a4

White's middlegame priorities are challenging the enemy queenside pawns, and a timely ♘d5 to open the center.

18 ...   c4

If Black defends the b-pawn with his queen, White has several attractive options, including 19 axb5 axb5 20 h4 and 20 &b3.

19 axb5   axb5

20 b3

28

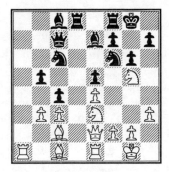

White realizes both priorities after 20...cxb3 21 ♗xb3 ♘a5 22 ♘d5!, with advantage.

20 ... b4!?

The first new move, designed to soften up d4 for a knight landing. Previously 20...♘a5 21 bxc4 bxc4 22 ♗a3! had been played and found to favor White.

The combination 20...cxb3 21 ♗xb3 ♘a5 22 ♘d5! ♘xd5 23 ♗xd5 ♖xd5 fails to 24 exd5 ♘b3 25 d6!. White has a clear edge after 25...♗xd6 26 ♖b1 or 25...♕xd6 26 ♗a3.

21 ♕xc4!

Black's innovation shines after 21 ♘xc4 bxc3 22 ♕e3 ♘d4!. Black also has excellent piece play after 21 cxb4 ♗xb4 and 22...♘d4. Black gets the upper hand after 23 ♗a3 ♗xa3 24 ♖xa3 ♘d4.

21 ... h6

A consequence of Black's last move. Now 22 ♘f3 ♗e6 23 ♕-moves bxc3 favors him.

22 ♘d5! ♘xd5
23 exd5 hxg5

It makes more sense for Black to trade off a pair of bishops – 23...♗xg5 24 ♗xg5 hxg5 – although White is still a tad better after 25 ♕xc6 ♕xc6 26 dxc6 ♖d2

27 ♖ac1. Another point is that 25 cxb4 (threatening 26 b5) ♖xd5 allows White to play for a win with 26 ♗e4!.

24 ♕xc6! ♕xc6
25 dxc6 bxc3

Post-mortem attempts to improve Black's chances with 25...♗f6 26 cxb4 ♗e6 27 ♗e3 e4 28 ♖ad1 or 25...♗e6 26 ♖a7 ♗c5 27 ♖b7 failed.

26 ♖xe5 ♗f6

Another try is 26...♗f5 (27 ♗xf5 ♖d1+ 28 ♔h2 ♗d6) to obtain bishops of opposite color and halt White's queenside pawns. But 27 ♖xe7 ♗xc2 28 b4 ♖d1+ 29 ♔h2 ♗d3 30 ♖d7 and b4-b5 breaks the blockade.

Now 27 ♖c5 ♗d4 seems to help Black, but 28 ♖c4 ♗e6 29 c7! ♖d6 30 ♗a3! wins.

27 ♖ea5 ♖fe8!

The best try. White's material begins to tell after 27...g4 28 hxg4 ♗xg4 29 ♗f4 or 27...♗e6 28 ♗xg5 ♗xg5 29 ♖xg5 ♖d2 30 ♖c1 and 31 ♖c5.

28 ♗xg5!?

White must act with dispatch since 28 ♔f1 allows 28...♖d2!, e.g. 29 ♗xd2 cxd2 30 ♖d1? ♖e1+ or

30 ♖d5 ♗a6+ 31 ♔g1 ♗xa1
31 ♖xd2 ♖e1+ 32 ♔h2 ♗e5+ and
Black is the one with winning
chances. The most accurate move
was 28 ♗e3!. Now Black's rooks
become dangerous.

28	...	♗xg5
29	♖xg5	♖d2
30	♖c1	♖ee2

This was a key idea behind
27...♖fe8. A unique situation arises
after 31 ♖a5 ♖xc2 (not 31...♖xf2
32 ♗e4 c2 33 ♖xc2 ♖xc2 34 ♖a8)
32 ♖xc2 ♖xc2 33 ♖a8 ♖c1+ 34 ♔h2
c2 35 ♖xc8+ ♔g7 36 c7, when both
players will queen on the c-file.

Black then wins with 36...♖h1+
37 ♔xh1 c1(♕)+ 38 ♔h2 ♕f4+.

31	♗xg6!	fxg6
32	♖xc3	♔h7
33	b4!	

Not 33 ♖f3 ♖c2! and the pawns
pose no threat.

33	...	♖e1+
34	♔h2	♖xf2
35	b5	

This was by far the best game
Fischer played in the tournament.
Why then did he fail to include it in
My 60 Memorable Games? The search
for an answer starts here.

35	...	♖b2
36	♔g3	

The king threatens to help
shepherd the pawns (36...♖ee2
37 ♔f3). Black can try to stop that
with 36...♖g1 with the idea of
37 ♔f3 ♗xh3! 38 gxh3! ♖xg5 39 c7
♖f5+ 40 ♔e4 ♖f8, drawing. White
cannot play for a win with 37 ♔h4
♖gxg2 38 ♖xg2 ♖xg2 39 b6 because
39...g5+! mates.

36	...	♔h6!

A good attempt to confuse White
(37 ♖gc5? ♖eb1).

37	♖cc5!	♖e3+
38	♔f4	♖eb3
39	♖gd5	

White, seeking a win at all cost,
avoids 39 h4 ♖b4+ after which a
draw is inevitable (40 ♔e3 ♖2b3+
41 ♔d2 ♖xh4 42 c7).

39	...	♖xg2
40	♖d8	♗e6?

On 41...♗xh3 42 ♖h8+ ♔g7
43 ♖xh3! ♖xh3 (or 43...♖f2+
44 ♔g4 ♖g2+) 44 c7 ♖f2+ 45 ♔g4
♖h8 Black draws. That would be a
just outcome to a sterling game. But
that's not the only reason the game
was omitted by Fischer.

Black missed a bid for a clear
advantage with 40...♖f2+! 41 ♔e5
♗xh3. The position resembles the
game – but with the major difference
that 42 ♖h8+ ♔g7 43 ♖xh3 ♖xh3
44 c7? loses to 44...♖h5+ 45 ♔d6
♖f6+ 46 ♔d7 ♖xc5. But 44 ♔d6
draws.

If, instead, 42 c7 Black has
42...♖f5+ 43 ♔d6 ♖d3+ 44 ♔c6
♖f6+ 45 ♔b7 ♗g2+ 46 ♔c8 ♖a3!.

41	♔e5	♗xh3

42 ♖h8+ ♔g7

43 ♖xh3! ♖xh3
44 c7

Now White is winning but there are several finesses to come.

44 ... ♖h8
45 ♖d5!

The natural 45 ♔d6 ♖b2 46 ♔c6 enables Black to complicate with 46...♔f6 47 b6 ♖e8 48 b7 ♖e6+ 49 ♔d5 ♖d2+ 50 ♔c4 ♖c2+ or 48 ♔b7 g5!.

45 ... ♖e2+

The threat was 46 ♖d8, and if 45...♖c2, then 46 b6.

46 ♔d6 ♔f6
47 b6 ♖b2
48 ♔c6 ♖c8?

The final error. Black could have drawn with 48...♔e6! 49 ♖d8 ♖c2+ 50 ♔b5 ♖h5+ and ...♖hc5!.

49 ♖d8 ♖c2+
50 ♔b7 ♖8xc7+
51 bxc7

White wins by a tempo now – and would win faster after 51...g5? 52 ♖d6+ and 53 ♖c6.

51 ... ♔f5

After five hours, a good swindle try would have been 51...♔e5, since

52 c8(♕) ♖xc8 53 ♖xc8 g5 54 ♔c6 g4 shuts the White's king out. But 52 ♖g8! ♔f5 53 c8(♕)+ transposes into the game and wins.

52 c8(♕)+ ♖xc8

53 ♖xc8! g5
54 ♔c6 g4
55 ♔d5 ♔f4

Or 55...g3 56 ♖f8+ ♔g4 57 ♔e4 g2 58 ♖g8+ and ♔f3.

56 ♔d4 ♔f3
57 ♔d3! Resigns

7

It was the games like the last one and the next that established Fischer's reputation for endurance. At Portorož he beat Sherwin when his New York rival blundered into a Lucena position with his 78th move. Earlier in the Interzonal he drew in 73 moves with Hector Rossetto when there were only two kings and a knight left on the board. Other players began to exaggerate his willingness to play until there was nothing remaining. Tal said Fischer played on in the last round at Bled 1961 "literally until there were only kings left." Tal's second, Alexander

31

Koblents, claimed Fischer's game with Gedeon Barcza at Zürich 1959 lasted until "there were only two kings on the board (and) Fischer played two more moves!" (The published scores don't back up either story.) Koblents added that when Fischer conceded Barcza the draw he wanted to post-mortem from move one because, he said, "Somewhere I could have played better." Barcza begged off, saying, "I have a wife and children. Who will feed them in case of my premature death?"

Fischer – Jacobo Bolbochán
Mar del Plata 1959
Sicilian Defense,
Four Knights Variation (B45)

1	e4	c5
2	♘f3	♘c6
3	d4	cxd4
4	♘xd4	♘f6
5	♘c3	e6
6	♘db5	♗b4
7	a3	♗xc3+
8	♘xc3	d5
9	♗d3!?	

This, rather than 9 exd5, shows supreme faith in the power of two bishops. On the only other occasion in which Fischer reached this position in a serious game (against William Addison three years later) he won a long endgame with 9 exd5 ♘xd5 10 ♗d2!? ♘xc3 11 ♗xc3 ♕xd1+ 12 ♖xd1.

In a 1968 simul against some of Greece's best players, Fischer won another long ending after 12...f6 13 f4 ♗d7 14 ♗c4 0-0-0 15 0-0

♖he8 16 ♖de1 ♖e7 and now 17 b4 ♔c7 18 b5 ♘b8 19 ♗b4.

9	...	dxe4

Black can insist on eliminating a bishop with 9...♘e5!.

10	♘xe4	♘xe4
11	♗xe4	♕xd1+
12	♔xd1	

12	...	♗d7

The books endorsed 12...f5 as Bolbochán had played seven years before in a game that went 13 ♗xc6+ (or 13 ♗f3 ♘d4) bxc6 14 ♖e1 ♔f7. That is the kind of position considered "equal" because a draw is likely. But the winning chances are not equal, and White can press with 15 c4 followed by b2-b3 and ♖e5.

13	♗e3	f5
14	♗f3	e5
15	b4!	

Better than 15 ♖e1 ♔f7 16 g3 ♖ac8 17 ♔c1 ♗e6 as in another Bolbochán game.

15	...	0-0-0
16	♔c1	♘d4

White is favored by 16...e4 17 ♗e2 ♗e6 18 ♔b2 and ♖ad1 (or 18...♘e5? 19 ♗xa7). But 16...♔c7, threatening 17...f4, is better.

17	♗xd4	exd4

The d-pawn looks weak but White's king can be stopped from reaching d3.

> **18 ♖e1   ♖he8**
>
> **19 ♔d2   ♗b5!**

White wins the pawn after 20 ♗e2 ♗xe2 but he has little after 20...♗c6.

> **20 ♖xe8   ♖xe8**
>
> **21 a4   ♗c4**
>
> **22 ♖c1**

With a threat of 23 c3 since 23...dxc3+? 24 ♖xc3 would cost the bishop.

> **22 ...   ♔b8**
>
> **23 c3   dxc3+**
>
> **24 ♖xc3   ♗f7**
>
> **25 a5   ♖e7**

In the last four moves Fischer converted one unexploitable asset, the weak d-pawn, for others, such as the more mobile king. Here 25...b6 would free Black from defending the b-pawn – but sentence him to defending the a-pawn after 26 a6!.

> **26 ♖e3   ♖d7+**

Rook trades favor White significantly (26...♖xe3? 27 ♔xe3 g5 28 ♔d4 etc) – so Black must allow the rook to attack pawns from behind.

> **27 ♖d3   ♖e7**
>
> **28 ♖d8+   ♔c7**
>
> **29 ♖h8   h6**
>
> **30 ♔c3   a6**

If Black tries 30...♖d7 and ...♗d5, White trades bishops and wins with ♖f8-f7+.

> **31 ♔d4   ♗e8**

Or 31...♖d7+ 32 ♔e5 ♖d2 33 ♖h7! and ♖xg7 wins.

> **32 ♖f8   ♗d7**

> **33 h4!   ♗c8**
>
> **34 ♗d5   ♗d7**
>
> **35 f4**

> **35 ...   g6?**

Like Taimanov in Game 90, Black is induced to put his pawns on light squares and tormented with threats of *zugzwang*. For example, 35...♗c8 36 ♖f7 ♖xf7 37 ♗xf7 ♔d6 38 ♗d5! soon runs Black out of moves.

Nevertheless, 35...g6? is the closest thing to a losing move in the game. With 35...♖e1!, as pointed out by Christopher Lutz, Black has real drawing chances, e.g. 36 ♖f7 ♖d1+ 37 ♔c5 ♖c1+ 38 ♗c4 ♔d8 39 ♔d5 ♖xc4 40 ♖xd7+ ♔xd7 41 ♔xc4 ♔c6!.

> **36 ♖f6   ♗e8**
>
> **37 ♗e6   ♗c6**
>
> **38 g3**

White may have had doubts about 38 ♖xg6 ♗xg2 39 ♖xh6, but it's also a win.

> **38 ...   ♖g7**
>
> **39 ♔e5**

Threat: 40 ♖f7+ and ♔f6.

> **39 ...   ♗e8**
>
> **40 ♗d5   h5**
>
> **41 ♖b6   ♔c8**

Not 41...♗c6 42 ♗xc6, and the
a-pawn dies.

42 ♗e6+ ♚c7

43 ♚f6 ♖h7

44 ♗d5 ♚c8

45 ♖e6!

Now 45...♗f7? 46 ♖e7 and White
wins.

45 ... ♚d8

46 ♖d6+ ♚c7

Black's quandary is illustrated by
46...♚c8 47 ♗g8 ♖c7 (47...♖h6 or
47...♖h8 loses the rook to 48 ♚g7)
48 ♗e6+ ♚b8 49 ♖d8+ and wins.

47 ♖b6 ♚c8

48 ♗g8 ♖c7

49 ♗e6+ ♚b8

Or 49...♚d8 50 ♖d6+ and wins.

50 ♖d6 Resigns

The threat is ♖d8+, e.g. 50...♚a7
51 ♖d8 ♗b5 52 ♚xg6.

8

Fischer had two favorite countries
to play in, Argentina and Yugoslavia.
Of the 15 international tournaments,
not counting the Interzonals and
Olympiads, in which he competed,

four were held in Argentina,
including his first, Mar del Plata
1959 and his last, Buenos Aires 1970
– and also his worst, Buenos Aires
1960. This was his favorite game
from Mar del Plata.

Fischer – Hector Rossetto
Mar del Plata 1959
Sicilian Defense,
Kan Variation (B41)

1 e4 c5

2 ♘f3 e6

3 d4 cxd4

4 ♘xd4 a6

5 c4

This had been considered a virtual
refutation of 4...a6 since the 1920s
but Black's system made a comeback
in the 1950s.

5 ... ♛c7

6 ♘c3 ♘f6

7 ♗d3

Fischer expressed the conventional
wisdom of the 1960s when he said
the restricting 7 a3 gave White a
major edge. But today 7...♗e7 8 ♗e3
0-0 9 ♖c1 ♘c6 and ...♘xd4 is one of
a few lines recognized as equal.

7 ... ♘c6

8 ♗e3 ♘xd4

Fischer recommended 8...♘e5! so
Black can meet 9 0-0 with 9...♘eg4!
and 9 ♖c1 with 9...♘fg4!.

9 ♗xd4 ♗c5

10 ♗c2 d6

11 0-0 ♗d7

12 ♘a4! ♗xd4

Black seems to lose this game
because he believes in the absolute
defensibility of his position even

after White controls b6. Here 12...♗xa4 13 ♗xa4+ ♔e7 is more promising.

13 ♕xd4 ♖d8

And so is 13...e5 followed by ...♗c6.

14 ♖fd1 0-0!

There was no reason to fear 15 ♕xd6 ♕xd6 16 ♖xd6 because of 16...♗xa4 and ...♘xe4.

15 ♖ac1 ♕a5

Black must delay the usual liberating advances (...d5 or ...b5), e.g. 15...b5 16 cxb5 axb5 17 ♘c3 after which b5 is a lingering target.

16 ♕b6!

A powerful move – used to similar effect by Viswanathan Anand in a 1995 Candidates match game with Gata Kamsky – that trades off the only active enemy piece. If Black tries 16...♕e5 17 ♖xd6 ♘g4 his attack dies in its tracks after 18 g3 ♕h5 19 h4 (19...♘e5 20 ♗d1 ♕g6 21 ♘c5).

16 ... ♕xb6

17 ♘xb6 ♗c6

18 f3

White is making slow progress – a good policy since Black may be

tempted into 18...d5? 19 cxd5 exd5, which leads to a textbook disadvantage after 20 e5 ♘d7 21 ♘xd7 ♖xd7 22 ♖d4.

18 ... ♘d7!

Black will have good counterplay after 19 ♘a4 ♘e5 20 ♗b3 g5! – and can defend his only weakness, d6, after 19 ♘xd7 ♖xd7 20 ♖d2 ♖fd8 and ...♔f8-e7.

19 ♘d5! ♗xd5?

Black shifts from watchful waiting to a strategy of making White's bishop "bad" and setting his own pawns on dark squares. That might work with queens on the board. But here he underestimates the force of White's b2-b4 and c4-c5 in an ending. The other way of transforming the position, 19...exd5 20 exd5 ♘e5, was adequate, according to Fischer, e.g. 21 dxc6 bxc6 22 b3 c5 23 ♗e4 ♖fe8. But 22 f4! favors White (22...♘g6 23 g3 or 22...♘xc4 23 ♗xh7+ ♔xh7 24 ♖xc4.

20 exd5 e5

21 b4 g6

A recurring theme now is the threat of bishop-takes-knight, since then c4-c5 would decide the game positionally. Black's last move avoids, for example, 21...a5 22 a3 axb4 23 axb4 ♖a8 24 ♗f5!, and it prepares ...f5 and ...♔g7-f6.

22 ♗a4! b6

"A knight is always badly placed on b6" proves true after 22...♘b6 23 ♗b3 and 24 c5.

23 ♖d3

Black must play 23...a5 (and if 24 a3 then 24...f5).

23 ... f5?

24 &Xa3!

White threatens &xd7 and &xa6, and he can meet 24...&f6 with 25 &c6!.

24 ...   &b8

White wins after 24...a5 25 bxa5 bxa5 26 &c6!, e.g. 26...&b6 27 &b1! &xc4? 28 &c3 &d2 29 &b2.

25 c5!   bxc5

The barricade policy (25...b5) leaves White with a protected passed pawn that must win (26 &b3 &f7 27 c6 &c7 28 &a5! and 29 a4).

26 bxc5   dxc5

27 &xc5   &g7

Black hopes to play ...&d6, to blockade the pawn and protect e5 (which 27...&d6 28 &e3 fails to do). After 27...&d7 28 &c7 &f6 29 &b3 his position would soon be hopeless.

28 &b3   &f7

29 d6

The main threat is 30 &c7 and &bb7.

29 ...   &d7

30 &c7

Doubling on the seventh rank is decisive. For example, 30...&f6 31 &bb7 &xc7 32 dxc7! &c8 33 &b3 &e8 34 &b8 &d6 35 &xc8 and &e6.

30 ...   &f8

31 &bb7   &xc7

32 bxc7!   &c8

White's winning method impresses "with simplicity and clarity," Russian author Leonid Verkhovsky said in a section of a 1989 book devoted to *zugzwang*.

33 &b3!

Black has no useful moves since &d7 allows &e6 and ...&-somewhere invites &b8!. The finale was:

33 ... a5 34 a4 h6 35 h3 g5 36 g4! fxg4 37 hxg4 Resigns

9

In his provocative 1964 article in *Chessworld,* Fischer listed the 10 greatest players of all time but seemed reluctant to include Alexander Alekhine (and omitted him in a similar list six years later). Fischer's criticism: "If you've seen one Alekhine game you've seen them all." He explained that Alekhine tried to get the superior center, shifted his pieces to kingside attack and delivered mate around move 25.

The same complaint may be lodged against Fischer, at least in his favorite &c4 line of the Sicilian

Defense. He followed a simple formula: safeguard the bishop at b3 and attack e6 with f2-f4-f5. If that secures control of d5, White has a variety of winning plans, beginning with a rook lift to h3 and queen to h5.

Fischer – Herman Pilnik
Santiago 1959
Sicilian Defense,
Sozin Variation (B88)

1	e4	c5
2	♘f3	♘c6
3	d4	cxd4
4	♘xd4	♘f6
5	♘c3	d6
6	♗c4	e6
7	♗b3	♗e7
8	0-0	0-0

A month later at Zürich, Joseph Kupper tried to exploit the absence of ♗e3 by way of 8...♘xd4 9 ♕xd4 0-0 10 f4 b6, threatening 11...d5 and 12...♗c5. But after 11 ♔h1 the formula worked perfectly: 11...♗b7 12 f5 e5 13 ♕d3 h6? (better 13...♖c8 14 ♗g5 ♖xc3!) 14 ♖f3 ♖c8 15 ♖h3 ♔h7 16 ♗e3 ♕d7? 17 ♘d5 ♗xd5 18 ♗xd5 ♘xd5 19 exd5 ♗f6 20 ♗xh6! gxh6 21 ♕e3 and wins.

9	♗e3	♗d7

This system, leaving out ...a6 in favor of ...♘xd4, ...♗c6 and ...b5, was quite popular at the time. Korchnoi went one step further at Rovinj-Zagreb 1970 and got an excellent game against Fischer with 9...♘xd4 10 ♗xd4 b5 11 ♘xb5 ♗a6.

10	f4	♘xd4
11	♗xd4	♗c6

Theory has paid little attention to 11...b5, although 12 e5 ♘e8 and 12 ♗xf6 gxf6 are not as bad for Black as they appear.

12	♕e2	

Better than 12 ♕d3 because 12...b5! 13 ♘xb5 ♗xe4 is with tempo.

12	...	♕a5?

The strength of a new opening idea is often judged by how well it responds to natural defenses. The text is a fine example of a routine move that is quickly punished. Black needs a quick ...b5 before White secures control of d5. Fischer had demonstrated, against Raymond Weinstein in the previous U.S. Championship, that 12...b5 13 ♘xb5 ♗xb5 14 ♕xb5 ♘xe4 should favor White following 15 f5. For example 15...d5 16 fxe6 fxe6 17 ♕c6 or 15...♗f6 16 ♕d3 – although 15...e5 16 ♗e3 ♗g5 is a better try (17 ♕e2 ♗xe3+ 18 ♕xe3 ♘f6 and ...a5-a4).

13	f5!	e5

This tempo-gainer is also natural, particularly since 13...exf5 14 ♖xf5 fuels White's initiative (14...♕b4 15 ♖d1 b5 16 g4 and now 16...h6 17 a3 ♕a5 18 ♗xf6 ♗xf6 19 ♖xf6 gxf6 20 ♖xd6 is promising).

14	♗f2	

But now 14...b5 15 a3 ♕c7 turns out to be much too slow. A Russian game, also played in 1959, ended soon after 14...♕c7 15 g4! ♘d7 16 h4 h6 17 ♔g2 ♘c5 18 ♗xc5 dxc5 19 g5! hxg5 20 hxg5 ♗xg5 21 ♕h5 ♗h6 22 f6!.

14 ...   ♗d8

This deserves a better fate. Pilnik, a Candidate three years before, decides to exchange off his worst piece, even at the cost of a pawn.

15 ♖ad1   ♗b6!

He would solve his most pressing problems after 16 ♖xd6 ♗xf2+ 17 ♖xf2 ♖ad8.

16 g4!

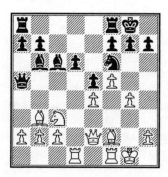

16 ...   h6?

Even with the bishop diverted from e7, Black believed he could hold up g4-g5 with ...h6 and ...♘h7. The alternatives were:

(a) 16...♗xf2+ 17 ♖xf2 ♕c5 18 g5 ♘e8 19 ♕h5 and there is no good way of meeting 20 g6 or 20 ♖d3 and 21 ♖h3.

(b) 16...♔h8 17 g5 ♘g8, a defensive formation Najdorf used in similar positions. But 18 ♖d3 (or 18 ♖xd6) ♗xf2+ 19 ♖xf2 ♖ad8 20 ♖h3 grants White a free hand on the kingside, e.g. 20...g6 21 ♕g4 h6 22 ♖xh6+ ♘xh6 23 ♕h4 and mates.

17 h4   ♘h7

Black may have counted on 17...♗d4 18 ♗xd4 exd4 19 ♖xd4 ♕e5 – only to discover now that 18 g5! keeps the attack rolling. A typical line would be 18...hxg5 19 hxg5 ♘h7 20 ♖d3 (or 20 g6) ♘xg5 21 ♖g3 ♗xc3 22 ♖xg5 ♗d2 and now 23 ♖xg7+! ♔xg7 24 ♕g4+ ♔h7 25 ♕h5+ ♗h6 26 ♗e3 and wins.

18 ♖d3!

This is superior to 18 ♖xd6 ♗xf2+ 19 ♖xf2 ♖ad8 with d-file play.

18 ...   ♔h8

19 g5   ♗d4

Not 19...hxg5 20 hxg5 ♘xg5 21 ♕h5+ ♘h7 22 ♖h3.

20 ♔h2!

The point of Black's last move was to discourage 20 ♕h5 by way of 20...♗xc3 and ...♗xe4. But there's no reason to worry about 20...♗xc3 21 bxc3 ♗b5 22 c4 ♗c6 since White has a choice of winning ideas, starting with 23 gxh6 gxh6 24 ♖xd6.

20 ...   ♗b5

21 ♘xb5   ♕xb5

22 c3!   ♗xf2

23 ♖xf2   ♕b6?

Better than this prelude to desperation was 23...hxg5 24 hxg5 g6 although 25 ♕d2 should win.

24 ♖g2   d5
25 ♗xd5   ♖ad8
26 ♕h5   g6
27 ♕xh6   ♖xd5

Otherwise 28 f6 ♖g8 29 ♗xf7 wins.

28 exd5   e4

White should avoid 28...gxf5 29 ♕xb6 and go for mate with 29 g6 fxg6 30 ♖xg6 ♕c7 31 ♖dg3 and ♖g7.

29 ♖dg3   ♕d6
30 h5!   ♖g8
31 hxg6   fxg6
32 f6   ♕xd5

There was no defense (32...e3 33 ♔g1).

33 ♕xh7+! Resigns

Although he only tied for fourth in a weak field at Santiago, Fischer established his credentials as a legitimate grandmaster when he finished =3rd a month later at Zürich, behind Tal and Gligorić. *Chess Review* worried whether his success was luring him onto a path that led off a cliff. "Do we have the moral right to encourage Bobby Fischer?" the magazine asked. "The path of glory leads to poverty."

10

As he prepared for the fourth FIDE Candidates tournament, Paul Keres went on a fishing trip with Vladas Mikenas, the veteran Estonian master. While they were relaxing they talked chess and discovered a dangerous sacrificial line in the Najdorf Sicilian. "To celebrate our success," Mikenas recalled, they decided Keres should save the idea for a game with Fischer, who was becoming the world's most devoted Najdorf-ile. As luck would have it, Fischer was due for Black against Keres in the first round when the Candidates began in September 1959. The timing was perfect and "the 'fish' went for the bait," Mikenas wrote.

Paul Keres – Fischer
Candidates Tournament,
Bled-Zagreb-Belgrade 1959
Sicilian Defense,
Najdorf Variation (B99)

1	e4	c5
2	♘f3	d6
3	d4	cxd4
4	♘xd4	♘f6
5	♘c3	a6
6	♗g5	e6
7	f4	♗e7
8	♕f3	♕c7

Needing a draw against Gligorić in the final round at Portorož to qualify for this Candidates Tournament,

Fischer made the stunning choice of the "Argentine Variation" – 8...h6 9 ♗h4 g5 10 fxg5 ♘fd7 – despite the complications of 11 ♘xe6 fxe6 12 ♕h5+ ♔f8 13 ♗b5!. After 13...♖h7! he had the better of it when a draw was agreed at move 32.

9	0-0-0	♘bd7
10	♗e2	b5
11	♗xf6	♘xf6

12	e5!?	♗b7
13	exf6!	

The soul of the "fishing trip variation." White is worse after 13 ♕g3 dxe5 14 fxe5 ♘d7 15 ♕xg7 ♕xe5 or 15 ♗f3 0-0.

13	...	♗xf3
14	♗xf3	

Black must navigate past pitfalls such as 14...♖c8 15 fxe7 ♕xe7 16 ♘f5! exf5? 17 ♖he1 (Better is 15...b4! 16 ♘d5! exd5 17 ♖he1 ♕c4 with muddy complications.).

14	...	♗xf6!

The immediate bishop-trap, 14...d5, allows 15 fxe7 ♕xf4+ 16 ♔b1 ♔xe7 and now 17 ♗xd5 ♖ac8 18 ♗b7 b4 19 ♘e4! (Nunn).

15	♗xa8	

Now an attractive idea is 15...♕c4 16 ♘e4 ♕xa2, although White should have the better chances after 17 ♘xf6+ gxf6 18 c3!.

15	...	d5!

Black is ready to coordinate his pieces, e.g. 16 ♗c6+ ♔f8! 17 ♘ce2 ♔e7 and ...♖c8 should win.

16	♗xd5!	

Imagine being Fischer – playing the first game of your first Candidates Tournament and realizing you are still in the prepared analysis of one of the greatest attackers in chess history.

He didn't need much time to consider 16...♕xf4+? 17 ♔b1 ♗xd4 18 ♗c6+ ♔e7 19 ♘e2 because White ends up with rook, bishop and knight and a continuing attack for the sacrificed queen.

More enticing is 16...b4 17 ♗c6+ ♔e7. After 18 ♘ce2 ♖d8 19 ♖d2! Black can draw with 19...♗xd4 20 ♘xd4 ♖xd4 21 ♖xd4 ♕xc6.

16	...	♗xd4!

White has more than enough compensation after 16...exd5 17 ♘xd5 ♕c5 18 ♖he1+ ♔f8 19 ♘f5.

17	♖xd4	exd5

18 ♘xd5

Whether this is White's first mistake has been debated for more than 50 years. It gives up the option of retaking on d5 with the rook, such as with 18 ♖e1+ ♔f8 19 ♖e5 and then 19...h5? 20 ♖exd5 ♔g8 21 ♖d7 ♕c6 22 ♘e4.

Black improves with 19...g6 and after 20 ♘xd5 masters have tested four defenses, all adequate but none entirely convincing. Among them: 20...♕a7 21 c3 ♔g7 22 f5! gxf5 23 ♘e3 and 20...♕c5 21 c3 ♔g7 22 f5 ♖c8 23 f6+ ♔h8 24 ♖de4.

18 ... ♕c5

19 ♖e1+ ♔f8

20 c3

The smoke at least recedes enough so we can count pieces: White's rook, knight and pawn are not quite enough for a queen, provided Black's king finds safety and his rook is freed. Fischer's notes cite one example of Black's task – 20...g6 21 g4 ♔g7 22 g5 ♖d8 23 ♘f6! and now he has to bail out with perpetual check, 23...♖xd4 24 ♖e8! ♖d8! 25 ♖xd8 ♕e3+.

20 ... h5!

21 f5?

Analysts also tried to save White's ingenious opening with 21 ♖e5, threatening 22 ♘f6. Fischer regarded 21...g6 22 f5 ♔g7! as fine for Black (23 f6+ ♔h6 24 g4 b4!).

21 ... ♖h6

22 f6

The black rook is only temporarily thwarted by this and Fischer believed his winning chances were only "slight" after 22 ♖ed1.

22 ... gxf6

23 ♘f4?

Mikenas said he and Keres had underestimated Black's chances when they prepared the opening, and he concluded the best White could achieve after 12 e5 was a draw. "But Keres persisted in seeking a win – and lost," he added. He may have had 23 ♘e3 in mind, but Black is worse after 23...♖g6 24 ♖d5 ♕c8 25 ♖xh5 or 23...♕e5 24 ♖d5 ♕f4.

23 ... h4

24 ♖d8+?

White should begin setting up a defensive screen with 24 ♖ee4.

24 ... ♔g7

25 ♖1e8 ♕g1+

26 ♔d2 ♕f2+

27 ♘e2 ♖g6

Black frees h6 for his king (28 ♖g8+ ♔h6 29 ♖h8+ ♔g5).

28 g3 f5!

And now it has f6. Black delays ...hxg3 because in some cases ...h3! and ...♕xh2 will be the key to winning. (The immediate 28...h3 loses the pawn to rook checks.)

29 ♖g8+ ♔f6

The h-pawn proves decisive after 30 ♖d6+ ♔e7 31 ♖dxg6 fxg6 32 ♖xg6 h3! and ...♕xh2.

30 ♖xg6+   fxg6
31 gxh4   ♕xh2?

Black wrongly assumes the h4-pawn will fall. He wins after 31...♕xh4! 32 ♖d6+ ♔f7 33 h3 ♕h6+! and 34...♕xh3, e.g. 34 ♔e1 ♕xh3 35 ♖xg6 ♕h4+ (not 35...♔xg6?? 36 ♘f4+) 36 ♖g3 f4.

32 ♖d4!   ♕h1
33 ♔c2

White must stop the queen raid (e.g. 33 ♘f4 ♕b1!).

33 ...   ♔e5
34 a4?

Trading pawns is certainly desirable but 34 ♘c1! and ♘d3+ may create an impregnable fortress.

34 ...   ♕f1
35 ♘c1   ♕g2+
36 ♔b3?

Now White's king and knight are separated and he must avoid 36...bxa4+ 37 ♔xa4 ♕c2+! 38 ♘b3 ♕xb2 or 37 ♖xa4 ♕d2 38 ♘a2 f4 and wins. The king had to retreat to d1 after which 36...♔f6 37 ♘d3 ♕f1+ leaves the outcome in doubt.

36 ...   bxa4+
37 ♔a3   ♕c2
38 ♘d3+   ♔f6
39 ♘c5   ♕c1!

Even if Black wins the knight for his f-pawn, White will draw if he can capture both queenside pawns and then post his rook on a protected fourth-rank square such as d4. That's a fortress because Black cannot promote his g-pawn, his king is barred from taking part in mating threats – and there are no other winning plans.

40 ♖xa4   ♕e3
41 ♘xa6?

Also lost is 41 ♖xa6+? ♔g7 42 ♘e6+ ♔h6 43 ♘d4 ♔h5. But the main question is whether Black can win after 41 ♖d4!.

Fischer gave an elaborate line that began with 41...f4 42 ♘d3 f3 43 ♔b3 ♔g7 and then 44 ♔a3 ♕e2 45 ♔b3 ♕d1+ 46 ♔c4 a5! 47 ♔b5 a4 48 ♔a5 ♕b3 49 ♔a6 a3 after which the rook loses its pawn support (50 bxa3 ♕xa3+ and 51...♕xc3) and defeat is a matter of time.

41 ...   f4
42 ♖d4   ♔f5!

Far superior to 42...f3 43 ♘c5 f2 44 ♘e4+ ♕xe4 45 ♖xe4 f1(♕) after which Black can't break through. Now however, 43 ♘c5 ♕e7! 44 b4 ♕xh4 and both of Black's passed pawns will cost material.

43 ♘b4   ♕e7!
44 ♔b3   ♕xh4
45 ♘d3   g5
46 c4   ♕g3
47 c5   f3

Since Black is eager to play ...f2, White could have set a trap with 48 c6 f2? 49 c7! ♕xc7 50 ♘xf2 ♕b6+ 51 ♔c3. However, 48...♕c7! shuts the door (49 ♖c4 g4 etc.).

48	♔c4	f2
49	♘xf2	♛xf2
50	c6	♛xb2
51	♔c5	♛c3+
52	♔d5	g4
53	♖c4	♛e5 mate

Now imagine being Fischer – playing the first game of your first Candidates Tournament and realizing you've just mated one of the greatest attackers in chess history in the center of the board.

11

By 1959 Fischer had become good friends with Svetozar Gligorić, the dean of Yugoslav players, who was 20 years his senior. But he wasn't entirely impressed with Gligorić's skill. In that 1964 list of the ten greatest players of all time, he included only three contemporary players, Boris Spassky, Mikhail Tal and Sammy Reshevsky. But in 1970, when he was asked on a Yugoslav TV show if he had changed his list, Fischer revised it to include Gligorić, as well as Tigran Petrosian and Mikhail Botvinnik.

Fischer – Svetozar Gligorić
Candidates Tournament,
Bled-Zagreb-Belgrade 1959
Sicilian Defense,
Sozin Variation (B57)

1	e4	c5
2	♘f3	♘c6
3	d4	cxd4
4	♘xd4	♘f6
5	♘c3	d6

6	♗c4	♗d7

Black's last is a finesse to reach a Dragon position: After 7 ♗e3 Fischer would be barred by 7...♘g4! from playing the system he used against Larsen. Black can't play 6...g6 without risking 7 ♘xc6 bxc6 8 e5 (which Reuben Fine overlooked in his book on the 1972 Fischer – Spassky match).

7	♗b3	g6
8	f3	♘a5

Gligorić wants to trade a knight for a bishop to make castling safe. For example, 9 ♗e3 ♖c8 10 ♕d2 ♘c4 and now 11 ♗xc4 ♖xc4 12 0-0-0 ♗g7 and 13...0-0 (13 ♗h6? ♖xd4).

But he might not have gotten a chance to castle anyway because of 13 ♘b3! ♕c7 (13...0-0 14 e5 dxe5? 15 ♘c5) 14 ♗d4, as in Fischer – Zuckerman, U.S. Championship 1966-7, which went 14...♗e6 15 e5! dxe5 16 ♗xe5 ♕c8 17 ♘a5 ♖c7 19 ♗xc7 and wins.

9	♗g5	♗g7
10	♕d2	h6
11	♗e3	♖c8
12	0-0-0	♘c4
13	♕e2!	

A Dragon rule of thumb, which Fischer challenges here, holds that White can't mate if he's given up his dark-squared bishop for a knight. The routine policy is 13 ♗xc4 ♖xc4 14 g4, followed by 15 h4 and perhaps 16 g5. But that weakens his own king position slightly and raises the possibility of ...♖xc3.

13	...	♘xe3
14	♕xe3	

14 ...   0-0

Black should challenge the dark squares with 14...♕b6! 15 ♕d2 ♕c5 as Luis Marini did against Fischer a year later at Mar del Plata. White won after 16 f4 h5? 17 ♘f3 ♗h6 18 e5!. But 16...b5 17 ♖he1 b4 is better, e.g. 18 ♘d5 ♘xd5 19 exd5 ♗g4 and now 20 ♗a4+ ♔f8 21 ♘f3 ♗c3! and Black wins.

Also 18 ♘a4 ♕a5 19 a3! ♖b8! favors him but not 19...♗xa4? 20 axb4 ♕a6 21 ♕d3!.

15 g4

Not 15 h4 h5! and Black can safely meet 16 g4 hxg4 17 h5 with 17...♘xh5 18 fxg4 ♗xg4 19 ♖dg1 ♘f6 and ...♗h5.

15 ...   ♕a5

16 h4

The attack is superior to the positional plan of 16 ♘d5 ♘xd5 17 exd5 ♗a4!.

16 ...   e6

A major concession, weakening the d-pawn in order to take control of d5. But it allows Black to meet 17 g5 hxg5 18 hxg5 with 18...♘h5 since there is no ♘d5.

17 ♘de2!

Retreats of well-posted pieces are often the most easily overlooked moves. But this one is recommended by three factors: (a) it opens up an attack on d6, (b) it protects against ...♖c5, ...♖fc8 and ...♖xc3, and (c) it prepares to use this knight to exchange off Black's after g4-g5 and ...♘h5.

17 ...   ♖c6

18 g5   hxg5

19 hxg5   ♘h5

20 f4   ♖fc8

21 ♔b1!

Fischer saw the trick of 21 f5? exf5 22 ♘d5 ♕xa2! and Black wins (23 ♗xa2 ♖xc2+ 24 ♔b1 ♖xb2+ 25 ♔a1 ♖xe2+).

21 ...   ♕b6

22 ♕f3

White prepares 23 f5, and if 23...exf5 then 24 exf5 ♗xf5 25 ♖xh5.

22 ...   ♖c5!

Another clever defense: 23 f5 exf5 24 ♘d5 ♕d8 25 exf5 ♗xf5 26 ♖xh5? fails to 26...♖xc2!.

23 ♕d3

Robert Hübner pointed out that 23 f5! exf5 24 ♖xh5! gxh5 25 ♕xh5 is strong. Computers found that 23 ♖xh5! gxh5 24 ♕xh5 and 25 f5 is also good, e.g. 24...♗e8 25 f5 exf5 26 ♘f4.

23 ...   ♗xc3

Black burns his bridges because he had no good way to defend d6 and also stop f4-f5. For example:

(a) 23...♖8c6 24 ♘a4!,

(b) 23...♗f8 24 f5 exf5 25 ♘d5 and then ♖xh5! and ♘f6+ must win,

(c) 23...♗b5 24 ♘xb5 ♕xb5 25 ♕xb5 ♖xb5 26 c3! ♖d8 27 ♖df1 and eventually f4-f5,

(d) 23...♗e8 24 ♕xd6 ♕xd6 25 ♖xd6 ♗xc3 with chances of endgame salvation. Another version is 23...a5 24 ♕xd6 ♕xd6 25 ♖xd6 ♗e8. A key point is that 24 a4? allows 24...♘xf4! 25 ♘xf4 ♖xc3! 26 bxc3 ♖xc3 (27 ♕xd6? ♖xb3+).

24 ♘xc3!   ♘xf4
25 ♕f3   ♘h5

Fischer's notes made no mention of 25...♖xc3 26 bxc3 e5 – probably because 26 ♕xf4! wins outright. Another defensive "sac" – 25...e5 26 ♘d5 ♖xd5 – would misfire because of 26 ♘e2!, since there is no defense to 27 ♘xf4 exf4 28 ♕xf4 and ♕h4.

26 ♖xh5!   gxh5
27 ♕xh5   ♗e8!

Black loses faster after 27...♔f8 28 ♕h8+ ♔e7 29 ♕f6+ ♔e8 30 ♖h1 ♗b5 31 ♗xe6!.

28 ♕h6!

Cutting off king escapes so that 29 g6 or 29 ♖h1 must win.

28 ...   ♖xc3
29 bxc3

More exact than 29 ♖h1 ♕d4!. But 29 g6! was an alternative win (29...♖g3 30 ♕h7+ ♔f8 31 ♕h8+ ♔e7 32 ♕h4+ ♔d7 33 ♕xg3 fxg6 34 ♗xe6+! or 29...♖xb3 30 ♕h7+ ♔f8 31 axb3).

29 ...   ♖xc3

Or 29...♕e3 30 ♖h1 ♕xc3 31 g6 ♕g7 32 ♕h2! and gxf7+ wins as pointed out by David Bronstein, who was much taken by this game.

30 g6!   fxg6
31 ♖h1   ♕d4
32 ♕h7+   Resigns

As in the Larsen game, White missed a faster mate (32 ♗xe6+).

12

By 1959 Fischer's games had already made an impression on opening theory – not in ancient lines such as the Bishop's Gambit and the Two Knights' Defense with 9 ♘h3, which he would revive in the 1960s – but in cutting edge variations. The following was only the first grandmaster game featuring Pal Benko's antidote to 6 ♗c4. Yet Black's crushing defeat threatened to push 6...♕b6 into retirement, a year after it had been introduced.

Fischer – Pal Benko
Candidates Tournament,
Bled-Zagreb-Belgrade 1959
Sicilian Defense, Sozin Variation (B57)

1 e4   c5

2	♘f3	♘c6
3	d4	cxd4
4	♘xd4	♘f6
5	♘c3	d6
6	♗c4	♕b6

Benko first used this move in the 1957 Hungarian Championship and used it one other time, at Portorož, before this game.

7	♘de2	e6
8	0-0	♗e7
9	♗b3	0-0
10	♔h1	♘a5
11	♗g5	

This points out a tactical flaw in ...♕b6/...♘a5. Black can't play 11...♗d7? because 12 e5! dxe5? 13 ♗xf6 hangs the bishop.

| 11 | ... | ♕c5! |

And this solves the problem while preparing ...b5-b4.

12	f4	b5
13	♘g3	

Since this opening was virtually being invented at the time, one can appreciate Fischer's common sense: He doesn't get fancy but just coordinates and protects his pieces and pawns (♗b3, ♗g5/f2-f4) and

directs them at the kingside (♘e2-g3 rather than 7 ♘b3). Nevertheless, he later concluded that 13...♘xb3 14 axb3 ♗b7 would equalize (15 ♘h5 ♔h8). Also good is 13...♗b7 and even 13...♔h8.

13	...	b4?
14	e5!	

This opens e4 up to White's knights and invites Black into 14...bxc3 15 exf6 ♗xf6 16 ♗xf6 gxf6 17 ♘e4 ♕f5 18 ♘xd6 with a crushing initiative, e.g. 18...♕g6 19 ♖f3 ♔h8 20 ♖g3 ♕h6 21 ♕g4!, threatening 22 ♕g8+!. No better is 15...gxf6 16 ♗h6 f5 17 ♘h5!.

| 14 | ... | dxe5 |

Here 15 ♘ce4 fails to 15...♕d4.

| 15 | ♗xf6 | |

Step two in the combination: 15...♗xf6 is refuted by 16 ♘ce4 ♕e7 17 ♘h5! (17...♔h8 18 ♘exf6 gxf6 19 fxe5 fxe5 20 ♘f6 and ♕h5). Or 16...♕c6 17 ♘xf6+ gxf6 18 ♕g4+ ♔h8 19 ♕h4.

| 15 | ... | gxf6? |

Fischer said Black could put up stiffer resistance with 15...bxc3! 16 ♘e4 ♕b4 17 ♕g4 ♗xf6 18 ♘xf6+ ♔h8.

Then 19 ♕h4 h6 20 ♘g4 cxb2! would prompt White to take the perpetual check – 21 ♘xh6 bxa1(♕) 22 ♘g4+ ♔g8 23 ♘f6+! – because he can end up with the worst of 21 ♖ab1 ♔h7 or 21 ♖ad1 e4.

If he tries, instead, to keep the attack going with 16 ♗xe5 cxb2 17 ♕g4 g6 18 ♗xb2, Black emerges with the upper hand (18...♘xb3 19 axb3 ♗b7).

| 16 | ♘ce4 | |

46

16 ...	♕d4

Black poses more problems with 16...♕c7. White is clearly better after 17 ♕g4+ ♔h8 18 ♕h4 ♖g8 19 ♘xf6 ♖g7 but not yet winning. Kasparov endorsed Fischer's claim that 17 ♘h5 f5 18 ♘hf6+ wins. But 17...♔h8 (18 ♘exf6 ♕d8) isn't so clear.

17	♕h5!	♘xb3

A form of resignation. Also lost was 17...♔h8 18 ♕h6 ♖g8 19 ♘xf6, 17...♔g7 18 ♖ad1 ♕xb2 19 ♕h4 ♗b7 20 ♘xf6! and 17...exf4 18 ♘f5! exf5 19 ♖xf4.

18	♕h6!

Not 18 axb3? because then 18...exf4! staves off immediate collapse.

18 ...	exf4

Black needs both ...exf4 and ...f5 to save himself but can only play one move at a time. Here 18...f5 would allow White to drive the queen away with 19 c3!, after which ♘h5 wins.

19	♘h5	f5

20	♖ad1!

A bit of technique would be required to win 20 ♘hf6+ ♗xf6 21 ♘xf6+ ♕xf6 22 ♕xf6 ♘xa1.

20 ...	♕e5

Black is mated after 20...♕xb2 21 c3!. He played out:

21 ♘ef6+ ♗xf6 22 ♘xf6+ ♕xf6 23 ♕xf6 ♘c5 24 ♕g5+ ♔h8 25 ♕e7 ♗a6 26 ♕xc5 ♗xf1 27 ♖xf1 Resigns

13

In his book *Grandmasters in Profile*, Dimitrije Bjelica included samples of handwriting and signatures that he had collected from top players. Some of their written comments were trivial, others tried to be profound. Botvinnik, for example, wrote "What is chess! This nobody knows." Fischer, however, wrote (in block letters): "My variation against the Caro-Kann is good but I have been a little unlucky with it."

Nothing illustrated Fischer's stubbornness more than his insistence on playing the Two Knights (3 ♘f3 ♗g4) Variation of the Caro. In the first 10 games he used it, Fischer managed a single win, three losses and six draws. The following game was typical. He continuously believed he was the one with winning chances, while Petrosian thought the opposite.

Fischer – Tigran Petrosian
Candidates Tournament,
Bled-Zagreb-Belgrade 1959
Caro-Kann Defense,
Two Knights Variation (B11)

1 e4 c6

Tal teased Fischer about his track record against the Caro by pushing his pawn to c6 at the start of one of their games at Curaçao – then holding it there several seconds before continuing on to c5, to begin the Sicilian he had intended all along.

2 ♘c3 d5
3 ♘f3 ♗g4
4 h3 ♗xf3
5 ♕xf3 ♘f6
6 d3 e6
7 g3? ♗b4
8 ♗d2 d4
9 ♘b1 ♗xd2+

Trading the dark-squared bishops and putting Black's center pawns on dark squares is dyed-in-wool Tarrasch dogma. But it also solves White's main development problem. Eight rounds earlier Keres played 9...♕b6 10 b3? a5 and then 11 a3 ♗e7! left Fischer's queenside in a mess that resulted in his ugliest defeat ever.

10 ♘xd2 e5

An improvement over 10...♕a5 11 a3 ♘bd7 12 ♕e2! with e4-e5 in mind, e.g. 12...h5 13 h4 ♘g4 14 ♗h3 ♘df6 15 0-0 0-0-0 16 ♘c4 and 17 e5 with advantage.

11 ♗g2 c5
12 0-0 ♘c6
13 ♕e2 ♕e7

Petrosian had beaten Fischer with this line 14 rounds before with 13...g5 14 ♘f3? h6 15 h4 ♖g8. Fischer indicated he was ready to improve with 14 c3 and if 14...♕e7 then 15 ♘f3 h6 16 cxd4 exd4 17 e5!.

14 f4 0-0-0
15 a3 ♘e8

16 b4! cxb4?

Very risky, particularly when 16...f6 would have given Black at least equality (17 bxc5 ♕xc5 18 fxe5 ♘xe5).

17 ♘c4?

Fischer pointed out that 17 fxe5 favors White after 17...♘xe5 18 axb4 ♔b8 (♖xa7 was threatened) 19 ♘f3 f6 20 ♕f2! ♕xb4 21 ♘xe5 fxe5 22 ♕f7.

But he underestimated 17 axb4!, which threatens 18 b5 ♘-moves 19 ♖xa7. For example, 17...♕xb4 18 fxe5 and 19 ♘c4 or 17...♔b8 19 b5 ♘b4 20 b6! axb6 21 ♘c4.

17 ... f6!
18 fxe5 fxe5
19 axb4 ♘c7!

The knight will have an excellent outpost at b5 and a better one at c3.

20 ♘a5 ♘b5

48

21	♘xc6	bxc6
22	♖f2	g6

Fischer said he realized his game was going downhill when Petrosian quickly played solid moves rather than 20...♘xb4. Here Black rejected 22...♕xb4 23 ♕g4+ ♖d7 24 ♖f7 ♖hd8 25 ♕xg7.

23	h4	♔b7
24	h5	♕xb4

Black missed a good chance for...♖hf8! on the last two moves. Now his king's insecurity becomes a factor.

25	♖f7+	♔b6
26	♕f2!	a5

It was too late for 26...♖hf8 because of 27 c4 – 27...♘c3 28 ♖axa7 or 27...♖xf7 28 ♕xf7 ♕c3 29 ♖b1! ♕xd3 30 c5+! ♔xc5 31 ♕e7+ and wins.

27	c4

27	...	♘c3?
28	♖f1?

Both players missed 28 ♕f6!, threatening, among other things, ♕g7 and ♖b7+, e.g. 28...♕d6 29 ♕g7 a4 30 ♖b7+ ♔c5 31 ♖e7. Fischer gave Black's best line as 28...♕c5 29 ♕g7 ♔a6 but White

would have a clear edge after 30 ♖a7+! ♕xa7 31 ♖xa5+ ♔xa5 32 ♕xa7+ ♔b4 33 ♕b6+ ♔a3 34 c5. The power of the queen against two rooks was an important lesson for Fischer, and one he used throughout the next decade. But even in that line 34...gxh5 35 ♕xc6 ♔b2! and ...♔c2 would be hard to win. In any case, the best defense, 28...♖df8, would have left the outcome uncertain.

28	...	a4
29	♕f6	♕c5
30	♖xh7!

Fischer rejected 30 ♕g7 ♖dg8 31 ♖b7+ ♔a6 32 ♕c7 because his queen can't escape rook attacks after 32...♖c8!.

30	...	♖df8!
31	♕xg6	♖xf1+
32	♗xf1	♖xh7
33	♕xh7	a3
34	h6!

The only defense against two black queens is two white queens.

34	...	a2
35	♕g8	a1(♕)
36	h7	♕d6

Fischer, who still thought he was the one with winning chances, felt Black should have forced him to sue for peace after 36...♘e2+ 37 ♔f2 ♘xg3.

37	h8(♕)	♕a7
38	g4	♔c5!

Black realizes his king is safer here – or on b4 – than on b6. Both players remembered their earlier game when Petrosian marched his king to a3, despite White's queen and rook, just before Fischer resigned.

39 ♕f8?

If White missed a win before adjournment it was 39 g5! so that 39...♕a1 loses after 40 ♕f8! and a trade of queens. Less clear is 39 ♕h2 ♕a1 40 g5 ♕c1.

39	...	♕ae7
40	♕a8	♔b4!
41	♕h2	♔b3!

The king is remarkably safe: 42 c5 ♕xc5 43 ♕g8+ ♔a3 44 ♕c2 can be met by 44...♕b4 45 ♕a8+ ♕a4.

42 ♕a1

With 42 ♕d2 White would threaten ♗e2-d1+ – and might win after 42...♕a3 44 ♕xc6. But Black's queen becomes too active after 42...♕h4 to entertain serious winning chances.

Fischer's last winning try was 42 c5! ♕xc5 43 ♕g8+!. Black needs to use his queens to defend his king after 43...♔a3 44 ♕c2 and that may allow White to push his g-pawn.

42	...	♕a3
43	♕xa3+	♔xa3
44	♕h6	♕f7!

Based on 45 ♕xc6 ♘d1! or 45 ♕d6+ ♔b3 46 ♕xe5 ♕f3!.

White's next move stops ...♕f3 and enables him to meet 45...♘d1 with 46 ♕c1+.

45	♔g2	♔b3
46	♕d2	♕h7

47 ♔g3? ♕xe4!

White overlooked this move (48 dxe4 ♘xe4+ 49 ♔h4 ♘xd2 50 g5 ♘xf1 51 g6 d3! and wins). Now he should play 48 g5.

48 ♕f2? ♕h1!

Draw

Black has good winning chances after 49 g5 e4 or 49 ♗g2 ♕h6 threatening ...♘d1 or ...♘e2-f4+. But, according to Fischer, Petrosian couldn't start thinking about a win after playing defense for so long.

Fischer only managed to win three games – and lost four – in the final 12 rounds of the Candidates Tournament. But after virtually guaranteeing Tal first prize, by losing a near-winning game to him in the penultmate round, he ended on a high note. Bjelica recalled going with him to a movie theater on the day before the final round to see *Lust for Life,* the Kirk Douglas film about Vincent Van Gogh. At one point

"Bobby whispered to me: 'If I don't beat Smyslov I'll cut off my own ear'." The next day he outplayed the former world champion by move 20 and won in 54 moves.

14

By the time Fischer was four, Arnold Denker had given up his own chess career but he remained a strong competitor until well into his 60s. Denker watched Fischer mature in Manhattan Chess Club tournaments and recalled him as a good-looking blond kid who never mastered social skills and even had trouble making eye contact. In one of the few times they met over the board, in the fourth round of the 1959-60 U.S. Championship, Fischer was trying to emerge from a shaky start. He had drawn two games (one from a lost position against Robert Byrne) and won the third after a Bisguier blunder. This game started a rally that led to Fischer's third national title.

Arnold Denker – Fischer
U.S. Championship,
New York 1959-60
*Queen's Gambit Declined,
Ragozin Variation (D38)*

1	d4	♘f6
2	c4	e6

This move order enables Black to avoid the static pawn structure of the Exchange Variation (3 ♘c3 d5 4 cxd5 ♘xd5, not 4...exd5).

3	♘f3	d5
4	♘c3	♗b4

Fischer had decidedly mixed results in this line and later switched to 4...c5. One of his two losses at Portorož (against Olafsson) continued 4...♗b4 5 cxd5 exd5 6 ♗g5 h6 7 ♗h4 c5 8 e3 ♘c6 9 ♖c1 c4?!.

Black went material-grabbing – 10 ♗e2 ♗e6 11 0-0 0-0 12 ♘d2 ♗e7 13 b3! g5? 14 ♗g3 ♗a3 15 ♖c2 ♘b4 16 bxc4 ♘xc2 17 ♕xc2 dxc4 18 ♘b5 ♗b4 and was much worse after 19 ♘c7 ♗xd2 20 ♘xe6!.

5	♗g5	h6
6	♗xf6	♕xf6
7	cxd5	exd5
8	♖c1	0-0
9	a3	♗xc3+
10	♖xc3	c6
11	e3	a5

Black's move enables him to rebuff the minority attack with 12 b4 axb4 13 axb4 ♕e7 (and 14 b5 ♕b4 15 ♕b3 ♖a1+). But it's also a waiting move that allows him to see where White places his bishop. On 11...♗g4 White would get a good game with 12 ♗e2! ♘d7 13 0-0 a5 14 ♕b3.

12 ♗d3

Against 12 ♗e2 Black takes the other diagonal with 12...♗f5! 13 0-0 ♘d7 and ...♕e7/...♘f6-e4.

12	...	♗g4!
13	h3	♗h5

Now 14 0-0 ♗xf3 15 ♕xf3 ♕xf3 16 gxf3 a4 (avoiding ♖b3) is harmless for Black, e.g. 17 e4? ♖d8.

14	g4	♗g6
15	♘e5	♗xd3
16	♕xd3	♕e7

17 ♕f5!

This stops ...♘d7 and prepares ♖g1 and g4-g5. The position is roughly equal.

17 ... ♖d8
18 ♖g1 ♘d7

If White realized how much trouble he was getting into he would seek refuge in an endgame with 19 g5 ♘xe5 20 dxe5 (not 20 gxh6? ♘g6) hxg5 21 ♕xg5.

19 ♘xd7 ♖xd7
20 g5 ♖d6!

This offers better winning chances than 20...g6 21 gxh6 ♔h7.

21 h4?

Black's position is promising after 21 gxh6 ♖xh6 or 21 g6 fxg6 22 ♖xg6 ♖f8. But 21 ♖g3 or even 21 ♔d2 were superior to this weakening move.

21 ... h5!

Unless White is willing to shed a pawn (22 g6? fxg6 23 ♖xg6 ♖xg6 24 ♕xg6 ♕xh4), the kingside will remain closed now.

22 ♔e2?

This costs a tempo because of Black's 23rd move.

22 ... g6!

If White retreats to c2 or d3, Black directs his firepower at the kingside

(...♕e6 or ...♖e6-e4). But if he goes in the other direction, ...b6 and ...c5 becomes very strong.

23 ♕f3 ♖e6

On e4, this rook will threaten ...♖xd4 as well as ...♖xh4.

24 ♔d2 ♖e4
25 ♕h3 ♕c7!

This diagonal is so useful that Denker should try 26 ♕g3!, since his survival chances are better after 26...♕xg3 27 fxg3. Black should persevere on the queenside with 26...♕b6 27 ♔c2 ♕b5.

26 ♖gc1 ♖ae8

The threat to the h-pawn, from ...♖g4 and ...♖ee4, prompts another White weakening.

27 f3 ♖4e6
28 ♖e1

On 28 b4? axb4 29 axb4 ♕e7 the double attack wins a pawn.

28 ... b6!

Black abandons ...♕b6-b5 or ...a4/...♕a5 in favor of the push of the c-pawn.

29 ♔c2

29 ... c5

Now 30 ♔b1 offers Black a pleasant choice between the 30...c4 and ...b5-b4 steamroller and increasing pressure on the e-file with 30...♕e7.

30 dxc5

White can't delay this for long (30 f4 ♕e7 31 f5 gxf5 32 dxc5 d4!).

30 ... d4!

Also good was 30...bxc5 31 ♖d1 ♕c6 (32 f4 ♕a4+ 33 ♔c1 d4).

31 cxb6 ♕xb6

32 ♖d3 ♖b8

Nothing spoils a good attack like a premature check. Here 32...♖c6+? 33 ♔b1 leaves Black with nothing better than 33...♖xe3 34 ♖dxe3 dxe3 35 ♕d7.

33 b3

But not 33 ♖b1 ♕c6+ 34 ♔d1 ♕c4!.

33 ... ♖c6+

34 ♔b2

After 34 ♔d2 the fastest wins are 34...♕c5! 35 ♖d1 ♖xb3! and 34...♕c7! with, among other ideas, 35...♖c2+ and 36...♖h2!.

34 ... ♖c3!

Without his only good defender, White's king is sentenced to a death march.

35 ♖xc3 dxc3+

36 ♔xc3 ♕xb3+

37 ♔d2 ♕a2+!

One move faster than 37...♕b2+ 38 ♔d3 ♖d8+ 39 ♔e4 ♕c2+ 40 ♔f4 ♕c7+ 41 ♔e4 ♕e7+ 42 ♔f4 ♕d6+ and mates.

38 ♔d3 ♖d8+

39 ♔e4 ♕c4+

40 ♔e5 ♖d5+

White resigns

The bitter end would be 41 ♔f6 ♕c6+ 42 ♔e7 ♕d6+ 43 ♔e8 ♕f8 mate.

15

Yefim Geller once complained that his fault was he tried to play perfect chess. "I look at a mass of variations and spend time and strength on them," he told Alexander Koblents. Geller said the ideal was the "golden mean" of Fischer, Tal and Botvinnik, who calculated neither too much nor too little.

How much Fischer calculated is not certain. Or, to be more exact, how far. In the following game, he begins a combination at move 15. He may have decided to play it when he visualized how strong 19...♗xc3 would be. Or he may have looked further and stopped when he appreciated Black's winning chances after 21...♖e1+. Or he may have kept calculating until he saw the favorable heavy piece endgame that could arise six moves after 24 fxg6.

Whatever the case, it's an impressive example of analysis.

Arinbjorn Gudmundsson –
Fischer
Reykjavik 1960
Grünfeld Defense (D95)

1	d4	♘f6
2	♘f3	

In *My 60 Memorable Games* Fischer called this move "solid but passive." However, he went further in *Chess Life* in October 1963 calling it "a common error."

He explained that it gave up the option of meeting the King's Indian with the Sämisch Variation ("undoubtedly his most effective weapon"). And, in a note that looks quaint today, he added that the Exchange Variation of the Grünfeld Defense is "no longer strong" because the knight can be pinned – 2...g6 3 c4 ♗g7 4 ♘c3 d5 5 cxd5 ♘xd5 6 e4 ♘xc3 7 bxc3 c5 8 ♗c4 0-0 9 0-0 ♗g4 – "and White's center must collapse."

But by the 1980s it was known that White has quite a good game after 8 ♖b1, for example.

2	...	d5
3	e3	g6
4	c4	♗g7
5	♘c3	0-0
6	♕b3	e6
7	♗e2	♘c6!

Threatening to win the two bishops with 8...♘a5. White can't support 8 c5 for long (8...b6 9 ♗b5 ♗d7).

Probably the best strategy against Fischer was 8 cxd5 exd5

9 ♗d2 and later ♘a4/♗b4.

8	♕c2	dxc4
9	♗xc4	e5!

10 dxe5

White gets the worst of 10 d5 ♘a5 or 10 ♘xe5 ♘xe5 11 dxe5 ♘g4 12 f4? (12 e6!) ♘xe5! 13 fxe5 ♕h4+.

10	...	♘g4

11 0-0

Fischer indicated the text was weaker than 11 e6 ♗xe6 12 ♗xe6 fxe6 13 0-0 when Black has nothing better than a draw by perpetual check (13...♖xf3 14 gxf3 ♕h4 15 fxg4 ♕xg4+).

11	...	♘cxe5
12	♘xe5	♘xe5
13	♗e2	c6
14	f4	

Even against the best line, 14 e4 ♕h4, Black stands well (15 f4? ♘g4 or 15 h3 g5! 16 f4 gxf4 17 ♗xf4 ♔h8 and 17 ♖xf4 ♕g3). White should be equal with 15 ♗e3 but ...

14	...	♘g4!

15 h3

15 ...   ♗f5!

Black is better after this shot, since 16 ♕b3 ♘f6 leaves White with a backward e-pawn and a slightly bad bishop at c1.

Fischer gave the key variation as 17 ♕xb7 ♘e4 18 ♕xc6 ♖c8 19 ♕a6 ♘xc3 20 bxc3 ♗xc3 21 ♗a3 ♗xa1 22 ♗xf8 ♗d4! (23 exd4 ♕xd4+ 24 ♔h1 ♔xf8) with advantage.

But more resistant is 18 ♘xe4 ♗xe4 19 ♗f3 when Black has a significant initiative – but White has a pawn.

16 e4   ♕d4+
17 ♔h1   ♘f2+
18 ♖xf2

Not 18 ♔h2 ♘xe4 and Black wins quickly after 19 ♗d3? ♘g3!.

18 ...   ♕xf2
19 exf5   ♗xc3!

The knight defends better than the bishop attacks after 19...♖fe8 20 ♘e4! ♕e1+ 21 ♔h2 ♗d4 (or 21...gxf5 22 ♘g3) 22 ♗e3! ♕xa1 23 ♗xd4.

20 bxc3   ♖ae8
21 ♗d3

Forced (21 ♗d1? ♖e1+ 22 ♔h2 ♕g1+ 23 ♔g3 ♖xd1).

21 ...   ♖e1+

22 ♔h2   ♕g1+
23 ♔g3   ♖fe8
24 ♖b1?

The losing move. White has to insert an exchange of pawns on g6 in order to deny Black another attacking line (...gxf5! followed by ...♔h8/...♖g8+ or ...♖8e6-g6+).

24 ...   gxf5!

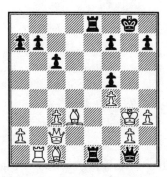

Now 25 ♗xf5 – to anticipate 25...♖8e6 – loses to 25...♖1e2 26 ♗xh7+ ♔h8 27 ♕f5 ♖xg2+ 28 ♔h4 ♖g7.

25 ♗d2   ♖xb1!

Now it's easy because the bishops run out of squares.

26 ♕xb1   ♕xb1
27 ♗xb1   ♖e2

White resigns

In view of 28 ♗c1 ♖e1.

16

This forgotten gem, against a minor Argentine master, shows how Fischer used optimism as an asset. Facing serious threats while still in the opening, he repeatedly rejects safe moves in favor of complex alternatives which hold out the prospect of a quick win. Fischer is the first to err – but his opponent immediately returns the favor and quickly loses.

Osvaldo Bazan – Fischer
Mar del Plata 1960
*Queen's Gambit Declined,
Ragozin Variation (D38)*

1	♘f3	♘f6
2	c4	e6
3	♘c3	d5
4	d4	♗b4
5	cxd5	exd5
6	♗g5	h6
7	♗h4	c5
8	e3	♘c6
9	♗e2	

This opening was highly controversial around 1958-62 because of Black's ability to grab pawns. At Bled 1961, Fischer grabbed and won against Portisch after 9 ♗b5 ♕a5! 10 ♗xc6+ bxc6 11 ♗xf6 ♗xc3+ 12 bxc3 ♕xc3+ 13 ♘d2 gxf6 14 ♖c1 ♕d3 15 ♖xc5 ♖g8!.

9	...	g5
10	♗g3	♘e4
11	♖c1	♕a5
12	0-0!	

White will obtain excellent compensation.

12	...	♗xc3
13	bxc3	♘xc3
14	♕e1	♘xe2+

Only White has serious winning chances in the 14...♘e4 15 ♕xa5 ♘xa5 16 dxc5 endgame.

15	♕xe2	c4

16 e4

In the post-mortem Bronstein recommended 16 ♘e5! followed by f2-f4 or ♕h5 and this was borne out by later games that went 16...♘xe5 17 ♗xe5 ♖g8 18 f4 with advantage.

16 ... ♗e6

Did Fischer know he was accepting a challenge? Or did he instinctively reject 16...dxe4 17 ♕xe4+ ♗e6 18 ♖xc4 ♕d5 and 16...0-0 17 exd5 ♕xd5 18 ♕xc4 ♗e6 as being too hard for Black to win because of the bishops of opposite color?

17 ♗c7?!

Objectively a bad, almost losing move – but this is not known for another 11 moves.

17 ... ♕xc7

Black should avoid 17...♕b5 18 a4 ♕xa4 19 exd5, which distinctly favors White. But he could have ducked the challenge with 17...b6, after which 18 ♖fd1 is unclear.

18 exd5 g4!

White has the upper hand after 18...♕d7 19 dxe6 ♕xe6 20 ♖fe1. And he has better chances than in the game after 18...0-0-0 19 dxc6 ♕xc6 20 ♘e5 or 19 dxe6 ♘xd4 20 ♕xc4.

19 ♘d2

The attack evaporates soon after 19 dxe6? gxf3 20 exf7+ ♔f8! 21 ♕xf3 ♕xf7.

19 ... ♘xd4

20 ♕e4!

The complications also favour Black after 20 ♕e3 ♕f4!. For example, 21 dxe6 ♕xe3 22 exf7+ ♔e7! 23 fxe3 ♘e2+ or 21 ♖xc4 ♕xe3 22 fxe3 ♘e2+ 23 ♔f2 ♗xd5 24 ♖c5 and now either 24...g3+ 25 hxg3 ♘xg3! 26 ♔xg3 ♖g8+ or just 24...♗xa2.

20 ... ♕f4!!

A magical move (21 ♕xf4 ♘e2+) that Black had to have seen much earlier, since 20...0-0-0 allows 21 dxe6! (much better than 21 ♕xd4 ♗xd5 or 21 ♖xc4 ♘c6 22 dxc6 ♗xc4 23 cxb7+ ♔b8).

21 ♖xc4!

Not 21 ♕e1 b5. After 21 ♕xf4 ♘e2+ 22 ♔h1 ♘xf4 23 dxe6 Black keeps his extra pawn with 23...♘xe6 26 ♖xc4 h5 but has greater winning chances with a two-pawn edge on the queenside after 23...b5 24 exf7+ ♔xf7.

21 ... ♕xe4!

Black has no real edge after 21...♕xd2 22 ♖xd4 ♕xa2 23 ♖c4!.

22 ♘xe4 ♘e2+

This knight remains trapped behind enemy lines for another eight moves yet plays a key role in the defense.

23 ♔h1 ♗d7?

Simpler is 23...f5! 24 dxe6 fxe4.

24 ♖e1 ♔f8

A clever way of stopping ♘d6+ and also enabling Black to meet 25 ♖xe2 with 25...♗b5.

But smoother is 24...♔e7 25 ♖xe2 ♖hc8! when there is no strong discovered check.

25 ♘f6?

With 25 ♘d6! White should not lose – and that was enough reason to kill its chances for inclusion in *My 60 Memorable Games*.

25 ... ♗b5

26 ♖b4 ♗a6

27 ♘d7+ ♔e7

Not 27...♔g7?? 28 ♖xg4+ and mates.

28 ♘c5

28 ... ♖he8!

This indirectly protects the knight and threatens 29...♔d6 30 ♘ moves ♘g3+.

| 29 | ♘xa6 | ♔d6! |
| 30 | ♖xb7 | |

White had nothing better (30 ♖d1 ♘c3).

30	...	♘g3+
31	hxg3	♖xe1+
32	♔h2	♖c8!
33	♖xf7	♖cc1

Mate on h1 is threatened.

White resigns

17

Fischer made a deep impression on Boris Spassky and David Bronstein when they met him at Mar del Plata 1960. They were struck by his strong opinions – such as predicting that Mikhail Botvinnik would easily defeat Tal in the world championship match about to begin in Moscow. They were also struck by his energy: After losing to Spassky in the second round, the American allowed only one draw in the remaining 13 rounds.

Fischer – Fridrik Olafsson
Mar del Plata 1960
Sicilian Defense,
3 ♗b5+ Variation (B51)

1	e4	c5
2	♘f3	d6
3	♗b5+	

The first – and only – time Fischer tried this in a serious game.

3	...	♗d7
4	♗xd7+	♕xd7
5	0–0	♘c6
6	♕e2	

Nicolas Rossolimo had popularized the logical plan of ♕e2/♖d1 and d2-d4 in the 1950s. White will decide on whether to play c2-c3 based on Black's next move or two. For example, on 6...e6 he goes directly to 7 ♖d1 and 8 d4 to exert pressure against d6.

6	...	g6
7	c3	♗g7
8	♖d1	

| 8 | ... | e5 |

Fischer's classical approach was illustrated in the post-mortem: Spassky and Bronstein suggested 8...f5, to regain control of d5, Spassky later gave 9 exf5 ♕xf5 10 d4 cxd4 11 cxd4 ♘f6 and ...♘d5 as a possible continuation. But Fischer dismissed 8...f5 out of hand. Olafsson's choice makes d2-d4 essential, since otherwise Black can build a potent initiative with ...0-0, ...♖ae8 and ...f5-f4.

| 9 | ♘a3 | |

Rossolimo played 9 d4 against Fischer two years later in the U.S. Championship and obtained enough play for the pawn after 9...exd4 10 cxd4 ♘xd4 11 ♘xd4 cxd4 12 ♘a3 ♘e7 13 ♘b5 ♘c6 14 ♗f4 ♗e5 14 ♗f4 ♗e5 15 ♗h6 0–0–0

16 f4! (This transposes into a line Spassky considered as insufficient compensation for White after 16 ♖ac1 ♔b8 17 b4).

9	**...**	**♘ge7**
10	**d4!**	**cxd4!**

White can favorably exploit the d5 hole after 10...♕c7 11 dxc5 dxc5 12 ♘c4 and ♘e3-d5. Kmoch evaluated 10...exd4 11 cxd4 ♘xd4 12 ♘xd4 ♗xd4 as worse than the text because White would have more than enough compensation after 13 ♘b5 ♘c6 14 ♗h6 or 14 ♗e3 or 14 ♗f4.

11	**cxd4**	**exd4**

White is certain to regain his pawn, and that means he will hold a positional edge unless Black dissolves his d6 pawn or obtains enough counterplay elsewhere. The easiest road to equality is 11...♘xd4! 12 ♘xd4 exd4 13 ♘b5 ♘c6 as in the Rossolimo game, e.g. 14 ♗f4 0–0 15 ♘xd6 ♘e5! or 15 ♗xd6 ♖fe8.

12	**♘b5**	**0–0**
13	**♘fxd4**	**d5?**

Black's failure to trade a pair of knights hurts him, compared with equality after 13...♘xd4 14 ♘xd4 d5:

(a) 15 ♘b3 ♖fd8,

(b) 15 ♘b5 a6 16 ♘c3 ♗xc3 17 bxc3 ♕e6, or

(c) 15 ♗g5 dxe4! 16 ♕xe4 ♖fe8 or 16 ♘b5 ♘d5! (17 ♕c4 ♘b6).

14	**♘b3!**	**a6**
15	**♘c3**	**d4**

The only middlegame issue to debate after this will be the weakness of Black's pawns. Kmoch recommended 15...♗xc3 16 bxc3 f5

to muddy the waters (17 e5 ♘d8). But 17 exd5! ♘xd5? 18 ♕f3 punishes.

16	**♘a4**	**♖ae8**

Black plays for ...f7-f5 but 16...♕c7! first would have stopped White's strong reply.

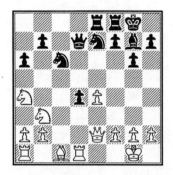

17	**♗f4!**	**♘d5**

The threat was 18 ♘bc5 ♕c8 19 ♘b6 because on 19...♕d8 White would have 20 ♘cd7!.

18	**♗g3**	**♕e7**

Olafsson may have counted on 18...f5 only to discover that it allows 19 ♕c4!, e.g. 19...fxe4? 20 ♘b6 or 19...b5 20 ♕xd5+ ♕xd5 21 exd5 bxa4 22 ♘c5 or 22 dxc6.

19	**♘ac5**	**♔h8**
20	**♖e1**	**♘b6**
21	**♖ac1**	**f5**
22	**♕d2!**	**♕f7**

White's edge is evident after 22...fxe4 23 ♘xe4! ♕b4 (else 24 ♘d6 or 24 ♗d6) 24 ♗d6 ♕xd2 25 ♘3xd2 ♖g8 26 ♘c5 and 25...♖f7 26 ♘g5.

23	**exf5**	**gxf5**

Playing for ...f4. On 23...♕xf5 White safely grabs on b7.

24	**♘d3**	

Good positional play (and clearly better than 24 ♘xa6? ♘c4 which loses).

24	...	♘d5
25	♗d6	♖g8
26	♘a5!	

Spassky praised this way of securing e5 for a bishop or knight. White's position improves with each trade now.

26	...	♘xa5
27	♖xe8	♖xe8
28	♕xa5	h6
29	g3!	♔h7
30	♘f4	♘xf4
31	♗xf4	♕e6

The d-pawn is easily blockaded – and wouldn't be a factor anyway after 31...d3 32 ♖c7 ♕e6 33 ♖xb7. Better was 31...♖e7 and ...♖d7.

32 ♗d2! ♖c8?

In time pressure, Olafsson finds a poor way of meeting the threat of 33 ♖e1 queen-moves 34 ♖xe8 and 35 ♕xf5+.

| 33 | ♖e1 | ♕f7 |
| 34 | ♖e7! | ♕g6 |

The queen-and-bishop ending (34...♕xe7 35 ♕xf5+ and 36 ♕xc8+) is quite lost.

| 35 | ♖xb7 | f4 |
| 36 | ♕d5! | |

This stops ...♕b1+-♕e4+. Black should now exchange on g3 – but may have feared 36...fxg3 37 ♖xg7+?? ♔xg7! (not 37...♕xg7 38 ♕f5+) 38 ♕d7+ overlooking 38...♕f7!. As the game goes White easily parries the perpetual check threats.

36	...	♖e8
37	♗xf4	♖e1+
38	♔g2	♕d3
39	♔h3!	♕g6

The attack turns around after 39...♕f1+ 40 ♔h4 ♕xf2 41 ♕f5+ and mates.

40	♖d7	h5
41	♔g2	h4
42	♖d6	**Resigns**

Black didn't resume play after this sealed move in light of 42...♕d3 43 ♕h5+ or 42...♕e8 43 ♕f5+ ♔g8 44 ♖xa6.

18

One day during the Mar del Plata tournament, Fischer dropped by the hotel room Spassky shared with Bronstein and noticed they had tournament bulletins of the most recent U.S.S.R. championship. "His eyes lit up and he exclaimed 'This is what I need!'" and eagerly asked permission to borrow them to copy, Spassky wrote in *Shakhmaty v SSSR*. It was familiarity with Soviet analysis that saved Fischer two months later in a marathon battle against another top Soviet grandmaster:

Mark Taimanov – Fischer
Buenos Aires 1960
Nimzo-Indian Defense (E51)

1	c4	♘f6
2	♘c3	e6
3	d4	♗b4
4	e3	0–0
5	♗d3	d5
6	♘f3	♘c6
7	0–0	dxc4
8	♗xc4	♗d6
9	♘b5	♗e7

Taimanov, in his notes to this game in the 1960 Soviet chess yearbook, recommended 9...e5 10 ♘xd6 cxd6 instead of this, which he considered a mistake.

10	h3	a6
11	♘c3	♗d6

But in fact the position has merely transposed into a variation normally reached via 7...a6 8 h3 dxc4, and which became a main line by the 1970s. Later, in 1960 at the Leipzig Olympiad, Fischer tried 11...b5 12 ♗d3 ♗b7 against another Nimzo-Indian connoisseur, Gligorić. Black equalized after 13 ♕e2 ♗d6 14 ♖d1 ♕e7 and ...e5 but lost.

12	e4	e5
13	♗e3	exd4

But now 13...b5 allows White the attractive option of 14 ♗d5! ♘xd5 15 exd5 (15...♘xd4 16 ♘xd4 exd4 17 ♕xd4).

14 ♘xd4

More aggressive is 14 ♗xd4!, aiming for e4-e5, e.g. 14...♘xd4 15 ♕xd4 b5 16 e5 with an edge, as in a 1975 Soviet game, Gulko – Dvoretsky.

14 ... ♗d7?

This is the kind of passive move a mature Fischer wouldn't have considered. A good alternative is 14...♘xd4 15 ♗xd4 b5 16 ♗e2 c5 and ...♗b7.

15 ♖e1 ♕e7?

And this should have turned out disastrously (better was 15...♘e5 16 ♗b3 c5).

16	♗g5!	♘xd4
17	♘d5!	

Far superior to 17 ♕xd4 ♕e5.

17	...	♕e5
18	f4!	♘f3+

Here Taimanov calculated 19 gxf3 ♕xb2 and concluded that Black had too many tactical resources. Among the lines to consider are:

(a) 20 ♖e2 ♕a3 21 ♗xf6 gxf6 22 ♘xf6+ ♔h8 23 ♘xd7 ♖g8+ 24 ♖g2 ♗c5+ 25 ♔h1 ♖xg2 26 ♔xg2 ♖g8+ 27 ♔h1 ♖g1+ and Black wins. But 25 ♔f2 is unclear, and

(b) 20 ♖e2 ♗c5+ 21 ♔h1 ♕d4 22 ♘xf6+ and 23 ♖d2 wins, and

(c) 20 ♖b1 ♕a3? 21 ♘xf6+ gxf6 22 ♗xf6 ♕c5+ 23 ♔h1 wins.

19 ♕xf3 ♕d4+

20 ♔h1   ♘g4!

"This move does honor to the ingenuity of Fischer," wrote Taimanov. Plainly worse are 20...♕xc4 21 ♗xf6 and 20...♘xd5 21 ♗xd5.

21 hxg4   ♕xc4

22 b3!

The queen doesn't have a good retreat (22...♕d4 23 ♖ad1 or 22...♕c5 23 e5).

22 ...   ♕b5

Now 23 f5 c6! is fine for Black (24 ♗e7 cxd5 25 ♗xd6 dxe4 and ...♖fe8).

23 a4   ♕a5

24 ♖ed1   ♗c6

Another crisis for Black. The text avoids 25 b4 and allows him to meet 25 ♘e7+ ♗xe7 26 ♗xe7 ♖fe8 27 b4 ♕b6 28 ♗c5 with 28...♗xe4!.

25 e5   ♗b4?

26 ♕e4

For the rest of the middlegame Taimanov has to choose between which favorable endgame he will play. He wrote that he didn't want to "sell too cheaply" his positional edge by winning a mere pawn with 26 ♗e7 ♗xe7 27 ♘xe7+ ♔h8 28 ♘xc6 bxc6 29 ♕xc6.

But from a psychological point of view, 26 ♗e7 is best. Rather than defend a long endgame, Fischer might have been tempted into 26...♗d2?!, which turns out badly after 27 ♗xf8 ♗xd5 28 ♕f2.

26 ...   ♗xd5

27 ♖xd5   ♕b6

28 f5

Now the psychological onus is on White – to prove he has something tangible after having amassed such a positional edge. He rejected 28 a5 ♕c6 29 f5 because of 29...b5! 30 ♖c1 ♕b7.

28 ...   ♗c3

29 ♖c1   ♗b2

30 ♖b1   ♗c3

31 ♖c1   ♗b2

Black won't fall for 31...♕xb3? 32 ♕f3. Taimanov felt 32 ♖c2 was promising because after 32...♕xb3 White can choose from among two strong pawn advances and a capture on c7. Black's crisis is over following 33 f6 ♖fc8 or 33 e6 fxe6 34 fxe6 c6. But he is losing after 33 ♖xc7.

32 ♖c4?   ♖ae8!

Black suddenly has threats of 33...f6 and 33...c6 and this triggers the sharpest calculations of the game.

33 f6   c6!

34 fxg7

Not 34 ♖d2 ♖xe5.

34 ...   cxd5

35 gxf8(♕)+ ♔xf8!

This shifts the tide again. After 35...♖xf8 36 ♕xd5 ♕xb3 37 ♗f6! White stands a bit better. But the text allows Black to meet 36 ♕xd5 with 36...♗xe5.

It's been suggested that 36...♕g6 is even better for Black (37 ♗f6 ♕h6+ 38 ♔g1 ♕e3+ 39 ♔f1 ♗xe5 or 37 ♗h4 ♕b1+ 38 ♔h2 ♗xe5+). But White's position is so strong that he has the edge after 37 ♗f4!. For example, 37...♗xe5, based on 38 ♗xe5 ♕h6+ 39 ♔g1 ♕e3+ and 39 ♗h2?? ♖e1 mate, loses a piece to 38 ♕c5+! ♔g8 39 ♗xe5 ♕h6+ 40 ♔g1.

36 ♕xh7!   ♗xe5

Of course not 36...♕g6?? 37 ♕h8+ ♕g8 38 ♗h6+ ♔e7 39 ♕f6+ and mates.

37 ♖f4!   ♕e6?

An almost automatic reaction by a grandmaster in time pressure – yet this is not nearly as good as 37...♗g7, with the idea of 38...♖e1+. Then 38 ♕f5 ♕e6 or 38 ♖f1 d4 39 ♗c1 ♕xb3 give Black serious winning chances.

38 ♖f1   b5?

For the second time in the game Fischer makes two bad moves in a row and this time he comes close to losing. After 38...♗g7 39 ♗c1 (39 ♗d2 ♕xg4) 39...♕e7 40 g5 ♕b4 41 ♗b2 d4 42 ♕f5 he loses. But 38...♗d4! was safe.

39 axb5?

This is the kind of automatic move, just before the time control, that haunts grandmasters afterwards. If 39 ♖e1!, as he intended, the pin wins (40 ♗f4 or 40 ♗h6+). For example, 39...d4 40 ♗h6+ ♔e7 41 ♗g7 f6 42 ♗xf6+ ♔xf6 43 ♖f1+.

Taimanov's explanation was: "My nerves gave out as often happens when you are not just out to win but

to 'punish' your opponent." (The reason he felt the need to punish him is that the previous day Fischer had announced, while standing next to Taimanov, "I start my winning streak tomorrow.")

39 ...   axb5

40 ♗d2

White realizes too late that 40 ♖e1 can be met by 40...♖a8 and ...♖a1.

40	...	♔e7!
41	♗b4+	♔d8
42	♖xf7	♖h8
43	♖f8+	♖xf8
44	♗xf8	♕f6!
45	♗c5	d4?

Just as the crisis ends, Black begins playing for a win. After 45...♕f1+ 46 ♗g1 ♗d4 White is tied up but secure enough to draw.

46 ♔g1!   ♕f4!

Black now realizes he must allow a bishop endgame...

47	♕e7+	♔c8
48	♕f8+	♕xf8
49	♗xf8	♗g3
50	♔f1	

50 ...   d3!

...which he can draw thanks to this resource. To free his king and win the d-pawn, White must allow the enemy king to become very active.

51	♗b4	♔d7
52	♗e1	♗f4
53	♗c3	♗g3
54	g5	♔e6?

Black makes the game interesting again. After 54...♔e7! 55 g6 ♔f8 White cannot make progress.

55	g6	♔e7
56	♗e1!	♗f4
57	♗h4+	♔f8
58	g3!	♗d6!

The natural 58...♗e3 loses to the maneuver ♗f6-e5-f4! and a king advance.

59	♔f2	♗c5+
60	♔f3	♔g7
61	♗g5	♔xg6
62	♗f4	♔h5!

Better than 62...♔f5 63 g4+ ♔e6, which may also draw but is much trickier. The text allows Black to meet 63 g4+ with 63...♔h4.

63	♔e4	♔g4
64	♔xd3	♔f3
65	♗c7	♗f2
66	♗d6	♗e1

Black must create a situation (with...b4) in which White will trade his g-pawn for the b-pawn. Then White can only win if he advances his last pawn in such a way that Black cannot give up his bishop for it.

67	♔d4	♔g4
68	♔c5	b4
69	♔b5	♔f5
70	♔c4	♔e6
71	♗c7	♔f5

72	♔d3	♔g4
73	♗d6	♗c3
74	♔c4	♗e1
75	♗xb4	♗xg3

Black holds this ending thanks to a striking discovery made by Yuri Averbakh, Taimanov's longtime rival. Averbakh gave a brief account of his analysis in 1953 and later expanded on it in *Shakhmaty v SSSR* in 1956 His thesis was that David Janowsky had misplayed a very similar ending in 1916 against José Capablanca. Averbakh discovered further that Black can draw with an unusual defensive strategy. "I didn't need to find anything," Fischer admitted after the game. "I remembered all (of Averbakh's) variations perfectly well."

76	♗c3	♗d6
77	♔d5	♗e7
78	♗d4	♗b4
79	♔c4	♗a5
80	♗c3	♗d8
81	b4	♔f4!!

After 81...♔f5 82 ♔d5 we've reached Capablanca – Janowsky, New York 1916. Black resigned because his king is cut off and can't get in front of the pawn (82...♗b6

83 ♗d4 ♝c7 84 b5 ♝d8 85 ♔c6 ♚e6 86 ♗b6 ♝g5 87 ♗c7 ♝e3 88 ♗d6 ♝f2 89 ♗c5 and 90 b6 etc.).

But Averbakh showed that the proper defense was attack from behind the pawn: 82...♚f4! 83 ♗e5+ ♚e3! 84 b5 ♚d3 85 ♔c6 ♚c4!.

82	b5	♚e4
83	♗d4	♝c7
84	♔c5	♚d3!
85	♔c6	♚c4!

To win White must preserve his pawn and force the bishop off c7. But he can't do both. For example, 86 ♗b6 ♝f4 87 ♗c7 ♝e3 and White can never execute the necessary blocking maneuver of ♗d6-c5 because Black can attack c5 twice.

| 86 | ♗b6 | ♝f4 |
| 87 | ♗a7 | ♝c7! |

Draw

More mistakes than in any other Fischer game but marvelous nonetheless.

19

In his first Olympiad, Fischer began with two bizarre games against little-known players: He defeated Teodor Ghitescu when the Rumanian blundered away his queen on the 14th move. Then, with the White pieces in a typical Dragon Variation, Fischer botched the attack against César Munoz of Ecuador and was lost by the 30th move. After a few draws and a rest day to steady himself, Fischer was ready for the following:

René Letelier – Fischer
Olympiad, Leipzig 1960
King's Indian Defense (E70)

| 1 | d4 | ♘f6 |
| 2 | c4 | |

Six months earlier at Mar del Plata, it was Letelier who avoided theory with 2 ♗g5. He resigned just before mate in a long endgame that began 2 ♗g5 c5 3 c3 ♕b6 4 ♕b3? cxd4 5 ♕xb6 axb6 6 cxd4 ♘c6 7 ♘f3 ♘b4 (This was the only serious game in which Fischer faced the Trompowsky Attack.).

2	...	g6
3	♘c3	♗g7
4	e4	0–0

Designed to provoke 5 e5 and then liquidate the center via ...d6 and ...c5. It has independent value if White responds 5 f3 because then 5...c5 6 dxc5 b6 is a promising gambit.

| 5 | e5 | ♘e8 |
| 6 | f4 | |

Black has reasonable chances after 6 ♘f3 d6 7 exd6 ♘xd6 and 8...♗g4 or 7 ♗f4 ♘c6 8 ♗e2 ♗g4.

| 6 | ... | d6 |
| 7 | ♗e3 | |

White wants to rule out Fischer's next move. After 7 ♘f3 dxe5 8 fxe5? ♗g4 9 ♗e2 c5! Black realizes his goal and the center collapses. Safe and solid is 8 dxe5 ♕xd1+ 9 ♘xd1 – but that isn't why White played 5 e5.

7 ... c5!?

Black should equalize after 7...dxe5 8 dxe5! ♕xd1+ 9 ♖xd1 because he can break in the center with 9...♘c6 10 ♘f3 f6!. The text is more ambitious but perhaps not quite sound – and may not deserve the exclamation point it is usually awarded.

8 dxc5 ♘c6
9 cxd6

The natural defense is 9 ♘f3 ♗g4 but 10 ♗e2 ♗xf3 11 ♗xf3 dxe5 favors Black a bit.

9 ... exd6

Now 10 exd6 ♘xd6 only helps Black (11 ♗e2 ♖e8 12 ♕d2 ♗e6).

10 ♘e4?

Here 10 ♘f3! was necessary and places the correctness of 7...c5 in doubt. Certainly White's chances are much better after 10...♗g4 11 ♗e2 dxe5 12 ♗c5 or 11...♕a5 12 exd6 than in the game.

10 ... ♗f5!
11 ♘g3?

If you're going to be a pawn grabber, you should grab pawns:

11 ♘xd6 ♘xd6 12 ♕xd6 ♕xd6 13 exd6 was ugly because of 13...♗xb2 14 ♖d1 ♘b4 15 ♔f2 (or 15 ♘e2 ♗c2!) 15...♘xa2. But after 16 ♘e2 it's not entirely lost – as White soon is in the game.

11 ... ♗e6
12 ♘f3 ♕c7!

Fischer believed 12...dxe5 was also winning but wanted "to fracture him in the middlegame." It would be interesting to know what mayhem he was hoping for after 12...dxe5 13 ♕xd8 ♖xd8 14 ♗c5. Probably he foresaw 14...exf4 15 ♘e4 and then a favorable 15...♗f5 or 15...♗xb2.

13 ♕b1

After 13 ♗e2 dxe5 14 ♗c5 Black has a crushing initiative with 14...♕a5+ 15 b4 ♘xb4 16 ♗xf8 ♔xf8! 17 0–0 exf4.

The text is a finesse that avoids the problems arising after 13 ♕c2 dxe5 14 f5 gxf5 15 ♘xf5 ♘b4! and then 16 ♕b3 ♗xf5 17 ♕xb4 ♘f6 18 ♕c5 ♕xc5 19 ♗xc5 ♖fd8 or 16 ♕b1 ♗xf5 17 ♕xf5 ♘d6 18 ♕b1 ♘xc4. But if you have to play artificial moves like ♕b1 this early as White, you're on very thin ice.

13 ... dxe5

14	f5	e4!

So that 15 ♕xe4 gxf5 16 ♘xf5 ♕a5+ wins. If instead 15 ♘xe4 ♗xf5, White finds himself in a nasty pin, e.g. 16 ♗c5 ♗xe4 17 ♕xe4 ♕a5+.

15	fxe6	exf3
16	gxf3	f5!

This makes a new threat (...f4) and enables Black to recapture on e6 with a rook.

17	f4	♘f6
18	♗e2	

Otherwise 18...♘g4 shortens the game.

18	...	♖fe8

Now 19 0–0 ♖xe6 20 ♗d2 ♘d4 21 ♗d3 ♕b6 is dreadful.

19	♔f2	♖xe6
20	♖e1	♖ae8

Black also might have won with 20...♖xe3!? with complications such as 21 ♔xe3 ♕b6+ 22 ♔f3 ♘g4 23 ♘h1 ♗xb2 or 22 ♔d2 ♖d8+ 23 ♗d3 ♘b4 24 ♖e3 ♘e4+. But his position deserves something clearer.

21	♗f3?	

The only way to keep the game going a bit longer was 21 ♗d2 and then 21...♘d4 22 ♕c1 or 22 ♕d3.

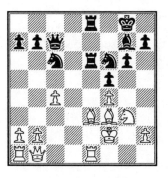

21	...	♖xe3!
22	♖xe3	♖xe3
23	♔xe3	♕xf4+!

White resigns

The problem finish is 24 ♔xf4 ♗h6 mate. White understandably had no interest in playing out 24 ♔e2 ♘d4+ or 24 ♔f2 ♘g4+ 25 ♔g2 ♘e3+ 26 ♔f2 ♘d4.

20

Fischer briefly played postal chess but virtually none of his games survive. One intriguing specimen is a miniature he apparently lost in *Chess Review*'s annual tournament, the Golden Knights, in 1955. The game A. W. Conger – B. Fischer began 1 d4 ♘f6 2 c4 g6 3 ♘c3 ♗g7 4 e4 d6 5 ♗g5 h6 6 ♗h4 0–0 7 f4 c5 8 d5 ♕a5 9 ♕d2 and now, instead of 9...e6!, he played 9...♕c7? 10 ♗d3 e6 and resigned after 11 ♘b5 ♕b6 12 ♘xd6!, although 12...♕xd6 13 e5 is not that clear. Here is a similar line.

László Szabó – Fischer
Olympiad, Leipzig 1960
King's Indian Defense (E70)

1	d4	♘f6
2	c4	g6
3	♘c3	♗g7
4	e4	0–0
5	♗g5	

Szabó points out a drawback to Black's fourth move. After the normal 4...d6 Black can meet 5 ♗g5 with 5...h6 and then 6 ♗h4 c5 7 d5 ♕a5! with the idea of 8 ♕d2 g5 9 ♗g3 ♘h5! or 8 ♗d3 g5 9 ♗g3

♘xe4! 10 ♗xe4 ♗xc3+ 11 bxc3 ♕xc3+ and 12...f5 as in a Spassky – Fischer rematch game.

But after 4...0-0 5 ♗g5 h6 White can retreat to e3 and gain a tempo later with f2-f3 and ♕d2.

5 ... d6

6 ♕d2 c5

7 d5

White is less than equal after 7 dxc5 dxc5 8 ♕xd8 ♖xd8 9 ♗xf6 ♗xf6 10 ♘d5 ♘c6 11 ♘xf6+ exf6.

7 ... e6

8 ♗d3 exd5

9 ♘xd5

After 9 cxd5 a6 10 a4 ♕a5 White's rook is undefended at a1 and therefore 11...b5 is threatened, e.g. 11 ♘ge2 b5 12 0–0 b4 or 11 ♖a3 ♖e8 12 ♘ge2 ♘bd7 13 0–0 ♘e5. The other capture, 9 exd5, is known to be unambitious in similar situations, and here White gets nothing that can pretend to be an edge after 9...♘bd7 10 f4 a6 11 a4 ♕a5 (12 ♘ge2 b5!).

9 ... ♗e6

Black plans 10...♗xd5 and doesn't fear the backward d-pawn after 10 ♘xf6+ ♗xf6 11 ♗xf6 ♕xf6 12 ♘e2 because of the piece play he gets after 12...♘c6, e.g. 13 ♖c1 a6 14 ♘c3 ♘d4 and ...b5.

10 ♘e2 ♗xd5

But he must act before ♘ec3 reinforces the knight. After 10...♘c6 11 ♘ec3 ♘d4 12 0–0 ♖e8 13 f4! White has a splendid middlegame ahead of him.

11 exd5

Fischer pointed out 11 cxd5 c4! and then 12 ♗c2 (not 12 ♗xc4? ♘xe4) 12...♘bd7 13 0–0 ♘c5 14 ♘c3 b5 with excellent play.

11 ... ♘bd7

One of the knights has to find a good square now (12 f4 ♕e8! and ...♘g4 or 13...♘e4 with at least a small plus for Black).

12 0–0 ♘e5

13 f4?

White has equality but no more with 13 ♘c3 After 13 ♖ae1 Black succeeds in exchanging off White's good bishop with 13...h6 14 ♗f4 ♘h5 15 ♗e3 but 15 ♗xe5! ♗xe5 16 f4 ♗g7 17 f5! is dangerous. Better is the equal 13...♘xd3.

13 ... ♘xd3

14 ♕xd3 h6!

The timing of this move in the King's Indian makes all the difference. Once White advances f4-f5 the bishop can retreat along a better diagonal.

15 ♗h4 ♖e8

Now 16 ♘c3 ♕b6 followed by ...♘g4 (17 f5 g5 18 ♗g3 ♘g4 or 17 h3 ♘h5).

16 ♖ae1 ♕b6!

In order of importance, Black's move (a) threatens the b-pawn, (b) unpins the knight, and (c) prepares to double rooks on the e-file.

17 ♗xf6?

The hard-to-find defense was 17 b3 ♘e4 18 f5! so that 18...g5 19 ♘c1 threatens ♖xe4.

17 ...   ♗xf6

18 f5   g5

19 b3

White seems to have solved his main problems and is ready for ♘g3-e4 or ♘h5. If he had safeguarded his queenside with 19 ♖b1 (to meet 19...♕a5 with 20 a3) Black would seize the e-file with 19...♖e7! 20 ♘g3 ♖ae8.

19 ...   ♕a5!

But this sets new problems because the main threat is not 20...♕xa2 but rather 20...♗d4+! (21 ♘xd4? ♖xe1 or 21 ♔h1 ♖e3 and ...♖ae8 with a crushing pin).

20 ♖c1??

Fischer said the best defense was 20 ♕b1, e.g. 20...♕d2 21 ♘g3. Now the game becomes a rout.

20 ...   ♕xa2

21 ♖c2

21 ...   ♖e3!

Undoubtedly overlooked by Szabó. But even after 21...♕a3 it's hard to imagine Black lasting long, e.g. 22 ♘g3 ♗d4+ 23 ♔h1 ♖e3 or 22 ♕h3 ♔h7 23 ♕h5 ♖e7 24 ♖f3 ♖ae8 25 ♖h3 ♕a1+ 26 ♔f2 ♗d4+.

22 ♕xe3   ♕xc2

23 ♔h1   a5!

24 h4   a4

White resigns

21

The teenaged Fischer was much more likely to try speculative pawn sacrifices in the openings than the Fischer of the late 1960s and '70s. At Mar del Plata 1960, for example, he tried 1 c4 ♘f6 2 ♘c3 g6 3 d4 ♗g7 4 g3 0-0 5 ♗g2 c5 6 ♘f3 cxd4 7 ♘xd4 ♘c6 8 0-0 ♘g4 9 e3 d6!? 10 ♘xc6 bxc6 11 ♗xc6 ♖b8. He even played a form of the Morra Gambit (1 e4 c5 2 ♘f3 a6 3 d4 cxd4 4 c3, against Korchnoi at Buenos Aires 1960). In the following game he repeats a pawn "sac" (...d5) that later became a major theme of hedgehog pawn structures.

William Lombardy – Fischer
U.S. Championship,
New York 1960-61
Sicilian Defense, 4 ♕xd4 (B53)

1	e4	c5
2	♘f3	d6
3	d4	cxd4
4	♘xd4	♘f6
5	f3	

Before the 1970s, Maróczy Bind pawn formations (as with 6 c4 here) were considered so favorable to White that elaborate methods like this were adopted to avoid blocking the c-pawn with ♘c3.

5	...	♘c6

The book lines were 5...e5 6 ♗b5+ ♗d7 7 ♗xd7+ ♘bxd7 8 ♘f5 d5 9 exd5 and 6...♘bd7 7 ♘f5 d5 8 exd5 a6 9 ♗xd7+ ♕xd7 10 ♘e3 with mixed chances.

6	c4	e6
7	♘c3	♗e7

Black doesn't spend a tempo on 7...a6 since 8 ♘c2! makes ...d6-d5 less likely to work.

8	♗e3	

Black is waiting for the opportunity for a temporary pawn sacrifice (...d5) that will punish the non-developing moves 5 f3 and 6 c4. Fischer won a game at Mar del Plata 1960 (versus Foguelman) that went 8 ♘c2 0-0 9 ♘e3 d5!? 10 cxd5 exd5 11 exd5? ♘e5 12 ♕b3 ♗c5 13 ♗d2 ♖e8 14 ♗e2 ♘g6! 15 ♘c2 ♘h4.

8	...	0-0
9	♘c2	

9	...	d5

Black could have prepared the break with 9...♖e8, e.g. 10 ♗e2 d5 11 cxd5 exd5 12 ♘xd5 ♘xd5 13 exd5 ♘b4 (14 ♗c4?? ♘xc2+ 15 ♕xc2 ♗c5 and wins). But 13 ♕xd5 ♕c7 14 ♔f2 is not as good for Black as in the game.

10	cxd5	exd5
11	♘xd5?	

After this Black is at least equal. Fischer conceded that Black would have been worse after 11 exd5! ♘b4 12 ♗c4 ♗f5 13 ♘xb4 ♗xb4 14 0-0 ♖c8. The pawn sacrifice was anticipated in a 1952 Soviet game, Yudovich – Simagin, which went 12 ♘xb4 ♗xb4 13 ♔f2 ♖e8 14 ♗d4 ♘xd5 15 ♗b5 ♗xc3 16 bxc3 (not 16 ♗xe8? ♕h4+) ♗d7 with advantage for Black.

11	...	♘xd5
12	♕xd5	

White understandably didn't want to open the e-file after 12 exd5 ♘b4 13 ♗c4 ♗f5 14 ♘xb4 ♗xb4+ 15 ♔e2 ♖e8 – and not 15 ♔f2? ♕h4+..

12	...	♕c7!

But now he must deal with threats to his queen (...♖d8) and king (...♗h4+). He should address the latter problem first, such as with

13 ♗e2 ♗h4+ 14 g3 ♗f6 15 0-0!.

13 ♕b5?   ♗d7

14 ♖c1?

Black would have obvious compensation after 14 ♕c4 ♗e6 15 ♕c3 ♖fd8 16 f4 (or 16 ♗e2 ♗f6 17 ♕a3 ♗e5) ♖ac8 17 ♔f2 ♕b8. But better was the nerves-of-steel defense, 14 ♕e2! ♗f6 15 ♔f2, with some survival prospects.

14 ...   ♘b4!

Black's attack requires no difficult-to-find moves after 15 ♕c4 ♕a5! 16 ♘xb4 ♗xb4+ 17 ♔f2 ♖ac8, e.g. 18 ♕d5 ♖xc1 19 ♗xc1 (not 19 ♕xa5?? ♖c2+) ♗e1+! 20 ♔e3 ♕b6+.

15 ♘xb4!

Proper panic: The endgame is only slightly inferior. White gets a strong centralized knight, anchored by an extra pawn, in return for the rook.

15 ...   ♕xc1+

16 ♗xc1   ♗xb5

17 ♘d5!   ♗h4+!

Without this move White wins. Now he has slim drawing chances.

18 g3   ♗xf1

The trappy 19 gxh4?! ♗c4 (19...♗g2? 20 ♖g1 ♗xf3 21 ♗h6! or

21 ♖g3! ♗xe4 22 ♘f6+) only hurts White's drawing chances.

19 ♖xf1   ♗d8

With no passed pawn or pawn majority, Black's hopes rest on undermining the knight on d5, then trading a pair of rooks and creating pawn targets for his remaining rook and king.

20 ♗d2

Black has a more difficult task after 20 g4! ♖c8 21 ♔d1 and ♗d2-c3.

20 ...   ♖c8

21 ♗c3   f5!

Since the best thing about White's game is the supported knight, he must avoid 22 exf5 ♖xf5 23 ♘e3 ♖h5, when Black wins easily.

22 e5   ♖c5!

Now a retreat to e3 or f4 runs into 22...♗a5! and ...♖xe5(+).

23 ♘b4   ♗a5

24 a3   ♗xb4

Black operates freely on light squares now.

25 axb4   ♖d5

26 ♔e2   ♔f7

27 h4

Not 27 e6+? ♔g6 which dooms the e-pawn. White avoids advancing his f-pawn because Black's other rook would invade via ...♖c8-c4-e4+.

27 ...   ♔e6

28 ♔e3   ♖c8

29 ♖g1   ♖c4

Black has two ways of breaking the dark-square blockade. The simplest technique, identified with Capablanca, is to return the Exchange at the right moment to reach a winning rook-and-pawn or king-and-pawn ending.

More complex is the temporary pawn sacrifice of...f4+ (and if gxf4 then ...♔f5). If White tries to stop that plan with 30 f4 he gives away e4 to a black rook and provides an invasion route of f7-g6-h5-g4 to the black king.

But both winning techniques depend on timing. For example, the ...f4+/gxf4/...♔f5 plan is doomed if, as is the case here, White can reply ♖g5+ or ♖xg7.

30 ♖e1?

A wait-and-see strategy, such as 30 ♖a1 a6 31 ♖g1, is best. Then 31...♖xe5+ 32 ♗xe5 ♔xe5 is probably winning after 33 b5 a5. But White can upset that with 32 ♔d3!, e.g. 32...b5 33 ♗xe5 ♔xe5 34 ♖e1+ and then 34...♔f6? 35 b3! ♖xb4 36 ♔c3 or 34...♔d5 35 b3 ♖xb4 36 ♔c3 ♖d4 37 ♖e7. Therefore, Black would have had to prepare an Exchange sacrifice by a series of maneuvers and probes, or try to find a more efficient way of

engineering ...f4+, with ...g6, then ...h6 and ...g5.

30	...	♖xc3+!
31	bxc3	♖xe5+
32	♔d2	♖xe1
33	♔xe1	♔d5
34	♔d2	♔c4
35	h5	b6!

This ensures an outside passed a-pawn, which must prevail once White's passes are exhausted. Lombardy, who in another U.S. Championship, played until adjournment at move 90 two queens down, doggedly continued:

36 ♔c2 g5 37 h6 f4 38 g4 a5 39 bxa5 bxa5 40 ♔b2 a4 41 ♔a3 ♔xc3 42 ♔xa4 ♔d4 43 ♔b4 ♔e3 White resigns

22

In the 1950s, Samuel Reshevsky compiled a remarkable match record, defeating Najdorf, Gligorić, Lombardy, Bisguier, and Donald Byrne. After he overpowered Benko, in a ten-game match in September 1960, veteran columnist Hermann Helms wrote in the *New York World, Telegram & Sun*: "Reshevsky looms as the powerhouse on the North American chess scene despite the ascendancy of teenage Bobby Fischer. A match between Reshevsky and Fischer would certainly be welcomed." Ten months later a best-of-16-game match between the two began. But the tension between them had been palpable for years. When they competed at the 20-player Buenos Aires 1960, Reshevsky was quoted by Taimanov as saying "I would settle for 19th – if Fischer placed 20th." The ill will helped poison, and ultimately shorten their match, which became the first Fischer fiasco to gain widespread media attention.

Fischer – Samuel Reshevsky
Second match game,
New York 1961
Sicilian Defense,
Dragon Variation (B72)

1	e4	c5
2	♘f3	♘c6
3	d4	cxd4
4	♘xd4	g6
5	♘c3	♗g7
6	♗e3	♘f6
7	♗e2	

Announcing he had prepared something special. Two years before in a U.S. Championship game, Reshevsky fell into a book trap (7 ♗c4 0-0 8 ♗b3 ♘a5? and could have resigned after 9 e5! ♘e8? 10 ♗xf7+! ♔xf7 11 ♘e6! dxe6 12 ♕xd8). Typically for a Fischer – Reshevsky game, he played until the 42nd move.

7	...	0-0
8	f4	d6
9	♘b3	♗e6

Fischer was well ahead of the curve in arguing that 9...a5 10 a4 ♗e6 was superior. Then 11 g4? is bad since White never has the a2-a3 move that proves essential to his attack in the game.

10 g4

Fischer showed a fondness for this move in Sicilians and Pirc/Moderns. For example, a game with Korchnoi

at Curaçao began 1 e4 d6 2 d4 ♘f6 3 ♘c3 g6 4 f4 ♗g7 5 ♘f3 0-0 6 ♗e2 c5 7 dxc5 ♕a5 8 0-0 ♕xc5+ 9 ♔h1 ♘c6 10 ♘d2 a5 11 ♘b3 ♕b6 12 a4 ♘b4 and in this Dragon-like position he allowed 13 g4? ♗xg4!, with advantage to Black after 14 ♗xg4 ♘xg4 15 ♕xg4 ♘xc2.

10 ... d5

Endorsed by theory since 1936 but after this game the debate resumed over whether 10...♘a5 was better.

11	f5!	♗c8!
12	exd5	♘b4
13	♗f3	

Alekhine had tried 13 d6 ♕xd6 14 ♗c5 against Botvinnik at Nottingham 1936 but the game petered out to perpetual check after 14...♕f4! 15 ♖f1 ♕xh2 16 ♗xb4 ♘xg4! 17 ♗xg4 ♕g3+.

13 ... gxf5

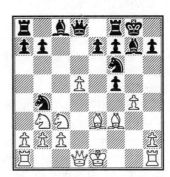

"I thought he was a little bit wild in the openings," Reshevsky said, many years later, of his pre-match evaluation of Fischer. "I knew he was original in the openings but I thought he took too many chances."

14 a3

This had been recommended by Luděk Pachman who analyzed 14...fxg4 15 axb4 gxf3 16 ♕xf3

73

♗g4 17 ♕g2 ♗h5 18 ♗d4 ♗g6 19 0-0-0 as favorable for White.

14 ...   fxg4

15 ♗g2

But there was no reason to trade off this fine bishop for a knight that will be kicked to a6 (and never make another move).

15 ...   ♘a6

16 ♕d3!

This stops the bishop from bolstering the kingside (...♗f5-g6) and enables White to force open a file with h2-h3, e.g. 16...♘c7? 17 0-0-0 ♘ce8 18 h3 g3 19 ♘e2 ♘d6 20 ♘xg3 and ♗d4.

16 ...   e6

Reshevsky thought 50 minutes on this, the first new move of the game. On 16...♘d7, which was played in a 1942 Soviet game, Fischer intended 17 0-0-0 ♘e5 18 ♕e2.

Then 18...♕c7 19 ♗d4 ♘g6! is fine for Black because his knight plugs up the g-file. A trade of dark-squared bishops will open c5 and e5 for Black's pieces.

White would probably not do better with 19 h3 after which 19...g3 20 ♖d4 (to stop ...♘c4 and prepare ♕h5/♖h4 or ♗f4) can be answered by 20...♘g6 21 ♖c4 ♕d6, with level chances.

A similar defense is 16...♕d6 with the idea of ...♕g6 as well as ...♘h5-f4. For instance, 17 0-0-0 ♘h5 18 h3 ♘f4 19 ♕e4 ♘xg2 and 20 hxg4 favors White.

17   0-0-0

After 17 d6 ♘d5! Black would suddenly have plenty of play (18 ♗xd5 exd5 19 ♕xd5 ♖e8).

17 ...   ♘xd5

Better chances are offered by 17...exd5 18 h3 g3 19 ♗d4 ♘h5!.

18 h3!   g3

With no knight to defend h7, Black must keep the h-file closed.

19 ♖hg1   ♕d6

20 ♗xd5   exd5

21 ♘xd5

The pretty 21 ♗d4 ♕f4+ 22 ♔b1 ♗f5 23 ♖xg3 leads to only an endgame edge after 23...♗xd3 24 ♖xg7+ ♔h8 25 ♖xf7+ ♕xd4 26 ♖xf8+ ♖xf8 27 ♘xd4 ♗e4.

21 ...   ♔h8

Now 22 ♗d4 ♗xd4! 23 ♕xd4+ f6 has much less bite.

22 ♗f4   ♕g6

23 ♕d2

Some annotators claimed 23 ♕f3 would have won more quickly (23...♗h6 24 ♖xg3 ♗xf4+ 25 ♕xf4 ♕e6 26 ♕d4+ or 23...♗e6 24 ♖xg3 ♗xd5 25 ♖xd5 ♕f6 26 ♖xg7! ♕xg7 27 ♖g5). Fischer shot back that 23...♗f5! 24 ♖xg3 ♕c6 saves Black. He didn't appreciate how much stronger 24 ♘e7 ♕f6 25 ♘xf5 ♕xf5 26 ♖xg3 was.

23 ...   ♗xh3!

74

| 24 | Rxg3 | Bg4 |
| 25 | Rh1 | Rfe8 |

Black parries the neat threat of 26 ♘e7 ♛e6 27 Rxg4! ♛xg4 28 Rxh7+! ♚xh7 29 ♛h2+. He is a move or two (...f5, ...Re4 or ...Rad8) away from weathering the storm.

| 26 | ♘e3 | ♛e4? |

But in time pressure, Reshevsky overlooks a combination. Necessary was 26...f5 so that 27 ♘xg4 fxg4 28 ♛h2 Rac8 29 Rxg4 could be met by 29...Re1+!.

| 27 | ♛h2! | |

Murderous, since 27...Bf5 fails to 28 Rxg7 ♚xg7 29 ♘xf5+ ♛xf5 30 ♘d4, e.g. 30...♛e4 31 ♛h6+ ♚g8 (31...♚h8? 32 Be5+) 32 Rg1+.

| 27 | ... | Be6 |

No one resigned or offered draws in Fischer – Reshevsky games until the board was nearly barren. But here 28 ♘d2! might have ended matters immediately.

28	Rxg7!?	♚xg7
29	♛h6+	♚g8
30	Rg1+	♛g6

The rest was: **31 Rxg6+ fxg6 32 ♘d4 Rad8 33 Be5 Rd7 34 ♘xe6 Rxe6 35 ♘g4 Rf7 36 ♛g5 Rf1+ 37 ♚d2 h5 38 ♛d8+ Resigns**

The match ended, with the score tied 5½-5½, because of a scheduling dispute that escalated into accusation, recrimination and eventually a forfeit in Reshevsky's favor.

23

The Bled tournament of 1961 was hyped by its sponsors as "The Tournament of the Century." Dedicated to the 30th anniversary of Alekhine's great victory at the Slovenian resort, it was intended to be the grandest round-robin since the 1930s. Even though Botvinnik, Euwe, Smyslov and Reshevsky refused their invitations, it attracted an exceptionally strong field, including six of the eight contestants from the previous Candidates tournament. Fischer's excellent form was evident in the first game.

Svetozar Gligorić – Fischer
Bled 1961
*King's Indian Defense,
Classical Variation (E98)*

1	d4	♘f6
2	c4	g6
3	♘c3	Bg7
4	e4	d6
5	♘f3	0-0
6	Be2	e5
7	0-0	♘c6
8	d5	♘e7
9	♘e1	♘d7
10	♘d3	f5
11	exf5	

This forces Black to make an early decision about pawn structure: He can concede e4 and use f5 as a jumping-off place for minor pieces. Or he can accept pressure on his center (11...gxf5 12 f4) and try to use the half-open g-file.

11 ...   ♘xf5!

12 f3   ♘f6

In the Reshevsky match Fischer showed that Black had a good game with 12...♘d4 13 ♘e4 b6, holding up c4-c5. Then 14 ♗g5 ♕e8 helps him create kingside chances with ...h6/...g5 and ...♕g6.

13 ♘f2!   ♘d4

14 ♘2e4

Play follows the basic ideas endorsed by opening experts at the time: White works from the outpost at e4, Black keeps the queenside closed and expands on the kingside. But later analysts suggested Black might have done just as well with 13...c6 and ...♕b6+, while White may have had superior options after 13...♘d4 in 14 ♗e3, 14 ♗d3 or even 14 ♖e1.

14 ...   ♘h5!

15 ♗g5

Perhaps better is 15 ♖f2 intending ♗f1!.

15 ...   ♕d7

Now if White allows 16...♘f4 Black has a splendid game, with prospects of ...h6 and, if ♗h4, then ...♘xg2!.

16 g3   h6

On the immediate 16...c5 White has a strong 17 ♘b5!, since 17...♘xb5 18 cxb5 and b2-b4 is excellent for him.

17 ♗e3   c5

A typical King's Indian choice: Black can be a pawn down or have a positionally ruined game (17...♘xe2+ 18 ♕xe2 g5 19 c5).

18 ♗xd4

White no longer has the c4-c5 break, he can't win the d6-pawn with 18 ♘b5 ♘f5 19 ♗d2 a6 and there wasn't much to 18 dxc6 bxc6 19 f4 because Black's pieces are annoyingly active after 19...♘xe2+ 20 ♕xe2 exf4 21 gxf4 ♖e8. Salo Flohr, in *Shakhmaty v SSSR*, recommended 18 ♖f2. But he said Gligorić "mistakenly supposed" that Fischer had blundered.

18 ...   exd4

19 ♘b5   a6!

The pawn can't be held by 19...♗e5 20 f4.

20 ♘bxd6   d3!

Black sets up ...♗d4+ and a sacrifice on g3. For example, 21 ♗xd3 ♗d4+ 22 ♔h1 ♘xg3+ 23 ♘xg3 (23 hxg3?? ♕h3 mate) ♕xd6 is playable for Black, e.g. 24 ♕c2 ♗h3 25 ♖fd1 g5. But once again Gligoric underestimated the Exchange sacrifice, 22 ♖f2!, with advantage.

21 ♕xd3   ♗d4+

But not 21...♗xb2? 22 ♘xc8! ♗xa1 23 ♘b6 ♗d4+ 24 ♕xd4! and wins, or 22...♖axc8 23 ♖ae1 with a solid positional edge.

22 ♔g2?

This lays a small trap (22...♕h3+ 23 ♔h1 and Black has no good move, e.g. 23...♗f5 24 ♕b3) and prepares a *zwischenzug* at move 23, compared with 22 ♔h1 ♘xg3+ 23 ♘xg3 ♕xd6.

Evans called this an example of the perfect chess game – perhaps because he and Fischer couldn't find any improvements for Black. However, Isaac Boleslavsky pointed out that White would do much better with 22 ♖f2!, which favors him after 22...♗xf2+ 23 ♔xf2 ♘f6 24 ♘xf6+ ♖xf6 25 ♘e4. Or 22...♗xb2 23 ♖b1 ♗d4 24 ♘xc8 ♖axc8 25 ♖b6!.

22 ... ♘xg3!

Fischer said he had to have foreseen this when he played 17...c5.

23 ♘xc8!

As noted before, 23 ♘xg3 ♕xd6 is fine for Black, and other captures on g3 allow mate.

23 ... ♘xf1
24 ♘b6! ♕c7!

The threat of ...♕xh2+ and mate brings Black close to a win.

25 ♖xf1 ♕xb6

White appears to be getting the worst of it (26 ♕d2 g5 and ...♖f4 or 26 b3 ♕c7).

26 b4!

This seals the draw since Black is losing after 26...cxb4 27 c5! ♗xc5 28 ♘xc5 ♕xc5 and now 29 ♕xg6+ ♔h8 30 ♕xh6+ ♔g8 31 ♖g1!.

26 ... ♕xb4

Fischer also rejected 26...♖f7 27 bxc5 ♗xc5 28 ♖b1, e.g. 28...♕a7 29 d6 ♗d4 30 ♕d2 followed by ♕xh6 or c5/♗c4.

27 ♖b1 ♕a5

28 ♘xc5!

Not 28 ♖xb7 ♖f7 29 ♖xf7 ♔xf7 30 ♕b1 ♕c7 and ...♖b8.

28 ... ♕xc5
29 ♕xg6+ ♗g7
30 ♖xb7

Fischer recalled how Gligorić wrote down Black's saving reply even while Fischer was looking for some way to play for a win.

30 ... ♕d4!
31 ♗d3 ♖f4
32 ♕e6+ ♔h8
33 ♕g6 Draw

24

"Chess players, as a rule, are very revengeful people," Tal wrote in his game collection, meaning they are always looking for a chance to retaliate against an opponent who inflicted a particularly memorable defeat on them. When Tal met Fischer in the second round at Bled, it was three months since he had lost a World Championship rematch (literally "revenge match" in Russian) to Botvinnik. Now it was Fischer's turn for payback, to avenge the 0-4 humiliation he suffered at Tal's hands in the 1959 Candidates Tournament.

Fischer – Mikhail Tal
Bled 1961
Sicilian Defense (B47)

1	e4	c5
2	♘f3	♘c6
3	d4	cxd4
4	♘xd4	e6
5	♘c3	♕c7

The ...♘c6/...e6 system was very new and given only half a page in Rolf Schwarz's 587-page book on the Sicilian (1961).

6 g3 ♘f6?

Tal plays a natural move – and finds himself lost by move ten. In fact, he gave 6...♘f6 two question marks in the tournament book. He explained that he planned to play 6...a6 and 7...♘f6 but "once a year or so" he reversed the move order in his calculations, and paid the price.

Essential was 6...a6 – yet several strong GMs have fallen into the same trap since 1961 – including

Benko, Judith Polgar and Yevgeny Vasiukov.

7 ♘db5!

And among the players who failed to punish 6...♘f6? by playing other seventh moves are Keres and Vlastimil Hort.

7 ... ♕b8

Black hopes to recoup with...a6.

8 ♗f4 ♘e5?

Fischer considered 8...e5 9 ♗g5 a6 10 ♗xf6 gxf6 11 ♘a3 b5 12 ♘d5 to be clearly in White's favor and indicated it was no better than the knight move. Yet two decades later a similar position in the Sveshnikov Sicilian was regarded as quite playable. Fischer was wrong – 11...♗xa3 12 bxa3 ♘e7 is better for Black than what happens to him in the game.

9 ♗e2!!

Botvinnik, who annotated this game for *Chess Life*, thought this was part of a trap set by White's sixth move (!). By watching h5 and f3, White prepares both ♕d4 and ♗xe5/f2-f4. For example, 9...a6 10 ♕d4 d6 11 ♖d1! axb5 12 ♗xe5 or 9...d6 10 ♕d4 ♘c6 11 ♕xd6!. In contrast, the immediate 9 ♗xe5 ♕xe5 10 f4 ♕b8 11 e5 a6 12 exf6 axb5 is better for Black than the game.

| 9 | ... | ♗c5 |

Black's position is so bad Tal suggested "9...♘g8!??" in his notes although White's superiority is clear after 10 ♕d4 f6 11 0-0-0. Also poor is the tricky 9...♗b4 10 ♕d4 ♘c6?! because of 11 ♗xb8 ♘xd4 12 ♘c7+ ♔e7 13 ♘xa8 ♘xc2+ 14 ♔d2.

10	♗xe5	♕xe5
11	f4	♕b8
12	e5	a6

Black is positionally crushed after 12...♘g8 13 ♘e4 ♗e7 14 ♕d2 and ♘bd6+.

| 13 | exf6 | axb5 |
| 14 | fxg7 | |

Also excellent is 14 ♘e4 ♗f8 15 ♕d4 g6 but Fischer's way is surer.

14	...	♖g8
15	♘e4	♗e7
16	♕d4	♖a4

Botvinnik recommended 16...♕c7. That enables Black to escape into a merely inferior endgame in lines such as 17 0-0?! ♖a4! 18 ♘f6+ ♗xf6 19 ♕xf6 ♕c5+ 20 ♖f2 ♕d4!). However 17 ♗d3 and ♘f6+ is close to winning.

| 17 | ♘f6+ | ♗xf6 |

After 17...♔d8 White wins with either 18 ♕b6+ or the flashy 18 ♘xg8 ♖xd4 19 ♘xe7.

| 18 | ♕xf6 | |

The threats include 19 ♗h5, 19.♗d3 and 19 ♕h6.

| 18 | ... | ♕c7! |

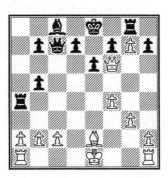

19 0-0-0!

In each of their two previous games, Fischer found enough sparkling moves to win most games. But he failed to follow them up and had to settle for a loss and a draw. This time his play remains at a consistently high level – with only one slip to come. Here he avoids:

(a) 19 ♗xb5? ♕a5+, which hangs a bishop,

(b) 19 ♗h5 ♖e4+ and 20...d5!, and

(c) 19 ♗d3 ♕c5! 20 ♗xh7 and now 20...♕e3+ 21 ♔f1? ♕f3+ 22 ♔g1 ♕e3+ 23 ♔g2 ♕e2+ 24 ♔h3 ♖xg7! 25 ♕xg7 ♕h5+ with perpetual check. But much better was 20 f5! with a likely win.

| 19 | ... | ♖xa2 |
| 20 | ♔b1 | ♖a6 |

Black had no defense to ♗h5, e.g. 20...♕a5 21 b3 or 20...♖a5 21 ♗h5 d5 22 ♖xd5! exd5 23 ♖e1+ and wins.

21 ♗xb5?

But once again Fischer plays too quickly and this time it lengthens the game considerably. With 21 ♗h5 d6 (21...d5 22 ♖xd5! ♖xg7 23 ♖d3! ♖g8? 24 ♖d8+!) 22 ♖he1 ♕e7 23 ♕h6 and ♕xh7 Black can resign. For example, 23...♔d7 24 ♕xh7 ♕e8 25 f5 e5 26 ♖xe5! or 25...♔c7 26 fxe6 ♗xe6 27 ♖xe6!.

21 ...   ♖b6

Tal pointed out 21...♖a5 22 ♕h6? ♖xb5 23 ♕xh7 allows 23...♖xb2+! 24 ♔xb2 ♕b6+ 25 ♔c1 ♕e3+ 26 ♖d2 ♕a3+ 27 ♔d1? ♕f3+ or 27 ♔b1 ♕b4+ with a perpetual check.

But White can sidestep the trap with 22 c4!.

22 ♗d3   e5

Also lost is 22...♕d8 23 ♕h6 f5 because of 24 ♕h5+ ♔e7 25 ♗e2 with the idea of 25...♖xg7 26 ♕h4+ ♔e8 27 ♗h5+.

The point of 22...e5, besides attacking the queen, is that 23 ♕xe5+ ♕xe5 takes Black from a hopeless middlegame to a merely wretched endgame.

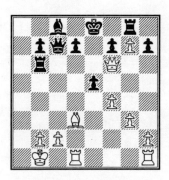

23 fxe5!   ♖xf6
24 exf6

A rare case when it was Fischer who gave up his queen for two rooks. Now 24...♕b6 25 ♖hf1 and 26 ♗xh7 is *kaput*.

24 ...   ♕c5

Black manages to trade off the pawns for a rook now (and 25 ♖hf1 ♕h5).

25 ♗xh7   ♕g5
26 ♗xg8   ♕xf6
27 ♖hf1   ♕xg7
28 ♗xf7+   ♔d8

29 ♗e6

White can choose between several winning plans. It may seem that 29 ♖d3 followed by the advance of the h-pawn is fastest but Black gets counterplay from lines such as 29...b6 30 h4 ♗a6 31 c4 ♕h7 32 ♔c2 b5. Perhaps 29 ♗d5 is a cleaner win but it's hard to resist doubling rooks on the seventh rank.

29 ...   ♕h6
30 ♗xd7   ♗xd7
31 ♖f7   ♕xh2
32 ♖dxd7+   ♔e8
33 ♖de7+   ♔d8
34 ♖d7+

Tal gave an alternative win: 34 ♖xb7 ♕h1+ 35 ♔a2 ♕d5+ 36 b3 ♕a5+ 37 ♔b2 ♕e5+ 38 c3 ♕e2+ 39 ♔a3 ♕a6+ 40 ♔b4 ♕d6+ 41 ♔b5 ♕d3+ 42 ♔b6 ♕e3+ 43 ♔a6 ♕e6+ 44 ♔a7 and wins.

That's fine for the armchair analyst – but the practical player would follow Fischer's example, which leaves White a much larger margin of error.

34	...	♔c8
35	♖c7+	♔d8
36	♖fd7+	♔e8
37	♖d1	b5
38	♖b7	♕h5

Or 38...♕xg3? 39 ♖h1 ♕e5 40 ♖h8+! ♕xh8 41 ♖b8+.

| 39 | g4! | ♕h3 |

Again Black can't take the pawn because 40 ♖h1 and the mate threat wins (40...♕d4 41 ♖h8+!).

40	g5	♕f3
41	♖e1+	♔f8
42	♖xb5	♔g7
43	♖b6	♕g3
44	♖d1	♕c7
45	♖dd6!	♕c8

The threat was 46 ♖g6+ ♔h7 47 ♖h6+ ♔g7 48 ♖bg6+ ♔f8 49 ♖h8+ and 50 ♖h7+.

| 46 | b3 | ♔h7 |
| 47 | ♖a6 | **Resigns** |

The threat of 48 ♖a7+ ♔g8 49 ♖dd7 has no answer.

25

Fischer's opening rounds at Bled look like a greatest-games collection. After facing Gligorić and Tal, he won this overlooked gem in Round Four – with another queen sacrifice – and overwhelmed Geller in Round Six.

Fischer – Fridrik Olafsson
Bled 1961
Sicilian Defense,
Dragon Variation (B35)

1	e4	c5
2	♘f3	g6
3	d4	cxd4
4	♘xd4	♗g7
5	♘c3	♘c6
6	♗e3	♘f6
7	♗c4	♕a5

This ends the "sac, sac, mate" formula since 8...♘xe4 is threatened (8 ♕d2? ♘xe4! 9 ♘xc6 ♕xc3! and 8 f3 ♕b4! 9 ♗b3 ♘xe4!).

8	0-0	d6
9	♘b3	♕c7
10	♗e2	0-0
11	f4	

More energetic is 11 g4, e.g. 11...a5 12 g5 ♘d7 13 a4 ♘b4.

| 11 | ... | a5 |
| 12 | a4 | |

A necessity since ...a4-a3 was threatened, and Black gets an easy game after 12 a3 a4 14 ♘d4 ♘xd4 14 ♗xd4 e5!.

| 12 | ... | ♘b4 |

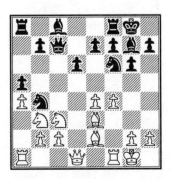

Both players have lost a tempo, Black with his queen, White with his bishop.

13 ♖f2!

This was the product of Fischer's first big think of the game. The rook (a) prepares to double on the f-file, (b) protects c2 in coordination with ♗f3 and ♘d5 and (c) is available to pressure d6 from d2 after ...e5.

Now 13...♗e6 14 ♘d4 ♗c4 15 ♗f3 slightly favors White (15...♖fd8 16 ♖d2 ♕c8 17 ♘db5), as does 13...♗d7 14 ♗f3 ♗c6 15 ♖d2 ♘d7 16 ♘d4 and ♘db5.

13 ... e5

A common theme in similar positions. Black takes the sting out of ♘d5 and enables his minor pieces to be liberated with ...exf4 and ...♘d7.

14 ♗f3 ♗d7
15 ♖d2! ♖fd8!

This is justified by 16 ♖xd6 ♗xa4 and 17 fxe5 ♗xb3 18 cxb3 ♘e8. Black's compensation is clear after 19 ♗b6! ♖xd6 20 ♕xd6! ♕c8!.

Black may have intended 16...♘e8 17 ♖d2 exf4 instead, because he would enjoy excellent chances on the dark squares after 18 ♗xf4 ♕xf4 19 ♖xd7 ♖xd7 20 ♕xd7 ♗e5.

16 ♔h1! ♗c6

A 1967 game ended abruptly after 16...♗h6? 17 ♕g1! ♖e8 18 f5 ♗xe3 19 ♕xe3 d5 20 fxg6 d4 21 ♕g5 and wins.

17 ♕g1 ♘d7

Otherwise 18 ♗b6. Black dreams of ...exf4 and ...♘e5.

18 f5!

This guarantees White a slight positional edge despite the messy

pawns after 18...gxf5 19 exf5 ♗xf3 20 gxf3 and ♘e4.

Also 19...d5 20 ♘xd5 ♗xd5 21 ♗xd5 ♘xd5 22 ♖xd5 ♕xc2 leaves White a bit ahead after 23 ♖b5!.

18 ... b6

Black will play ...♘c5 and retake with the d-pawn if White plays ♘xc5. On the immediate 18...♘c5 White has a slight edge after 19 ♖ad1 (because 19...♘xb3? allows 20 ♗b6).

19 ♖ad1 ♘c5

Here 19...♘xc2 comes to mind since Black is better after 20 ♖xc2 ♗xa4 21 ♘xa4? ♕xc2 22 ♘xb6 ♘xb6 23 ♗xb6 ♕xb3. But 21 ♘a1! ♗xc2 22 ♘xc2 favors White's minor pieces.

20 ♘b5 ♕e7

Now 20...♗xb5 21 axb5 ♘xb3 loses to 22 ♗xb6, while 21...♖ab8 22 ♘xc5 and 23 c3.

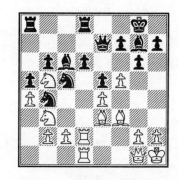

21 ♘xd6! ♘xc2

Not 21...♗xa4 22 ♗xc5 bxc5 23 ♕xc5.

22 ♘xc5

Here 22 ♖xc2 ♖xd6 23 ♘xc5 bxc5 24 ♗xc5 ♖xd1 25 ♕xd1 leaves White a pawn ahead. But 22...♗xa4! upsets the applecart.

22	...	♘xe3
23	♕xe3	bxc5
24	♗e2!	

Another big think. The bishop is headed to c4 and d5. White probably rejected Boleslavsky's recommendation of 24 b3 because of 24...c4 25 ♘xc4 ♖xd2 26 ♕xd2 gxf5. But 27 exf5 e4 28 ♗e2 is strong.

24	...	♗xa4
25	b3	♗e8
26	♗c4	a4

Fred Reinfeld prepared a book of Fischer's games before his death in 1963 and in it he gave a sample of Black's difficulty: 26...♕a7 27 fxg6 hxg6 28 ♖f1 (28 ♕g5! is better) ♖d7 and now not 29 ♗b5? ♖xd6 but 29 ♘xe8 ♖xe8 30 ♖xd7 ♕xd7 31 ♖xf7 and White wins. (The book appeared in 1967 as *Great Games by Chess Prodigies* with 68 pages devoted to Morphy, Reshevsky and Capablanca – and 178 to Fischer).

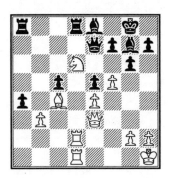

27 ♗d5!

So that 27...♖a7 28 ♘xe8 ♖xe8 (28...♕xe8? 29 ♗xf7+ and ♖xd8) 29 fxg6 hxg6 30 ♖f2 ♕f8 31 bxa4.

27	...	♖xd6!

Black is clearly worse following 27...♖ab8 28 ♘xe8 ♕xe8 29 bxa4

when 29...♕xa4 would be met by 30 ♗xf7+.

28	♗xa8	♖d4

Black tries to complicate in view of the hopelessness of 28...♖xd2 29 ♖xd2 and ♗d5.

29	fxg6	hxg6
30	bxa4	♗xa4

Black could have tried 30...♕a7 31 ♗d5 ♕xa4 but he can't hold out long after 32 ♖f1.

31	♖a1!	♕f8?

Black could have saved himself with 31...♕d8! 32 ♗d5 ♗c6! (33 ♗xc6 ♖xd2 34 ♖a8 ♖d1+ or 34 ♗d5 ♖xd5 35 exd5 ♕xd5). This is why 31 ♖b1! was best.

32 ♗d5!

Not 32 ♖xd4 exd4 33 ♕a3 ♕xa8 34 ♕xa4 ♕xa4 35 ♖xa4 d3 and Black wins.

32	...	♗h6
33	♖xd4!	♗xe3

Or 33...cxd4 34 ♕g3 and wins.

34	♖dxa4	♕h6
35	♖f1	♗f4
36	g3!	

If the bishop moves, 37 ♖a8+ wins.

36	...	♕h3

37 ♖aa1! ♗xg3

38 ♖a8+ Resigns

In view of 38...♔g7 39 ♖xf7+ ♔h6 40 ♖h8+.

26

Fischer's career record with certain strong grandmasters improved markedly as he matured. Following his disastrous start against Tal, he scored 3½-1½ in their last five games. And after scoring 4-7 with only one win, in his first 11 meetings with Gligorić, he was 5-0 in their last five non-training games.

But there was one major exception: Yefim Geller. In between their first game, below, and their last, which Fischer won, Geller amassed the best record of any Fischer rival – five wins, two draws and one loss.

Fischer – Yefim Geller
Bled 1961
Ruy Lopez,
Steinitz Defense Deferred (C72)

1	e4	e5
2	♘f3	♘c6
3	♗b5	a6
4	♗a4	d6
5	0-0	

A fairly unusual move in 1961, when 5 c3 or 5 ♗xc6+ were endorsed by theory. Today, Black usually replies with a neutral move such as 5...♗d7, but at the time 5 0-0 was controversial because of:

5	...	♗g4
6	h3	♗h5

To save this variation – which seemed to be on life-support after this game – masters soon began adopting 6...h5, since 7 hxg4? hxg4 8 ♘e1?? ♕h4 is suicide for White. Fischer said he would have replied 7 d4 and if 7...b5 8 ♗b3 ♘xd4 then 9 hxg4 hxg4 10 ♘g5, a line whose merits are still in doubt (10...♘h6 11 ♗d5 ♗e7 or 11 g3 ♗e7 12 f4 c6).

7 c3 ♕f6?

Geller had no poker face and his expressions during the game were revealing. Fischer recalled how he looked very pleased with himself after coming up with this new move.

8	g4!	♗g6
9	d4!	

This offers a sacrifice Black felt he should accept in view of 10 ♗g5 and d4-d5. He could have reduced the damage with 9...b5 10 ♗c2 ♕d8 – but that would admit he'd wasted two moves. Better is 9...h6 10 ♖e1 b5 11 ♗c2 ♕d8 but White commands a comfortable edge after 12 a4.

9	...	♗xe4?
10	♘bd2	♗g6

Black can temporarily keep the center closed with 10...♗xf3 11 ♘xf3

84

e4 12 ♖e1 d5. But Fischer noted how strong 13 ♗g5 was:

(a) 13...♕e6 14 c4! with a powerful liquidation of the center, or

(b) 13...♕d6 14 c4! dxc4 (or 14...f6 15 cxd5 ♕xd5 16 ♗b3) 15 d5! and wins, and,

(c) 13...♕g6 14 ♕b3 b5 15 ♕xd5 bxa4 16 ♘e5!.

Besides, Geller still seemed happy with his position.

11   ♗xc6+   bxc6

12   dxe5

Fischer believed 12 ♕a4 ♔d7 was safe for Black. But Keres pointed out the precariousness of Black's situation after 13 dxe5 dxe5 14 ♘c4 ♗d6 15 ♖d1 ♖e8 16 ♘xd6 cxd6 17 ♕b4! and then 17...♔c7 18 ♕a5+ ♔d7 19 ♕c5 or 18...♔b7 19 ♗e3 c5 20 ♗xc5.

12   ...   dxe5

Fischer made no mention of 12...♕d8, perhaps because 13 ♕a4 ♕d7 14 ♖e1 d5 15 e6! fxe6 16 ♘e5 so clearly favors White.

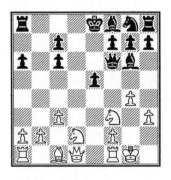

13   ♘xe5!

Harold Lommer, a prominent endgame composer, reported on Bled 1961 for the brief-lived *American Chess Quarterly*. He recalled how around this move Geller "seemed very sure of his position and moved rather quickly, then suddenly stopped and gasped. Something must have gone very, very wrong." What Geller overlooked is unclear but he surely saw 13...♕xe5?? 14 ♖e1.

13   ...   ♗d6

There is no safe harbor for the king any more (13...0-0-0 14 ♕e2 ♔b7 15 ♘b3 and ♘a5+). But it was unclear, even to the grandmaster spectators, how bad Black's position was. Fischer regarded 14 ♘xc6 h5 as risky but his king is safe after 15 ♘c4 or 15 ♖e1+ ♔f8 16 ♘f3.

14   ♘xg6!

One of those Fischer moves that looks ridiculous at first: White allows the opening of the h-file and trades a strong knight for a nothing bishop – and only slowly reveals its power.

White doesn't fear 14...hxg6 because of 15 ♘e4 ♕h4 16 ♘xd6+ cxd6 17 ♕xd6 ♕xh3?? 18 ♖e1+. Nevertheless Geller spent about half an hour on his reply.

14   ...   ♕xg6

15   ♖e1+

Geller's "clock kept ticking away valuable minutes while he scratched his head pondering his position," Lommer wrote. "He was smoking so many cigarettes that he was soon enveloped in a white halo of smoke."

15   ...   ♔f8

After 15...♘e7 16 ♘c4 0-0-0 17 ♕a4 Black's king jumps from the frying pan to fire. Instead, he pins his hopes for king safety on f8 and for counterplay in the opening of the h-file.

16 ♘c4   h5

17 ♘xd6   cxd6

Fischer believed 17...♕xd6 was best but didn't say how he would proceed. Keres, in the tournament book, recommended 18 ♕xd6+ cxd6 19 ♗f4 ♖d8 20 ♖ad1 d5 21 ♖d4 (although there is something to be said for 21 ♗c7 ♖d7 22 ♗b6 ♘h6 23 f3).

But more in keeping with the tempo of the game is 18 ♕a4! after which 18...hxg4 19 ♗f4 and now 19...♕c5 20 ♖e5 or 19...♕f6 20 ♕b4+ ♘e7 21 ♗xc7 ♖e8 22 ♖e7! are winning for White.

18 ♗f4   d5?

After this Black had 45 minutes left for 22 moves. Tal, an interested bystander since Fischer was his chief rival for first prize, suggested 18...♖d8 after the game. But 19 g5 leaves Black without a good continuation, e.g. 19...♘e7 20 ♕f3 and ♖e2/♖ae1.

19 ♕b3!   hxg4

Geller spent 40 of those 45 minutes glumly calculating variations such as 19...♘e7 20 ♖xe7 ♔xe7 21 ♕b7+ or 19...♘f6 20 ♕b7! as in the game (20...♖e8 21 ♖xe8+ ♘xe8 22 ♖e1 ♕f6 23 ♕c8 and wins).

20 ♕b7!

Much better than 20 ♕b4+ ♘e7 21 ♕xe7+ ♔g8.

20 ...   gxh3+

21 ♗g3

21 ...   ♖d8

22 ♕b4+   Resigns

"The roof almost caved in at the tumultuous burst of applause," Lommer wrote. "It was almost as though the spectators were greeting in applause the next world's champion."

27

Perhaps the least known of Fischer's combinations was also the longest. Fischer's opponent, Arthur Bisguier, had achieved some excellent positions against him since they first met five years before and was in fine form at Bled, where he defeated Geller, Keres and Najdorf . But at move 14 Fischer grabs a white pawn in what appears to be a highly double-edged position. Over the course of the next 15 moves, Bisguier rejects one drawish opportunity after another because his winning prospects appear too good to waste. Only at move 30 does it become clear Fischer has seen much further than him.

Arthur Bisguier – Fischer
Bled 1961
Queen's Gambit Declined,
Semi-Tarrasch Defense (D42)

1	d4	♘f6
2	♘f3	d5
3	c4	e6
4	e3	c5
5	♘c3	♘c6
6	cxd5	

Fischer's opening repertoire reflected an odd philosophy: every position, even one of pure symmetry, contained within it the possibilities for an advantage – for Black as well as White. The key was finding the right moment to break symmetry. For example, on 6 a3, White can meet 6...a6 with 7 dxc5 ♗xc5 8 b4, with advantage. But in the eighth game of his Candidates match with Petrosian, Fischer broke the pattern earlier with 6...♘e4!? 7 ♕c2 ♘xc3 8 bxc3 ♗e7. The position soon turned in his favor after 9 ♗b2 0-0 10 ♗d3 h6 11 0-0 ♘a5.

6	...	♘xd5
7	♗d3	♗e7
8	0-0	0-0
9	a3	cxd4
10	exd4	♘f6

Fischer never showed much interest in playing against hanging pawns (9...♘xc3 10 bxc3).

11	♗e3	b6
12	♖c1	♗b7
13	♕e2	

This gives Black a chance to sharpen the position that 13 ♗b1 ♖c8 14 ♕d3 would not.

13	...	♘g4

Black decides to punish the apparently inexact ♗e3. Bisguier gets into endgame trouble only because he, in turn, decides to punish Black's dogmatism. White's position is not worse after 14 ♖fd1 ♘xe3 15 ♕xe3 ♗f6 16 ♗e4 or 14 ♗b1 ♘xe3 15 fxe3 ♕d6 16 ♕d3. But why not preserve the bishop?

14	♗f4	♘xd4!!

"This is unbelievable," Euwe wrote, "considering the many obvious resources which White has at his disposal, which will soon become clear."

15	♘xd4	♕xd4

Now 16 ♗xh7+! ♔xh7 17 ♕xg4 ♕f6 is only a slight edge for Black. However, White appears to get an edge with his next two moves.

16	♕xg4	♕xd3
17	♖fd1	♕g6!

Black has seen through 17...♕a6 18 ♗e5 g6 19 ♖d7 ♗c5 20 ♕h4! or 19...♖fe8 20 ♖xe7 ♖xe7 21 ♕g5 and 19...♖ae8 20 ♖xe7 ♖xe7 21 ♗f6, winning. He opts instead to ruin his pawns in order to keep an extra one.

18	♕xg6	fxg6!
19	♖d7	♗c5

Not 19...♖xf4 20 ♖xe7 ♗d5? 21 ♘xd5 exd5 22 ♖cc7.

20 ♗e3

White invites ...♗xe3 – which remains an error for four moves.

20 ... ♗c6!

White would have the upper hand after 20...♗xe3 21 fxe3 ♗c6 22 ♖d6. It's not clear who has the edge after 21...♖f7 22 ♖xf7 ♔xf7 23 ♘b5 ♔f6 (24 ♖c7 ♗e4 25 ♖xa7 ♖d8).

21 ♖c7

21 ... ♖fc8!

If Black had inverted his move order, with 21...♗xe3 22 fxe3 ♖fc8 23 ♖xc8+ ♖xc8, White's king would be a tempo ahead of the game after 24 ♘b5 ♗d7 25 ♖xc8+ ♗xc8 26 ♘xa7 ♗d7 27 ♔f2. The knight is freed after, for example, 27...♔f7 28 ♔e2 ♔e7 29 ♔d3 ♔d6 30 ♔c4.

In fact, White can do better with 23 ♘b5! (after 21...♗xe3 22 fxe3 ♖fc8), because then 23...♖xc7 24 ♘xc7 wins outright, and 23...♗d7 24 ♘xa7! or 23...♗b7 24 ♘d6 ♖xc7 25 ♖xc7 ♗d5 26 e4 ♗b3 27 ♘c8! favors White.

22 ♖xc8+?!

Again White plays for a win, passing up a likely draw in 22 ♘b5! ♗xb5 23 ♖xc8+ ♖xc8 24 b4.

22 ... ♖xc8

Now 23 ♗xc5 bxc5 24 f3 ♔f7 offers Black good winning chances.

23 ♘b5!

Black can transpose into the note to White's 22nd with 22...♗xb5 23 b4. But he has better:

23 ... ♗d7!

The outlines of a winning edge appear after 24 ♗xc5 ♖xc5 25 ♖xc5 bxc5 26 ♘xa7 ♔f8.

24 b4

The bid to create a fortress fails after 24 ♘xa7 ♖a8 25 ♖xc5 bxc5 26 ♗xc5 ♔f7 28 b4 ♖b8 29 f3 ♗a4.

Bisguier may have been misled by thinking Fischer would answer 24 b4 with 24...♗xb5 25 bxc5 bxc5 26 ♖xc5 ♖xc5 27 ♗xc5 and try to win with the extra, doubled pawn.

24 ... ♗xe3

25 ♖xc8+ ♗xc8

There are no more tricks for White since 26 ♘xa7 ♗xf2+ and 27...♗d7 wins easily.

26 fxe3 ♗d7!

Or perhaps White had assumed Black would choose 26...a6 27 ♘d6 ♗d7 28 ♘c4 b5 29 ♘e5, when his chances in the good-♘-vs.bad-♗ ending are slim.

27 ♘d6

When Black made his 14th move he almost certainly had calculated this far – and still further, because he probably saw that 27 ♘xa7 b5 traps the knight. In contrast with the note to move 21, the white king is denied c4 in this variation and will run out of moves following 28 ♔f2 ♔f7 29 ♔e2 ♔e7 30 ♔d3 ♔d6 31 ♔d4 e5+ 32 ♔e4 g5. Then Black's king can pick off the knight. But the winning task would be hard after 29 ♔f3 e5 or 29...♔e7.

In fact, as the game goes, White can draw by creating an impregnable fortress: 27...♔f8 28 ♘e4 ♔e7 29 ♔f2 ♗c6 30 ♘c3, as Karsten Müller pointed out. Black can get his king to e5 but can't penetrate White's shield.

27 ... ♔f8

28 e4? e5!

Although the defender usually benefits from a trade of pawns, here Black needed to stop 29 e5 and ♔f2-e3.

29 ♔f2 ♗c6

30 ♘c4

After the pawn swap, the bishop will dominate the knight, making *zugzwang* possible. But 30 b5 is met by 30...♔e7! 31 ♘c8+ ♔d8 and if 32 ♘xb6 (or 32 ♘xa7 ♗xe4) then 32...♗xb5 33 ♘d5 ♔d7. Black's chances are increasing.

30 ... ♗xe4

31 ♘xe5 ♔e7

32 ♘c4 ♔e6

The pawn endings (such as 33 g3 ♔d5 34 ♘d2 ♔d4 35 ♘xe4 ♔xe4 36 h3 h5) are lost.

33 ♘e3 ♔e5

34 ♔e2 ♔d4

35 ♔d2 ♗c6!

Zugzwang looms (36 ♔e2? ♔c3).

36 g3 ♗d7

37 ♘d1

Or 37 ♘c2+ ♔c4 38 ♘a1 ♗f5 and 37 h4 h5 38 ♘g2 ♔c4 39 ♘f4 ♗f5 and wins in either case.

37 ... ♔e4

Since 38 ♔e2 ♗g4+ and ...♗xd1 is hopeless, White must allow the king to reach g2.

38 ♘e3 ♔f3

39 ♔d3 g5

40 ♔d4 ♗e6

41 ♔e5

The h-pawn was lost after 41 ♔d3 ♗h3 and ...♔f2. The rest of the game went:

41 ... ♔xe3 42 ♔xe6 ♔f3 43 ♔f5 ♔g2 44 ♔xg5 ♔xh2 45 g4 b5 46 ♔f5 ♔g3 47 g5 g6+ White resigns

A curious incident occurred after Bled ended while Fischer toured Yugoslavia and was stricken with what the *New York Times* called apparent appendicitis. He was in

Zagreb for a simul when he suddenly felt abdominal pains. Bjelica recalled: "We postponed the exhibition and raced off to Banja Luka in an ambulance. During that time I could see what great love he had for chess. Bobby gripped his stomach with one hand, and in the other he held Keres' book, *My Greatest Games*. Fischer refused to have an appendectomy and the pain slowly receded. He spent three days in the hospital, playing offhand games and thumbing through Keres."

28

Fischer played no more serious games in 1961. He passed up the U.S. Championship, the only time he failed to accept his invitation between 1957 and 1967, and didn't return to chess until his second Interzonal, at Stockholm. Again he started slowly, and it was only in the fourth round, against the new grandmaster Lajos Portisch, that he began to impress, when he played one of the most instructive rook-and-pawn endgames of the 20th Century.

Fischer – Lajos Portisch
Interzonal, Stockholm 1962
Caro-Kann Defense (B10)

1	e4	c6
2	♘c3	d5
3	♘f3	dxe4
4	♘xe4	♘d7
5	♗c4	♘gf6
6	♘eg5	♘d5

Unlike the comparable position with 3 d4, here 6...e6 7 ♕e2 ♘b6? is refuted by 8 ♘e5!.

| 7 | d4 | h6 |

8	♘e4	♘7b6
9	♗b3	♗f5
10	♘g3	♗h7
11	0-0	e6
12	♘e5	♘d7

Black must try to exchange off at least one pair of minor pieces and avoid lines such as 12...♗e7 13 ♘h5 0-0? 14 ♕g4!.

13	c4	♘5f6
14	♗f4	♘xe5

He is more constricted after 14...♗e7 14 ♕e2 0-0 16 ♖ad1 ♖e8 17 ♖fe1.

15	♗xe5	♗d6
16	♕e2	0-0
17	♖ad1	♕e7

White's bishop is his best piece but trading it off (17...♗xe5? 18 dxe5 ♘d7 19 ♖d6!) leaves Black in a bind.

18	♗xd6	♕xd6
19	f4	

White enjoys a textbook edge in space – four occupied ranks versus three, with a no-man's-land in between. The logical next step is to improve the scope of his rooks, such as with f4-f5.

| 19 | ... | c5? |

Kmoch showed his Viennese school caution when he recommended a waiting policy of 19...♖fe8! (and 20 f5? ♗xf5 or 20 ♕f3 ♖ad8 21 f5 e5!).

20 ♕e5!   ♕xe5
21 dxe5

White can try to dominate the d-file with 21 fxe5 ♘g4 22 ♖f4 ♘e3 23 ♖d2 cxd4 24 ♖fxd4. But Black complicates matters with 23...♖ad8!, e.g, 24 ♔f2? g5! or 24 d5 b5!?.

21 ...   ♘e4
22 ♖d7!   ♘xg3
23 hxg3   ♗e4

Black appears to be holding the balance (24 ♖fd1 ♗c6 25 ♖7d6 ♖fc8! and ...♔f8 followed by ♖c7).

24 ♗a4!

By taking away ...♗c6 White threatens 25 ♖e1.

24 ...   ♖ad8
25 ♖fd1   ♖xd7
26 ♖xd7   g5!
27 ♗d1!

A new threat: 28 ♗f3.

27 ...   ♗c6
28 ♖d6   ♖c8
29 ♔f2   ♔f8
30 ♗f3   ♗xf3
31 gxf3

After 31 ♔xf3 ♔e7 White has few prospects, since the king raid, 32 fxg5 hxg5 33 ♔g4, allows 33...f5+! 34 ♔xg5 ♖g8+ and ...♖g4(+).

He also achieves nothing from 32 ♔e3 f5. And 32 f5 exf5 33 ♖xh6, as in the game, is at least equal for Black after 33...♖d8.

31 ...   gxf4?

The trade opens a window of opportunity at move 33, compared with 31...♔e7 32 f5 exf5 33 ♖xh6 ♖c6!.

32 gxf4   ♔e7

33 f5!

"When a young player is good at attacking or at combinations, this is understandable," Alexander Kotov wrote in *Shakhmaty v SSSR*. "But a faultless endgame technique at the age of 19 is something rare. I can only recall one other chessplayer who at that age was equally skillful at endgames – Vasily Smyslov."

Fischer's play here has a Smyslov-like quality. At each point when it appeared Black had equalized (at move 23, 26 or 32) White finds a new resource, such as the threat of 34 f6+ ♔e8 35 ♖d1! and ♖h1.

33 ...   exf5
34 ♖xh6   ♖d8

Now the king-and-pawn ending (34...♖c6? 35 ♖xc6 bxc6) will lose because the white king invades (36 ♔g3 ♔d7 37 ♔h4!).

The instructive main line is 36...f6 37 ♔f4 ♔e6 38 exf6 ♔xf6 39 a3 a6 40 a4 a5 41 b3! – the first mini-*zugzwang* – ♔e6 42 ♔g5 ♔e5 43 ♔g6 ♔f4 44 ♔f6 ♔xf3 45 ♔xf5 ♔e3 46 ♔e6 ♔d3 47 ♔d7! ♔c3

(47...♔d4 48 ♔d6 explains White's last move) 48 ♔xc6 ♔xb3 49 ♔b5!.

35 ♔e2?   ♖g8

36 ♔f2   ♖d8?

Black could have taken advantage of White's inaccuracy with 36...f4!, threatening 37...♖g5.

Then 37 e6 is a winning try (37...fxe6 38 ♖h7+). But 37...♖d8 is safe (38 ♔e2? ♖d6!).

37 ♔e3!   ♖d1

White's pawns are faster after 37...f4+ 38 ♔xf4 ♖d4+ 39 ♔f5 ♖xc4 40 ♖h7, threatening 41 e6.

38 b3   ♖e1+

Black gains a tempo on the game after 38...♖a1 39 ♔f4? ♖xa2. But White does better with 39 ♖h2! ♔e6 40 ♔f4 f6 41 ♖h6! or 39...♖d1 40 ♔f4 ♖d3 41 ♖h8.

Because ♔f4 is so strong in these positions, 38...♖d4! 39 f4 ♖e4+ 40 ♔f3 ♖e1 would have drawn, e.g. 41 ♖f6 ♖a1 42 ♖xf5 ♖xa2.

39 ♔f4   ♖e2

40 ♔xf5   ♖xa2

41 f4   ♖e2

42 ♖h3   ♖e1!

The rook is best placed on the e-file as we'll see.

43 ♖d3!!

The rook invasion, 43 ♖h8, fails to 43...♖e3 and then 44 ♖b8 ♖xb3 or 44 ♖c8 ♔d7.

Therefore, White tries to provoke ...b6 with his threat of ♖d5. For example, 43...♖e2 44 ♖d5 b6 and now 45 ♖d3! ♖e1 46 ♖h3.

This is the same position that occurred in the diagram but with the critical addition of ...b6 – and White wins after 46...♖e2 47 ♖h8 ♖e3 48 ♖b8! ♖xb3 49 ♖b7+ and ♔f6.

43 ...   ♖b1

Black concedes the e-file. But now what? On 44 ♔e4 ♖e1+ 45 ♔d5 ♖f1 he holds.

44 ♖e3!

A new plan – 45 e6 will create a passed f-pawn.

44 ...   ♖b2

Black can defend with passes, such as 44...♖h1. White seems to win after 44...a5 45 e6 fxe6 46 ♖xe6+ ♔d7 47 ♖e3 but not after 47...a4 48 bxa4 ♖b4.

Nor is White winning after 44...a6 45 e6 b5 with 46 exf7+ ♔xf7 47 ♔e5 bxc4 48 bxc4 ♖d1 49 ♖h3 ♖d4.

45 e6   a6

46 exf7+   ♔xf7

47 ♔e5!   ♖d2

Black cannot permit ♔d5.

48 ♖c3!

This is not as mysterious as it may seem: Black is denied counterplay from ...b5 (compared with 48 f5 b5 49 cxb5 axb5 50 ♖c3 c4!, which draws).

48 ...   b6

| 49 | f5 | ♖d1 |

Active defense fails: 49...♖e2+ 50 ♔d5 ♖f2 51 ♔c6 ♖xf5 52 ♔xb6 ♔e6 53 ♔xa6 ♔e5 54 ♖d3! ♔e4 55 ♖d7. Black's king is cut off and White will create a Lucena position, e.g. 55...♖h5 56 ♔b5 ♖g5 57 b4 cxb4+ 58 ♔xb4 and 59 c5.

| 50 | ♖h3 | b5? |

Even now Black could have drawn by deflecting the king, 50...♖e1+ 51 ♔d5 ♖b1 (52 ♔c6 a5 53 ♔xb6 a4).

| 51 | ♖h7+ | ♔g8 |
| 52 | ♖b7 | bxc4 |

Or 52...b4 53 ♔e6! as in the game.

| 53 | bxc4 | ♖d4 |
| 54 | ♔e6! | |

This is the first of three points in which Black's chances are crippled because of the bad placement of his rook: 54...♖xc4 55 ♖b8+ ♔h7 56 f6 and White wins because 56...♖e4+ 57 ♔f5! threatens both the unfortunate rook and 58 f7.

| 54 | ... | ♖e4+ |
| 55 | ♔d5! | |

White must force a trade of his f-pawn for the c-pawn. He has nothing after 55 ♔f6 ♖xc4 56 ♖b8+ ♔h7 57 ♔f7 ♖b4.

55	...	♖f4
56	♔xc5	♖xf5+
57	♔d6!	♖f6+
58	♔e5	

Black's rook lacks the "checking distance" (58...♖f5+??). If the attacked rook goes to f1 White wins with the Lucena-like 59 c5 ♖c1 60 ♔d6 ♖d1+ 61 ♔c7 a5 62 c6 a4 63 ♔b8 ♖d8+ 64 ♔a7.

58	...	♖f7
59	♖b6!	♖c7
60	♔d5	♔f7

The a-pawn couldn't be saved anyway (60...♖d7+ 61 ♔c6 ♖a7 and now 62 ♖b8+ ♔f7 63 c5 and ♔b6 wins).

| 61 | ♖xa6 | ♔e7 |

For the third time Black is victimized by bad rook placement because White has:

| 62 | ♖e6+! | ♔d8 |
| 63 | ♖d6+ | |

Since Black loses the pawn endgame (63...♔c8 64 ♖c6) he must allow his king to be cut off from the queening square.

63	...	♔e7
64	c5	♖c8
65	c6	♖c7
66	♖h6	♔d8

Last trap: 67 ♔d6? ♖d7+! and Black draws.

| 67 | ♖h8+ | ♔e7 |
| 68 | ♖a8 | **Resigns** |

White wins with ♔d6 after Black's king moves.

29

The Interzonal organizers scheduled a three-day break after the fourth round so that most of the players would enjoy a rest day. Even though Fischer had to play off the Portisch adjournment, he got a virtual day off in his next game, thanks to the astonishing depth of his opening preparation. He took less than 10 minutes to achieve a winning position.

István Bilek – Fischer
Interzonal, Stockholm 1962
Sicilian Defense,
Najdorf Variation, 6 ♗g5 (B97)

1	e4	c5
2	♘f3	d6
3	d4	cxd4
4	♘xd4	♘f6
5	♘c3	a6
6	♗g5	e6
7	f4	♕b6

This move was given a question mark by Vladimir Simagin, the Russian openings authority, in 1963. That reflected the volatile nature of the opening: In international games played in 1962, Black was winning nearly twice as many games as White in this variation. By 1963 the ratio was reversed.

8	♕d2	♕xb2
9	♖b1	♕a3
10	e5	dxe5
11	fxe5	♘fd7
12	♗c4	♗e7?

This game provoked a forest's worth of published analysis, which ended when a devastating improvement was discovered for White at move 16. Fischer, undismayed, tried to save the opening by finding an earlier improvement for Black. First he tried 12...♕a5, which has its own problems, and then 12...♗b4, which appears to be best.

13	♗xe6!	0-0
14	0-0	

All these moves had been played in a highly-publicized game, Dückstein – Euwe, Chaumont 1958, which White won convincingly after 14...fxe6 15 ♘xe6 ♘c6 16 ♘d5! and then 16...♗c5+ 17 ♔h1 ♘cxe5 18 ♘xf8. Euwe led the mourners who pronounced the Poisoned Pawn Variation dead...

14	...	♗xg5
15	♕xg5	h6!

...but it was revived by this move in this game...

| 16 | ♕h4 | |

...and reinterred when 16 ♕h5! was found. Three articles, in Soviet and Rumanian magazines, in 1963, showed that White's initiative was too strong after 16...♕xc3 17 ♖xf7! ♕xd4+ 18 ♔h1 ♔h8 19 ♖bf1 or 16...fxe6 17 ♘xe6 ♖xf1+ 18 ♖xf1 ♕e7 19 ♕f5.

16 ...   ♕xc3!

Euwe, annotating the Dückstein game, analyzed 16...♘xe5 and 16...fxe6. Fischer's move, which threatens 17...♘xe5 and 17...♕e3+, turns the tables.

17 ♖xf7!

After long thought, Bilek finds the best practical chance. Quieter moves (17 ♖b3 ♕c5 18 ♖g3 fxe6) lead nowhere.

17 ...   ♖xf7
18 ♕d8+

Again best. White runs out of ammunition after 18 ♖f1 ♘xe5! or 18 ♗xf7+ ♔xf7 19 e6+ ♔g8 20 e7 ♘f6 (21 ♕xf6 ♕e3+ 22 ♕f2 ♕xe7).

18 ...   ♘f8
19 ♗xf7+ ♔xf7
20 ♖f1+ ♔g6

The only move (20...♔g8?? 21 ♖xf8+ ♔h7 22 ♖h8+ ♔g6 23 ♕e8+ ♔g5 24 ♘f3+ and wins).

21 ♖xf8

Attempts to fine-tune the attack by way of 21 ♕e8+ ♔h7 22 ♖xf8 fail to 22...♕e1+! 23 ♖f1 ♕e3+ followed by ...♗d7 and ...♕xd4.

21 ...   ♗d7!

This threatens 22...♕xd4+ and prepares ...♘c6. But 21...♕e1+ 22 ♖f1 ♕xe5 was also good.

22 ♘f3

Black has enough material to win two games after 22 ♖f6+ ♔h7! 23 ♖xh6+ ♔xh6!.

22 ...   ♕e3+
23 ♔h1 ♕c1+
24 ♘g1 ♕xc2

Black's nonchalance is astonishing. He doesn't fear 25 ♖f6+ because the king can simply retreat. Nor is 25 e6 ♗c6 26 ♘f3 impressive because of 26...♕b1+ 27 ♘g1 ♕e4! and Black has an easy win.

25 ♖g8

Throughout his later career, Fischer won games that convinced skeptics he'd been too greedy – just as Tal won games that seemed to show he'd been more lucky than sound. As a result, annotators often searched for missed wins by Fischer's opponents, just as other analysts hunted for refutations of Tal's sacrifices. The quest for "Bilek's Missing Win" began here.

A leading candidate was 25 ♕e7, threatening 26 ♕f7+ and 26 ♖xb8 – since 25...♕xa2 26 ♕d6+ ♗e6?? 27 ♕d3+! leads to mate. But it fails the key test of 25...♕c4! 26 ♖f3! ♔h7 27 ♖g3 ♕g8, when White cannot strengthen his attack (28 ♘f3 ♗f5 29 ♘h4 ♘c6!).

That suggested White needed something more subtle, such as 25 h3. By creating *luft* it frees the knight for duty. However, Black has the only winning chances in the endgame that arises after 25...♗c6 26 ♘f3 ♘d7! 27 ♕xa8 ♘xf8 28 ♕xf8.

Finally, the champions of White's cause found 25 h4!, which provides both *luft* and the attacking potential of h4-h5+. For example, 25...♗c6 26 ♘f3 ♘d7 is mated by 27 h5+!! ♚xh5 28 ♕h4+ ♚g6 29 ♕g4+ ♚h7 30 ♘g5+!. This spawned enormous analysis and counter-analysis stretching well past move 40.

The conclusion? Black's chances are greater after lines such as: 25...♚h5, when the king is remarkably safe.

25 ...   ♕f2!

26 ♖f8?

White goes through the motions of making threats. After 26 ♘f3 ♕f1+ 27 ♘g1 ♗c6 he can resign. But 26 h3! would keep the game alive, e.g. 26...♕f1 27 ♖f8 ♕e1 28 e6! ♗xe6?? 29 ♕d3+ and wins, or 28...♕xe6! 29 ♘f3.

26 ...   ♕xa2

27 ♖f3   ♚h7!

Forfeits

The flag-fall was anti-climactic since Black's king is now secure (28 ♖g3 ♕g8 or 28 h3 ♕d5 29 ♖f8 ♗c6). Fischer took 35 minutes, a little more than a fifth of Bilek's two hours and a half.

30

Fischer's opening range was deepening by 1962. He could answer 1 e4 with 1...e5 or 1 d4 with 1...d5, for example, as he did at Curaçao. And while he still relied on relatively few openings, they ranged from the cutting-edge Najdorf Sicilian to long-discarded ideas of Wilhelm Steinitz. Despite its success in this game, 5 ♕e2 inexplicably failed to catch on.

Fischer – Eugenio German
Interzonal, Stockholm 1962
Petroff Defense (C43)

1	e4	e5
2	♘f3	♘f6
3	d4	

An oddity of Fischer's repertoire is that he repeatedly avoided the main Petroff (3 ♘xe5) lines. In fact, against Bisguier in the 1959-60 U.S. Championship he played the notorious drawing line 3 ♘xe5 d6 4 ♘f3 ♘xe4 5 ♕e2 and only won when Black tried too hard to win.

3	...	exd4
4	e5	♘e4
5	♕e2!?	

This makes an ugly impression – but if it succeeds it could be the refutation of 3...exd4. Black's knight is attacked and 5...d5 is met by 6 exd6.

This game was the first serious attempt to resuscitate 5 ♕e2 since a Steinitz – Pillsbury game from St. Petersburg 1895-6, which went 5...♗b4+ 6 ♔d1!? d5 7 exd6 f5 8 ♘g5 0-0 9 ♕c4+ ♔h8 10 ♕xb4. Black ruined his initiative and lost after 10...♘c6 11 ♕a3 ♘xf2+ 12 ♔e1 ♘xh1 13 dxc7, and the verdict that remained on the opening books was that only a Steinitz could make 5 ♕e2 work. Fischer never revealed what improvement he had in mind but 6 ♘bd2 ensures at least a small edge.

5	...	♘c5
6	♘xd4	♘c6
7	♘xc6	bxc6

After 7...dxc6 8 ♘c3 Black must anticipate problems on the d-file from 9 ♗e3 and 10 ♖d1. But 8...♗e7 9 ♗e3 ♕d7 is a likely solution.

| 8 | ♘c3 | ♖b8 |

This was commended at the time but 8...♗a6 9 ♕g4 and now 9...♕e7 or 9...h5 10 ♕g3 h4 or 10 ♕f4 ♗xf1 may be better.

| 9 | f4! | ♗e7 |
| 10 | ♕f2! | |

This gains control of key dark squares because 10...d6 11 ♗e3 ♖xb2? loses a piece to 12 0-0-0! (12...♖b8 13 ♗xc5 or 12...♘a4 13 ♘xa4 ♖xa2 14 ♘c3).

| 10 | ... | d5 |
| 11 | ♗e3 | ♘d7 |

| 12 | 0-0-0 | 0-0 |

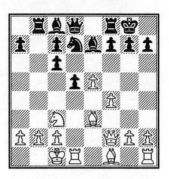

13 g4!

Dr. Tarrasch's prescription for such positions was ♘a4 followed by blockading with a minor piece on c5. But Fischer prefers a kingside pawn storm to the pitfalls of 13 ♘a4 ♖b4 14 b3 ♖xa4!? 15 bxa4 ♘b6.

| 13 | ... | ♗b4 |
| 14 | ♘e2 | |

Now, however, 14 ♘a4 makes sense since 14...♖b4 isn't available. Then 14...♘b6 15 ♘c5? ♗xg4 16 ♘a6 is unclear. But 15 ♘xb6! axb6 16 f5, followed by ♗f4 and ♕g3 is stronger. Black's queenside is healthy then but it offers no counterplay.

| 14 | ... | ♘b6 |

Black must have appreciated, from reading Tarrasch if not Nimzovich, that 14...c5 was the thematic move. To play it, however, he has to evaluate some difficult, unequal-material positions.

On 15 c3 Black can play 15...♗a5 because 16 ♖xd5 ♗b7 skewers rook. But 16 ♗xc5 ♘xc5 17 ♕xc5 ♗b6 is more hard to judge. Black has compensation for his pawn – but

White can counter-sacrifice with 18 ♕xd5! ♕xd5 19 ♖xd5 ♗b7 20 ♗g2 with mixed chances.

Black's best may be to decline the offer and flee into a bishops-of-opposite-color ending with 19...♗xg4 20 ♘d4 ♗e6.

15	♘d4	♕e8
16	c3	♗e7
17	f5	c5!

Black is properly alarmed. He realizes his counterplay is stillborn after 17...♘a4 18 ♘b3 (18...♗a3 19 bxa3 ♘xc3 20 ♖e1 ♕xe5 21 ♗d4) and on other moves White wins on the kingside with f5-f6.

18	♘b5	d4!

Black will have excellent compensation after 19 cxd4 cxd4 20 ♘xd4 (not 20 ♗xd4 ♕c6+) ♘a4 and ...c5. Also promising is 19...c4 with the idea of 20 ♘c3 ♘a4.

19	♗f4!	dxc3?

Black's nerves fail – or perhaps he just missed White 21st and 22nd moves. There were four candidates worth considering:

(a) 19...♗b7 20 ♖g1 a6,

(b) 19...♘a4 and if 20 ♕c2 then 20...a6, and

(c) 19...a6 20 ♘xc7 and now 20...♕a4? 21 f6 favors White. But 20...♕c6 21 f6 ♕xc7 (rather than 21...♖xh1? 22 ♗g2) 22 fxe7 ♕xe7 should suffice.

(d) 19...♘d5! puts White in trouble, e.g. 20 f6! ♖xb5! 21 fxe7 ♘xe7 22 ♗xb5 ♕xb5.

20	♘xc3	♘a4

21	♗b5!!	♖xb5
22	♘xa4	

Black needed the knight for counterplay. Left with the wrong minor pieces on the board, he has no answer to f5-f6.

22	...	♖b4
23	♘c3	♗b7
24	♖he1	♔h8

There was no good defense to 25 f6. For example, 24...♕c8 25 f6 gxf6? 26 ♗h6 fxe5 loses quickly to 27 ♖xe5! ♖e8 28 ♖xe7! ♖xe7 29 ♕f6.

No better is 25...♗d8 26 f6. For example, 26...♕e6 27 ♕xc5 ♕b6 28 ♕xf8+! and mates. Relatively best is 26...♖c4 when White should win after 27 ♕h4! ♖xf4 28 ♕g5 ♖xf6 29 exf6 ♗xf6 30 ♕xc5.

25	f6!	♗d8
26	♗g5	♖d4

Desperation. The threat was 27 ♖xd8 ♕xd8 28 fxg7+. Black is losing after 26...g6 27 ♗h6 ♖g8 28 e6! or 27...♖xg4 28 ♗g7+! ♔g8 29 ♕xc5.

27	fxg7+	♔xg7
28	♗f6+	♔g8
29	♕h4!	

There is no defense to ♕g5 mate.

29	...	🨢xd1+
30	🨞xd1	**Resigns**

Black avoids mate with 30 🨢xd1? ♕xe5!.

31

Stockholm was a 23-round marathon but by the 15ᵗʰ round Fischer had a commanding lead. Draws in the remaining seven games would have easily assured his qualification for the next Candidates Tournament. But Fischer's main opponent was history. He was intent on surpassing Alexander Kotov's record in winning the 1952 Interzonal. This game, from the next-to-last-round, put him within reach. But he fell just short of Kotov's winning percentage and three-point margin of victory.

Mario Bertok – Fischer
lnterzonal, Stockholm 1962
Queen's Gambit Declined,
Tartakower Variation (D53)

1	d4	d5
2	c4	e6
3	🨞c3	🨝e7
4	🨞f3	🨞f6
5	🨝g5	0-0
6	e3	h6
7	🨝h4	b6
8	cxd5	🨞xd5

A basic premise of the Tartakower Variation is that by trading two sets of minor pieces Black can defend the hanging or isolated pawn more easily.

9	🨝xe7	♕xe7

10	🨞xd5	exd5

11	🨝e2

In *My 60 Memorable Games* Fischer analyzed 11 🨢c1 🨝e6 12 ♕a4 c5 13 ♕a3 🨢c8 and gave one continuation, 14 🨝e2, which he said was equal after 14...♔f8 and double-edged after 14...♕b7.

But by the time of the 1972 world championship match he had found 14 🨝b5, with the idea that 14...🨞d7 15 0-0 leaves Black vulnerable to 🨝xd7 and dxc5. Spassky, one of the acknowledged Tartakower experts during the 1960s, had never lost with it – until Fischer beat him in the sixth match game after 14...a6 15 dxc5 bxc5 16 0-0 🨢a7 17 🨝e2 🨞d7 18 🨞d4!. But best is Geller's 14...♕b7!.

11	...	🨝e6

Another page of the Tartakower plan calls for developing the bishop here, not on b7, so that Black can occupy the b-file with heavy pieces.

12	0-0	c5
13	dxc5	

Fischer called this a mistake and said 13 🨞e5 🨞d7 was better – although only equal. In fact, Black would stand excellently after 14 🨞d3 c4 15 🨞f4 b5. In the years since 1962 White has obtained small edges with 13 ♕d2 or 13 ♕a4 – and it was realized that Bertok's real mistake was his next move.

13 ...   bxc5

14 ♕a4?

A better plan is 14 ♘e5 ♘d7 15 ♘d3! and ♘f4, since ...c4 leaves the d-pawn more vulnerable than in the last note (that is, without dxc5/ ...bxc5).

14 ...   ♕b7

15 ♕a3   ♘d7

16 ♘e1

The knight heads to f4 but the pressure on d5 isn't quite enough to balance Black's queenside initiative as we'll see at move 19. White might have done better with 16 ♗a6 ♕b6 17 b3.

16 ...   a5!

Black's powerful plan of ...♕b4 had been made famous in Rubinstein – Nimzovich, Carlsbad 1907 (1 d4 d5 2 ♘f3 e6 3 c4 c5 4 cxd5 exd5 5 ♘c3 ♘c6 6 ♗f4 cxd4 7 ♘xd4 ♗b4 8 e3 ♘f6 9 ♘xc6 bxc6 10 ♗d3 0-0 11 0-0 ♗d6 12 ♗g3 ♗xg3 13 hxg3 c5 14 ♖c1 ♗e6 15 ♕a4 ♕b6 16 ♕a3 c4 17 ♗e2 a5! 18 ♖fd1 ♕b4!).

17 ♘d3   c4

18 ♘f4   ♖fb8

19 ♖ab1?

White's knight maneuver made sense but he fails to follow it through. The alternatives are:

(a) An assault on d5 with 19 ♗f3 ♘f6 20 ♖fd1. But Black's c-pawn proves too strong after 20...♕xb2 21 ♕xb2 ♖xb2 22 ♘xd5 ♘xd5 23 ♗xd5 ♗xd5 24 ♖xd5 and now 24...c3 25 ♖dd1 c2 26 ♖dc1 ♖ab8 and ...♖b1.

(b) An attack on e6 (which Fischer used successfully in the Spassky game in a slightly different setup). Here 19 ♘xe6 fxe6 20 ♗g4 offers White slight chances of saving a half point after 20...♖a6 21 b3 cxb3 22 axb3 ♕xb3 23 ♕e7 ♘f8 24 ♖a3.

(c) Liquidating everything with 19 e4, as recommended by Keres and not mentioned by Fischer. After 19...dxe4 20 ♘xe6 fxe6 21 ♗xc4 or 19...♕xb2 20 ♕xb2 ♖xb2 21 exd5 ♗xd5 22 ♖fe1 White should have no fear. What Keres *et al* overlooked was 21...♗f5! in place of 21...♗xd5? in the last line (22 ♗xc4 ♖b4 23 ♖ac1 ♘e5 and wins).

(d) Surrendering a pawn, 19 b3 cxb3 20 axb3 ♕xb3 21 ♕e7, offers slim compensation (21...♖e8 22 ♕d6 ♕b6 23 ♕a3).

19 ...   ♗f5

20 ♖bd1   ♘f6

21 ♖d2

This loses in the middlegame, whereas 21 ♗f3 ♕xb2 33 ♕xb2 ♖xb2 23 ♘xd5 ♘xd5 is a lost ending. For example, 24 ♖xd5 ♗e6 25 ♖c5 ♖c8 26 ♖xa5 c3 27 ♖a8 ♖xa8 28 ♗xa8 f5! and the c-pawn wins. Or 24 ♗xd5 ♖c8 25 e4 ♗e6!.

21 ... g5!

Now 22 ♘h5 ♘e4 23 ♖c2 ♕b4! wins à la Nimzovich (and is much cleaner than 23...♘g3? 24 fxg3).

22 ♘xd5?! ♘xd5

23 ♗xc4

White has even less compensation after 23 ♗f3 ♗d3.

23 ... ♗e6

24 ♖fd1?

White preserves his dignity a bit longer with 24 ♗xd5 ♗xd5 25 f3 Euwe suggested 25 ♕d6, on the grounds that 25...♗xg2 26 ♕xh6 was "very risky." In fact, 26...♖a6! would end the game speedily.

24 ... ♘xe3!

25 ♕xe3 ♗xc4

The rest warrants no comment:

26 h4 ♖e8 27 ♕g3 ♕e7 28 b3 ♗e6 29 f4 g4 30 h5 ♕c5+ 31 ♖f2 ♗f5 Resigns

32

In one of his last articles, Mikhail Botvinnik said the tempo of Fischer's attacks resembled those of Morphy. The principal difference was that Paul Morphy launched his attacks from open positions while Fischer launched his from modern, semi-open ones, he wrote. But games like the following bear a stronger resemblance to victories of Alexander Alekhine around 1930 or Garry Kasparov about 1990. Fischer shared a prize for it (not the first brilliancy prize, as claimed in *My 60 Memorable Games*, but the second). With a bit of irony he noted that if he had played the move many annotators considered best (25 ♘xe7+) he wouldn't have won any prize. ("They don't give medals for endgame technique!")

Fischer – Julio Bolbochán
Interzonal, Stockholm 1962
Sicilian Defense,
Najdorf Variation, 6 h3 (B90)

1	e4	c5
2	♘f3	d6
3	d4	cxd4
4	♘xd4	♘f6
5	♘c3	a6
6	h3	

This was the first time Fischer tried this naive-looking move, seeking positions akin to the Keres attack (5...e6 6 g4). One of its chief benefits is that the default strategy of the Najdorf – 6...e5 7 ♘de2 ♗e6 – allows White a nice game after 8 g4 ♗e7 9 ♗g2 and ♘g3-f5 (or 8...d5 9 g5! ♘xe4 10 ♘xe4 dxe4 11 ♕xd8+ and ♗g2).

6	...	♘c6
7	g4	♘xd4
8	♕xd4	e5
9	♕d3	♗e7

10 g5

Although obvious, this move was an improvement over 10 b3?, which had been punished in a celebrated game, Gereben – Geller, Budapest 1952.

10 ...   ♘d7

11 ♗e3

Now 11...b5 12 a4 b4 13 ♘d5 with advantage.

11 ...   ♘c5?

Fischer believed that 11...♗xg5 12 ♗xg5 ♕xg5 13 ♕xd6 ♕e7 was only a small edge for White (14 ♕xe7+ ♔xe7 15 ♘d5+ ♔f8 16 0-0-0 g6).

12 ♕d2   ♗e6

13 0-0-0   0-0

White's king can become an issue after 13...♕a5 and ...b5. For example, 13...♕a5 14 ♔b1? ♘xe4 wins for Black. But 14 a3 b5 15 ♔b1 followed by 16 f4 (or 16...0-0? 17 ♘d5) favors White.

14 f3

More exact was 14 ♔b1, to prevent 14...♕a5 (by 15 ♘d5!).

14 ...   ♖c8

15 ♔b1!

White has won the battle of the opening: Enemy counterplay is severely limited.

15 ...   ♘d7

16 h4   b5

17 ♗h3!   ♗xh3

This concedes d5 but other moves do nothing to impede White's attack (17...♖b8 18 h5 or 17...♖e8 18 ♘d5 ♗f8 19 h5). Reinforcing d5 with 17...♘b6? costs material (18 ♗xb6 ♕xb6 19 ♘d5 ♕d8 20 ♘xe7+ ♕xe7 21 ♕xd6).

18 ♖xh3   ♘b6

19 ♗xb6   ♕xb6

20 ♘d5   ♕d8

21 f4

But here 21 ♘xe7+ ♕xe7 22 ♕xd6??, as suggested by more than one annotator, loses to 22...♖fd8!.

The text threatens 22 f5 followed by f5-f6 or g5-g6.

21 ...   exf4

22 ♕xf4   ♕d7

23 ♕f5!   ♖cd8

The pressure mounts (23...♕xf5? 24 ♘xe7+ or 23...♖fd8? 24 ♕xd7 and 25 ♘b6),

24 ♖a3!?

An Alekhine/Kasparov-like move – striking at another wing in order to stretch the enemy defenses. The direct 24 ♖c3 was also strong (24...♖fe8 25 ♘c7).

24 ...   ♕a7

25 ♖c3!

Technicians would win a pawn with 25 ♘xe7+ and 26 ♖xa6 but Fischer wanted to deliver a knockout in the middlegame. A candidate for such a blow is 25 ♘f6+ since 25...gxf6 26 gxf6 ♔h8 27 ♕g5 ♖g8 28 fxe7! wins. But 25...♗xf6! 26 gxf6 ♕c5 is not as clear.

25 ...   g6!

Black could not allow 26 ♖c7 and saw that 25...♖d7 exposes the first rank to the idea mentioned above, 26 ♘f6+! ♗xf6 27 gxf6 g6 28 ♕g5 ♔h8 29 ♕h6 ♖g8 and now 30 ♖c8! mates.

26 ♕g4   ♕d7

27 ♕f3!

Better than 27 ♕f4 because White needs that square for a knight and wants to retain the possibility of ♕b3.

27 ...   ♕e6

28 ♖c7!

Black seems to have improved his position since 25...g6 but his queen finds itself embarrassed now, e.g. 28...♖d7? 29 ♘f4. As the game goes the only hiding place is h8.

28 ...   ♖de8

Fischer pointed out how 28...♖fe8 29 ♖f1 ♖c8 30 ♖a7 leaves White with a bind (30...♖a8 31 ♖xa8 ♖xa8 32 ♘c7).

29 ♘f4   ♕e5

30 ♖d5   ♕h8

This looks awful – but one can imagine Korchnoi refusing a draw with Black against a lesser player because he has the prospect of ...h6!.

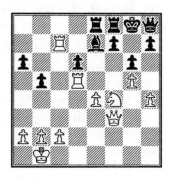

31 a3!

White makes *luft* before he continues the attack with ♕b3 or begins to harvest pawns with ♖a7.

On 31 ♕b3 ♗d8 32 ♖d7 ♖xe4 and White has lost his big advantage. For example, 33 ♕g3 ♗e7 34 a3 h6.

31 ...   h6

Or 31...f6 32 ♕b3! ♖f7 33 ♖xd6! and wins.

32 gxh6   ♕xh6

The a2-g8 diagonal proves remarkably vulnerable from now on. For example, Black loses quickly on 32...♗xh4 33 ♘xg6! fxg6 34 ♕b3!.

33 h5   ♗g5

Black recognizes that 33...g5 34 ♘e2 and ♘d4-f5 is asphyxiation.

34 hxg6!

White regains his material at a profit after 34...♗xf4 35 gxf7+ ♖xf7 36 ♖xf7 ♔xf7 37 ♖h5! (better than 37 ♖f5+).

34 ...   fxg6

There is great temptation now to try 35 ♖xg5 ♕xg5 36 ♕b3+, since 36...♔h8 37 ♕h3+ ends the game. Black is losing even after the superior 36...d5 37 ♘xd5 ♔h8 and now 38 ♕h3+ ♕h5 39 ♕d7 ♕h6 40 ♘f6!.

35 ♕b3!

But this is faster. The only way to avoid a lethal discovered check is 35...♔h8. But that allows 36 ♘xg6+ ♕xg6 37 ♖xg5! ♖f1+ 38 ♔a2 – which wins, thanks to 31 a3. For example, 38...♕xg5 39 ♕h3+ ♔g8 40 ♕xf1. (More than one annotator alleged Fischer had overlooked a faster win with 40 ♕h7+ ♔f8 41 ♕h8+ ♕g8 42 ♕h6+. But this backfires because Black's 41st move is a countercheck.)

Also winning is the routine 36 ♖xg5 ♖xf4 37 ♖d5 and eventually ♖xd6.

35 ...   ♖xf4

36 ♖e5+   ♔f8

37 ♖xe8+   Resigns

In view of 37...♔xe8 38 ♕e6+ and mates.

33

Fischer's terrific Interzonal result raised expectations extraordinarily high. In retrospect, he wasn't as strong as he seemed. Fischer hadn't played particularly well against the stronger players at Stockholm and his weaknesses were exposed at Curaçao when he lost his first two games, to Benko and Tal. After missing an easy win in the third round (but eventually winning), he was close to tears after losing to Korchnoi. When he faced Keres at the end of the first cycle at Curaçao, Fischer appeared to be playing the role of a spoiler rather than contender.

Fischer – Paul Keres
Candidates Tournament,
Curaçao 1962
Ruy Lopez (C96)

1	e4	e5
2	♘f3	♘c6
3	♗b5	a6
4	♗a4	♘f6
5	0-0	♗e7
6	♖e1	b5
7	♗b3	d6
8	c3	0-0
9	h3	♘a5
10	♗c2	c5
11	d4	♘d7

This became known as the "Keres Variation" after this game (although it had been tried before). Black prepares to exchange twice on d4 and apply pressure with ...♗f6 and ...♘c6.

12	dxc5!	dxc5
13	♘bd2	♕c7
14	♘f1	♘b6
15	♘e3	♖d8
16	♕e2	♗e6

White has a strong ♘d5! coming up. He stands better after 16...f6 17 ♘h4 ♗f8 18 ♘d5! as later played by Gligorić or 17 ♘d5 ♘xd5 18 exd5 ♘b7 19 a4 ♗d7 20 ♘h4 as recommended by Fischer.

17 ♘d5!

By indirectly trading e-pawns, White opens the center for his superior heavy pieces.

Fischer gave 17...♗xd5 18 exd5 f6 19 h4 ♘xd5 20 h5 and ♕e4 or 19...♘ac4 20 h5 ♘d6 21 ♕d3! e4 22 ♖xe4 as favoring White.

17	...	♘xd5
18	exd5	♗xd5
19	♘xe5	

White's tactical resources include a discovered attack on the queen after ♗f4 and a combination of ♖ad1xd5 and ♕e4.

Among the futile defenses are:

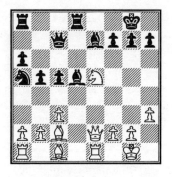

(a) 19...♖e8? 20 ♕d3! attacking the bishop and h7;

(b) 19...♗d6 20 ♕d3!, ditto (20...♗xe5 21 ♕xh7+ ♔f8 22 f4!);

(c) 19...♗e6? 20 ♘xf7 with ♕xe6 or ♕xe7 to come;

(d) 19...♗f8 20 ♕h5 g6 21 ♕h4 ♗g7 22 ♘g4 followed by ♗g5/♘f6+, and

(e) 19...f6 20 ♕h5! fxe5 (20...g6 21 ♘xg6) 21 ♗xh7+ ♔f8 22 ♖xe5 ♗f7 23 ♖f5 ♗f6 24 ♖xf6! gxf6 25 ♗h6+ ♔e7 26 ♖e1+ ♗e6 27 ♗f5 ♖d6 28 ♗f4 as pointed out by Fischer.

19	...	♖a7
20	♗f4	♕b6
21	♖ad1	g6

This anticipates the threats of 22 ♗xh7+ or 22 ♖xd5. The only alternative Fischer gave in his notes was 21...♗xa2 and it's not surprising that this is punished by 22 ♖xd8+. For example, 22...♗xd8 23 ♘c4! or 22...♕xd8 23 b4! cxb4 24 cxb4 ♗xb4 (24...♘c4 25 ♘c6!) 25 ♕e4! ♗xe1 26 ♕xh7+ and White wins material (26...♔f8 27 ♕h8+ ♔e7 28 ♗g5+ f6 29 ♘g6+ ♔d7 30 ♗f5+ ♔c7 31 ♗f4+).

Black's difficulties are also underlined by 21...♕f6 and then

22 ♖xd5 ♖xd5 23 ♕e4 ♕h4 24 g3 ♖xe5 25 ♕xe5 and ♕b8+ wins.

22 ♘g4   ♘c4

The knight only gets into trouble here but 22...♘c6 23 ♗e4! is no better, e.g. 23...♖ad7? 24 ♖xd5 ♖xd5 25 ♕f3.

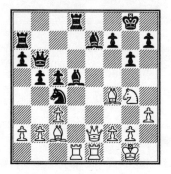

23 ♗h6

The last rank becomes naked to a rook check. White's superiority in the center is so great that 23 b3 ♘a3 24 ♗d3 would win faster.

23 ...   ♗e6

This plugs the e-file but only temporarily. After 23...♘xb2 White has 24 ♖xd5 ♖xd5 25 ♗e4 winning material (25...♖d8 26 ♕xb2 f5 27 c4!). But the outcome is unclear after 25...♖h5! 26 ♕xb2 g5! and ...♖xh6.

24 ♗b3!   ♕b8

To avert ♕e5. On 24...♗xg4 25 ♖xd8+ ♕xd8 26 hxg4 ♕d5 (26...♘d6 27 ♕e5! ♗f6 28 ♕xd6! or 27...♗f8 28 ♗xf8 ♕xf8 29 ♕xc5) 27 ♖d1 ♕e6 White can slowly build up his position (28 ♗xc4 bxc4 29 ♕d2 ♖a8 30 ♖e1 ♕d6 30 ♕e2) or enter the favorable endgame (28 ♕xe6 and ♗xc4).

25 ♖xd8+   ♗xd8

Black loses quickly after 25...♕xd8 26 ♗xc4 bxc4 27 ♕e5! or 26...♗xc4 27 ♘f6+! ♔h8 28 ♕e5.

26 ♗xc4   bxc4

27 ♕xc4!

Not just winning a pawn but threatening 28 ♖xe6 fxe6 29 ♕xe6+ and mates with ♕e8. Of course, 27...♗xc4 28 ♖e8 is mate.

27 ...   ♕d6

28 ♕a4   ♕e7

No improvement is 28...♕d7 29 ♖d1!.

29 ♘f6+   ♔h8

30 ♘d5   ♕d7

31 ♕e4!

The pressure, based on 31...♗xd5 32 ♕e8+, mounts.

31 ...   ♕d6

32 ♘f4   ♖e7

33 ♗g5

Once again Fischer misses a knockout (33 ♗f8!).

33 ...   ♖e8

34 ♗xd8   ♖xd8

Or 34...♕xd8 35 ♕e5+ ♔g8 36 ♘d5! and 35...f6 36 ♕xc5 ♗xa2 37 ♖xe8+ ♕xe8 38 c4 (better than 38 ♕b6 ♕e1+ 39 ♔h2 ♕e5).

35	♘xe6	♕xe6
36	♕xe6	fxe6
37	♖xe6	♖d1+
38	♔h2	♖d2
39	♖b6	♖xf2
40	♖b7!	♖f6
41	♔g3	**Resigns**

Keres didn't resume this adjourned position, whose outcome is transparent after 41...♔g8 42 b4 cxb4 43 cxb4 ♖d6 44 a4 ♖d3+ 45 ♔h2 etc.

34

Mikhail Tal said after the 1959 Candidates Tournament that most of Fischer's losses were due to his "repeating the same, and to a considerable extent, inferior opening systems." By 1962 he seemed most vulnerable in the 6 ♗e2 Najdorf Variation. He nearly lost to Geller in that line at Stockholm and did lose to him with it in the second round at Curaçao. Tal was eager to pose another test.

Mikhail Tal – Fischer
Candidates Tournament,
Curaçao 1962,
Sicilian Defense,
Najdorf Variation, 6 ♗e2 (B92)

1	e4	c5
2	♘f3	d6
3	d4	cxd4
4	♘xd4	♘f6
5	♘c3	a6
6	♗e2	e5
7	♘b3	

Three days before, Fischer lost to Geller after 7...♗e7 8 0-0 0-0 9 ♗e3 ♕c7 (this is unnecessary before White has played f2-f4) 10 a4 ♗e6 11 a5 ♘bd7 and now 12 ♘d5! ♘xd5 13 exd5 ♗f5 14 c4 ♗g6? 15 ♖c1 ♘c5 16 ♘xc5 dxc5 17 b4! with a considerable edge.

7	...	♗e6

This move had been discredited since Najdorf had lost with it in the 1953 Candidates Tournament – to Geller.

8	0-0

This game helped revive 7...♗e6 but in the 1970s it was realized that the bishop move has a drawback: After 8 f4 White has 9 f5 or 9 g4 coming up, e.g. 8...♕c7 9 g4! exf4 10 g5 ♘fd7 11 ♗xf4 with an excellent game.

8	...	♘bd7
9	a4	♗e7
10	f4	♕c7
11	♗e3	0-0
12	a5	

In the Geller – Najdorf game, Black had inserted ...♖ac8 but allowed a strong ♖a4!. Fischer's next move anticipates that at the cost of isolating his a-pawn.

12	...	b5!
13	axb6	♘xb6
14	f5	♗c4
15	♗xb6?	

This logical move, to secure control of d5, was book – but also bad. Geller's second game with White against Fischer at Curaçao saw the superior 15 ♔h1! and then 15...♖fc8 16 ♗xb6 ♕xb6 17 ♗xc4 ♖xc4 18 ♕e2 ♖b4 19 ♖a2! ♕b7 20 ♘a5 ♕c7 21 ♘d5 ♘xd5 22 exd5 gave White another clear edge. (Black later drew thanks to an Exchange sacrifice.)

Black can improve with 18...♖ac8 19 ♖a2 ♗d8! after which he has no major problems.

| 15 | ... | ♕xb6+ |
| 16 | ♔h1 | ♗b5! |

A difficult move to foresee. Black prepares 17...♗c6!, seizing the initiative.

17 ♗xb5

Despite the attention this position had drawn in its short history, few grandmasters realized White was worse. But Fischer believed White should try to draw with the opposite colored bishops after 17 ♘xb5 axb5 18 ♕d3.

17	...	axb5
18	♘d5	♘xd5
19	♕xd5	♖a4!
20	c3	♕a6!

In theory White has excellent chances because of d5 and the "good-knight-versus-bad-bishop."

But in practice White lacks a realizable plan, whereas Black has a minority attack (...♖c8 and ...b4). A good illustration of the dangers was Fischer's game with Unzicker at the Varna Olympiad later in 1962. White meandered about – 21 h3 ♖c8 22 ♖fe1 h6 23 ♔h2 ♗g5 – and suddenly found himself resigning after 24 g3? ♕a7 25 ♔g2 ♖a2 26 ♔f1 ♖xc3!.

| 21 | ♖ad1 | ♖c8 |
| 22 | ♘c1 | |

Dreaming of reaching d5.

| 22 | ... | b4! |

Now 23 cxb4 ♖xb4 24 ♘d3 ♕d4 or 23 b3? ♖a5 are horrible.

| 23 | ♘d3! | bxc3 |
| 24 | bxc3 | |

| 24 | ... | ♖a5? |

Fischer called this a "lemon" that denied him a quick win that would come from 24...♖xc3 (Then 25 ♘xe5 dxe5 26 ♕xe5 is refuted by 26...♗b4! 27 ♕xc3 ♕xf1+!.) Kmoch and Viktor Lyublinsky, in separate annotations, thought highly of 24...♖xc3 25 f6! ♗xf6 26 ♘xe5! (citing 26...♗xe5?? 27 ♕xf7+ or 26...dxe5 27 ♕d8+!). But they underestimated 25...gxf6! because 26 ♘f2 or 26 ♘c1 loses to 26...♖d4 (27 ♖xd4 ♕xf1 mate).

| 25 | ♕b3 | ♖a3 |
| 26 | ♕b1 | ♖axc3 |

| 27 | ♘b4! | ♕a7 |
| 28 | ♘d5 | ♖3c6 |

White's position has improved markedly in four moves but he must avoid lines such as 29 f6? ♗xf6 30 ♘xf6+ gxf6 31 ♖xf6 ♕e3!.

29	♕b3	♗f8
30	h3	♖a6
31	♖b1	♖a3

Black's winning plans include:

(a) doubling rooks on the seventh rank, (b) trading queens followed by winning the e-pawn, and (c) creating a last-rank mate threat with ...h5-h4.

| 32 | ♕b5 | ♕d4 |
| 33 | ♖fe1 | ♖g3 |

After 33...♖a2 34 ♕d7 Black can't continue 34...♖cc2? because 35 ♖b8 threatens 36 ♖xf8+.

| 34 | ♕e2 | ♕d3 |
| 35 | ♕h5 | ♕c2 |

And here 35...♖c2 36 ♖b7! gives White a winning attack, e.g. 36...g6 37 ♘f6+ ♔g7 38 ♕h7+ ♔xf6 39 ♖xf7+.

36	♕e2!	♕xe2
37	♖xe2	h5
38	♖a2	♖d3
39	♖a7	h4!

After 39...♖d4 40 f6 ♖xe4 White saves himself with 41 ♖bb7 ♖d4 42 fxg7 ♖xd5 43 ♖xf7!.

And he would win after 41...♖e1+ 42 ♔h2 h4 43 ♖xf7 ♖cc1?? with 44 ♖f8+! ♔xf8 45 fxg7+ ♔g8 46 ♘f6 mate. But Black is saved by 42...♖f1 or 43...♖f1.

| 40 | f6 | g6 |
| 41 | ♔h2! | |

Tal requires his opponent to make a critical choice with his next move – the sealed move.

| 41 | ... | ♖xd5!?! |

But Tal confessed that when the adjournment envelope was opened Black's move "came like a thunderbolt." It was easy to dispose of 41...♖d4? 42 ♖bb7 ♖xe4 by way of 43 ♖xf7 ♖d4 44 ♖xg7+! ♗xg7 45 ♖xg7+ ♔f8 46 ♘e7! and wins.

But no one in the Soviet delegation saw Fischer's move coming. They must have expected 41...♖d2 42 ♖bb7 ♖cc2 after which 43 ♖b8 ♖xg2+ is only a draw. White can also try 43 ♘e3 ♖c3 44 ♖b8 ♖xe3 45 ♖xf8+ ♔h7 46 ♖fxf7+ ♔h6 but he is worse after 47 ♖h7+ ♔g5 48 f7 ♖g3.

| 42 | exd5 | ♗h6 |
| 43 | ♖e7 | |

White must watch the e-pawn (43 ♖d7 e4!) as well as a potential mating attack. For example, 43 ♖bb7? ♗f4+ 44 ♔h1?? ♖c1 mate.

On 44 ♔g1 ♗e3+ 45 ♔h2 ♗xa7 46 ♖xa7 Black has 46...♖c5 47 ♖a8+ ♔h7 48 ♖f8 g5!.

43	...	♗g5
44	♖f1	♗f4+
45	♔g1	g5

46 ♖b1

Black faces another crisis. White is ready to threaten ♖bb7.

Trading rooks is almost always bad for Black and here 46...♖c1+ 47 ♖xc1 ♗xc1 48 ♖d7 ♗e3+ 49 ♔f1 ♗c5 50 ♔e2 is lost.

On 46...♗e3+ 47 ♔f1 ♖c2 Black is still alive but following 48 ♔e1 he must be careful.

46 ... e4!

On this square the pawn denies White f3, so 47 ♖bb7 ♖c1+ is a perpetual check.

47 ♖xe4 ♔h7!

48 ♖e7 ♔g6

49 ♖bb7 ♔xf6

50 ♖xf7+ ♔e5

The powerfully centralized king and danger of rook checks ensure Black at least a draw, e.g. 51 ♖b5 ♖c1+ 52 ♔f2 ♖c2+ 53 ♔f3 ♖c3+ 54 ♔g4 ♖g3+ and White is playing to lose.

The conclusion was uneventful:

51 ♖fc7 ♖a8 52 ♖b1 ♔xd5 53 ♖d1+ ♔e6 54 ♖c2 ♖a3 55 ♔f2 ♖b3 56 ♖e2+ ♔f5 57 ♖d5+ ♔f6 58 ♖e4 Draw

35

Into the early 1960s, Soviet players who had met him described Fischer as a chess-mad American who was willing to play five-minute chess at any hour. Tal recalled how he had already packed his bag to leave at the end of Zürich 1959 when he got a call from Fischer's room, elsewhere in their hotel. "I'm flying to New York in the hour," he said.

"But if you agree to play some blitz I'll give up my ticket." But by the time of Curaçao, when Tal was playing Fischer for the last times, the Latvian began to appreciate him as a player of considerably greater depth, especially in the endgame. Game 34 was one example of that and the following, from the 11th round, was a second. The opening skirmishing is intriguing because both players seem to believe they had caught their opponent in a rare, virtually new sideline.

Fischer – Mikhail Tal
Candidates Tournament,
Curaçao 1962
Sicilian Defense,
Löwenthal Variation (B32)

1	e4	c5
2	♘f3	♘c6
3	d4	cxd4
4	♘xd4	e5

Neither Tal nor Fischer had ever played this then-trendy opening before, and they never would again.

5	♘b5	a6
6	♘d6+	♗xd6
7	♕xd6	♕f6

An unusual concept: Instead of cobbling a pawn structure on dark squares (...d6) to shield his holes, Black bets on superior development and an explosive ...d5 sacrifice.

8	♕d1	♕g6
9	♘c3	♘ge7
10	h4!	

When an opening is young, such as 5...a6 was in 1962, natural moves such as 10 ♗e3 are tried. But often they are rejected (here because of

10...d5! 11 ♘xd5 ♘xd5 12 ♕xd5
♗e6 or 11 exd5 ♘b4) in favor of
eccentric but effective alternatives,
such as 10 h4, threatening 11 h5.

10	...	h5
11	♗g5	d5!?
12	♗xe7	

Today this opening has been more
or less retired by 12 exd5! ♘b4
13 ♗xe7!, which sentences Black to
a poor ending after 13...♔xe7
14 ♗d3! ♘xd3+ (14...♕xg2 15 ♗e4
and 16 a3) 15 ♕xd3 ♕xd3 16 cxd3.

12 ... d4!

Tal knew that 13 ♗c5 dxc3 14 f3
cxb2 15 ♖b1 b6 had turned out well
for Black in a recent game. White
also has to work to avoid getting the
worst of it after 13 ♘e2 ♘xe7
14 ♘g3 ♗g4!.

13 ♗g5!

Fischer is first to improve.

13	...	dxc3
14	bxc3	♕xe4+
15	♗e2	f6
16	♗e3	♗g4!

After 16...♕xg2? 17 ♗f3 ♕g6
18 ♕d6 White stands better since
18...♗d7 19 ♖b1 0-0-0?? 20 ♗b6 is
help-mate.

17	♕d3!	♕xd3
18	cxd3	♗xe2
19	♔xe2	0-0-0
20	♖ad1?	

Regardless of who surprised
whom in the opening, Black would
have a slight edge even after the
superior 20 ♖hd1 ♘e7 21 ♖ac1.
Now he should double on the d-file
before ...♘e7.

| 20 | ... | ♘e7 |
| 21 | d4! | |

The dogmatic 21 c4, putting
pawns on the opposite color
squares of the bishop, gives White
a perfectly miserable position after
...♘f5-d4. The text amounts to a
sacrifice of the c-pawn.

21	...	♘d5
22	♖c1	♖he8
23	♖hd1	f5

Alexander Khalifman considered
23...♖d7 24 dxe5 ♘xe3 better (or
23...exd4 24 cxd4+ ♔d7 25 ♔f3 g6
26 ♖c5).

24 ♗g5! ♖d7?

Tal fails to find a Tal-like resource:
24...exd4+ 25 ♔f1 (better than 25 ♔d3
♖d7 26 cxd4+ ♖c7) dxc3! 26 ♗xd8
♖xd8.

111

Then Black has winning chances following 27 ♔e2 b5 28 a3 ♔c7 29 ♔d3 ♔c6 30 ♔c2 ♔c5 31 ♔b3 ♖b8 32 ♖e1 a5 33 ♖e5 a4+ and ...♔c4.

Tal gave 27 ♖d3! instead but then 27...b6!! is a superb reply since 28 ♖cd1 ♔c7 29 ♖xd5?? ♖xd5 30 ♖xd5 c2 wins because there is no ♖c5+. On 28 a3 ♔c7 29 ♖cd1 ♖d6, Black retains his edge.

25	dxe5	♖xe5+
26	♔f3	♖e4
27	♖d3	♖c4
28	♖cd1!	

White's pieces are well placed and his king is ready to raid the kingside after 28...♘b6? 29 ♗e3! ♖xd3 30 ♖xd3 ♘d7 31 ♗d4.

28	...	♖xc3
29	♖xc3+	♘xc3
30	♖c1	♖c7

More active is 30...♖d3+ 31 ♔f4 ♔d7 32 ♔xf5 ♘xa2. But after 33 ♖e1! White has the only winning chances, e.g. 33...♔c6 34 ♖e6+ ♖d6 35 ♖g6.

31	♗f4	♖c6
32	♗e5!	

After 32 ♗d2 ♘xa2! 33 ♖xc6+ bxc6 34 ♔e3 c5! Black draws because the knight is not trapped. (Or 34 ♔f4 c5 35 ♔xf5 c4.)

32	...	♘d5!

The bishop and faster king win after 32...♘xa2 33 ♖xc6+ bxc6 34 ♔f4! c5 35 ♔xf5 c4 36 ♗xg7 c3 37 g4! c2 38 ♗b2.

33	♖d1!	

But here Black would have sealed off the kingside after 33 ♖xc6+ bxc6 34 ♗xg7 ♔d7 and draws.

33	...	♘f6

Tal passes up another sacrifice, a temporary one – 33...♔d7! 34 ♖xd5+ ♔e6 35 ♖a5 b6 or 34 ♗xg7 ♔d6.

34	♔f4!	g6

On 34...♖c4+ (or 34...♖c2) White plays 35 ♗d4, with good winning chances, rather than 35 ♔xf5? ♖xh4.

35	f3!	♘d7
36	♗d6	♖c2?

Black would not lose after 36...♘b6, and ...♘c4 discourages ♔g5xg6.

37	g3	

This is what White had in mind after 34 ♔f4. Even though two pawns up, Black would lose following 37...♖xa2? 38 ♔g5 or 38 ♖c1+ first.

37	...	♖e2?

Tal's idea was to defend the g-pawn this way but even now 37...♖c6 38 ♔g5 ♘b6 (39 ♔xg6 ♘c4) might hold.

38	♔g5	♖e6
39	♗f4	♘f8

40 ♖d6   a5!

Trap: the pawn ending is drawn after 41 ♖xe6? ♘xe6+ 42 ♔xg6 ♘xf4+ 43 gxf4 b5.

41 ♔h6!

Now ♔g7 is a lethal threat, e.g. 41...b5 42 ♔g7 ♖xd6 43 ♗xd6 ♘e6+ 44 ♔xg6.

41 ...   ♖e2

42 ♖d2

But 42 ♔g7? ♘e6+ 43 ♔xg6 ♘xf4+ 44 gxf4 ♖xa2 offers nothing.

42 ...   ♖e7

43 ♗d6

White sealed here and must have analyzed at least as far as the first of the *zugzwangs* at move 45.

43 ...   ♖h7+

44 ♔g5   ♖f7

Black runs out of squares after 44...♘d7? 45 ♔xg6 ♖h8 46 ♔g7 ♖e8 47 ♔f7!, e.g. 47...♖h8 48 ♖c2+ ♔d8? 49 ♗e7 mate or 47...♖e3 48 ♖c2+ ♔d8 49 ♗c7+ and 50 ♗f4+.

45 ♖b2!   f4

46 ♗xf4

Also winning is 46 ♗xf8 ♖xf8 47 g4!.

46 ...   ♖f5+

47 ♔h6   b5

48 ♗d6   b4

49 g4!

White may be winning after 49 f4 ♔d7 50 ♗xf8 ♖xf8 51 ♔xg6 and then 51...♖g8+ 52 ♔xh5 ♖xg3 53 ♖e2!. But the text is surer.

49 ...   ♖xf3

50 g5!   ♘e6

Tal analyzed 50...♔d7 51 ♗xf8 ♖xf8 52 ♔xg6 ♖h8 and then launched into a long line that went

53 ♔g7 ♖c8 54 ♖e2! ♖c4 55 g6 ♖xh4 56 ♔h7 ♖g4 57 ♖e5! wins.

But much simpler is 53 ♔f7 (threatening g6-g7) ♖h7+ 54 ♔f6 ♖h8 55 ♖d2+ ♔c7 (55...♔e8? 56 ♔g7! wins the rook) 56 g6.

51 ♔xg6   ♖d3

52 ♗e5   ♖e3

Otherwise ♔xh5 wins.

53 ♔f5!   ♘f8

54 ♖g2!   ♖f3+

55 ♗f4   ♔d7

56 g6!   ♘e6!

White's bishop controls both queening squares, a1 and h8, and that means 56...♘xg6 57 ♖xg6 ♖f2 58 a3! bxa3 59 ♖a6 followed by ♖xa5 and ♔g5 must win.

57 g7!   ♖xf4+

Black is also lost after 57...♘xf4 58 g8(♕) ♘xg2+ 59 ♔e4.

58 ♔e5   ♖f8

59 gxf8(♕)   ♘xf8

60 ♔d5   a4

61 ♖g7+   ♔e8

62 ♔d6   b3

63 a3!   Resigns

The final *zugzwang:* 63...b2 64 ♖e7+ ♔d8 65 ♖b7.

36

This little-known exhibition game, arranged in summer 1962 by Danish TV, is a good example of Fischer's sense of justice. Even in a game with nothing at stake but ego he wouldn't let Larsen get away with what he considered indulgences in the opening. Fischer plays for an edge with Black, grabs a pawn and ignites a sparkling battle of imaginations.

Bent Larsen – Fischer
Exhibition, Copenhagen 1962
Bird's Opening (A02)

1	f4	♘f6
2	♘f3	g6
3	d3	d5

Fischer may have been influenced by one of his early games when he crushed an amateur by exploiting a hole at e3 (after 3 b3 ♗g7 4 ♗b2 0-0 5 d3?! d5 6 ♘bd2? ♘g4! 7 ♗xg7 ♘e3 8 ♕c1 ♔xg7).

Later in his career, Fischer preferred setups with ...d6, allowing White to transpose into a Closed Sicilian, as in a 1971 Larsen – Fischer Candidates match game that went 1 f4 c5 2 ♘f3 g6 and now 3 e4 ♗g7 4 ♗e2 ♘c6).

4 ♘bd2

With colors reversed (1 d4 f5 2 c4 d6 3 ♘c3 ♘f6 and ...♘bd7/...♕c7 followed by ...e5) this has been called Antoshin's Variation.

4	...	d4

Now 5 ♘b3 c5 6 c3 (not 6 ♘xc5?? ♕a5+) would challenge Black's strategy. White may have rejected this because of 6...dxc3 7 bxc3 c4

since 8 dxc4? ♕xd1+ 9 ♔xd1 is no fun to play, even in an exhibition.

5	c3	dxc3
6	bxc3	♘d5!

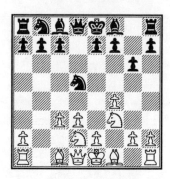

7	♕a4+!	♘c6

Not 7...♗d7 8 ♕d4 with advantage.

8	♘e5	♗g7

And here White wins after 8...♘xc3? 9 ♕c4!. A real alternative was 8...♘b6 since 9 ♘xc6 ♘xa4 10 ♘xd8 ♔xd8 is nothing for Black to fear. White would probably stay in the middlegame – or is it still the opening? – with 9 ♕c2 ♘xe5 10 fxe5.

9 ♘e4!

Black has the better of 9 ♘xc6 ♕d7 because of the vulnerability of c3, e.g. 10 ♘b1 ♕xc6 11 ♕xc6+ bxc6 12 ♗d2 ♖b8.

9	...	♘b6!

This breaks the pin favorably (10 ♘xc6 ♘xa4 11 ♘xd8 ♔xd8) and prompts White to offer a gambit "on spec."

10	♕b3?!	♘xe5
11	fxe5	♗xe5!

Black has a positional edge after 11...0-0 12 d4 ♗e6 or 12 ♗f4 ♗e6. But allowing White to emerge from the opening relatively unscathed may have offended Fischer's sense of jurisprudence. He wants material.

12 ♕b5+   ♘d7
13 ♗h6!   c6
14 ♕b3   ♘f6

Now 15 ♘g5? ♕d5 and Black is on the road to victory.

15 ♗g7   ♖g8
16 ♗xf6   exf6
17 d4

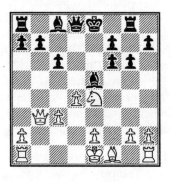

17 ...   f5!

Also favorable is 17...♗c7 18 ♘c5 b6!.

18 ♘f2

But there's not a scintilla of compensation in 18 dxe5 fxe4 19 ♖d1 ♕g5 or 18 ♘c5 ♕h4+ 19 ♔d2 ♗xd4!.

18 ...   ♗f4
19 e4!   dxe4
20 ♗c4   ♖g7

Black may have been scared off 20...♕e7 21 0-0 b5 by 22 ♗xf7+ ♕xf7 23 ♕xf7+ ♔xf7 24 ♘xe4. But 24...g5 25 g3 ♗f5 26 ♖ae1 ♖ge8 wins (not 26...♖ae8 27 ♖xf4! gxf4 28 ♘d6+).

21 0-0   b5?!

Simplest is 21...♗e3! 22 ♖ae1 ♗xf2+ 23 ♖xf2 f5 since 24 ♖xe4+

fxe4 25 ♗f7+ is refuted by 25...♔e7!.

22 ♘xe4!   bxc4

Now 23 ♕a3 is refuted by 23...♕h4!.

23 ♕xc4   ♗e3+
24 ♔h1   ♗f5!

Not 24...♗d7 25 ♘f6+ ♔f8 26 ♕c5+ ♕e7 27 ♘xd7+.

25 ♕xc6+   ♔f8
26 ♘d6   ♖b8

Not 26...♗e6? 27 ♖ae1! and White is suddenly better.

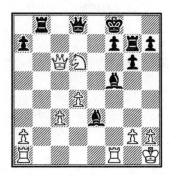

27 ♕c5

It was too early for desperation – 27 ♖xf5 gxf5 (27...♖b6? 28 ♘xf7!) 28 ♘xf5 is refuted by 28...♗g5.

27 ...   ♕b6

Both first ranks become vulnerable now. For example, 28 ♕a3 ♔g8 29 ♖ae1 ♗d3 30 ♖f3 ♗d2 or 29 ♖fe1 ♗g5 30 ♘e8 ♗h4!.

28 ♕e5   ♗g5

Also good was 28...f6 29 ♕xf6+ ♔g8 (30 ♕e5 ♕c7).

29 ♖ae1!

Threatening ♕e8+.

29 ...   ♕d8

Another trap was 29...♗d7 30 ♖xf7+! and White wins. The text would allow Black to coordinate his pieces with 30 ♘xf5 gxf5 31 ♖xf5 ♔g8.

30 g4 ♗f6

Also winning was the immediate 30...♗e7 because 31 ♘xf7 ♔xf7 32 gxf5 ♗f6! 33 ♕e6+ ♔f8 is quite safe.

31 ♕d5

Also lost is 31 ♕f4 ♗e7 32 ♖xe7 ♕xe7 33 ♘xf5 ♕b7+ or 33 gxf5 gxf5 34 ♘xf5? ♕b7+ 35 ♖f3 ♕xf3+ and mates.

31 ... ♗e7!

32 gxf5?

Here 32 ♖xe7 ♕xe7 (not 32...♔xe7? 33 gxf5 ♕xd6 34 f6+) 33 gxf5 ♕e2 is lost but offered better chances than the game.

32 ... ♕xd6

33 ♕xd6 ♗xd6

34 f6 ♖g8

35 c4

With only a piece for a pawn, White manages to create play (35...♖b2? 36 c5!).

35 ... g5!

36 c5 ♗f4

37 h4

Last trap: on 37...h6 38 h5! White's 39 ♖e7 or 39 d5 would create more trouble than Black expected, e.g. 38...♖e8? 39 d6 ♖xe1? 40 ♖xe1 and White wins.

37 ... ♖g6!

38 d5 ♖xf6

39 hxg5 ♗xg5

40 d6 ♖c8!

Simplest. Black gives back the piece and keeps two extra pawns. **White resigned** after: **41 ♖xf6 ♗xf6 42 d7 ♖xc5 43 ♖e8+ ♔g7 44 d8(♕)**

♗xd8 45 ♖xd8 ♖c1+ 46 ♔g2 ♖c2+ 47 ♔g3 ♖xa2.

37

In the first round of the Olympiad at Bulgaria's Golden Sands resort in Varna, Fischer found himself paired with an unknown Asian opponent. As he prepared his scoresheet, he tried in vain to figure out how to spell Black's name. Fischer looked at his opponent's scoresheet but couldn't decipher the writing. Then he looked at the name card on the side of the table but the Cyrillic lettering wasn't much help. Finally, he solved the mystery. In the place on the scoresheet for White he wrote "Fischer." And in the place for Black he added, "A Mongolian."

Fischer – Sharav Purevzhav
Olympiad, Varna 1962
Sicilian Defense,
Dragon Variation (B77)

1	e4	c5
2	♘f3	d6
3	d4	cxd4
4	♘xd4	♘f6
5	♘c3	g6
6	♗e3	♗g7
7	f3	♘c6
8	♕d2	0-0
9	♗c4	♘d7

This maneuver (...♘b6 and ...♘a5-c4) to neutralize both bishops was all the rage. It had been analyzed by Leonid Shamkovich and Yacov Estrin four months before in the May 1962 issue of *Shakhmatny Bulletin,* and that seemed to make it a good choice because Fischer had allowed ...♘c4xe3 in Game 11.

But, as the tournament book pointed out, playing even a very new move against "the living chess encyclopedia" was highly risky.

10 0-0-0   ♘b6

11 ♗b3   ♘a5

12 ♕d3!

Shamkovich and Estrin cited two of the opening's tricks: 12 ♗h6? ♘ac4 13 ♕g5 e5! wins for Black (14 ♘de2 ♗f6!), and 12 ♕e2 a6! threatens to trap a knight with 13...e5.

Fischer's move was an innovation. By keeping his queen on the d-file he can meet 12...♘xb3+ 13 axb3 d5 with 14 ♘de2! and exd5 (This is why 10 0-0-0 is superior to the move then endorsed by theory, 10 h4.)

12 ...   ♗d7

13 h4!

White's 12th move bought him a tempo or two (before Black plays ...♖c8 and ...♘bc4). This move points out Black has only one minor piece defending the king.

13 ...   ♖c8

14 h5   ♘bc4

15 hxg6   hxg6

After the game 15...fxg6 was recommended since 16 ♗h6 would be refuted by 16...♗xh6! 17 ♖xh6

e5, threatening ...♕g5+. On other moves to preserve White's bishops, he loses the initiative, e.g. 16 ♗g5 ♘xb3+ 17 cxb3 ♘e5 or 17 axb3 ♕a5 or 17 ♘xb3 ♘xb2!.

However, 16 ♔b1 is good preparation for ♗h6. Then 16...♘xb3 17 axb3 ♘xe3 18 ♕xe3 favors the knights over the bishops, e.g. 18...♕e8 19 f4 e5 20 fxe5 ♕xe5 21 ♘f3 and ♘d5.

16 ♗h6!

16 ...   e6??

This is logical, stopping ♘d5 and enabling the queen to defend the kingside. But as often occurs, here logic is calamitous.

It was too late for 16...♗xh6+ 17 ♖xh6 e5 because of 18 ♖dh1 exd4 19 ♘d5 with a winning attack. But Black must try the other forcing line, 16...e5!.

Then 17 ♗xg7 ♔xg7 18 ♘db5 ♗xb5 19 ♘xb5 a6 20 ♘xd6? ♕g5+ 21 ♔b1 ♖fd8! allows Black's queen to play, e.g. 22 f4 ♕xf4 23 ♕h3 ♖h8.

But 18 ♘de2! ♕g5+ 19 ♔b1 is strong in view of 20 g3 and 21 f4. Or 19...b5 20 ♗xc4 ♘xc4 21 b3 ♘a5 and the d6 pawn falls.

17 f4!

White clears the way for ♕h3. Now 17...♕f6 18 e5 dxe5? 19 ♗g5! loses outright, and 17...♗xh6 18 ♖xh6 ♔g7 19 ♕h3 ♖h8 20 ♖h1 ♕g8 21 f5! wouldn't last much longer.

| 17 | ... | e5 |
| 18 | ♘f5! | |

Based on 18...gxf5 19 ♗xg7 ♔xg7 20 ♕g3+ ♔f6 21 ♕g5+ and mates.

| 18 | ... | ♗xf5 |
| 19 | exf5 | ♘xb2 |

A desperate try that falters because of a neat tactical point.

20 ♔xb2

Not 20 ♕h3? ♖xc3!.

| 20 | ... | e4 |

21 ♗xg7!

Black missed a mate (21...exd3 22 f6).

| 21 | ... | ♔xg7 |
| 22 | ♘xe4 | **Resigns** |

38

Fischer's notes to the following historic struggle in *My 60 Memorable Games* are odd because he chiefly quoted the world champion's own annotations in the October 1962 *Chess Life.* Fischer expressed little

of his own viewpoint – except to deny Botvinnik's claim that White was better after 23 moves and that the game would have been drawn even if Black had found the right 51st move.

Mikhail Botvinnik – Fischer
Olympiad, Varna 1962
Grünfeld Defense (D98)

1	c4	g6
2	d4	♘f6
3	♘c3	d5

"Fischer very rarely plays the Grünfeld Defense," Botvinnik wrote. In fact, this is the earliest known game of his with 3...d5.

4	♘f3	♗g7
5	♕b3	dxc4
6	♕xc4	0-0
7	e4	♗g4
8	♗e3	♘fd7
9	♗e2	♘c6
10	♖d1	♘b6
11	♕c5	♕d6

This position regained the spotlght in 1986 when Anatoly Karpov scored a memorable world championship match victory over Garry Kasparov with 12 e5 ♕xc5 13 dxc5 ♘c8 14 h3 ♗xf3 15 ♗xf3 and then 15...♗xe5

16 &xc6 bxc6 17 &d4. But Black should equalize after 17...&f4 and...e5.

12 h3   &xf3

So that 13 &xf3 ♕xc5 14 dxc5 ♘c4 15 &c1 ♘d4 with excellent piece play.

13 gxf3   ♖fd8

But 13...♕xc5? 14 dxc5 &xc3+ 15 bxc3 ♘a4 16 ♔d2 only puts the knight in danger of &b5 (and 16...a6 17 ♖b1). Botvinnik agreed afterward with Soviet openings expert Semyon Furman, who said 13...e6 equalizes.

14 d5   ♘e5

15 ♘b5

Botvinnik rejected 15 f4 ♘ec4 16 &xc4 ♕xc5. But White has the superior 16 e5! ♕xc5 17 &xc5 ♘xb2 18 ♖b1, regaining the pawn with advantage. Fischer indicated he would have avoided all this by way of 15...♘ed7 16 ♕b5 e5!.

15 ...   ♕f6!

A strong idea, based on the assumption that the kingside is exploitable – and that the queen won't be trapped.

16 f4   ♘ed7

17 e5

Botvinnik reached this very position in preparations for his 1958

championship match with Smyslov and concluded that Black's queen was in trouble. For example, 17...♕f5 18 ♕b4 a5 19 ♕d4 c5 20 dxc6 bxc6 21 &g4 or 17...♕h4 18 ♕a3 g5 19 ♖d4!.

17 ...   ♕xf4!

But this was a nasty surprise.

18 &xf4

Fischer joked that after 18 ♕xb6?? ♕e4! 19 f3 ♕h4+ 20 &f2 ♕b4+ it was important to play "...axb6! (toward the center)."

18 ...   ♘xc5

19 ♘xc7   ♖ac8

20 d6   exd6

Now 21 ♖xd6 ♘cd7! embarrasses White's pieces (22 e6 ♖xc7 23 ♖xb6 &e5!).

21 exd6   &xb2

22 0-0   ♘bd7

In their annotation battle, Botvinnik claimed he stood better despite the loss of a pawn and called this move inferior to 22...♘cd7 23 &f3 &e5 24 &xe5 ♘xe5 25 &xb7 ♖b8, which would minimize White's edge. Fischer, who liked Black's position, said he couldn't disagree more with giving back a pawn.

23 ♖d5   b6

24 &f3?

But they agreed this was the wrong diagonal. Botvinnik was more optimistic and felt that after 24 &c4 the threat of ♖e1-e7 would be strong. However, Fischer pointed out that White cannot make progress after 24 &c4 ♘e6 25 &h2 ♘d4, e.g. 26 ♖b1 &c3 27 ♖c1 &b2, etc.

24 ...   ♘e6!

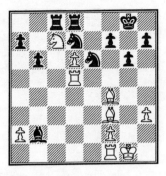

25 ♘xe6

After this, White's inferiority is obvious. Botvinnik believed 25 ♗h2 ♘d4 26 ♖xd4!? ♗xd4 27 ♖e1 was good for him – but Fischer said 27...♗c5 and ...♘f6 was good for him.

Who is right? Fischer, based on variations such as 27...♗c5 28 ♖e7 ♘f6 29 ♗b7? ♖xc7! or 28 ♘d5 ♔g7 followed by ...♗d4 and ...♘f6.

25	...	fxe6
26	♖d3	♘c5
27	♖e3	e5!

Not 27...♗d4 28 ♖a3 e5 because of 29 ♗g5 ♖xd6 30 ♗e7 ♖d7 31 ♗g4.

28	♗xe5	♗xe5
29	♖xe5	♖xd6
30	♖e7	♖d7
31	♖xd7	♘xd7
32	♗g4	♖c7

Having won back the second rank (31 ♖fe1 ♖cc7) Black has excellent winning chances, particularly if White traded here with 33 ♗xd7?. But Fischer's conviction that he would be winning after an exchange of minor pieces came back to haunt him at move 41.

33	♖e1	♔f7
34	♔g2	

Botvinnik criticized his use of the bishop, which should have gone to d5 when it could and now belongs on e6.

34	...	♘c5
35	♖e3	♖e7

Not 36 ♔f3?? h5! and the bishop is trapped.

36 ♖f3+

White is angling for a trade of rooks, which would allow him to set up a solid line of defense with his king on e3 or d4, a pawn on f4 and bishop on c2. But here, for example, 36 ♖xe7+ ♔xe7 37 ♗d1 ♔d6 38 ♔f3 ♔d5 39 ♔e3 ♔c4 would lose.

36	...	♔g7
37	♖c3	♖e4
38	♗d1	♖d4

Where does the rook do the best job of restriction? Botvinnik felt 38...♖e1! was right and 39 ♗c2 ♖c1 would win.

Fischer was not sure about 39 ♗f3. But it's not hard to visualize Black winning after 39...♔f6 40 a3 ♔e5 and ...♔d4, e.g. 41 ♖e3+ ♖xe3 42 fxe3 ♘e4! 43 ♗g4 b5 44 ♗d7 ♘d6 45 ♔f3 a6 46 ♔e2 ♘c4.

39	♗c2	♔f6
40	♔f3	♔g5
41	♔g3	

41 ... ♘e4+?

As Botvinnik pointed out, White is almost in *zugzwang:* a king move allows ...♔h4, for example, and a rook move permits a strong ...♖c4. That means a "pass" such as 41...♖b4 is very strong, e.g. 42 a3 ♖d4 and White is just about out of moves.

42 ♗xe4   ♖xe4

43 ♖a3

"Natural and bad," wrote Botvinnik, who believed 43 ♖c7 would draw easily. But even then 43...♖a4 44 ♖xh7 ♖a3+ is an excellent winning try.

43 ...   ♖e7

And here 43...a5! 44 ♖b3 ♖b4 leads to a won pawn ending, e.g. 45 ♖xb4 axb4 46 f4+ ♔f5 47 ♔f3 ♔e6 48 ♔e4 ♔d6 49 ♔d4 b5 etc.

Better for White is 44 ♖f3 but after 44...♖a4 45 a3 b5 he is losing.

44 ♖f3   ♖c7

45 a4   ♖c5

Fischer sealed this move, the best available, and both teams spent hours analyzing the position. It became an obsession. Tal recalled how he, Boleslavsky and Spassky worked on it for hours. Botvinnik, Geller, Keres and Furman analyzed all night in another room of their hotel. When Tal went to the room of Donald and Robert Byrne, to offer a draw in the adjourned D. Byrne – Tal game, he found the Byrnes were working on it too. Unfortunately for Fischer, the attractive 45...♖c4 allows 46 a5! bxa5 47 ♖f7, with a draw.

46 ♖f7   ♖a5

47 ♖xh7!!

A stunningly implausible method of drawing: White allows his opponent two connected passed pawns.

47 ...   ♖xa4

48 h4+!   ♔f5

The pawns are paralyzed after 48...♔f6 49 ♖b7! ♖a5 50 ♔g4 b5 51 f4 a6 52 ♖b6+ ♔f7 53 ♖b7+.

49 ♖f7+   ♔e5

50 ♖g7   ♖a1

51 ♔f3   b5?

Here is where the dog is buried, as the Russians say. Botvinnik's notes claimed White draws even after 51...♔d4 52 ♖xg6 b5 53 h5 b4 54 h6 b3 55 ♖g4+! ♔c5 56 ♖g5+ ♔b4 57 ♖g4+ ♔a3 58 ♖h4! b2 59 h7 b1(♕) 60 h8(♕).

Fischer disputed that claim with his longest note in all of *My 60 Memorable Games.* He said 56...♔b4 was an error because White could draw immediately with 57 ♖g7. Instead he recommended 56...♔c6! 57 ♖g6+ ♔b7! 58 ♖g7+ ♔a6! 59 ♖g6+ ♔a5 60 ♖g5+ ♔a4 61 ♖g4+ ♔a3 62 ♖h4 b2 63 h7 b1(♕) 64 h8(♕) – reaching the same position as Botvinnik after his 60 h8(♕).

Fischer then claimed a win for Black with 64...♕b3+ 65 ♔e2 ♕d1+ 66 ♔e3 ♖b1.

But Botvinnik eventually shot back in two ways. First he pointed out White is drawing after 67 ♕f8+ ♕a2 68 ♕c5!.

Moreover, Botvinnik said that one of his students, a youngster from Baku named Garik Kasparov, had found a second draw – 67 ♖c4 ♖b3+ 68 ♖c3!. Despite the many checks, Black cannot make progress (68...♕e1+ 69 ♔d3 ♕f1+ 70 ♔d2 ♕xf2+ 71 ♔d3). Botvinnik hinted that his opponent had been out-analyzed by a 13-year-old schoolboy. Fischer never replied – and this is unfortunately the closest we ever got to a Fischer – Kasparov match.

52 h5!

This resource, discovered by Geller around 5 a.m., seals the draw.

52	...	♖a3+
53	♔g2	gxh5
54	♖g5+	♔d6
55	♖xb5!	h4
56	f4	♔c6
57	♖b8	h3+
58	♔h2	a5

59	f5	♔c7
60	♖b5	♔d6

Botvinnik pointed out that "in any textbook on the endgame" you would find that this is a draw without the f-pawn. There was nothing left to say:

61 f6 ♔e6 62 ♖b6+ ♔f7 63 ♖a6 ♔g6 64 ♖c6 a4 65 ♖a6 ♔f7 66 ♖c6 ♖d3 67 ♖a6 a3 68 ♔g1 Draw

Botvinnik's three-volume game collection omits the final comment he made in *Chess Life:* "'Too many mistakes?' the reader may justly ask. Yes, there were rather a lot!" Fischer's comment in *Chess Life* was more direct: "Botvinnik swindled me."

39

Before the U.S. – U.S.S.R. match, Miguel Najdorf made three bets with Larry Evans – that Fischer would lose to Botvinnik, that Evans would lose to Spassky and that the Americans would lose the match. Najdorf lost the first but won the other two wagers. Yet it was Fischer who made a remarkable prediction when he faced Najdorf in the U.S. – Argentina match. Fischer said he would win in 25 moves. He took only 24:

Fischer – Miguel Najdorf
Olympiad, Varna 1962
*Sicilian Defense,
Najdorf Variation 6 h3 (B90)*

1	e4	c5
2	♘f3	d6
3	d4	cxd4

4	♘xd4	♘f6
5	♘c3	a6
6	h3	b5?

7 ♘d5!

A strong move which enables White to exploit Black's expansion with c2-c4. Fischer committed a rare blunder in *My 60 Memorable Games* when he said White would meet 7...e6 advantageously with 8 ♘xf6+ ♛xf6 9 c4 – overlooking 9...d5! with the threat of ...♝b4+. (The ...d5 idea was a recurring blind spot for Fischer – see Games 55 and 94.)

White can retain an edge instead with 9 ♝d3! ♝b7 10 0-0 followed by c2-c3/a2-a4.

7 ... ♝b7

"Of course not 7...♘xe4 because of 8 ♛f3," wrote Kmoch in *Chess Review*. Yet this was Black's best according to Fischer. He gave 8...♘c5 after which 9 ♘f6+ gxf6 10 ♛xa8 ♝b7 11 ♛a7 ♛c7 grants Black excellent compensation for the Exchange (and is better than 11...f5 12 b4! ♝g7 13 bxc5 ♝xd4 14 ♛xb7 ♝xa1 15 c6 as suggested by Georgi Popov in the tournament book).

A sterner test of 8...♘c5 is 9 b4! since 9...♘b7? allows 10 ♛c3 and

♘c7+. Black appears to be safe after 9...e6 10 bxc5 exd5 11 ♛xd5 ♖a7 – but not after 9...♘cd7 10 ♛c3 ♖a7 11 ♝xb5!.

8 ♘xf6+ gxf6

9 c4! bxc4?

After this Black is in major trouble. Better was the ugly 9...b4 10 ♛a4+ ♛d7 or even 9...♝xe4 10 cxb5 ♝g7 11 ♛g4 ♝g6 12 ♘f5 0-0. Popov suggested White "stands excellently" after 9...b4 10 ♝e2! ♝xe4 11 ♝f3 but 11...♝xf3 12 ♛xf3 ♖a7 is unclear.

10 ♝xc4 ♝xe4

Also bad is 10...♛a5+ 11 ♝d2 ♛e5 because of 12 ♛b3! ♛xe4+ 13 ♔d1, e.g. 13...e6 14 ♖e1! ♛xd4 15 ♛xb7 ♛a7 16 ♛c8+ and ♝xe6.

11 0-0! d5!

The game wouldn't have reached move 20, let alone Fischer's prediction of 25, if Black had played 11...e6 12 ♖e1 and allowed a sacrifice on e6.

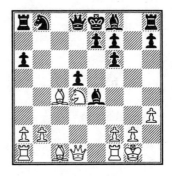

12 ♖e1

From now on both players have to consider the possibility of ♖xe4, and if ...dxe4, then either ♝xf7+ or a queen move to b3 or h5. This can't be stopped by artificial means, e.g. 12...h5 13 ♖xe4! dxe4 14 ♕b3! ♕xd4 15 ♗e3 or 12...♖g8 13 ♖xe4! dxe4 14 ♕h5 ♖g6 15 ♕xh7 ♖g7 16 ♕xe4 ♖a7 17 ♘f5 with a winning attack in either case.

12 ... e5?

This was the last major choice Black made. His move is superior to 12...♘d7 13 ♘c6 ♕c7 14 ♗xd5 or 12...e6 13 ♕h5 ♗g6 14 ♕xd5. But two captures come into consideration.

(a) Fischer felt White had a winning position even though two pawns down after 12...♗xg2 13 ♔xg2 dxc4 14 ♕f3 ♘d7 15 ♘f5, e.g. 15...e6? 16 ♖xe6+! or 15...♖g8+ 16 ♔h1 e5 17 ♗e3. But this is dubious after 14...♖g8+ 15 ♔h1 ♖a7 and, if need be, ...♖d7.

(b) He concluded that Black's best was 12...dxc4 13 ♖xe4 ♕d5 14 ♕f3 e6, which he didn't evaluate. (But it's hard to imagine Black surviving after 15 ♗f4 and ♖ae1.)

13 ♕a4+!

A case when making the most forceful move before the less forceful one of a combination is the correct procedure. On 13 ♖xe4? dxe4 14 ♕a4+ Black can play 14...♕d7! 15 ♗b5 axb5 16 ♕xa8 exd4.

13 ... ♘d7

But now 13...♕d7? just loses to 14 ♗b5.

14 ♖xe4!

Not 14 ♘c6? ♘c5! when Black's crisis is over.

14 ... dxe4
15 ♘f5 ♗c5

Mates begin to appear in the might-have-been lines. One is 15...♖g8 16 ♗xf7+! ♔xf7 17 ♕b3+ ♔e8 18 ♕e6+.

On 15...♖a7, White has 16 ♗xf7+! ♔xf7 17 ♕b3+ ♔g6 18 ♘h4+ ♔g7 and instead of perpetual check, there is 19 ♗h6+! ♔xh6 20 ♕g3 with the unstoppable mate threat of ♘f5+.

16 ♘g7+! ♔e7

Not 16...♔f8 17 ♗h6 ♔g8 18 ♕b3 and the game is over (18...♕e7 19 ♘f5 and ♕g3+).

17 ♘f5+ ♔e8
18 ♗e3

The exchange of bishops sets up a devastating knight check at d6 or queen checks along the a3-f8 diagonal. But note that if White had played this two moves ago, Black could castle.

18 ... ♗xe3
19 fxe3 ♕b6

To stop 20 ♕b4!.

20 ♖d1!

The 1962 Soviet chess yearbook wrote: "Of course, a strong move, but still more energetic is 20 ♗xf7+ ♔xf7 21 ♕xd7+ ♔g6 22 ♕g7+ ♔xf5 22 ♕g4 mate."

But Fischer pointed out that 20...♔d8! lets Black live (21 ♖d1 ♕b5) – although after 22 ♕a3 it's not clear how long that might be.

20 ... ♖a7

On 20...♖d8 White grabs the a-pawn because then 22 ♗b5 becomes a killing threat.

21 ♖d6!

Again 21 ♗xf7+ ♔d8! or 21 ♘d6+ ♔e7 fail.

21 ... ♕d8

The immediate 21...♕c7 loses to 22 ♖c6 (faster than Fischer's 22 ♖xf6 ♖f8) ♕d8 23 ♕a3.

And 21...♕xb2 22 ♗xf7+ should not last long, for example 22...♔xf7 23 ♖xd7+ ♖xd7 24 ♕xd7+ ♔g6 25 ♕g7+ and mates, or 22...♔d8 23 ♕a5+ ♖c7 24 ♗e6 ♕b5 25 ♖xd7+.

22 ♕b3

Analyst Eliezer Agur claimed a faster win in 22 ♕a3 followed by ♗b3-a4 or ♗e2-h5. A sample variation runs 22...♖g8 23 ♖d1 ♖c7 24 ♗b3! ♖g6 25 ♗a4 and Black has no good moves. But Fischer's move wins at least a queen.

22 ... ♕c7

Or 22...♖f8 23 ♘g7+ ♔e7 24 ♕a3! and a lethal discovered check.

23 ♗xf7+ ♔d8

24 ♗e6 Resigns

Black can chose between various degrees of hopelessness including (a) 24...♕c8 25 ♕b6+, (b) 24...♕c1+ 25 ♔h2 ♔c8 26 ♘e7+, (c) 24...♖b7 25 ♕d1 ♕c8 26 ♕g4 – or, as Fischer gave, 25 ♕a4 ♕c8 26 ♕a5+ ♔e8 27 ♕xa6 ♔d8 28 ♗xd7 with a winning endgame. (He didn't see how crushing 25 ♕d5! ♔c8

26 ♖xd7! would have been.) Kmoch called this a "knight-odds" treatment of Najdorf. One day later Najdorf redeemed his honor by crushing Portisch in 22 moves with a double pawn sacrifice. "I only win and lose brilliantly," he explained.

40

Although his experience had ranged from weekend Swiss System opens to Candidates Tournaments, Fischer had never played much team chess until he succeeded Reshevsky as first board in the Olympiads. Reshevsky managed only a plus-one score at Munich 1958 and Tel Aviv 1964, and often drew in fewer than 30 moves. But Fischer fought in every game. At Leipzig 1960 he won ten, drew six and lost two. At Varna 1962 he began with a blistering 8½-1½ before slowing down to a final score of 11-6. His ability to win with Black in games like the following kept the Americans in the medal race until the last round.

Max Blau – Fischer
Olympiad, Varna 1962
Sicilian Defense, 4 ♕xd4 (B53)

1	e4	c5
2	♘f3	d6
3	d4	cxd4
4	♕xd4	

This, with c2-c4, was regarded as a valid way of playing for a win while avoiding Najdorf/Dragon theory.

4	...	♘c6
5	♗b5	♗d7

6	♗xc6	♗xc6
7	c4	♘f6
8	♘c3	g6

A basic premise of 4 ♕xd4 states: When White sets up a Maróczy Bind pawn structure, Black should fianchetto. But when White adopts the more aggressive plan of 7 ♘c3 and 0-0-0, Black plays ...e6/...♗e7. Typical play here would be 9 0-0 ♗g7 10 ♕d3 0-0 11 ♘d4 ♕b6.

9	♗g5	♗g7

10 ♘d5?

Blau tries to exploit the temporary pin on f6 at a prohibitive loss of time. Better was 10 0-0 0-0 11 ♕e3.

10	...	0-0!

Now 11 ♘xf6+ exf6 is nearly winning for Black (12 ♗h4 ♗xe4; 12 ♗e3 f5), and 11 ♗xf6 exf6 12 0-0 f5 is excellent for him.

11	♕d3	♗xd5!

Good enough to equalize – at least – is 11...e6 12 ♘xf6+ ♗xf6 13 ♗xf6 ♕xf6 (14 ♘d4 d5 15 ♘xc6 bxc6). After the superior text Black has two pawns to harass before White manages to castle.

12 exd5

Black gets a nice game from 12 cxd5 ♕b6 but even better is

12...♕a5+!, e.g. 13 ♗d2 ♕a4 or 13 ♕d2 ♕a6! 14 ♕b4 ♖ac8.

12	...	♘d7

Now 13 ♕e2 is answered by 13...♕a5+ 14 ♗d2 ♕a6! 15 ♗g5 ♘b6 (16 ♗xe7? ♖fe8).

13	♕d2	♖c8
14	♖c1	b5!

Black's more active pieces give him the edge after 15 cxb5 ♖xc1+ 16 ♕xc1 ♕a5+ 17 ♕d2 ♕xb5 (18 b3 ♘b6).

15	b3	bxc4
16	bxc4	♘c5
17	0-0	

If White averts ...♘e4 he allows a nasty 17...♕a5+.

17	...	♘e4
18	♕e3	♘xg5

Here 19 ♘xg5 ♕d7 20 ♖fe1 may hold Black's advantage to a manageable level.

19 ♕xg5? ♖c5!

Now 20 ♘d2 invites 20...♕c7 and a threat of 21...e6. For example, 21 ♖fe1 e6 and now 22 ♘b3 ♖xc4 23 dxe6 fxe6 24 ♖xe6 ♗e5! traps the rook. Also bad for White is 24 ♖xc4 ♕xc4 25 ♕e7 a5! and 26...a4, e.g. 26 h3 a4 27 ♘c1 ♗d4.

20	♕e3	♕c7

And here 21 ♘d2 (which could also have come about via 20 ♘d2 ♕c7 21 ♕e3) is met strongly by 21...♖a5, since 22 ♖c2? ♖xd5 hangs a pawn. But 21 ♖c2 ♖xc4 22 ♖xc4 ♕xc4 23 ♕xa7 ♗f6 24 ♖d1 defends better.

21 ♘d4

21 ...   ♗xd4!

Black's heavy-piece pressure against c4 is much more effective than the immediate 21...♖xc4 22 ♘c6!, e.g. 22...♖xc1 23 ♘xe7+ and 24 ♖xc1.

22 ♕xd4   ♖c8

23 ♖c2

White must lose material but can draw if he liquidates enough pawns. Best was probably 23 ♕e3 (or 23 ♖fe1) ♖xc4 24 ♖xc4 ♕xc4 25 ♕xe7 although after 25...♕xd5 26 ♕xa7 ♖a8 Black has the kind of advantage he can nurse for another 40 moves.

23 ...   ♖xc4

24 ♖xc4   ♕xc4

25 ♕xa7   ♕e4!

Centralizing gives Black better chances with equal material than he would have had a pawn up in the last note. If White tries to break Black's hold with 26 ♕e3 ♕xe3 27 fxe3 he lands in a lost endgame (27...♖a8 28 ♖a1 ♖a3 29 ♔f2 f5 and ...♔f7-f6-e5).

And 26 a4 ♖c5 27 ♕a8+ ♔g7 28 ♖d1 ♕d4! just loses a pawn.

26 h3   ♖c4!

Black doesn't even allow 27 a4. On 27 ♕b8+ ♔g7 28 ♕b2+ f6 he has ...♖c2 coming up (and 29 ♕d2 ♖d4 30 ♖e1 ♖xd2 31 ♖xe4 ♔f7 is lost).

27 ♖d1   ♔g7

Black threatens 27...♖a4.

28 ♕b7   ♕e2

29 ♖f1   ♖a4

30 ♕b3   ♖xa2

31 ♕c3+   f6!

The immediate 31...♕e5? 32 ♕xe5+ dxe5 isn't convincing after 33 ♖d1 with the idea of 34 d6, e.g. 33...♖a6 34 ♖c1 ♖d6 35 ♖c5.

32 ♕e1   ♕e5!

Clearer than 32...♕xe1 33 ♖xe1 ♔f7 34 ♖d1, e.g. 34...f5 35 g3 ♔f6 36 ♔g2 ♔e5 37 ♖e1+ or 36...♖a5 37 f4.

33 f4

Or 33 ♕xe5 fxe5! 34 ♖d1 ♔f6 (35 g3 e4).

33 ...   ♕xd5!

Thanks to White's make-or-break last move, Black can also seek an endgame with 33...♕d4+ 34 ♔h2 ♔f8 35 ♕e6 ♕d2 36 ♕e4 f5. But Fischer tended to avoid rook endings whose outcome was less than 100 percent certain. Black can go for the kill now since his king will be magically safe on h6 – or even g3.

34 ♕xe7+ ♔h6

Best here is probably 35 ♖f3 (threatening 36 ♕f8+ ♔h5 37 g4+). But Black makes slow progress with 35...♕d1+ 36 ♖f1 ♕d2 37 ♕e4 d5 38 ♕f3 ♕d4+.

35 ♕f8+ ♔h5

White missed his chance for ♖f3 because now it loses outright to 36...♕d1+ (37 ♔h2 ♕xf3 or 37 ♖f1 ♕d2 38 g4+ ♔h4 39 ♕xf6+ ♔g3!).

36 g4+ ♔h4

37 ♕xf6+

Black would have met 37 ♕h6+ with 37...♔g3 and mates. But here 37...♔g3 38 ♕c3+ ♔h4 39 ♖f2 makes him start over again.

37 ... ♔xh3

38 ♕c3+ ♔xg4

39 ♕c8+ ♔h4

40 ♕d8+ ♔h5

White resigns

The only defenses to 41...♕g2 mate are 41 ♕g5+ ♔xg5 and the faster losses of 41 ♖f2 ♕c5! and 41 ♖f3 ♕d1+ 42 ♖f1 ♕g4+.

41

Fischer's form varied considerably in 1962, from Stockholm to Curaçao to Varna, and he finished the year with his closest brush with failing to win the U.S. Championship. But in several of his victories, such as the following, he seemed more dominant than he did in any other year of his career.

Fischer – Karl Robatsch
Olympiad, Varna 1962
Center Counter Defense (B01)

1	e4	d5
2	exd5	♕xd5
3	♘c3	♕d8?!

A 19th Century idea with a 20th Century twist. Black hopes to disrupt White's development with a fianchetto bearing down on d4.

4	d4	g6

Fischer – Addison, Palma de Mallorca 1970, went 4...♘f6 5 ♗c4 ♗f5?! 6 ♕f3 ♕c8 7 ♗g5! ♗xc2 8 ♖c1 ♗g6 9 ♘ge2 with a strong initiative.

5	♗f4!	♗g7

Black would have a comfortable game after 6 ♘f3 ♘h6 and ...♘f5 or 6 ♘b5 ♘a6 and ...c6.

6	♕d2!

Fischer's move, an innovation, allows him to carry out a strong setup reminiscent of "sac, sac, mate." But it depends on the soundness of the pawn sacrifice: 6...♗xd4? 7 0-0-0 ♘c6 8 ♗b5 ♗d7 9 ♘d5! (much better than 9 ♗xc6 ♗xc6 10 ♕xd4? ♕xd4 11 ♖xd4 ♗xg2) e5 10 ♘f3 and wins.

The alternative grab is 6...♕xd4 7 ♕xd4 ♗xd4 but White has a terrific ending after 8 ♘b5 ♗b6 9 ♘xc7+.

6 ... ♘f6

7 0-0-0 c6

Fischer felt 7...♘d5 8 ♗e5 0-0 was better (9 h4 h5).

8 ♗h6 0-0?

And here Fischer said the king belonged on the queenside after 8...♗xh6 and ....♗f5.

9 h4! ♕a5

Timing matters: on 10 ♗e2 ♗e6! 11 h5 ♘bd7 and Black's king may escape – 12 ♗xg7 ♔xg7 13 hxg6 fxg6 14 ♕h6+ ♔f7 15 ♘f3 ♔e8.

10 h5!

The formula threat is 11 hxg6, 12 ♗xg7 ♔xg7 and 13 ♕h6+.

10 ... gxh5

The key alternative is 10...♘xh5 11 ♗e2 ♘f6, after which 12 ♗xg7 ♔xg7 13 ♕h6+ ♔g8 14 g4! and 19 g5 must win.

11 ♗d3 ♘bd7

White is in no hurry to exchange on g7 since 11...♗f5?? 12 ♕g5! loses immediately.

12 ♘ge2 ♖d8

13 g4! ♘f8

The game is over soon after 13...♘xg4 14 ♖dg1 – and immediately after 13...hxg4? 14 ♗xg7 ♔xg7 15 ♕h6+.

14 gxh5 ♘e6

15 ♖dg1 ♔h8

Or 15...♔f8 16 ♗xg7+ ♘xg7 17 ♕h6 ♘g4 18 ♕xh7 and 19 ♕h8+ or 19 f3 wins.

16 ♗xg7+ ♘xg7

17 ♕h6 ♖g8

Also lost was 17...♘e6 18 ♘f4.

18 ♖g5! ♕d8

19 ♖hg1 ♘f5

Equivalent to resignation. Fischer would have liked to finish off with 19...♕f8 20 d5! which points out how fragile the defense is (20...cxd5 21 ♘xd5 and 22 ♘xf6). After 20...♗d7 White has 21 d6! ♘f5 22 ♕xf8 ♖axf8 23 ♗xf5 and Black must try 23...♖xg5 24 ♖xg5 h6 – which loses after 25 dxe7 ♖b8 26 ♖g3! ♗xf5 27 ♖f3.

20 ♗xf5 Resigns

42

Fischer next made news by turning down his invitation to play in the first Piatigorsky Cup, which featured Petrosian, Keres, Gligorić, Reshevsky and Benko. Instead he entered a July 4th weekend tournament which began two days after the Piatigorsky. Fischer never explained publicly why he passed up the strongest tournament of 1963 to play in a Swiss System open offering a $750 top prize. But his action was understood as a slight to Jacqueline Piatigorsky, who was sponsor of both the Cup and the ill-fated

Reshevsky match two years before. Later Fischer wrote an over-the-top article in *Chess Life*, in which, among other things, he claimed that at least five of his Western Open games were of a higher quality than all but one of the Piatigorsky games. When passions cooled he didn't include any of the Western games in his 60 Memorable ones. But the following was a worthy candidate.

Hans Berliner – Fischer
Western Open, Bay City 1963
Queen's Gambit Declined,
Semi-Tarrasch Variation (D41)

| 1 | d4 | ♘f6 |
| 2 | c4 | e6 |

Berliner, who won the next world correspondence championship, was known for elaborately prepared openings and Fischer didn't want to find out what he had planned against a King's Indian or Grünfeld.

3	♘c3	d5
4	cxd5	♘xd5
5	e4	♘xc3
6	bxc3	c5
7	♘f3	cxd4
8	cxd4	♗b4+

After this line was temporarily discredited, by a Spassky win in the 1969 world championship match, Fischer switched to 8...♘c6 9 ♗c4 b5 and made a 29-move draw with Spassky in the 1972 championship match.

9	♗d2	♗xd2+
10	♕xd2	0-0
11	♗d3	

White's center looks impressive but if he can't find a way to capitalize on it in the middlegame it will be a liability in the endgame.

For example, a queen trade after 11 ♗c4 ♘c6 12 0-0 b6 13 ♖fd1 ♗b7 14 ♕f4 ♕f6! 15 ♕xf6 or 15 ♕e3 ♖fd8 16 e5 ♕h6!, as in Reshevsky – Fine, Hastings 1937-8 is excellent for Black. As Fischer put it, "The more pieces that are exchanged, the less valuable a pawn center is."

11	...	b6
12	0-0	♗b7
13	♖fd1	

A smoother way of coordinating forces is 13 ♖ac1 ♘c6 14 ♗b1 followed by ♖c3 or ♖fd1.

| 13 | ... | ♘c6 |

Black can meet 14 ♕f4 with 14...♕f6, as in the Fine game. White should settle for 14 ♕e3.

| 14 | ♕b2? | ♕f6! |

Now the d-pawn is frozen and becomes the main topic of debate after, for example, 15 e5 ♕f4.

| 15 | ♖ac1 | ♖fd8 |
| 16 | ♗b5 | |

Black's pressure is also evident after 16 ♗b1 ♖ac8 17 ♖c3 ♕f4.

| 16 | ... | ♖ac8 |
| 17 | ♘e5?! | |

White cannot find a plan or even improve the position of his pieces because of trades (17 ♖c4 ♘e7). Berliner's solution is bold: he trashes his textbook center in return for tactical chances on the c- and d-files.

17 ...   ♘xe5

18 dxe5   ♕f4

After 18...♖xc1 19 ♕xc1! White stands better than in the game.

19 ♖xc8   ♖xc8

On 20 f3 Black has a strong plan of 20...h5 followed by ...h4 and ...♖c5.

20 ♕d4

The threats of mate (21 ♕d8+) and of 21 ♕d7 ♖b8 22 ♕c7 save White's e-pawns for the moment.

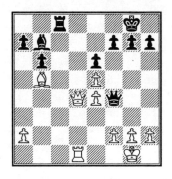

20 ...   g5!

Black needed *luft* and there are two reasons why this way is best:

The first is strategic. To defend e4 White must eventually play f2-f3 (or ♗f3) but that will invite ...g4 now. The other reason is tactical. Black rejects 20...h6 because of 21 f3 ♖c5 22 ♗e8 ♖xe5 23 ♕d6!.

(White can also try 20...h6 21 ♕d7 with the idea of 21...♕xe4?? 22 ♕xc8+ ♗xc8 23 ♖d8+ ♔h7

24 ♗d3. But Black is close to winning after 21...♖c1!.)

21 f3

The ♕d7 idea fails immediately (21 ♕d7 ♖c2 22 f3 ♕xe5 23 ♕xb7 ♕xb5) but could be hidden by 21 ♗d3 because of 21...♖c5 22 ♕d7! ♖c1 23 ♕d8+ ♔g7 24 ♕f6+!.

21 ...   g4!

Annotators – who often play the role of mind-readers – claimed Fischer chose this because he saw 21...♖c5 was faulty on account of 22 ♗e8, threatening 23 ♗xf7+.

Then 22...♗c8 23 g3 ♕xf3 would lose to 24 ♗xf7+! ♕xf7 25 ♕d8+ ♔g7 26 ♖f1. Or 25...♕f8 26 ♕xg5+ ♕g7 27 ♖d8+.

However, 22...♔g7! is a sufficient reply: 23 g3 ♕xe5 24 ♕xe5+ ♖xe5 and now 25 ♖d7? ♗c6! 26 ♖xf7+ ♔g8 27 ♖e7 ♔f8 wins.

Fischer's method is more convincing.

22 ♗e2   gxf3

But here 22...♖c2 was better. For instance, 23 g3 ♕h6 24 ♕d3 ♖xa2 25 f4 ♗a6 and a queen endgame, 26 ♕d8+ ♔g7 27 ♖d2.

23 gxf3

Of course, 23 ♗xf3 is desirable but after Black stops the nuisance checks with 23...♔g7, he can pick off a winning pawn with ...♖c5.

23 ...   ♔h8!

Now 23...♖c2 is poor because of 24 ♔h1 ♖xe2?? 25 ♖g1+ or 24...♔g7 25 ♖g1+ ♔h6 26 ♕d1!.

24 ♔h1   ♗a6!

Without this trick (25 ♗xa6?? ♕xf3+ and ...♖g8 mates) a draw was likely. Black still has a lot of work to

do after 25 ♕d2 ♕xd2 26 ♖xd2
♗xe2 27 ♖xe2 ♔g7 even if he wins
a pawn, e.g. 28 ♔g2 ♖c5 29 f4 ♖c3!
30 f5! ♖c5 31 fxe6 fxe6 32 ♖d2.

25	♕f2?	♗xe2
26	♕xe2	♕xe5
27	♖g1	f5!

To win, Black: (a) eliminates
threats to his king by controlling the
a1-h8 diagonal, (b) ties White's
queen to e4, and that frees him to
(c) create a passed queenside pawn.

28	♕d3	fxe4
29	fxe4	♖f8
30	♕c2	♕f6

Part of Fischer lore is that he spent
the previous night playing speed
games for substantial stakes against
a Midwestern expert, Norbert
Leopoldi, and his caution (30...b5!)
is a symptom of tiredness.

31	♖g2	♕d4
32	h3	♕a1+
33	♖g1	♕e5

White loses the pawn ending
after 34 ♖g2 ♖f1+ 35 ♖g1 ♖xg1+
36 ♔xg1 ♕c5+.

34	♕e2	b5
35	♕c2	b4
36	♕d3	a5
37	♕c2	♕f6
38	♕c4	♕f3+
39	♔h2	♖d8

The threat of ...♖d2+ liquidates,
e.g. 40 ♖g2 ♕f4+.

40	♕c2	♕c3
41	♕xc3+	bxc3
42	♖c1	

42	...	♖d3!

A case when a rook is not best
placed behind a passed pawn
(42...♖c8 43 ♖c2) but rather on a
rank to cut off the enemy king.

After **43 ♖b1 ♔g7 44 ♖b5 a4
45 ♖c5 a3 46 ♔g2 ♖e3 47 ♖c4 ♔f6
48 h4 ♔e5 49 ♔f2 ♖h3 50 ♔g2 ♖d3
51 h5 ♔f4 52 h6 ♔e3 53 ♖c7 ♔d2**
White resigns

43

By late 1963 Bisguier had already
lost eight straight times to Fischer
and was developing a Bobby
complex. After agreeing to play in
a Labor Day weekend tournament,
the New York State Open, he had
second thoughts when he discovered
Fischer was committed to playing.
Bisguier feared he wouldn't even
finish second if, as usual, he lost to
Fischer. But he agreed to compete
when he was assured of an amount
equal to the second prize regardless
of his result.

Fischer – Arthur Bisguier
New York State Open,
Poughkeepsie 1963
Two Knights Defense (C59)

1	e4	e5
2	♘f3	♘c6

3   ♗c4

Fischer hadn't played this move since a U.S. Junior Championship game in which his opponent shocked him with the Wilkes Barre Variation, 3...♘f6 4 ♘g5 ♗c5!?, which he had never seen. In *Chess Life*, Fischer recalled how he almost burst out laughing at seeing an opponent overlook 5 ♘xf7. But after 5...♗xf2+ 6 ♔xf2 ♘xe4+ 7 ♔e3? ♕h4 he was lucky to avoid losing.

Fischer added that he was content with a draw since he had no chance for first place – and because he had already clinched the prize for best score by a player under 13, since he was the only player under 13.

3   ...   ♘f6

4   ♘g5   d5

5   exd5   ♘a5

6   ♗b5+

Bronstein "actually blundered away a piece" in the 1958 Olympiad with 6 d3 h6 7 ♘f3 e4 8 dxe4 ♘xc4, Fischer wrote in *Chess Life*. In truth, Bronstein's game was played in 1956, Bronstein planned the sack in advance, he got permission from his team to do it – and he won.

6   ...   c6

7   dxc6   bxc6

8   ♗e2   h6

9   ♘h3

A move superbly suited for Fischer, whose love of the two bishops trumped the risks (... ♗xh3). He blamed "vigorous Russian propaganda" for discrediting 9 ♘h3 after Steinitz used it unsuccessfully against Tchigorin in the 1890s – the last times 9 ♘h3 was used in grandmaster chess until this game.

9   ...   ♗c5

When 9 ♘h3 was later adopted by Nigel Short and Gata Kamsky, opponents preferred 9...g5 or 9...♗d6. But White stood well after d2-d3, 0-0, ♔h1 and ♘g1.

10   0-0   0-0

11   d3   ♗xh3

Bisguier, unaware of the antique theory, nevertheless improves over a Steinitz – Tchigorin game that went 11...♘d5 12 c4 ♘e7 13 ♔h1 ♗xh3 14 gxh3 ♘f5 15 f4 with advantage to White. Boleslavsky, among others, believed Black was better off avoiding ...♗xh3 altogether, and should use the time White spends on ♔h1 and ♘g1 to bring his own knight back into the game (...♘b7, ...♗b6 and ...♘c5).

12   gxh3   ♕d7

13   ♗f3

Wholly wrongheaded is 13 ♗g4? ♘xg4 14 hxg4 f5. In the magazine article, Fischer added that 13 h4 "is too materialistic even for me."

13   ...   ♕xh3

14   ♘d2

So was 14 ♗g2 ♕h4 15 ♕e1 ♖fe8! 16 ♕xa5 ♘g4 17 h3 ♗xf2+ 18 ♖xf2 (18 ♔h1? ♕g3! and wins) ♕xf2+ 19 ♔h1 e4!. For example,

20 hxg4 exd3 and Black wins. Or 20 ♕d2 exd3 21 ♕xf2 ♘xf2+ and ...dxc2.

14	...	♖ad8
15	♗g2!	♕f5

Black would like to play 15...♕h4 but White safely wins at least a pawn with 16 ♘f3 ♕h5 17 ♕e1!.

16	♕e1	♖fe8
17	♘e4	♗b6

18 ♘xf6+

Fischer's instinct told him 18 b4 ♘b7 19 b5 was "more like it" and that idea is justified by 19...cxb5? 20 ♘xf6+ and ♗xb7. But at the board he had second thoughts about ...♘d5-f4. On 19...♘xe4 20 ♕xe4 ♕xe4 21 ♗xe4 White's superiority is obvious, and he can try for even more with 20 ♗xe4 ♕g4+ 21 ♔h1 ♗a5 22 ♕d1.

18	...	♕xf6
19	♔h1	c5

Bisguier said he expected to get excellent play from 20...c4 but underestimated Fischer's reply. They agreed that 19...g5! was best, to stop f2-f4.

20	♕c3!	♘c6

Black's knight gets to d4 now but it's only temporary. He is a move

late with 20...g5 (21 f4! gxf4 22 ♗xf4).

21	f4	♘d4
22	♕c4	

Fischer rejected 22 fxe5? ♕xe5 23 ♗f4 ♕e2! in favor of dislodging the knight with c2-c3.

22	...	♕g6!

Black still has a menacing attack if he can play ...♕h5 and ...♘f5. Fischer dismissed 22...♕e6 with the comment that 23 ♕a4 ♕d7? loses material to 24 ♕xd7 ♖xd7 25 c3 ♘c2 26 ♗c6.

However, Black has better in 23...♖e7 24 c3 ♘f5, threatening ...♖xd3. White must avoid 25 ♗e4? ♘g3+! 26 hxg3 ♕h3+ 27 ♔g1 c4+, which loses, and he would be worse after 25 ♕e4 ♘h4 26 f5 ♕f6 or 26 fxe5 ♘xg2.

23	c3	♘f5?

Bisguier feared Fischer. Against anyone else he would have gone for 23...♘c2! 24 ♖b1 exf4, threatening 25...♖xd3.

24 fxe5

Again 24 ♗e4 ♕h5, threatening ...♘g3+, is dubious.

24	...	♖xe5
25	♗f4	♖e2

Black plays to win, rather than equalize with 25...♘e3.

26 ♗e4   ♖xb2?

A blunder that sharply curtails the game. Following the correct 26...♖e8! Black's threat of 27...♖8xe4 would likely force 27 ♗f3. Then 27...♖xb2 is perfectly safe and the position is in balance. For example, 28 ♖ae1 ♖xe1 29 ♖xe1 ♕f6, e.g. 30 ♕d5 ♘e7.

Fischer noted that if instead, 27 ♖g1? ♕h5 28 ♖af1 Black wins with 28...♘e3! e.g. 29 ♕b5 ♖xe4 30 dxe4 ♘xf1 31 ♖xf1 ♕g4 or 31 ♕e8+ ♔h7 32 ♖xg7+ ♔xg7 33 ♗e5+ ♕xe5 34 ♕xe5 f6! and the king eludes checks.

27 ♗e5!

This wins the pinned knight. Fischer games are often decided by a centralized bishop (e.g. Games 2, 4, 25, 76). Like Game 93, two centralized bishops dominate here.

27	...	♖e8
28	♖xf5	♖xe5
29	♖xe5	**Resigns**

44

In the same September 1963 issue of *Chess Life* in which Fischer boasted of the quality of his Western Open games he made a more daring claim. Annotating a game of his that began 1 ♘f3 ♘f6 2 g3 g6 3 ♗g2 ♗g7 4 0-0 0-0 5 d3 d6 he concluded "Black stands better!...Now whatever White does, Black will vary and get an asymmetrical position and have the superior position due to his better pawn structure." He meant that on 5 e4, Black has 5...c5! and on 5 c4, Black responds 5...e5!.

Fischer's faith in Black's ability to get the upper hand in symmetrical positions was also shown in his treatment of the Semi-Tarrasch, the 1...c5 English, and the Neo-Grünfeld. His notes to the following game indicated that after eight or so moves only Black could think of winning – and that White should play for a draw.

Robert Byrne – Fischer
U.S. Championship,
New York 1963-64
Neo-Grünfeld Defense (D79)

1	d4	♘f6
2	c4	g6
3	g3	c6
4	♗g2	d5
5	cxd5	cxd5
6	♘c3	♗g7

Fischer presented his case for Black's superiority in his game with Miroslav Filip at Varna, which went 7 ♘f3 0-0 8 0-0 ♘e4!, an old idea of Euwe's.

7 e3

In his *American Chess Quarterly* notes Fischer criticized this as "somewhat passive" compared with 7 ♘h3 0-0 8 ♘f4, which rules out ...e5 by concentrating on d5. White later passes up the similar 10 ♘f4, which leads to a lifeless middlegame that Fischer regarded as best.

7	...	0-0
8	♘ge2	♘c6
9	0-0	b6
10	b3	♗a6
11	♗a3	♖e8

Nine out of ten masters, as Fischer might say, would coordinate their heavy pieces with 11...♕d7 and ...♖fc8. But there is little in the position for either side after, say, 12 ♖e1 ♖fc8 13 ♖c1 followed by ♘f4 and ♗f1.

12 ♕d2

In retrospect 12 ♖e1, and then 12...♖c8 13 ♖c1, does a better job of discouraging ...e5. But White would have to be sure that this move order didn't just encourage the break by making ...♘xe5-♘d3 more powerful. For example, 13...e5 14 dxe5 ♘xe5 15 ♘xd5 ♘xd5 (not 15...♖xc1 16 ♘xc1!) 16 ♕xd5? ♘d3 17 ♖xc8 ♕xc8 18 ♖d1 ♕c2.

Inserting 16 ♖xc8 ♖xc8 doesn't help. White loses after 17 ♕xd5? ♗xe2 18 ♖xe2 ♕a6! forks the rook and bishop. He is in a bad pin after 17 ♗xd5? ♖d8 (18 ♘f4 ♘d3!).

12 ...   e5!

Fischer gave both his 11th and 12th moves exclamation points in his initial notes – and gave White's next a question mark. He explained that the potential knight outposts at e4 and d3 outweighed the isolation of the d-pawn.

13 dxe5   ♘xe5
14 ♖fd1

Taking on d5 loses a piece (14 ♘xd5 ♘xd5 15 ♗xd5 ♗xe2), so White is faced with the familiar "Which rook?" dilemma. Byrne's choice is natural, leaving c1 for the QR. Moreover, if White is going to attack d5 with ♘f4 he needs to get out of the a6-e2 pin first.

In his first notes, Fischer said 14 ♖ad1 would be met by 14...♘e4 15 ♘xe4 dxe4 16 ♗xe4 ♕xd2 17 ♖xd2 ♘c4 18 ♗xa8 ♘xd2 19 ♖d1 ♘c4 20 bxc4 ("best") ♖xa8 with a strong endgame for Black.

But Yuri Averbakh embarrassed Fischer by finding 20 ♗c6! after which White wins, e.g. 20...♖c8 21 bxc4 ♖xc6 22 ♖d8+ or 20...♘xa3 21 ♗xe8 ♗xe2 22 ♖d7!. This revelation was particularly painful since the first articles Fischer had written for *Chess Life* were compilations of errors he found in Soviet analysis, responding to Russian allegations that he was lacking in "self-criticism."

Fischer later wrote that after Averbakh's analysis appeared, he spent an evening "just staring at the position" with 14 ♖ad1 until he found a resource – 14...♕c8 – that would vindicate 12...e5. For instance, 15 ♘xd5 ♘xd5 16 ♗xd5 ♖d8 17 f4 ♖xd5! 18 ♕xd5 ♗b7, leads to a winning attack or better endgame for Black. After the superior 15 ♗b2 ♕f5 he claimed Black "keeps the initiative."

Evans, in his syndicated newspaper column, gave a slightly different version. After seeing Averbakh's analysis, Fischer "brooded over this problem for weeks" before finally coming up with 14...♕c8, he wrote. "After this Bobby stopped publishing analysis."

14 ...   ♘d3!

The threat of 15...♘e4! is potent. For example,

(a) 15 ♘d4 ♘e4 16 ♘xe4 dxe4 17 ♗b2 ♖c8 and Black's pieces begin to dominate, or

(b) 15 ♘f4 ♘e4 16 ♘xe4! dxe4! (16...♗xa1? 17 ♘d6) 17 ♖b1 ♖c8 18 ♘xd3 ♗c3! and ...♗xd3. Fischer also gave (c), the sickly 15 f3 and concluded 15...♗h6 16 ♘f4 d4! or 16 f4 ♗g7 and ...♘e4 was excellent for Black.

15 ♕c2   ♘xf2!

This would have been unsound if White had developed the right rook at move 14.

16 ♔xf2

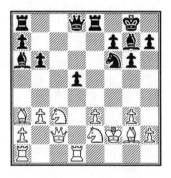

16 ...   ♘g4+

When he showed off this game a few weeks later at the Marshall Chess Club, Fischer joked "I'm sure Tal will say I shoulda played rook takes pawn – but I don't believe it."

After 16...♖xe3 17 ♔xe3 ♘g4+ 18 ♔d2 ♖c8 Black has lots of play – but for a rook and knight he deserves

something more concrete. White can even defend with 19 ♘xd5 ♖xc2+ 20 ♔xc2.

17 ♔g1   ♘xe3
18 ♕d2   ♘xg2!

This game was played in a separate room, away from spectators, who were hearing Nicolas Rossolimo describe 18 ♘xd1 as necessary – and 18...♘xg2 as incomprehensible.

19 ♔xg2   d4!

The attacked knight can't move, and 20 ♕c2 ♖c8 solves nothing.

20 ♘xd4   ♗b7+
21 ♔f1

This looks artificial but it avoids the chief drawback to 21 ♔g1 – 21...♗xd4+ 22 ♕xd4 ♖e1+ and wins (23 ♖xe1 ♕xd4+ or 23 ♔f2 ♕xd4+ 24 ♖xd4 ♖xa1 25 ♖d7 ♖c8 26 ♗b2 ♖h1!). Another way of avoiding that tactic is 21 ♔f2. But then 21...♕d7 and ...♕h3 is too much, e.g. 22 ♖ac1 ♕h3 23 ♘f3 ♗h6 24 ♕d3 ♗e3+ after which 25 ♕xe3 ♖xe3 26 ♔xe3 ♖e8+ 27 ♔f2 ♕f5 is over.

21 ...   ♕d7!

Fischer called Byrne's **resignation** here "a bitter disappointment." The key point, missed by Rossolimo among other high-rated spectators, is

22 ♕f2 ♕h3+ 23 ♔g1 ♖e1+!! and then 24 ♖xe1 ♗xd4 followed by ...♕g2 mate. In 1998 the *British Chess Magazine* listed 23...♖e1+!! as one of the greatest moves ever played – even though it was never played.

45

The following was the most dramatic game Fischer won from Benko in a series that hadn't been as one-sided as might be supposed. Benko had crushed Fischer positionally in their first game, at Portorož, and won in 27 moves at Buenos Aires 1960. Their four previous U.S. Championship games resulted in one Benko loss and three draws. Fischer's reputation for Benko-bashing was based on the four wins, three draws and one loss in their two Candidates tournaments. (And that included one Fischer victory that could easily have been a loss.) In *Chess Life*, Fischer explained that he passed up a promising queen sacrifice, 13 ♕xe5 ♘g4! 14 ♕xg7+!. Among the reasons was that he had already assured himself of the brilliancy prize when he won Game 44 seven rounds previous.

Fischer – Pal Benko
U.S. Championship,
New York 1963-64
Pirc Defense (B09)

1	e4	g6
2	d4	♗g7
3	♘c3	d6
4	f4	♘f6

5	♘f3	0-0
6	♗d3	

A rare move at the time, this soon replaced the more popular 6 ♗e2 c5 and 6 e5 dxe5.

6	...	♗g4?

This plausible strategy, to win control of d4, was recommended in opening books of the day, such as Rabar and Timet's *Sahovska Otvorenja*, which gave 7 0-0 ♘c6 as promising.

Benko had experience with 6...♘bd7 7 0-0? (a book move in 1963) e5!, based on 8 dxe5 dxe5 9 fxe5 ♘xe5 10 ♘xe5 ♕d4+ and ...♕xe5. But he knew that 7 e5! hands White an obvious edge.

7	h3!	♗xf3
8	♕xf3	♘c6
9	♗e3	e5

On 9...♘d7 White has 10 e5!, which is much stronger than the ECO-recommended 10 ♕f2.

10	dxe5!

Black's play is justified after 10 fxe5? dxe5 11 d5 ♘d4 12 ♕f2 c6!.

10	...	dxe5
11	f5	gxf5

In *Chess Life*, Fischer said 11...♘d4 12 ♕f2 gxf5 made little difference. By the time *My 60 Memorable Games* appeared he was able to cite a 1964 game that went 13 exf5 b5 14 0-0 c5 15 ♘e4 c4 16 ♘xf6+ ♕xf6 17 ♗e4 followed by c2-c3 and ♖ae1 with a potent initiative.

Slightly better is 12...b5 and 13 0-0 c5. White has a slight edge after 14 ♘xb5 ♘xb5 15 ♗xb5 ♘xe4 16 ♕f3 ♘d2 17 ♗xd2 ♕xd2 18 ♗d3 e4.

12 ♕xf5!

Here 12 exf5? would allow a good line-clearing offer, 12...e4! (13 ♘xe4 ♘e5).

12 ... ♘d4

Later 12...♕d7 was recommended but 13 ♕xd7 ♘xd7 14 ♘d5 ♖fc8 15 ♗b5 is hardly pleasant for Black.

13 ♕f2

Fischer said he was tempted by 13 ♕xe5. Then 13...♘g4 forces him into a dangerous-looking sacrifice, 14 ♕xg7+ ♔xg7 15 hxg4, e.g. 15...♘e6 16 e5 ♖h8 17 ♗h6+ ♔g8 18 ♘e4! or 15...♖e8 16 0-0-0 ♖e6 17 e5.

But after the game he appreciated that 15...♘c6 is a tough defense.

After 13 ♕f2 White enjoys a choice between queenside castling followed by g4-g5, and ♘e2-g3 or kingside castling followed by ♕g3 and doubling on the f-file.

13 ... ♘e8

Black is several moves away from having to deal with major threats yet his passive situation is semi-critical. Benko may have talked himself out of 13...c5 14 ♗g5 ♕d6 15 0-0-0 but he needs counterplay desperately.

14 0-0 ♘d6

The knight can support ...f5 or ...c5-c4. For example, 15 ♘e2 f5 or 15 ♘d5? f5 16 ♗xd4 fxe4! and Black is back in the game.

15 ♕g3!

Fischer took a considerable time before choosing this over 15 g4. Both moves discourage 15...f5, e.g. 15 ♕g3 f5 16 ♗h6 ♕f6 17 ♗xg7 ♕xg7 18 ♕xg7+ ♔xg7 19 exf5 ♘6xf5 20 ♖ae1 with a great endgame. But the queen move allows White to take aim at Black's most vulnerable point, h7.

15 ... ♔h8

16 ♕g4! c6

Fischer felt Black's next was the losing move but this one can share the guilt. The last chance for counterplay was 16...c5 even though 17 b3 ♖c8 18 ♘d5 keeps White on top (18...f5 19 exf5 ♘6xf5 20 ♗xd4! ♕xd5 21...♗b2, e.g. 21...♘e3 22 ♖xf8+ and ♕e4).

17 ♕h5 ♕e8?

Black meets the threat of 18 ♗xd4 exd4 19 e5 with 19...f5 – but he misses an exquisite finesse. He had to play 17...♘e6 or 17...c5.

18 ♗xd4   exd4

19 ♖f6!!

By freezing the f-pawn, White threatens mate in two (20 e5 and 21 ♕xh7).

19 ...   ♚g8

20 e5   h6

Trap: Black keeps the game alive after 21 ♖xd6 ♕xe5!.

21 ♘e2   Resigns

The attacked knight cannot move (21...♘b5 22 ♕f5!) and 21...♗xf6 22 ♕xh6 is instant death.

46

Fischer overhauled his 1 e4 e5 repertoire in the early-to-mid-1960s and there are several theories of why: One is that he was influenced by the games of Steinitz. Another is that he was trying to avoid prepared Ruy Lopez defenses. But perhaps the most influential factor was his claim that he'd found a surefire way for Black to equalize against the Lopez – and presumably didn't want

it to be played against him when he was White. Fischer never said what he had in mind but he apparently meant 4...b5 and 5...♘a5. Yet he never repeated this experiment:

William Addison – Fischer
U.S. Championship,
New York 1963-64
Ruy Lopez (C70)

1	e4	e5
2	♘f3	♘c6
3	♗b5	a6
4	♗a4	b5
5	♗b3	♘a5
6	d4	

More accurate is 6 0-0 since after Black defends the e-pawn, d2-d4 has more oomph. As White against Sven Johannessen at Havana 1966 he secured a positional advantage after 6...d6 7 d4 ♘xb3 8 axb3 f6 9 c4 ♗b7 10 ♘c3.

6	...	exd4
7	♕xd4	♘e7
8	c3?	

Since Black is developing slowly, 8 ♘c3 or 8 0-0 are more promising. For example, 8 0-0 d6 (threatening the Noah's Ark-like ...c5-c4) can be answered by 9 ♕c3! ♘xb3 10 axb3 ♗b7 11 ♖e1 after which Black may have to castle queenside.

8	...	♘xb3
9	axb3	♗b7
10	♗f4	

More consistent was 10 b4 so that 10...d5 11 e5 leaves Black with dark-square holes. But 10...f5! is good, e.g. 11 ♘bd2 fxe4 12 ♘xe4 ♘f5.

10 ...   d5!

Now 11 exd5 ♘xd5 12 ♕e5+ ♕e7 favors Black's bishops.

11 e5   c5!

This shot, based on 12 ♕xc5?? ♘f5, greatly improves the future of the b7-bishop. It also ensures that both of White's most positionally desirable moves – b3-b4 and e5-e6 – will have to be sacrifices, and probably unsound.

12 ♕d3   ♘g6

13 ♗g3

White would love to trade this piece. For example, 13 ♗g5 ♗e7 14 ♗xe7 ♕xe7 15 ♕e3 seems only slightly in Black's favor. Black can't dodge the exchange with 13...♕d7 14 0-0 h6? because of 15 e6!.

Also 13...♕c7 14 0-0 ♘xe5 is dangerous after 15 ♘xe5 ♕xe5 16 ♕d2 and ♖e1. But 13...♗e7! is strong after all because of 14 ♗xe7 ♕xe7 15 ♕e3 d4!. For example, 16 cxd4 cxd4 17 ♘xd4 ♘h4!.

13 ...   ♗e7

14 ♘bd2   ♘f8!

White may have toyed with the idea of 14...0-0 15 h4, in order

to swap bishops with 16 h5 and 17 ♗h4. He is worse after 15...f6 16 exf6 ♗xf6 17 h5 ♖e8+ 18 ♔f1 ♘e5 but there are chances for him after a trade of minor pieces and b3-b4/ ♘f3. Better is 15...♖e8.

15 0-0   ♘e6

Black's delay in castlng means he can harass White's with ...g5-g4. On the other wing, 16 b4 cxb4 17 ♘b3 bxc3 isn't worth a pawn.

16 ♖ad1   g5!

17 h3   h5

18 ♖fe1   ♕b6

19 ♘f1   d4!

This bars White's only good maneuver, ♘e3-f5, and is based on 20 cxd4? cxd4 21 ♘xd4? ♖d8, which costs material.

20 ♘3d2   g4

21 h4

The threat was 21...h4 22 ♗h2 g3! 23 fxg3 c4! and 24...dxc3+.

21 ...   ♕c6!

Black is careful not to allow c3-c4, e.g. 21...0-0-0? 22 c4! followed by ♘e4 and ♘fd2 with chances to make a stand.

22 ♕e4?

141

Better was 22 ♘e4 0-0-0 23 c4!.

22	...	0-0-0
23	♕xc6+	♗xc6
24	c4	♔d7!

With the d-file sealed, Black's fastest winning idea is to put rooks on a8 and b8 followed by ...a5-a4 or...bxc4.

25	♖a1	♖a8
26	♘e4	♗xe4!

This rules out reinforcing the knight with ♘fd2 or getting counterplay from 26...♖hb8 27 ♘f6+ ♗xf6 28 exf6 ♖b7 29 ♘d2.

27	♖xe4	♘g7

The plausible 27...♖hb8 28 ♖a2 ♘d8, with the idea of ...♔e6 and ...♘c6-b4, is rudely interrupted by 29 e6+.

28 ♘d2?

White's survival chances are close to zero after this. Not much better is 28 f3 bxc4 29 bxc4 ♘f5 or 28 e6+ ♘xe6! 29 ♖e5 ♔c6.

This was the last moment when b3-b4 offered any hope. For example, 28 b4!? bxc4 29 bxc5 ♗xc5 30 ♖c1 or 28...♘f5 29 bxc5 ♗xc5 30 cxb5 axb5 31 ♖c1 with faint chances of a reprieve.

28	...	♘f5
29	♖f4	♔e6
30	♘e4	bxc4
31	bxc4	♖hb8

Decisive. On 32 ♖a5 ♖xb2 33 ♘xc5+ ♗xc5 34 ♖xc5 d3 White must play 35 ♖d5 d2 36 ♔f1, leaving Black to choose between 35...♖c8/36...♖xc4! and 35...a5/ 36...a4, both winning.

32	♖a2	♖b4
33	♘d2	♘xh4

Threat: 34...♗g5.

34	♗xh4	♗xh4
35	♖e4	♗g5
36	f4	gxf3
37	♘xf3	♗e3+
38	♔h2	♖xc4

White resigns

47

On the eve of the 1963-64 U.S. Championship, Evans offered this appraisal of his friend in *Chess Life*: "Fischer is a genius who is versed in all the latest wrinkles and never plays any line unless thoroughly prepared – armed with a thousand-and-one subtle opening innovations. He is stubborn, opinionated and prepared to follow the 'truth' wherever it may lead ... Another interesting sideline is that he plays about 50 percent stronger with the White pieces (it is hard to remember when he last lost with White)!" In the only previous game in which Fischer had White, Evans drew comfortably in 27 moves.

Fischer – Larry Evans
U.S. Championship,
New York 1963-64
Bishop's Gambit (C33)

1	e4	e5
2	f4!	

This move created a sensation when it was played on a demonstration board at the playing site, the Henry Hudson Hotel. Fischer had lost a well-known game to Spassky's King's Gambit at Mar del Plata 1960 and later wrote an article "A Bust to the King's Gambit" for *American Chess Quarterly*, a magazine edited by...Larry Evans.

2	...	exf4
3	♗c4	♛h4+

Fischer's choice of the Bishop's Gambit is unusual – but Evans' reply is positively bizarre. The queen check hadn't been played at the grandmaster level since Spielmann – Levenfish, Moscow 1925. Modern players prefer 3...♞f6 and/or a quick ...d5.

4	♔f1	d6
5	♞c3	♗e6!
6	♕e2	c6?!

Black's policy of containment in the center only works if he keeps the house of kingside cards intact. Better was 6...♞c6.

7	♞f3	♛e7

After 7...♛h5 White can play 8 ♞d5! with a serious edge.

8	d4	♗xc4
9	♕xc4	g5

In Fischer's "Bust" he advocated 1 e4 e5 2 f4 exf4 3 ♞f3 d6 4 d4 g5 5 ♗c4 h6. Gambit fans tried to revive the opening by attacking Black's pawns with 5 h4 g4 6 ♞g1 and ♞ge2.

A similar policy would work here – 10 h4 g4 11 ♞e1 ♗h6 12 ♞d3. But Fischer has a sharper plan.

10 e5!

In principle, White's development should warrant sacking a second pawn. But what specifically does he have after 10...dxe5 11 dxe5 ♞d7?

Black equalizes after 12 ♞e4 ♞xe5 13 ♞xe5 ♛xe5 14 ♗d2 ♛d5! as Fischer pointed out. Similarly, 11 ♞xe5 ♞d7 12 h4 ♞xe5 13 dxe5 0-0-0 14 hxg5 ♛xg5.

Most likely, Fischer would have made it a real gambit – 11 ♗d2! with the idea of 11...♞d7 12 h4 and White has promising play.

10 ... d5

If the center remains closed, Black will be overwhelmed on the kingside. That means ...f6 becomes a must after this.

11 ♕d3 ♞a6

Black can see that h2-h4 will hurt so he hurries to castle and prepare ...f6 and ...♞b4. After 11...h6 12 h4 g4 13 ♞e1 he is clearly worse, and following 12...♗g7? 13 hxg5 hxg5 14 ♖xh8 ♗xh8 15 ♕h7, he's losing.

12 ♘e2   ♘b4
13 ♕d1   0-0-0?

Again 13...h6 is strategically bankrupt (14 c3 ♘a6 15 h4 ♗g7 and now 16 ♕d3 g4 17 ♘h2 f3 18 ♘g3 followed by ♘f5 with good play.).

But Black passed up 13...f6! 14 c3 ♘a6 15 h4 g4 and ..fxe5. White should play 15 exf6 and then 15...♕xf6 16 h4 g4 17 ♘e5, e.g. 17...f3 18 ♘g3 ♗d6 19 ♗g5 with complex play.

14 c3   ♘a6
15 h4!

Now 15...f6 16 exf6 costs a pawn.

15 ...   g4
16 ♘h2   h5

Since Black's kingside will be open to invasion now, it seemed like time to scorch the earth with 16...f3 (17 gxf3 ♕xh4). But 18 fxg4 favors White.

17 ♘xf4

17 ...   ♕xh4?

Modern players tend to forget how well grounded in positional principles is the King's Gambit. Black's kingside is a mess (17...f6?

18 ♘g6; 17...♕e8? 18 ♘xh5 f5 18 ♘g3) and this pawn grab smacks of frustration. But 17...♕d7 and ...♘e7/...♘c7 offered greater resistance.

18 ♔g1!   ♘h6?

White threatened 19 ♘xg4 ♕e7 20 ♘xh5. But Black's knight is doomed on this square since it can never reach f5 and cannot be defended for long after White plays ♗e3/♕d2.

19 ♘f1   ♕e7
20 ♘xh5

Material is equal but there is nothing Black can do to stop ♘fg3, ♗e3, ♕d2, ♖f1 and eventually ♗g5 and/or ♘f6.

20 ...   ♖g8
21 ♘fg3   ♖g6
22 ♘f4   ♖g5
23 ♗e3   ♘c7

If Black tries to untangle with 23...f6, White just keeps developing pieces. e.g. 24 ♕d2 ♘c7 (24...fxe5? 25 ♘xd5 and ♗xg5) 25 ♘fh5.

24 ♕d2   ♖g8
25 ♘fe2!

White wins a piece, completing one of the most one-sided strategic routs in a King's Gambit since the 1880s.

25 ...   f6

26 exf6 ♕xf6
27 ♟xh6 ♟d6

Black didn't **resign** until after:

28 ♖f1 ♕e6 29 ♟f4 ♖de8 30 ♖h6 ♟xf4 31 ♕xf4 ♕e7 32 ♖f6 ♞e6 33 ♕e5 ♞g5 34 ♕xe7 ♖xe7 35 ♖f8+ ♖xf8 36 ♖xf8+.

48

When Mikhail Botvinnik, the paragon of preparation, was readying himself for a match with Fischer in 1970, he made an elaborate study of the American's games. Among his most telling insights is that Fischer liked "clear positions" so much that he was prepared for simplification whenever he held positional plusses. This ran counter to a common tenet of the Soviet School, that in favorable positions you should avoid exchanges unless they lead to a quickly realizable advantage. The following game shows a typical Fischer decision: At move 32 he trades queens even though there is good reason to believe he has a faster win by other means. It may be a faster win – but it's not a clearer, more certain win.

Donald Byrne – Fischer
U.S. Championship,
New York 1963-64
*Sicilian Defense, Closed Variation
(by transposition) (B25)*

1 g3 c5!

Fischer wrestled with the problem of how to answer 1 g3 since Benko surprised him with it in the first round at Curaçao. In that game Fischer replied in the same way he

would against 1 ♞f3 – with 1...♞f6, 2...g6 and 3...♟g7. But Benko used the difference in move order to play 2 ♟g2 and 3 e4! and 4 d4.

That left Fischer with a choice of playing into one of two systems new to him – a closed Sicilian (...c5) in which he had already committed a knight to f6 or a Pirc Defense. He chose the latter (...d6) and lost.

2 ♟g2 ♞c6
3 d3 g6
4 e4 ♟g7
5 f4 e6

Black is playing a Closed Sicilian with ...♞ge7 while White avoids ♞c3 in favor of ♞bd2. White's knight turns out to be more of a problem piece than Black's.

6 ♞f3 ♞ge7
7 0-0 ♖b8
8 ♞bd2 d6
9 a4 0-0

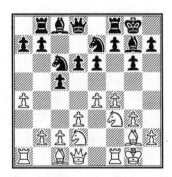

10 c3?!

White faced three questions in the opening. He answered the first at move nine when he signaled he would open the a-file after...b5. The second question was how to deal with the long term pressure on b2, and this move answers it at the cost of creating a new target at c3. The third question was how to develop the queen knight. The ♘h4/♘df3 option is modest but so is 10 ♘c4 and ♘e3 after ...a6/...b5. Byrne delays a decision.

10	...	a6
11	g4	b5
12	axb5	axb5
13	♘h4	b4!

There was no urgency for 13...f5 14 gxf5 exf5 since Black can stop f4-f5 by other means.

14 c4

White had to cede d4 because 14 ♕c2? allows 14...bxc3 15 bxc3 ♘d4! 16 ♕d1 ♘b5!.

14 ... ♘d4

The pawn structure favors Black and he can overwhelm the queenside with ...♕c7, ...♗d7 and eventually ...♖a8.

15 g5

If White had all day he might carry out an ambitious plan of ♘hf3, h2-h4-h5 and ♘h2-g4. But taking precautions with 15 ♘hf3 ♗d7 16 ♘b3 appears better.

15	...	♗d7
16	♘2f3	♕c7
17	♘xd4	♗xd4+
18	♔h1	♗g7

The bishop retreat anticipates ♘f3xd4 and clears the way for ...♘c6-d4 – if Black doesn't act in the center with...♗c6 and ...d5 instead.

19	♖b1	♖a8
20	♗e3	♖a2
21	♕d2	♖e8!

This discourages f4-f5, which would have been effective after 21...♘c6 22 f5!.

22 ♕f2 ♗c6

23 d4

The benefit of Black's 21st move is evident after 23 f5? exf5 24 exf5 ♘xf5 25 ♘xf5 gxf5 (26 ♕xf5? ♖xe3).

23	...	cxd4
24	♗xd4	♗xd4
25	♕xd4	♗a8

This is an over-finesse, since 25...♗b7 has the same plusses (such as clearing the square for ...♘c6) while avoiding the minus of a White counterattack on the a-file. It would also render Black extra options (...b3 and ...♗a6).

26 ♖a1

On 26 ♖fd1 ♖d8 27 b3 Black carries out his knight maneuver with 27...♘c6 28 ♕e3 e5 29 f5 ♘d4 with advantage.

26 ... e5!

After 26...e5 27 fxe5 dxe5 28 ♕f2 Black has 28...♕xc4, protecting f7. Note that 26...♖xa1 27 ♖xa1 e5 could transpose into the game, particularly since 28 ♖a7 exd4 29 ♖xc7 loses to 29...d3!.

27 ♕d2

Not 27 ♕f2 ♖xa1 28 ♖xa1 ♕xc4.

27 ... ♖xa1

28 ♖xa1 exf4

Black keeps his d-pawn (rather than 28...♕xc4 29 ♕xd6) because it will support the new outpost at e5.

29 b3 ♘c6

30 ♕xf4?

White should insert 30 ♘f3, not fearing 30...♘e5 31 ♘xe5 dxe5 32 ♕xb4 ♖b8 33 ♕a5!.

30 ... ♘d4

31 ♕e3!

Black begins to pluck pawns after 31 ♖b1 ♕e7.

31 ... ♘c2!

Not 31...♘f5? 32 exf5!. Black can also play for a win with 31...♕c5 but the text gives him a choice of two winning lines.

32 ♕a7

White loses the *desperado* contest after 32 ♖a7 ♕xc4!.

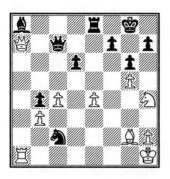

32 ... ♕xa7

Black's endgame is so easily won after this that it is hard to criticize Fischer for passing up the chance to win faster with 32...♗b7!. That threatens 33...♖a8 as well as 33...♘xa1. For example, 33 ♖a4 ♖a8 34 ♕f2 ♖xa4 35 bxa4 b3. The key tactic is ...♖xe4!, and it appears in variations such as 33 ♖c1 ♖xe4! 34 ♕f2 ♕e7 (35 ♗xe4 ♗xe4+ 36 ♘f3 ♘d4) and 33 ♕a5 ♕c8 34 ♖f1 ♘e3!.

33 ♖xa7 ♘d4

34 ♖d7

After 34 ♖a4 Black can win with 34...♘xb3 35 ♖xb4 ♘d2 but much better is 34...♖b8!. Then 35 e5 ♗xg2+ 36 ♔xg2 dxe5 37 ♘f3 is refuted by 37...♘xb3 38 ♘xe5 ♘c5 and the b-pawn runs on.

34 ... ♘xb3

35 ♖xd6 ♘c5

36 ♖b6 b3

37 ♔g1 ♗xe4!

Again Black chooses the clearest. Of course, 37...♘xe4 38 ♖xb3 ♘xg5 should win eventually but now the b-pawn must win material.

38 ♘f3 ♖a8!

Superior to 38...♗c2 39 ♖b5 and ♘d4 White can now avoid Black's combination with 39 ♔f1 but after 39...♖a2 he can safely resign.

39 ♖b5 b2

40 ♖xb2 ♖a1+

41 ♔f2 ♘d3+

The game ended with:

42 ♔e3 ♘xb2 43 ♔xe4 ♘xc4 44 ♔f4 ♖a2 45 ♔g3 ♘d6 46 ♗h3 and **White resigns**

49

Despite his 11-0 victory in the U.S. Championship, Fischer refused his invitation to the next Interzonal, at Amsterdam, because he considered the top prize of $300 too low. Just before the tournament began in May 1964 Fischer was interviewed by a Moscow correspondent of the Russian news service APN. Their brief Q & A went:

"But this deprives you of the chance to fight for the world championship title for at least three years."

"I know."

"What provoked your decision?"

"I don't want to play."

In fact, he didn't return to serious chess for 19 months, until the Capablanca Memorial in August 1965. It was Tal who captured the absurdity of the situation: For once, Bobby wanted to play chess – but someone else stopped him. He was barred by U.S. passport authorities from traveling to Fidel Castro's island. (It was not the last time he would come into conflict with the State Department.)

But extraordinary arrangements were made for him to play by long distance. Fischer sat at what was known as the "Capablanca table," a favorite of the Cuban, in the sealed off, back room on the Marshall Chess Club's second floor, with a window to his left so he could look out on the club's backyard. As usual following Fischer's absences, he returned with openings that were new to him – as well as ideas in heavily-analyzed lines very familiar.

Karl Robatsch – Fischer
Capablanca Memorial,
Havana 1965
Sicilian Defense,
Najdorf Variation 6 ♗c4 (B86)

1	e4	c5
2	♘f3	d6
3	d4	cxd4
4	♘xd4	♘f6
5	♘c3	a6
6	♗c4	e6
7	a3	

By securing the bishop a sniper's nest at a2, he solves White's most pressing problem in the opening but at the cost of a tempo. Fischer, who understood the arcana of 6 ♗c4 better than anyone, believed the tempo mattered. A year later at the Havana Olympiad he challenged Stein to a skittles game and after 7 ♗b3 ♗e7 8 f4! b5 9 f5 e5 10 ♘de2 ♗b7 11 0-0 he told Stein in Russian that Black's position was hopeless.

7	...	♗e7
8	0-0	0-0
9	♗a2	b5
10	f4	♗b7
11	f5	

Robatsch, then the leading advocate of 7 a3, used to like 11 e5 until it was found that 11...dxe5 12 fxe5 ♘d5 13 ♘e4 ♘b4! equalizes.

11	...	e5
12	♘de2	♘bd7

Black's weapons include pressure on the c-file and against e4, the blocking maneuver of ...♘bd7-b6-c4, and the wrecking power of a sacrifice on c3. But taking the e-pawn this early is toxic – 12...♘xe4?

13 ♘xe4 ♗xe4 14 ♘g3 ♗b7 15 f6!
♗xf6 16 ♘h5, e.g. 16...♗e7 17 ♕g4
g6 18 ♗h6.

13 ♘g3   ♖c8

The Exchange "sac" is in the air
now, e.g. 14 ♘h5? ♘xh5 15 ♕xh5
♖xc3! 16 bxc3 ♘f6 and ...♘xe4
leaves White with a position only a
computer would love.

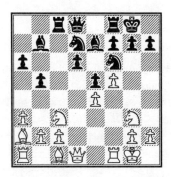

14 ♗e3

White must give up a bishop for a
knight. But where? On b6, as in the
game, on c4 (after ...♘b6-c4) or on
f6? For example, 14 ♗g5 ♘b6
15 ♗xf6 ♗xf6 16 ♖f3 and then
16...♘c4 17 ♗xc4 ♖xc4 18 ♖d3.
At the 1959 Candidates tournament
Olafsson tried to preserve his
bishops and played 15 ♘h5. But
then instead of Fischer's unsound
15...♖xc3? Black should equalize
with 15...♘c4!.

14 ...   ♘b6

White's 14th move was a novelty,
although hardly a major surprise,
and Fischer thought 17 minutes over
this.

15 ♗xb6

Black has an easy game after
15 ♔h1 ♘c4 16 ♗xc4 ♖xc4 and

...♕a8. By eliminating the knight
this way White can secure control of
d5 with ♘h5xf6+.

15 ...   ♕xb6+
16 ♔h1   ♕e3!

The queen hinders virtually all
White plans here, and if driven back
to h6 or g5, it will stop ♘h5 and
threaten ...♘g4. For example, 17 ♖f3
♕h6 18 ♕e2 ♖c5 19 ♖d1 ♖fc8 and
...a5. Or 17 ♘h5 ♘xe4 18 ♕g4
♕g5! and 18 ♘d5 ♗xd5 19 ♗xd5
♗g5!. Robatsch took 45 minutes
trying to find a solution.

17 ♘d5   ♗xd5!

Black preserves his best kingside
defensive piece.

18 ♗xd5   ♗d8

This seemed more promising than
18...♘xd5 19 exd5 ♗h4 20 ♖f3
(20 ♘h5 f6!) ♕h6 21 ♘e4 when it's
not clear how Black can improve
his position. But 20...♕d4! seeks a
very good endgame, 21 c3 ♕xd1+
22 ♖xd1 ♗xg3 22 ♖xg3 f6.

19 a4

White needs a new target since
Black has too free a hand after 19 c3
or 19 ♗b3 – and because 19 ♗b7?
♖c7 20 ♗xa6? ♕b6 costs a piece.

19 ...   ♗b6
20 axb5

There is no bishop-trap now after
20 ♗b7 but 20...♖c4, threatening
...♖xa4 or ...♖d4, is strong.

20 ...   axb5
21 ♖a6

White finally appears ready for
♖f3.

21 ...   b4!

But it turns out that 22 ♖f3 is met by 22...♘g4! and 23...♘f2+.

22 ♘h5

White can batten down the hatches with 22 ♗b3 ♗c5 23 ♕f3 but Black retains an edge after 23...♕d4. Robatsch's move was based on a trap: 22...♘xh5 23 ♕xh5 ♖xc2, and now 24 ♕xf7+! wins.

22 ...   ♘xd5

23 ♕g4

Superior to 23 ♕xd5 ♖xc2 and 24...♖c1 (or 24 ♕xd6?? ♕e2) – but not as scary as it appears.

The optical problem with 23 exd5! is that it junks the theme of exploiting d5 but doesn't get enough tactical compensation. But this was White's best chance, e.g. 23...♖c4 24 ♕d3!.

23 ...   g6

24 exd5   ♖xc2

Now 25 ♘f6+ ♔g7 26 ♖xb6 fails to 26...♖c1!. In fact, Black's king is as safe as White's now. For example, 25 ♘f6+ ♔g7 26 ♘e4 h5! 27 f6+ ♔h6! or 27 ♕h4 ♖c1 28 ♕f6+? ♔h6 (and 28 ♖a1 ♖xa1 29 ♖xa1 ♖c8 30 f6+ ♔g8) is poor.

25 fxg6   hxg6

26 ♘f6+   ♔g7

27 ♘h5+

White must acquiesce to a bad ending 27 ♕h4 ♖f2! (28 ♕xf2 ♕xf2 29 ♖xf2 ♗xf2 30 ♖xd6 ♖a8). Note the many land mines in this position. After 27 ♕h4 Black would draw after 27...♖h8? 28 ♘e8+! ♖xe8 29 ♕f6+ ♔h6 30 ♕h4+ – or lose after 28...♔g8?? 29 ♕f6 ♖h7 30 ♖a8!.

27 ...   ♔h6!

Once again this square is remarkably safe.

28 ♘f6   ♖f2

This stops 29 ♕h4+ ♔g7 30 ♕h7 mate.

29 ♖aa1   ♖a8!

Role reversal: Instead of an attacker stretching the defender's pieces beyond their limits, here the defender does the stretching (and the threatening, 30...♖xa1).

30 ♕xb4   ♔g7

Black avoids the final pair of traps – 30...♖xf6? 31 ♕h4+ and 30...♖xa1 31 ♘g4+ ♔g5?? (31...♔g7!) 32 h4+!.

31 ♕xd6

On 31 ♘g4 Black has a choice between a won ending (31...♕f4 32 ♕xf4 ♖xf4 33 h3 ♖xf1+

150

34 ♖xf1 f5) and a won middlegame (31...♖xf1+ 32 ♖xf1 ♕d3 since 33 ♕e1 f5 34 ♘xe5 dxe5 35 ♕xe5+ ♔h6 36 ♕f4+ g5! fizzles).

31	...	♕e2
32	♘e8+	♖xe8
33	♖fe1	♕g4

White resigns

Members of the Najdorf cult know the Postscript: After the game Robatsch telephoned New York to ask where he went wrong. Fischer replied, "The whole variation is worthless."

50

Even numbers figured prominently in Fischer's performance at the Capablanca Memorial: In the field of 22, Fischer began with two victories, including an elegant endgame win from Smyslov in the second round. His shortest game was a 22-move win over Tringov. In the even-number rounds Fischer suffered two losses. This game was played in the 16th round on Sept. 16. And in the end, he finished second, in a tie with two other grandmasters.

Fischer – Jan Hein Donner
Capablanca Memorial,
Havana 1965
Ruy Lopez, Marshall Attack (C89)

1	e4	e5
2	♘f3	♘c6
3	♗b5	a6
4	♗a4	♘f6
5	0-0	♗e7
6	♖e1	b5
7	♗b3	0-0

8	c3	d5
9	exd5	♘xd5

Fischer demolished Seidman in the 1960-61 U.S. Championship in the once-wild 9...e4 10 dxc6 exf3 line. Play went 11 ♕xf3 ♗g4 12 ♕g3 ♗d6 13 f4 g5? 14 d4 ♔h8 15 ♖e5! gxf4 16 ♗xf4 ♘h5 17 ♖xh5! ♗xh5 18 ♘d2 with a big positional edge.

10	♘xe5	♘xe5
11	♖xe5	c6
12	d4	♗d6
13	♖e1	♕h4
14	g3	♕h3
15	♗e3	

15	...	♗g4

"An interesting, scarcely explored alternative possibility" is 15...h5, wrote Leonard Barden in a 1963 book on the Ruy Lopez. He cited the game Boleslavsky – Saigin, Minsk 1961 in which Black obtained excellent play after 16 ♕f3 h4 17 ♘d2 ♗g4 18 ♕g2 hxg3 19 fxg3 ♕h5.

But this new idea disappeared after one test in international chess, and it came in the sixth round at Havana. Fischer improved against R.G.Wade with 17 ♗xd5! cxd5

18 ♘d2 ♗e6 19 ♗f4. Although they drew – after 19...♗g4 20 ♕g2!? ♕xg2+ 21 ♔xg2 h3+ 22 ♔g1 ♗xf4 – there was no GM interest in 15...h5 after that.

16 ♕d3   ♘xe3!?
17 ♖xe3   c5

This was Geller's new positional treatment of the Marshall, an attempt to improve over the hyper-analyzed 16...♖ae8 and 17...♖e6.

18 ♗d5

The delayed fianchetto is attractive but Fischer felt it was inferior to 18 ♕f1! ♕h6 19 ♘d2 and ♘f3, which gave him a winning edge (that he squandered) against Donner a year later at the second Piatigorsky Cup.

18 ...   ♖ad8
19 ♘d2   ♗b8?

Better was 19...♗c7 because...

20 ♗g2   ♕h6

21 d5!

...then this would have been refuted by 21...c4 22 ♕d4? ♗b6.

Fischer's move improves over 21 ♖ae1, which Ciocaltea used to draw with Geller in this tournament after 21...cxd4 22 cxd4 ♗a7 23 ♘b3 ♗e6 and ...♗xb3.

Theory hasn't advanced much since 1965 and Geller's innovation remains unclear after 19...♗c7 20 ♗g2 ♕h6 21 ♘f3 ♗b6. Play could peter out with a repetition of moves – 22 ♘e5 ♗e6 23 ♘f3 ♗g4 (but White can keep matters alive with 23 ♘c6 cxd4 24 cxd4 ♖d6 25 ♖ae1).

21 ...   c4

This was sharply criticized but if White is allowed to play 22 ♖ae1 or 22 c4 the game is strategically decided. For example, 21...♖d6 22 c4! f5 23 f4 and 24 ♖ae1 leaves Black without play. Or 21...f5 22 ♖e7 f4 23 ♘e4.

22 ♕d4   ♗f5

Now 22...f5 allows 23 ♖e6 since 23...♕xe6 24 dxe6 ♖xd4 25 cxd4 f4 26 d5! is a hopeless ending. But 22...♗h3, to pressure d5 after ...♗xg2 and ...♕h5, was a better try.

23 b3!   ♖c8?

It seems that 23...cxb3 24 axb3 and 25 c4 only helps White. But Black overlooked the possible blockade of 24...♖d7 25 c4 bxc4 26 bxc4 ♖c8 and ...♗c5. For example, 27 c5 ♗a7 28 ♕c4 ♖dc7! (not 28...♗xc5? 29 ♕xc5) and now 29 d6? ♗xc5? 30 dxc7! ♗xe3 31 ♘e4. But 29...♖xc5! turns the game around. Better for White is 29 ♖ae1 with a last-rank mate threat. After 29...♖d7 White would win with 30 c6 ♗xe3 31 ♖xe3 because of his passed pawns.

24 bxc4   ♗d6

Black threatens 25...♗c5, for example 25 ♖f3 ♗c5 (not 25...♗g4? 26 ♕xg4 ♕xd2 27 ♖xf7!) 26 ♕f4

♕xf4 27 ♖xf4 ♗d3 with untidy complications.

25 ♕b6! ♗f4

Otherwise White pockets another pawn.

26 ♕xh6 ♗xh6

27 f4 g5

This only looks strong when compared to 27...bxc4 28 ♗f1.

28 ♖e5 ♗d3

Black is left with at least the will to resist after 29 fxg5 ♗g7; 29 cxb5 axb5 30 d6 ♖xc3 and 29 ♗h3 ♖ce8. Fischer spent 16 minutes to decide on:

29 c5!! ♖xc5

30 d6

Black's rook is attacked and 30...♖xe5 31 fxe5 g4 is lost after 32 ♘b3 ♗e3+ 33 ♔h1 ♗c4 34 ♖d1.

30 ... ♖xc3

31 d7 gxf4

32 ♖ae1

Or 32 ♖e8 ♗g5 33 ♖ae1 fxg3 34 hxg3 ♖c2 and now 35 ♘f3 ♗f6 36 ♖d1! and wins.

32 ... ♗g7

33 ♖e8 ♗d4+

34 ♔h1 ♗f6

Or 34...♗b6 35 gxf4 and ♖g1, as in the game.

35 gxf4! Resigns

Opening the file decides (35... ♗f5 36 ♖g1 and ♗h3+).

51

Today when the chief defense to 1 e4 of many leading GMs is the Petroff or the Ruy Lopez Berlin Defense, it's hard to recall how for more than a decade Fischer regularly exposed himself to the risks of the Poisoned Pawn Variation. His opponents knew the likelihood of facing a Najdorf Sicilian was extremely high when facing Fischer. And they knew, since 1962, that he would meet 6 ♗g5 with 6...e6 7 f4 ♕b6, the sharpest response to the sharpest attack. Yet despite the theoretical minefield this created for him, Fischer always seemed to be ready to accept a challenge against a heavily prepared opponent. Case in point:

Georgy Tringov – Fischer
Capablanca Memorial,
Havana 1965
*Sicilian Defense,
Najdorf Variation 6 ♗g5 (B97)*

1 e4 c5

Fischer took 17 minutes over this – only because he arrived late.

2 ♘f3 d6

3 d4 cxd4

4 ♘xd4 ♘f6

5 ♘c3 a6

6 ♗g5 e6

7 f4 ♕b6

8	♕d2	♕xb2
9	♖b1	♕a3
10	e5	dxe5
11	fxe5	♘fd7
12	♗c4	♗b4
13	♖b3	

The heavy sacrifices can begin with 13 ♘xe6 – e.g. 13...♗xc3 14 ♘c7+ ♔f8 15 0-0! ♕c5+ 16 ♕e3! ♕xc4 17 e6! with a virulent attack.

But Black refutes 13...fxe6 14 ♖xb4 ♕xb4 15 ♗xe6 with 15...h6!. For instance, 16 ♗f7+ ♔xf7 17 ♕d5+ ♔g6 18 ♕d3+ ♔h5!.

Trickier is 15 0-0 in that last line, with the idea of 15...♕xc4 16 ♘e4! ♕xe4 17 ♕d6!. But again Black has a winning defense in 15...♕c5+! 16 ♖f2 ♕xc4 17 ♘e4 ♕xe4 18 ♕d6 because there is 18...♕e1+ 19 ♖f1 ♕xf1+! 20 ♔xf1 ♖f8+ and 21...♔f7.

13	...	♕a5
14	0-0	0-0

Three months later in the 1965-66 U.S. Championship, Robert Byrne sprung a spectacular prepared line, 15 ♗f6! gxf6 16 ♕h6!. But his opponent wasn't Fischer, as he had hoped – it was Evans, who lost after 16...♕xe5 17 ♘f5!! exf5 18 ♘e4 and ♖g3+.

What Fischer had in mind isn't certain but his close friend Bernard Zuckerman faced 15 ♗f6 in the next U.S. Championship and defeated Byrne in the endgame following 15...♘xf6! 16 exf6 ♖d8 17 ♖xb4! ♕xb4 18 ♕g5 g6 19 ♖f4! ♖xd4! 20 ♕h6 ♕f8.

Tringov evidently had an improvement because he repeated Byrne's moves against Palmasson in the 1966 Olympiad and won because Black varied with 19...b6 and then 20 ♖h4 ♕f8 21 ♕e3 ♖a7 22 ♘e4 ♖ad7?? 23 ♖xh7! Resigns (23...♔xh7 24 ♘g5+ and ♕h3-h7 mate).

15 ♘xe6?!

Another ingenious try which had worked well before. One 1964 game went 15...♘c5 16 ♘xf8 ♘xb3 17 ♗xf7+ ♔h8 18 ♘g6+! hxg6 19 ♕f4 and mates (19...♕c5+ 20 ♔h1 ♕d4 21 ♘e4).

15	...	fxe6
16	♗xe6+	♔h8

The attack dies now after 17 ♖fb1 ♗xc3.

17	♖xf8+	♗xf8

Black is probably also winning after 17...♘xf8 18 ♗xc8 ♘c6 (19 ♗xb7 ♕b6+ 20 ♕e3 ♕xb7 21 a3 ♗xc3 22 ♖xb7 ♗d4) but this is more direct.

18 ♕f4

All this had been analyzed, in Russia and elsewhere, to the conclusion that the ♕f7-g8 mate threat forced 18...♕xe5, with the idea of 19 ♕f7 ♕e1+. But that left White at least equal following

---

19 ♕xe5 and ♗xc8.

If Black tries 18...♕c5+, White has 19 ♔f1! (not 19 ♔h1 ♘c6 20 ♘e4 ♕xc2 threatening ...♕d1+ and mates) and here Gulko – Dubinin, Moscow 1963, ended in a win for White after 19...♘c6 20 ♘e4 and ♕f7. A key point is that 19...♘f6 allows 20 ♗xc8!.

18 ...   ♘c6!

The attack turns traitor.

19 ♕f7

19 ...   ♕c5+

20 ♔h1

Now on 20 ♔f1 as in Gulko – Dubinin, Black has 20...♘f6 21 ♗xc8 ♘xe5 22 ♕e6 ♘eg4, threatening 23...♕f2 mate and 23...♕xc8.

There's an ingenious alternative in 20 ♗e3!?, to deflect the queen. Black then might dream of a brilliancy prize with 20...♘f6 21 ♗xc5 ♗xc5+ 22 ♔h1 ♘xe5 23 ♕c7 ♗xe6. But after 24 ♕xc5 ♗xb3 25 axb3 White is winning. In fact, 20 ♗e3 is refuted simply by 20...♕xe3+ 21 ♔f1 ♕c1+ 22 ♔e2 ♘d4+ and ...♘xe6, or 22 ♔f2 ♗c5+.

20 ...   ♘f6!

The killer: 21 exf6 ♗xe6 22 fxg7+ ♗xg7 23 ♕xe6 ♕xg5 and Black wins. Also 21 ♗xf6 ♗xe6 22 ♕xe6 gxf6 23 ♕xf6+ ♗g7.

21 ♗xc8   ♘xe5!

22 ♕e6   ♘eg4

White resigns

He had no defense to the threats of 23...♘f2+ and 23...♖xc8. As in Game 29, White drowned in Najdorf complications that had been navigated well in advance by Fischer. This time White took two hours and 20 minutes, Black just over one hour.

52

Jacqueline Piatigorsky made it clear there wouldn't be a second Piatigorsky Cup in 1966 if Fischer refused his invitation as he had in 1963. This time Fischer said yes – but he was clearly rusty. After the first half of the double-round tournament he was alone in next-to-last place, with a 3½-5½ score, and appeared headed for his worst result since 1959. Fischer's turnaround began in the 10th round:

Fischer – Samuel Reshevsky
Second Piatigorsky Cup,
Santa Monica 1966
Ruy Lopez (C92)

1	e4	e5
2	♘f3	♘c6
3	♗b5	a6
4	♗a4	♘f6
5	0-0	♗e7
6	♖e1	b5
7	♗b3	d6
8	c3	0-0
9	h3	♘d7

The Tchigorin maneuver enjoyed a brief revival in the period 1955-68 but with the idea of giving up, rather than fortifying, the center.

10	d4	♘b6
11	♘bd2	exd4
12	cxd4	d5

Black solves his QB problem after 13 e5 ♗f5.

13 ♗c2!

But 13...dxe4 14 ♗xe4 favors White solidly (14...♘d5 15 ♕c2), as does 13...♘b4 14 ♗b1 dxe4 15 ♗xe4 ♘4d5 16 ♘b3 because of the stellar outpost for the knight at c5.

13	...	♗e6
14	e5	♕d7

After 14...♘b4 15 ♗b1 c5 White secures a different outpost, d4, with 16 dxc5 ♗xc5 17 ♘b3 ♗e7 18 ♘fd4. Then he can operate with threats of pushing his f-pawn or capturing on e6 followed by ♕g4.

15 ♘b3 ♗f5

But here if White occupies c5 with a pawn – 16 ♘c5 ♗xc5 17 ♗xf5

♕xf5 18 dxc5 – he has no more than equality after 18...♘d7! 19 ♕xd5 ♘b4 20 ♕e4 ♕xe4 21 ♖xe4 ♘c2 22 ♖b1 ♘xc5.

16 ♗g5

So that 16...♗xg5 17 ♘xg5 h6 is met by 18 e6! fxe6 19 ♘c5 with a big edge.

16 ... ♖fe8?

This is a poor attempt to improve on a 1959 Spassky – Tal game that went 16...♗b4 17 ♖e2 ♖fe8 18 ♖c1 ♘c4 19 ♘a1! with advantage to White. Reshevsky called his move a "tactical error...from which I was unable to recover," hinting that he overlooked White's 20th move. Best may be 16...f6 17 exf6 ♗xf6 although 18 ♘c5 and ♖c1 assure White a positional pull.

17 ♗xe7 ♖xe7

18 ♖c1!

White's superiority would be obvious after 18...♗xc2 19 ♕xc2 ♘b4 20 ♕d2 a5 21 a3.

18 ... ♘b4

But with only a pair of knights left, Black can live with 19 ♗xf5 ♕xf5 20 a3 ♘d3 21 ♕c2 ♕g6 22 ♘h4 ♕g5 23 ♕xd3 ♕xh4.

19 ♘c5! ♗xc2

The addition of ♘c5 makes itself felt after 19...♕c8 20 ♗xf5 ♕xf5 and now 21 ♕b3 ♘c6 22 ♘xa6.

20 ♕d2!!

Clearly better than 20 ♘xd7 ♗xd1 21 ♘xb6 cxb6 22 ♖exd1 ♘xa2. White would retain some edge with 20 ♖xc2 ♕f5 21 ♖ce2 since 21...♘xa2? 22 ♕b3 traps the knight. But the text ensures a huge disparity in minor pieces.

20 ... ♕e8

By protecting the rook Black avoids 20...♕c8 21 ♕xb4 ♗g6 22 ♘xa6.

21 ♕xb4 a5

22 ♕c3 ♗g6

Reshevsky rejected 22...♗f5 because of 23 ♘h4 ♗c8 24 f4. There would be scant hope of salvation after 24...♕d8 25 f5 ♖e8 26 ♕g3.

23 ♘h4! ♘a4

In the tournament book Reshevsky said he took "desperate measures," apparently hoping for play such as 24 ♘xa4 bxa4 25 ♕a3 ♖b8 26 ♖c5 ♖b4! 27 ♖xd5 ♕a8.

24 ♕b3! ♘xc5

25 ♖xc5 c6

26 ♖ec1 ♖e6

27 f4! f5

A supremely ugly move but 27...♗e4 28 f5 ♖h6 29 ♕g3 and 30 f6 was lost.

28 a4

White wants to inflict maximum damage on the queenside before harvest time. But 28 ♕c2 ♖a6 29 g4 was safe enough to win.

28 ... bxa4

29 ♕xa4 ♖b8

30 ♕a3 ♕d8

31 ♘xg6 hxg6

Now 32 ♖xa5 ♖xb2!.

32 ♖xc6 ♖xc6

33 ♖xc6 ♕h4

34 ♖xg6?

Fischer likely saw that 34...♕xf4 loses to 35 ♕e7! since on 35...♕c1+ 36 ♔h2 ♕f4+ he wins with 37 ♖g3 ♕h6 38 e6 ♖f8 39 ♕d7 and e6-e7.

But 34 ♕d6! was better because Black has set a devilish trap...

34 ... ♔h7!

35 ♖g5 ♖b4?

...that would have drawn after 35...♕xf4 36 ♕e7 ♖g8! preparing 37...♔h6!. Then 37 ♖h5+ ♔g6 38 ♖h4 ♕e3+ 39 ♔h2 ♖h8! 40 ♖xh8 ♕f4+ is perpetual check.

36	♕f3!	♚h6
37	g3!	♕xh3
38	♕xd5	**Resigns**

In view of 38...♖xb2 39 ♕e6+ ♚h7 40 ♕g6+ and mates, or 38...♖b6 39 ♕g8.

53

Most international players are forced to overhaul their opening repertoire as they age because their favorite variations have become too familiar or neutralized by new ideas. Fischer's problem with his favourite Black lines was different: By the mid-1960s he was too strong for some of them. Solid variations that he used to equalize when he was a teenager were no longer appropriate when grandmasters were playing to draw with him from move one. For example, the Fianchetto Variation of the King's Indian with 6...♘c6:

Jan Hein Donner – Fischer
Second Piatigorsky Cup,
Santa Monica 1966
King's Indian Defense,
Fianchetto Variation (E68)

1	d4	♘f6
2	c4	g6
3	g3	♗g7
4	♗g2	0-0
5	♘c3	d6
6	♘f3	♘bd7

Fischer helped popularize 6...♘c6 7 0-0 e5, which offers sharp middlegames after 9 d5 ♘e7 or an ending after 9 dxe5 ♘xe5 10 ♘xe5 dxe5 10 ♗g5 ♕xd1 11 ♖axd1 c6. He

had even beaten Donner in the 9 dxe5 line at Zürich 1959 – but that required many little mistakes by White. In fact, Darga – Fischer, Bled 1961 was drawn soon after 11...c6, and not long afterwards Fischer swore off grandmaster draws and adopted 6...♘bd7.

7	0-0	e5
8	e4	c6
9	♖b1	

Donner was impressed when Portisch played this move against Najdorf in the first round of the Piatigorsky tournament and got an excellent game after 9...♖e8 10 h3 a5 11 ♖e1 exd4 12 ♘xd4 ♘c5 13 ♗f4.

9	...	a6!

A fine waiting move, which prepares ...b5 as in an Old Indian, as well as ...exd4/...c5 followed by ...♘e5 and ....♗e6.

10 b4?

This concedes c4 without much in return.

10	...	exd4
11	♘xd4	♖e8

Now 12 ♕c2 ♘e5 allows Black fine play (13 ♘a4 b5 or 13 ♘ce2 b5).

12 h3   ♘e5

13 ♕e2   b5!

14 cxb5   cxb5!

Capturing toward the center is also quite good, since 14...axb5 15 f4 could be answered by 15...♘c4 (16 ♘xc6? ♕b6+), or 15...♕b6 (16 fxe5 dxe5 or 16 ♗e3 ♘c4 17 ♗f2 ♕a6) or even 15...♘h5!?. But Black's idea is to exert pressure on e4 and the c-file with ...♗b7 and ...♖c8.

15 ♖d1

An instinctive move – but this rook will be needed to defend the e-pawn while the other rook ends up looking silly on b3.

15 ...   ♗b7

16 f4?

There was no ideal square for the QB but the text is grossly weakening. Rudolf Marić likened White's position to a soap bubble: "It expands until it explodes."

16 ...   ♘c4

Black threatens 17...♘xe4 18 ♘xe4 f5.

17 ♕d3   ♖c8

18 ♔h2

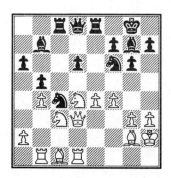

18 ...   ♕c7!

Black will batter the e-pawn with ...♕b8-a8 and ...♖e7/...♖ce8 – and displays great care by choosing this move over 18...♕b6. One difference is 18...♕c7 stops 19 ♗b2 (19...♘xb2 20 ♖xb2 ♕xc3). Another is that 19 ♘b3, with the idea of ♘d2xc4, can be met by 19...♘a3! 20 ♗xa3 ♕xc3 – since 21 ♕xc3 ♖xc3 22 e5 fails to 22...♗xg2 23 exf6 ♗e4.

19 ♖b3

A cheerless move. Donner later said he should have tried 19 ♘d5 and dream of ♘c6 after 19...♘xd5 20 exd5. But Black obtains a commanding position by 20...♗xd4! (or 20...♘b6!) 21 ♕xd4 ♖e2, e.g. 22 f5 ♘e5 or 22 ♗b2 ♘xb2 23 ♖xb2 ♖xb2 24 ♕xb2 ♕c2 25 ♖d2 ♕xb2 26 ♖xb2 ♖c3.

19 ...   ♖e7!

20 ♖e1   ♖ce8

Now 21 ♖e2, preparing ♘d5, is answered by 21...♕b8, e.g. 22 ♘d5 ♘xd5 23 exd5 ♖xe2 24 ♘xe2 ♕a7! with a punishing threat of ...♕f2 (25 ♕f3 ♗xd5 26 ♕xd5 ♖xe2 or 25 ♘c3 ♕f2 26 ♘e4 ♕xa2).

21 ♘c2   ♕c8!

Virtually winning a pawn. White should at least try 22 ♘a3 – as ugly as that looks (22...♘xa3 23 ♖xa3 ♖c7 and ...♖c4-d4, or 22...♕a8 23 ♘xc4 bxc4 24 ♕xc4 d5). Note the subtle difference in queen moves. This one is better than 21...♕b8 because...

22 ♘e3   ♘xe3!

23 ♖xe3

23 ...   ♘xe4

...now 24 ♘xe4 ♗xe4 25 ♖xe4 ♖xe4 26 ♗xe4 allows 26...♕xc1. That would win despite the bishops of opposite color (27 ♖b1 ♕c4 or 27 ♗d5 ♖e1 and ...♖d1).

24 ♗xe4   ♗xe4

25 ♕xd6?   ♖d7

White can resign: 26 ♕xd7 ♕xd7 27 ♖xe4 ♖xe4 28 ♘xe4 ♕d1 etc.

26 ♕c5   ♖c7

27 ♘xe4   ♖xc5

28 ♘xc5   ♗d4

White resigns

54

In an interview in *New In Chess* in 1990, Lajos Portisch recalled how he and Fischer once compared notes about their methods of study: "Lajos, is it true that you work eight hours a day?" the American asked. "And I said, 'Why are you asking? People also think you work eight hours a day.' Then Bobby said, 'Oh, yes, but they think I am crazy.'" Ever since they first met at Bled 1961 Fischer had been giving the Hungarian lessons in the opening and ending. But at Santa Monica, it was a difference in their

understanding about piece values that stood out.

Lajos Portisch – Fischer
Second Piatigorsky Cup,
Santa Monica 1966
Nimzo-Indian Defense (E45)

1 d4   ♘f6

2 c4   e6

3 ♘c3   ♗b4

4 e3   b6

5 ♘e2   ♗a6

6 ♘g3

Since the main point of Rubinstein's 4 e3 was to break the pin with 5 ♘e2 and 6 a3 Fischer made a valid point when he criticized this as inconsistent. But 6 a3 ♗xc3+ 7 ♘xc3 d5 was known to be inoffensive after 8 b3 0-0 9 a4 ♘c6.

When Evans tried to create a bind against him in the 1965-66 U.S. championship with 10 ♗e2 dxc4 11 ♗a3! ♖e8 12 b4, Fischer broke out in memorable fashion. First he played 12...♘e7 13 0-0 ♘ed5 14 ♖c1 c6 15 ♗f3 b5 16 a5 ♕c7 17 ♕c2 ♖ad8 18 ♖fd1 ♗b7 and then confounded his opponent with 19 ♖d2 ♘xc3 20 ♕xc3 c5!!. The threats of ...♗xf3 and ...cxd4 gave him a decisive edge.

6 ...   ♗xc3+!

The 1965 edition of *Modern Chess Openings* gave three alternatives that favored White (6...h5, 6...♘c6 and 6...c5) and one that allegedly equalized (6...0-0), but no mention of this, today's main line.

7 bxc3   d5

8 ♕f3   0-0

9 e4

Nimzo-Indian players have had to master positions like 9 cxd5 exd5 10 ♗xa6 ♘xa6 11 ♕e2 ♕c8 12 0-0 c5 ever since Botvinnik won the game of his life against Capablanca at AVRO 1938. Fischer felt this version was equal and later experience with 13 ♗b2 and 13 f3 supported him.

9	...	dxe4
10	♘xe4	♘xe4
11	♕xe4	♕d7!!

A stunningly nonchalant move – and, Portisch confessed, "a very unpleasant surprise." He had only considered 11...♘d7 12 ♗d3 ♘f6 13 ♕h4. But Fischer's move offers a temporary rook sacrifice (12 ♕xa8 ♘c6) knowing that the queen will be trapped and have to give herself up for the other rook.

Primers teach beginners that a queen and a pawn is equal to two rooks. Despite this, many masters prefer having the rooks. Yet Fischer readily went into endings with the queen and an extra pawn – and won, e.g. versus Bisguier, Stockholm Interzonal 1962, Donald Byrne, Western Open 1963, and versus Bilek, Havana 1965.

12 ♗a3

White is positionally worse after 12 ♗d3 f5 13 ♕e2 ♘c6 and ...♘a5.

12	...	♖e8
13	♗d3	

Fischer recommended 13 0-0-0 as more "consistent"(!).

13	...	f5

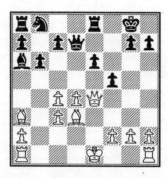

14 ♕xa8

And he called this "very bad judgment." White's pawn at c4, will be condemned once there is no white queen to defend it. Then the rooks-plus-bishop are no match for queen-plus-knight.

Portisch's *mea culpa* was that he realized how bad his position was and thought this was his best drawing chance. For example, 14 ♕e2 ♘c6 15 0-0 e5 16 d5 e4 is awful for White.

14	...	♘c6
15	♕xe8+	♕xe8
16	0-0	♘a5
17	♖ae1	

Fischer believed he should have improved his queen position before cashing in. He gave 17...♕a4 18 ♗b4 ♗xc4 19 ♗xc4 ♘xc4 20 ♖xe6 a5 21 ♗e7 ♘d2 22 ♖fe1 ♘e4 23 f3 ♕xa2! and wins.

161

However, White can fight a bit harder with 23 ♖e5 (23...♕xa2 24 ♖xf5) or 23 ♗h4 (e.g. 23 ♗h4 g5 24 f3).

17	...	♗xc4
18	♗xc4	♘xc4
19	♗c1	c5
20	dxc5	

White needs files for his rooks and targets for his bishop. His chances of drawing would be close to zero after 20 d5 e5.

20	...	bxc5
21	♗f4	h6!

It is crucial for Black to control the dark squares, such as by driving the bishop into submission with ...g5 and ...f4. Now 22 h4 is met by 22...e5! 23 ♗xe5 ♘xe5 24 f4 ♘f3+ 25 gxf3 ♕a4 and the win, after picking up two pawns, should be easy.

22	♖e2	g5

23 ♗e5

No better was 23 ♗e3, which Portisch claimed would have drawn after 23...♕b5 24 f3 e5 25 ♗f2. But 24...♘e5! and ...♘d3 would likely have won.

23	...	♕d8!
24	♖fe1	

Futile was 24 f4 ♘d2! 25 ♖fe1 ♘e4 followed by ...♕d5 or ...♕d3.

24	...	♔f7
25	h3	f4
26	♔h2	a6
27	♖e4	♕d5!

On the previous move, this would have given White a chance to threaten the a-pawn with ♗b8. But here Black threatens 28...♘e3 as well as 28...f3 29 gxf3 ♘d2.

28	h4	♘e3!
29	♖1xe3	

Or 29 f3 ♕d2 30 ♖g1 ♕f2. The remainder:

29 ... fxe3 30 ♖xe3 ♕xa2 31 ♖f3+ ♔e8 32 ♗g7 ♕c4 33 hxg5 hxg5 34 ♖f8+ ♔d7 35 ♖a8 ♔c6 White resigns

55

Fischer's late comeback made the Piatigorsky Cup a battle between him and Spassky, who recalled how up to 1,500 spectators (in a hall that seated 800) were on hand for the final rounds. The following game was Fischer's last victory and tied him for first place. But in the next round he could only draw with Spassky, who finished ahead of him by winning on the last day.

Fischer – Miguel Najdorf
Second Piatigorsky Cup,
Santa Monica 1966
Sicilian Defense (B44)

1	e4	c5
2	♘f3	♘c6

This was Najdorf's first game against Fischer with Black since the debacle at Varna. He wrote in the tournament book that he "did not consider it wise to try" the Najdorf Variation against Fischer because he "is one of the greatest specialists in this opening."

3	d4	cxd4
4	♘xd4	e6
5	♘b5	

Fischer never allowed his opponents to steer the game into a Scheveningen Variation.

5	...	d6
6	♗f4	e5
7	♗e3	

Now on 7...a6 8 ♘5c3 ♘f6 Fischer got excellent play against Badilles, in one of the 1967 exhibition games in Manila, with 9 ♗c4!. Play continued 9...♗e7 10 ♘d5 ♘xd5 11 ♗xd5 0-0 12 ♘c3 ♔h8 13 0-0 ♗e6 14 ♗b3! ♘a5 15 ♘d5.

| 7 | ... | ♘f6 |

Book at the time was 8 ♘1c3 a6 9 ♘a3 b5 and then the unclear 10 ♘d5 ♘xd5 11 exd5 ♘e7.

8	♗g5	♗e6
9	♘1c3	a6
10	♗xf6	gxf6
11	♘a3	♘d4?

Najdorf had prepared 11...♕b6 but at the board didn't like the looks of 12 ♘c4 ♕d4 13 ♘e3! ♗h6 14 ♕f3. For example, 14...0-0-0 15 ♗d3 ♖hg8 18 ♘f5!.

12 ♗c4?

After 12 ♘c4 ♖c8 White has a slight edge. Najdorf recommended 12...f5 instead but when Taimanov tried that against Fischer in 1971 White got the edge after 13 exf5

♘xf5 14 ♗d3 ♖c8 15 ♗xf5 ♖xc4 16 ♗xe6.

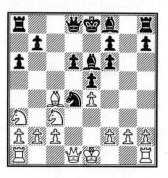

| 12 | ... | b5? |

Both players miss the magic-move 12...d5! (13 exd5 ♗xa3 14 bxa3 ♕a5 15 ♕d2 ♖c8 or 13 ♘xd5 ♗xa3 14 bxa3 ♖c8 15 ♗b3 ♕a5+). Fischer later analyzed 12...d5! in the tournament book. Yet 11...d5! apparently never occurred to him until Game 94.

13 ♗xe6 fxe6

The threat of a check on h5 is always a factor now – but never played. For example, 14 ♕h5+ ♔e7 15 ♘e2 ♕e8 is a minimal White edge.

14 ♘e2! ♘c6

The opponents agreed in the post-mortem that 14...♘xe2 had to be played followed by either 15...d5 (Fischer) or 15...h5 (Najdorf) – although in the latter case 16 0-0-0 d5?! 17 ♕f3 distinctly favors White. Fischer took 13 minutes on his reply – his longest "think" in the game.

15 ♘g3 ♕d7

Fischer endorsed 15...d5 or 15...♕a5+ 16 c3 b4 (17 ♘c4 ♕c5 18 ♘e3 bxc3 19 ♖c1 ♕b5). But 15...h5 is fine (16 ♘xh5 ♕e7).

| 16 | c4 | ♘d4 |
| 17 | 0-0 | b4 |

Premature. Black should try 17...♖c8 (and if 18 ♘e2 then 18...b4 19 ♘c2 ♘xc2 20 ♕xc2 d5). But Najdorf had not given up hope of ...0-0-0.

18 ♘c2   ♘xc2

This concedes that his blockade strategy has failed and he must complicate before White opens the queenside with a2-a3 (and perhaps the kingside as well with f2-f4).

19 ♕xc2   h5!

20 ♖fd1   h4!

White would have had a much easier task if he had stopped this counterplay with 20 h4!.

21 ♘f1   ♖g8

22 a3!

"Very well played," said Najdorf. Now 22...♕b7? 23 ♕a4+.

22 ...   h3

23 g3   bxa3

24 ♖xa3   ♕c6

Here 24...d5, hoping the threat of 25...♗xa3 will buy Black time for 25...d4, would fail to 25 ♖f3.

25 ♕e2!

This makes 25 ♕h5+ a real threat and avoids 25 ♘e3 ♗h6.

25 ...   f5

26 c5!

White uses the threat well – 26...dxc5 can't be played because of 27 ♕h5+ ♔e7 28 ♖ad3 (28...♔f6 29 ♕h4+ ♔g6 30 exf5+ exf5 31 ♕xh3). Or 26...♕xc5 27 ♕h5+ and exf5.

26 ...   ♕xe4

27 ♕xe4   fxe4

28 cxd6

Black's grand center is in ruins and 28...0-0-0 29 ♖xa6 ♔b7 is lost (30 ♖a4 ♖xd6 31 ♖xd6 ♗xd6 32 ♖xe4).

28 ...   ♗h6

Hoping for 29 ♘e3 ♗xe3 30 ♖xe3 ♖b8 with counterplay.

29 ♖a5!   ♔d7

30 ♖xe5   ♗g7

31 ♖xe4   ♗xb2

At least now Black's pieces are coordinated and he has an outside passed pawn to frighten White with.

32 ♘e3   a5

33 ♘c4   ♖gb8

34 ♖h4   ♔c6

35 ♖h7

A postal player has the liberty to analyze lines like 35 ♖xh3 a4 36 d7 a3 out to the end. The practical player will win the Exchange this way.

35	...	♗d4
36	♖c7+	♔d5
37	d7!	

White's winning ideas include ♘b6+ and ♖c8.

| 37 | ... | a4 |
| 38 | ♘b6+ | |

A faster win was 38 ♖c8 ♖xc8 39 ♘b6+ ♔c5 and now not 40 dxc8(♕)+? ♖xc8 41 ♘xc8 a3 but 40 ♖c1+! ♔xb6 41 ♖xc8!.

38	...	♖xb6
39	♖c8	♖d6!
40	♖xa8	♖xd7
41	♖xa4	e5

Najdorf said he should have resigned here but it was worth playing on to see if Fischer found...

| 42 | ♔f1 | ♖b7 |
| 43 | f4! | |

...this surprising move. White seems to invite ...♖b2 (or, after fxe5 the invasion of ...♖f7+-f2+). But the threat of fxe5, winning a piece, counts more.

43	...	♔e6
44	fxe5	♖f7+
45	♔e2	♖f2+
46	♔d3	♗xe5
47	♖e1	**Resigns**

The pawn ending is lost after 47...♖f5 48 ♖a5 and a double capture on e5.

56

After a relatively brief (for him) respite of two months, Fischer

returned to the board in the 17th Olympiad, at the Havana Libre (nee Hilton) hotel in October 1966. The U.S. team was considerably stronger than the one that finished sixth, and lost 0-4 in the U.S.S.R.-U.S. match, at the previous Olympiad. But there was no confidence about bringing home medals. As captain Donald Byrne put it, "Fischer will play first board. On second, third and fourth we'll play without Fischer. Unfortunately we have only one Fischer."

Fischer – Joaquim Durão
Olympiad, Havana 1966
Caro-Kann Defense (B10)

1	e4	e6
2	d3	c5
3	♘f3	♘c6
4	g3	g6
5	♗g2	♗g7
6	0-0	♘ge7
7	c3!	

Fischer understood, as few others did at the time, that White should delay ♘bd2 in favor of c2-c3/ d2-d4!. After 7 ♘bd2 0-0 8 c3 d6 Black might equalize with ...f5 before White acts in the center.

| 7 | ... | 0-0 |

On 7...d5 Fischer liked to continue 8 ♕e2 and if 8...0-0, then 9 e5.

| 8 | d4 | d6? |

Black should establish a presence in the center, either earlier with ...e5 or ...d5, or here with 8...cxd4 9 cxd4 d5, as in Game 84.

This looks like one of those amorphous positions that offers White only the tiniest of advantages. But three somewhat paradoxical moves simply alter the picture.

9   dxc5!

As soon as White creates the "ideal" pawn centre, he liquidates it.

9   ...   dxc5

10   ♕e2   b6

Stopping White's next move with 10...e5 would give him excellent prospects after 11 ♖d1 ♕c7 12 ♘a3!.

11   e5!

White will put e4 to better use than Black will put d5.

11   ...   a5

12   ♖e1

Rather than seize the open file with 12 ♖fd1, White overprotects his only potential weakness.

12   ...   ♗a6

13   ♕e4

Thanks to moves 9, 11 and 12, White has an almost effortless kingside attack (13...♗d3 14 ♕h4 or 14 ♕g4 ♗f5 15 ♕h4). Black can flee into the endgame with 13...♕d3 but he would be worse because of the liability at b6.

13   ...   ♖a7!

14   ♘bd2   ♗d3

Black should play 14...♖d7 so that 15 a4, which secures c4 for the knight, can be met by 15...♖d5!, forcing White to worry about his e-pawn. Worse is 15 ♘c4 b5 16 ♘d6? because of 16...♘xe5. But White can improve with 16 ♘e3 and ♘g4.

15   ♕h4   ♘d5

White's position is so strong now that he can sacrifice the e-pawn: 15...♕c7 16 ♘e4 ♘xe5 (16...♘f5 17 ♘f6+) 17 ♘xe5 ♗xe5 18 ♘f6+ or 17...♕xe5 18 ♗f4 ♕f5 19 ♗d6, threatening 20 g4 and 20 ♗xe7.

16   ♕xd8   ♖xd8

17   a4!   ♖ad7?

Black fails the first test of the endgame. A credible bid for counterplay was 17...g5! – 18 ♘xg5 ♘xe5 (19 f4 ♘g4 20 ♘de4 ♖ad7) or 18 h3? ♘de7 and ...♘g6.

18   ♗f1!

The tournament book recommended 18...♘de7 after which 19 ♗xd3 ♖xd3 20 ♔g2 ♗h6! enables Black to rid himself of his other bishop (21 ♘c4 ♗xc1 22 ♖exc1 ♘c8 23 ♖a3 ♖8d5 24 ♖b3 ♘d4!).

But this is too optimistic. Even in that line White enjoys an advantage with 25 ♘xd4 cxd4 26 ♔f1. Moreover, the best answer to 18...♘de7 is simply 19 ♘c4, since ...♗xc4 will allow White's bishop to assume a commanding post at b5.

18   ...   ♗xf1

19   ♔xf1   ♘de7

Black shouldn't decentralize the knight he needs to defend b6. True,

19...♗h6 20 ♘c4 or 20 ♘e4 is unpleasant. But there was still time for 19...g5!.

20	♘c4	♘c8
21	♗g5	♘6e7
22	♘fd2	h6

White now ties Black's pieces to the defense of b6.

23	♗xe7!	♖xe7
24	♖a3!	♖c7
25	♖b3	♖c6
26	♘e4	♗f8
27	♔e2	♗e7
28	f4	♔f8?

Essential was 28...h5, leaving White to decide between two plans. The most promising is expansion on the kingside (h2-h3 and g2-g4-g5). The second is a timely liquidation with ♘ed6 (The immediate 29 ♘ed6 ♘xd6 30 exd6 ♗xd6 31 ♖xb6 ♖xb6 32 ♘xb6 offers Black hope after 32...♗c7 33 ♘c4 h4.)

29	g4!	♔e8
30	♖f1	♖d5?

Passivity is fatal. After 30...♔d7 31 ♔e3 ♔c7 Black can solve his b6 problem and meet 32 f5 exf5 33 gxf5 gxf5 34 ♖xf5 with 34...♖f8, intending ...♖g6 or ...f6.

31	♖f3	♖d8
32	♖h3!	♗f8
33	♘xa5!	

"A '*petite combinaison*' in the style of Capablanca," said the tournament book. It is based on 33...bxa5 34 ♘f6+ ♔e7 35 ♖b7+ and mates.

33	...	♖c7
34	♘c4	♖a7

Or 34...♖c6 35 a5! and wins.

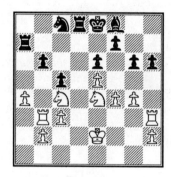

35	♘xb6	

This wins, of course. But 35 ♘f6+ ♔e7 36 a5! would shorten the game. The reason is that 36...bxa5? allows ♘xa5! and ♘c6+. Black's rook can never leave the second rank because of the ♖b7+ mating idea.

35	...	♘xb6
36	♖xb6	♖da8
37	♘f6+	♔d8
38	♖c6	♖c7

This time the mate was 38...♖a4? 39 ♖d3+. The text loses another pawn but 38...♖b8 39 ♖d3+ ♔e7 40 ♖cd6 would be instant death.

39	♖d3+	♔c8
40	♖xc7+	♔xc7

| 41 | Rd7+ | Kc6 |
| 42 | Rxf7 | c4 |

Else White wins the bishop with Nh7.

43	Nd7	Bc5
44	Nxc5	Kxc5
45	Rc7+	Kd5
46	b4!	**Resigns**

In view of 46...cxb3 47 Kd3 and 48 c4 mate.

57

Fischer popularized, if not invented, several of the positional ideas taken for granted in openings today. This goes beyond mere theoretical novelties in one variation or another. For example, in the following game Black pushes his c-pawn, the bedrock of the Benoni, to c4. This had been considered highly dubious in similar positions – until this game.

Arturo Pomar – Fischer
Olympiad, Havana 1966
Modern Benoni Defense (A69)

| 1 | d4 | Nf6 |
| 2 | c4 | c5 |

A new weapon for Fischer.

3	d5	e6
4	Nc3	exd5
5	cxd5	g6
6	e4	d6
7	Be2	Bg7
8	f4	0-0
9	Nf3	Re8
10	Nd2	

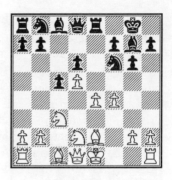

| 10 | ... | **c4!** |

Previously 10...Ng4 (11 Bxg4 Qh4+) had been analyzed found wanting, and 10...a6 11 a4 Ng4 was considered only adequate.

Quieter alternatives such as 10...b6 and 11...Ba6 or ...Na6-c7 followed by ...b6/...Ba6 only came into fashion in the 1980s.

But Fischer's move declares Black's intention to batter e4 with ...Nbd7-c5. This theme later appeared in different move orders, such as 8 Nf3 0-0 9 0-0 Re8 10 Nd2 Nbd7 and now 11 f4 is answered by 11...c4 12 Bf3? b5 or 12 Bxc4 Nc5.

11 Bf3?

Black has the edge now, as he would after 11 Bxc4 Nxe4. White's problem is that he has no time exploit the d4 hole with Nf3-d4 because Black's ...Nbd7-c5xe4 is faster, and 11 0-0 b5 12 Nxb5?? loses to 12...Qb6+.

The most popular line is 11 a4 Na6 12 0-0 Nc5 13 Bf3 with complex play after 13...b6 14 e5 or even 13...Bh6 14 e5.

| 11 | ... | Nbd7 |
| 12 | 0-0 | b5! |

There are many wins here and Black can be excused for wanting to avoid the counterplay of 28...♗d7 29 ♗e7 and ♖d5.

29	d7	♖ed8
30	♗a4	b3
31	♖fe1	♔g7

Black takes his time (31...c3? 32 ♗xd8 ♖xd8 33 ♖xe6! with a likely draw, or 32...c2? 33 ♗c7! and White wins).

32	♗xd8	♖xd8
33	♖d6	♗f6
34	♖ed1	♗g5!

Black controls the queening square at c1 and threatens ...♖b8 and ...b2. The win could still slip after 34...c3 35 ♖xe6! fxe6 36 ♗xb3.

35	♖b6	h6
36	♖c6	

As ugly as it looks, White should create *luft* with 36 g3.

36	...	♖a8!
37	♗b5	♗xd7!
38	h4	♗xc6
39	♗xc6	c3!
40	hxg5	c2
41	gxh6+	♔h8

White resigns

58

It was at Havana that Fischer sprang his most important new idea of the 1960s, the improved Exchange Variation of the Ruy Lopez. He first used 5 0-0 to beat Portisch in 34 moves, then two days later faced Gligorić, who must have been searching for a better defense. It didn't show. (Fischer's third victim, Eléazar Jimenez, put up little resistance a week later and lost in 33 moves.)

Fischer – Svetozar Gligorić
Olympiad, Havana 1966
Ruy Lopez,
Exchange Variation (C69)

1	e4	e5
2	♘f3	♘c6
3	♗b5	a6
4	♗xc6	

At the Capablanca Memorial, Fischer thought two minutes – actually more because of the transmission delays – before playing 4 ♗a4 against Smyslov. Evidently he was considering 4 ♗xc6 but decided to keep his interest in it secret, as it turned out, for another 14 months.

4	...	dxc6
5	0-0!	

The opening books of the day ridiculed this and gave "5...♗g4! and if 6 h3 then 6...h5!". Isaac Boleslavsky, for example, considered only 7 d3 ♕f6 8 ♗e3 ♗xf3 9 ♕xf3 ♕xf3 10 gxf3 ♗d6, with a Black edge.

Nevertheless, 5 0-0 had been the favorite line of the Dutch master

Barendregt who kept trying to bolster White's chances. His efforts seemed doomed after he lost a 1962 game that went 7 d3 ♕f6 8 ♘bd2 ♘e7 9 ♖e1 ♘g6 10 d4 ♗d6 11 hxg4 hxg4 12 ♘h2 ♖xh2! 13 ♔xh2?? ♕xf2 and ...♔e7/...♖h8+. But the discovery of 13 ♕xg4! turned matters around. White is slightly better after 13...♖h4 14 ♕f5 because 14...♕xf5? 15 exf5 loses a pawn. Since there were no major improvements for Black after 6...h5, the line appeared well worth a try at the grandmaster level.

5	...	f6
6	d4	♗g4

Portisch went into what became a main line: 6...exd4 7 ♘xd4 c5 8 ♘b3 ♕xd1 9 ♖xd1 and now instead of 9...♗d7, he played the book-endorsed 9...♗d6 10 ♘a5! b5 11 c4 ♘e7. But after 12 ♗e3 he was soon losing – 12...f5 13 ♘c3 f4 14 e5! ♗xe5 15 ♗xc5 (or 12...♔f7 13 ♘c3 ♖b8 14 e5! fxe5 15 ♘e4).

7 c3!

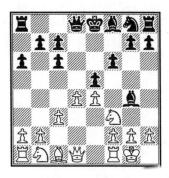

Actually this is a very old move and clearly better than 7 dxe5 which had turned out poorly after 7...♕xd1 8 ♖xd1 ♗xf3 9 gxf3 fxe5 10 f4 ♘f6.

7	...	exd4

8	cxd4	♕d7

In a comparable position (5...♗g4 6 h3 h5) the gambit is unsound (7 d4?! ♗xf3 8 ♕xf3 ♕xd4! 9 ♖d1 ♕c4). But here 8...♗xf3 9 ♕xf3 ♕xd4 10 ♖d1 ♕c4 11 ♗f4 offers more than enough compensation. Annotators endorsed 8...c5 9 d5 ♗d6 and ...♘e7, yet their recommendation has gone largely ignored since 1966. Would Fischer have taken up the challenge with 10 h3 ♗h5 11 g4!? ♗f7 12 ♖e1 and 13 e5?

9	h3!	♗e6

After 9...♗h5 10 ♘e5! White gets a better endgame, as Fischer showed against Jimenez.

10	♘c3	0-0-0
11	♗f4	♘e7

Black loses because he never found a way to neutralize both the bishop on f4 and ♘a4-c5. Here he could exchange off the bishop with 11...♗d6 but prefers to gain a tempo with ...♘g6 first.

Fischer showed how the attack explodes after 11...g5 12 ♗g3 h5 – with 13 d5! cxd5 14 ♖c1 and then 14...dxe4? 15 ♘a4! ♔b8 16 ♖xc7!! ♕xd1 17 ♖c8+! ♔xc8 18 ♘b6 mate or 17...♔a7 18 ♗b8+ and ♘b6 mate.

But he made no mention of 12...g4 (instead of 12...h5). Then 13 hxg4 ♗xg4 and ...♗xf3/...♕xd4 or ...♘e7-g6/...h5-h4.

White could try 13 d5 since he's slightly better in the ending after 13...cxd5 14 exd5 ♗xd5 15 ♘xd5 ♕xd5 16 hxg4 ♕xd1 – and has good attacking prospects after 13...♗xd5?! 14 exd5! gxf3 15 ♕xf3 cxd5 16 ♖ac1. But 13...gxf3 14 dxe6 ♕xe6 is nothing special.

12 ♖c1

12 ... ♘g6

Black misses a second chance for 12...g5! 13 ♗g3 g4 14 hxg4 ♗xg4. For example, 15 d5 ♗h6 16 ♖c2 ♖he8 and Black has coordinated his forces.

13 ♗g3 ♗d6

Black would like to play ...f5 but 13...f5 14 d5 fxe4 15 dxe6 ♕xd1 is a dubious endgame (16 ♖fxd1 exf3 17 gxf3 followed by f3-f4-f5). Also, 13...♗c4 14 ♖e1 f5 15 ♕a4 only helps White's queenside prospects.

14 ♘a4!

The lining up of rook against king creates a new tactic (15 d5 cxd5?? 16 ♘b6+).

14 ... ♗xg3?

The losing move, according to Gligorić. Black must be able to meet ♘c5 with ...♗xc5. That suggests 14...♕e7 since 15 ♘c5? allows 15...♗xc5 16 ♖xc5 ♕xc5!. However, White has a nice edge with 15 ♗xd6! ♕xd6 16 ♘c5 or 15...cxd6 16 d5.

Fischer recommended another waiting policy, 14...♔b8 15 ♘c5 ♕e7. But White has too strong a game after 16 ♕a4. The right way is

15...♗xc5 16 ♖xc5 f5!, e.g. 17 exf5 ♗xf5 18 d5? ♗e4!.

15 fxg3 ♔b8

Black must allow ♘c5 since 15...b6 16 d5! is not an option (16...cxd5?? 17 ♘xb6+). If Black is going to become desperate soon, now was the time for 15...♕d6 16 ♘c5 ♗xh3!?, which works much better than in the game (17 gxh3 ♕xg3+ or 17 e5 fxe5 18 gxh3 exd4 19 ♘e4 ♕d5).

16 ♘c5 ♕d6
17 ♕a4

17 ... ♔a7?

Now 17...♗xh3 18 e5! is less successful than in the last note. Fischer said Black is still breathing after 17...♗c8 18 ♖c3 ♘f8. For example, 19 e5 ♕d5 20 ♖b3 ♔a7 and ...♘d7 or ...♘e6.

18 ♘xa6!

Since Black cannot allow 18...bxa6 19 ♖xc6, Gligorić panicked.

18 ... ♗xh3
19 e5! ♘xe5

White wins eventually after 19...fxe5 20 ♘c5+ ♔b8 21 gxh3 – but 21 ♖c3! and ♖a3 would have been more in keeping with the flow of the game.

20	dxe5	fxe5
21	♘c5+	♚b8
22	gxh3	e4
23	♘xe4	♛e7
24	♖c3	b5
25	♛c2	**Resigns**

The tournament book reported that "various grandmasters" – Fischer identified them only as "spectators" – saw the position near the end and believed Black had drawing chances: They thought he had one rook more than White, since a player of Gligorić's ability couldn't be so lost after only 20 moves.

59

Fischer's final score at Havana was 15-2, or 88.2 percent. Yet once again he failed to win the prize for best score on first board – because Tigran Petrosian scored 11½-1½ or 88.4 percent. Fischer lost his chance to catch him in his next-to-last round game. Florin Gheorghiu offered a draw on the 15th move but Fischer refused and was ground down in 50 moves. Perhaps his defensive heroics in this game from the seventh round of the finals had made him feel indestructible.

Sven Johannessen – Fischer
Olympiad, Havana 1966
Benko Gambit Declined (A57)

| 1 | d4 | ♘f6 |
| 2 | ♘f3 | c5 |

Another new position for Fischer. On 3 c4 he would continue 3...cxd4 4 ♘xd4 e6.

| 3 | d5 | b5 |

| 4 | c4 | ♗b7 |

Better than 4...e6, which transposes into the Blumenfeld Gambit. Now 5 a4 bxc4 6 ♘c3 and 7 e4 was considered best at the time.

5	g3!?	g6
6	♗g2	bxc4
7	♘c3	♗g7
8	0-0	0-0
9	♘e5	d6
10	♘xc4	♘bd7

White's choice of development is modest but not without sting. A 1984 Soviet game went 10...♗a6 11 ♘e3 ♘bd7 12 ♛a4 with a small edge for White.

| 11 | ♖e1 | ♗a6 |
| 12 | ♛a4 | ♛c8 |

Black stands well after 12...♗xc4 13 ♛xc4 ♖b8, e.g. 14 ♖b1 ♘e5 15 ♛a4 ♛c7 16 ♗f4 ♖b4 17 ♛c2 ♖fb8. But Fischer likes his bishops – and doesn't seem to mind ♘a5-c6.

| 13 | ♘a5 |

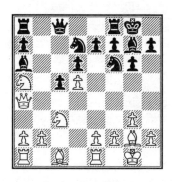

| 13 | ... | ♘b6 |

Black wants to know which piece is going to c6. The square turns out to be very useful to White after 13...♖e8 (not 13...♖b8? 14 ♘c6)

14 ♗g5 ♖b8 15 ♖ab1 ♖b4 16 ♕c6 and then 16...♘e5 17 ♕xc8 ♖xc8 18 ♘c6.

14 ♕h4

But on 14 ♕c6 ♕b8! White has to save his queen from...♖c8. He has nothing but a repetition of moves after 15 ♗h3 ♗c8 16 ♗g2 ♗a6 – and the worst of 16...♗d7 17 ♕b7 ♕xb7 18 ♘xb7 a5.

14 ... ♖e8

15 ♗g5 ♕c7

Since the knight is unprotected on a5, White has to beware ...♘bxd5.

16 ♘c6 ♗b7

But on c6 the knight is vulnerable to ...♘bd7 and ...e6xd5.

17 e4

However, f2-f4 and e4-e5 appear faster.

17 ... ♘bd7

Bad was 17...♗xc6? 18 bxc6 ♕xc6? 19 e5 ♘fd5 20 ♘xd5 ♘xd5 because of 21 e6!, which threatens ♖ad1.

18 f4 ♔h8!

Calculated insouciance: Black seems to have taken the slightest of precautions. Yet he threatens the bishop with 19...♘g8! and 20...f6, and keeps the idea of ...e6xd5 and ...♘xd5 alive.

19 e5!? dxe5

20 fxe5

In an East German book on the tournament, Boleslavsky took White to task for missing a golden opportunity to upset the American champion. He argued that 20 ♘xe5 was much stronger, citing, for example, 20...♘xe5 21 fxe5 ♘d7 22 e6 fxe6 23 ♖xe6.

After 20 ♘xe5 ♔g8, with ...e6 in mind, there are two critical continuations:

(a) 21 ♘c6 and now 21...c4, opens up the b6-g1 diagonal so that Black can meet 22 ♘xe7+ with 21...♖xe7 23 ♖xe7 ♕c5+.

The main line is 22 ♔h1 ♕b6 23 ♖ab1 e6! and White's knight is in trouble. He is lost after 24 b3 exd5 25 ♘e7+ ♖xe7! 26 ♖xe7 d4 27 bxc4? ♗xg2+ 28 ♔xg2 ♕c6+ and worse following 27 ♕h3 dxc3 28 ♗xf6 ♘xf6 29 ♖xb7 ♕e3 because of ...c2.

Good for Black is 24 f5 exf5! 25 ♕xc4 ♘g4!. Safest is the equal 21...e6.

(b) 21 ♘c4 and now Agur gives 21...♘b6 22 d6 ♕c8 23 ♘xb6 axb6 24 ♗xb7 ♕xb7 25 dxe7 ♘g4! and ...♗d4+.

But this is refuted by 23 ♖xe7 ♖xe7 24 ♘xb6 axb6 25 dxe7 and now 25...♘g4? 26 e8(♕)+ or 25...♖xg2 26 ♗xf6! ♗f3 (26...♗b7 27 ♖d1!) 27 ♗xg7 ♔xg7 28 ♖f1 ♗b7 29 f5!.

However, Black has a better reply to 22 d6 in 22...♕b8! 23 ♘xb6 ♗xg2! and then 24 ♘xa8 ♗xa8 25 ♖e2 ♕b7 26 ♖f1 exd6 or 24 ♖xe7 ♕xb6!.

| 20 | ... | ♘xd5! |
| 21 | ♘xd5 | ♕xc6 |

If the king still stood on g8, White would win with ♘f6+ or ♘e7+.

| 22 | e6 | ♘e5! |

Not 22...fxe6?? 23 ♘f4! and White wins.

| 23 | ♖xe5 | |

The attack falls apart after 23 exf7 ♘xf7. But 23 ♗h6! f6! 24 ♖xe5! fxe5 25 ♖f1 ♕xe6 should draw.

| 23 | ... | ♗xe5 |
| 24 | exf7 | ♖f8 |

25 h3?

White may have counted on 25 ♘f4 but 25...♗d4+ 26 ♔h1 ♕b6 27 ♗xb7 ♕xb7+ wins. Black can also put in a bid for the brilliancy prize with 26...♖xf7! 27 ♗xc6 ♗xc6+ 28 ♘g2 ♖f2.

In any case, 25 ♖e1 ♗d4+ 26 ♗e3 was a must.

| 25 | ... | ♖xf7 |
| 26 | ♘f4 | ♖xf4! |

White resigns

In view of 27 ♗xc6 ♗d4+ 28 ♔h2 ♖f2+ 29 ♔g1 ♖xb2+. Fischer took only 77 minutes – an hour less than his opponent.

60

The year 1966 ended with Fischer's last U.S. Championship. He had repeatedly called for the national championship to be doubled in length, remembering how a loss to Mednis in the 11-round 1962-3 tournament nearly ended his streak of first place finishes at four. The following was the last of his 90 Championship games.

Arthur Bisguier – Fischer
U.S. Championship,
New York 1966-67
Sicilian Defense (B50)

1	e4	c5
2	♘f3	d6
3	c3	

Bisguier's losing streak against Fischer had reached 11 games and he had begun adopting rare sidelines as White but still got the worst of it.

3	...	♘f6
4	♗d3	♘c6
5	♗c2	♗g4
6	d3	

More accurate is 6 h3 since 6...♗h5 would deny Black the fianchetto option (7...g6? 8 g4).

| 6 | ... | g6 |

Book, as of 1967, was 7 h3 ♗xf3 8 ♕xf3 ♗g7 9 ♕e2 0-0 10 0-0 b5 with equality.

| 7 | ♘bd2 | ♗g7 |
| 8 | h3 | ♗d7! |

Exchanging on f3 when White can recapture with a knight allows White to play d3-d4 quickly and solve the problem of what to do with his QN.

9 0-0   0-0

Now 10 d4 grants Black enough counterplay to equalize with 10...cxd4 11 cxd4 ♘b4 12 ♗b1 ♗b5 13 ♖e1 ♘d3.

10 ♘h2?

The best solution to the problem-knights was 10 ♖e1 and ♘f1. The f2-f4 plan has no bite when Black's e-pawn is unmoved.

10 ...   b5

11 f4   b4!

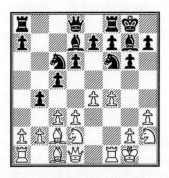

Fischer thrived on this attack on the center's base. Compare this with Game 48 and Kramer – Fischer from the 1957-8 U.S. Championship: 1 ♘f3 ♘f6 2 g3 g6 3 ♗g2 ♗g7 4 0-0 0-0 5 d3 d6 6 e4 c5 7 c3 ♘c6 8 ♘e1 ♖b8 9 f4 ♘e8! 10 ♗e3 ♗d7 11 ♘d2 b5 12 e5? dxe5 13 ♗xc5 exf4 14 ♖xf4 ♘c7 15 ♖f1 b4! 16 ♕c2 bxc3 17 bxc3 ♘b5 19 d4 ♖c8 19 ♕b2 ♘xc3! 20 ♕xc3 ♘xd4 and Black won.

12 ♘c4

Or 12 ♕f3 bxc3 13 bxc3 ♘e8! and the threat of ...♗xc3 proves annoying (14 ♗b2 ♘c7 and ...♘b5).

12 ...   d5!

13 ♘e5?!

White didn't like the hole created at d4 after 13 exd5 ♘xd5 14 ♕f3 e6

or 13 ♘e3 bxc3 14 bxc3 d4. But the text does worse pawn damage.

13 ...   bxc3

14 bxc3   dxe4

Now 15 ♘xd7 ♘xd7 or 15 ♘xc6 ♗xc6 16 dxe4 ♗xe4 costs White a pawn.

15 dxe4   ♘xe5

16 fxe5   ♘e8

17 ♘f3

White seizes the initiative with 17 ♕d5, threatening ♖d1 – but it ends in Black's advantage after 17...♘c7 18 ♕xc5 ♘e6 19 ♕d5 ♕c7.

17 ...   ♘c7

18 ♖f2   ♗b5

19 ♗g5

Black's queen is at least as useful as White's (after 19 ♖d2 ♕e8 and ...♕c6, or 19 ♕e1 ♘e6 and ...♕c7) so Bisguier allows a trade.

19 ...   ♕xd1+

20 ♖xd1   ♖fe8

21 ♗b3   c4!

On the one hand, this surrenders d4 and hamstrings his bishop. But on the other, Black solves the problems of defending the c-pawn, allows his knight to take up the excellent e6 square and denies d5 to White's bishop.

22 ♗c2   ♘e6

23 ♗e3   ♖eb8

24 ♖b1!

Since ♖bf1 means nothing now because of ...♗e8, it's White's turn to stop a threatened invasion (...a6/...♖e8/....♖b2).

In the post-mortem, 24 ♘d4 was suggested, e.g. 24...♗d7? 25 ♘f5 or

24...♗xe5 25 ♘xe6 fxe6 26 ♗d4 ♗xd4 27 ♖xd4 ♖d8 28 ♖fd2. However, in the last line 26...♗c7! and ...♖f8 retains solid winning chances.

White can also try 24 ♘d4 ♗xe5 25 ♘xb5 ♖xb5 26 ♗a4 ♖a5 27 ♗c6 and ♗d5 but again his chances are not as good as in the game.

24	...	a6
25	♖ff1	♗e8
26	♔f2	♘d8

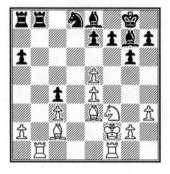

27 ♖xb8?

Trading off all rooks can only succeed if all invasion routes for the black king are sealed off. White is betting that he can always guard squares such as b2 and e5, a tall order.

Better was 27 ♘d2!, and if 27...♗xe5 then 28 ♘xc4 ♖xb1 29 ♖xb1 ♗xc3 30 ♘b6 ♖b8 31 ♘d5. The main point is 31...♖xb1 32 ♗xb1 ♗f6 allows White to sharply reduce his losing chances with 33 ♘xf6+ exf6 34 ♗d4 or 33 ♗c5 (and 32...♘c6? 33 ♘c7).

27	...	♖xb8
28	♖b1	♖b5!
29	♖xb5	axb5
30	♔e2	h6

31	♔d2	g5!

White should have prevented this expansion with 31 h4. Now 32 g4 ♘c6 33 ♗d4 leaves Black with a variety of winning ideas including 33...e6 and ...♘xd4/...♖f8.

32	h4	g4
33	♘d4	e6?
34	♗f4	

Black should have stopped 34 h5! with 33...h5.

White may have rejected 34 h5 ♗xe5 35 ♗xh6 because of 35...♗xd4 36 cxd4 f6, which dooms the h-pawn. But 37 ♔c3 ♗xh5 38 a4 or 38 ♔b4 should draw.

34	...	h5!
35	♗g5	♘b7
36	♗f6?	

This would create an impregnable fortress after 36...♗xf6 37 exf6 and e4-e5/♔e3-f4. For example:

(a) 37...♘c5 38 e5 ♘d7 39 ♘xb5 ♘xe5 40 ♘d6 ♗c6 41 g3 and 42 a4 (White can also try 39 a4 since 39...bxa4? 40 ♗xa4 ♘xf6 41 ♗xe8 ♘xe8 42 ♘e2 followed by ♔e3-d4 or ♘f4).

(b) 37...e5 38 ♘f5 ♔h7 39 ♘g7! ♗d7 40 ♘xh5.

36	...	♗h6+
37	♗g5	

White believes all four doubled pawns are safe if his king reaches f4. But a better practical try is 37 ♔e2, forcing Black to choose between ideas such as 37...♘c5 and ...♘d7, 37...♗f4 followed by ...♗g3, and a king raid via h7-g6. He also has tricks. For example, 37 ♔e2 ♘c5 38 g3 ♘d7 39 ♘xb5 ♘xf6 40 ♘c7 (not 40 ♘d6 ♗f8!) seems to draw.

But Black wins a pawn with 40...♗a4! 41 ♗xa4 ♘xe4. Also lost is 38 ♔f2 ♗d2 39 ♘e2 ♗c6.

37	...	♗xg5+
38	hxg5	♔g7
39	♔e3	♔g6
40	♔f4	♘c5
41	g3	

White should pass (41 ♗b1 ♘a4 42 ♘e2 ♘b2 43 ♘c1 ♘d1 44 ♘e2). The dearth of tempi comes back to haunt him at move 43.

41	...	♗d7

Black might win after 41...♘d3+ 42 ♗xd3 cxd3 43 ♘b3 (43...♗c6 44 ♘d2 ♗b7 45 ♘b3 h4!?) but the text is a higher-percentage play.

42	a3	♗e8!

White's king is required to defend g5 while his bishop must watch both d3 and a4. That leaves only the knight to move – but 43 ♘e2 ♘d3+! 44 ♗xd3? cxd3 loses immediately. Something has to give.

43	♗b1	♘a4
44	♘e2	♘b2

Again with the idea of 45...♘d3+.

45	♘d4	♘d1!
46	♘e2	♘f2!

47	♔e3	♘h3

A remarkable route for the knight that was on d7 at move 39.

48	♘f4+	♔xg5
49	♘g2	

Quite lost is 49 ♘xh3+ gxh3 50 ♔f2 h4.

49	...	f6
50	exf6	♔xf6
51	♘h4	

White's king is shut out by Black's next move but 51 ♔d4 e5+ 52 ♔d5 would lose to 52...♘g1 and ...♘e2.

51	...	e5!
52	♗c2	♗d7
53	♗b1	♘g5

The knight begins another tour, headed for g6.

54	♗c2	♘f7
55	♗b1	

55	...	♘h8!
56	♗c2	♘g6

White must allow the h-pawn to advance (57 ♘g2 ♔g5 and ...h4).

57	♘xg6	♔xg6
58	♔f2	♔g5
59	♔g2	h4
60	♔h2	h3!

The g-pawn is hopelessly blockaded after 60...hxg3+?? 61 ♔xg3.

61	♔g1	♔f6
62	♔h2	♔e7

With the enemy king confined to the vicinity of h1, all Black needs to win is king access to a4.

63	♔g1	♔d6
64	♔f2	♔c5
65	♔g1	♔b6
66	♔h1	♔a5
67	♔g1	♗c6

68	♔h2!	♗b7!

On the immediate 68...♗xe4 White also queens: 69 ♗xe4 ♔a4 70 ♗f5 ♔b3! 71 ♗xg4 e4 72 ♗xh3 ♔xc3 73 g4 ♔d2? (73...e3 wins) 74 g5 c3 75 g6. Note that 68 ♔h1? – which is often incorrectly given in databases – would have lost to 68...♗xe4+! (69 ♗xe4 ♔a4 70 ♗f5 ♔xa3 71 ♗xg4 ♔b3).

69 ♔g1

Or 69 ♗d1 ♗xe4 70 ♗xg4 ♔a4 71 ♗d7! ♗g2! 72 g4 e4 73 g5 e3 74 ♗g4 ♔xa3.

69	...	♗xe4!
70	♗xe4	♔a4
71	♗f5	

Another nice line runs 71 ♗c6 ♔xa3 72 ♗xb5 ♔b3 73 ♗d7 ♔xc3 74 ♗xg4 ♔d3! 75 ♗xh3 c3 75 ♗f5+ e4 and 76...c2. Or 75 ♗d1 e4 76 g4 ♔d2!.

71	...	♔b3!!

Black needs a tempo, not the a-pawn, to win.

72	♗xg4	e4
73	♗xh3	

Or 73 ♗f5 e3 74 ♔f1 h2.

73	...	♔xc3
74	g4	♔d2

White resigns

The point of Black's 68th move is repeated – he queens with check. Endgame connoisseur Walter Korn compared Black's play to a study but he was overstating the case when he claimed 74...e3 75 ♗f1 ♔d2 76 g5 e2 77 ♗xe2 ♔xe2 78 g6 c3 would draw. Black still wins after 75...♔b2 76 g5 c3 77 g6 e2!, for example.

61

Max Euwe was among the admirers who said the ending in which Fischer excelled was rook and bishop versus rook and knight (Games 35 and 90). But there is another candidate – endings with bishops of opposite color and one pair of rooks. Fischer won some examples of this not-so-rare ending that other grandmasters might have concluded were drawn. His games with Pachman at Havana 1966, Maric at Skopje 1967, Hort at Palma 1970, and Parma at Rovinj-Zagreb 1970 are memorable. But the following is the most impressive of the lot.

Fischer – Győző Forintos
Monte Carlo 1967
Ruy Lopez, Breyer Variation (C95)

1	e4	e5
2	♘f3	♘c6
3	♗b5	a6
4	♗a4	♘f6
5	0-0	♗e7
6	♖e1	b5
7	♗b3	d6
8	c3	0-0
9	h3	♘b8
10	d4	♘bd7
11	♘h4	

This gambit (11...♘xe4 12 ♘f5) was popular from about 1961 to 1967, then disappeared for no compelling reason.

11	...	exd4
12	cxd4	♘b6
13	♘d2	

The offer still holds (13...♘xe4 14 ♘xe4 ♗xh4 15 ♕h5). But Fischer later switched to 13 ♘f3 and obtained a big positional edge against Barczay at Sousse following 13...d5? (13...c5!) 14 e5 ♘e4 15 ♘bd2 ♘xd2 16 ♗xd2 ♗f5 17 ♗c3.

| 13 | ... | ♘fd5? |

Superior was 13...c5 with pressure on e4 after 14 ♗c2 cxd4 15 ♘hf3 ♖e8 and ...♗b7.

| 14 | ♘hf3 | ♘b4 |

15 d5!

The position has transposed into a variation usually reached via 9...♘d7 10 d4 ♘b6 11 ♘bd2 exd4 12 cxd4 ♘b4 13 d5. White's move lays claim to c6 for a knight, e.g. 15...♗f6 14 ♘f1 a5 15 a3 ♘a6 16 ♗c2 and 17 ♘d4.

| 15 | ... | c5 |

Also good is 15...♘d3 16 ♖e2 ♗f6 and ...♘xc1.

| 16 | dxc6 | ♘xc6 |
| 17 | ♘f1 | ♗f6? |

Black should drive the bishop off b3 first (17...♘a5).

18 ♗e3!

White needn't spend a tempo on 18 ♖b1 because he wins material with 18...♗xb2? 19 ♕c2! (an idea not available after 17...♘a5 18 ♗c2 ♗f6). For example, 19...♗xa1 20 ♕xc6 or 19...♘c4 20 ♗xc4 ♗xa1 21 ♗b3 ♘b4 22 ♕d2.

| 18 | ... | ♘a5 |
| 19 | ♗d4! | ♗b7 |

The difference between the knights on f1 and b6 is illustrated by 19...♘xb3 20 axb3! ♗b7 21 ♘g3 ♖e8 22 ♘h5, e.g. 22...♖xe4? 23 ♖xe4 ♗xe4 24 ♗xf6 gxf6 25 ♕d4.

20 ♘g3   ♘bc4

21 ♗xc4   ♘xc4

22 ♘h5   ♘e5

This accepts an inferior endgame – but one with bishops of opposite color – and that explains its appeal compared with the difficult middlegame of 22...♗xd4 23 ♕xd4 f6 24 ♘f4.

23 ♘xe5   dxe5

24 ♗c5   ♕xd1

Worse was 24...♖e8 25 ♕g4 and ♖ad1 – and 24...♗e7? (25 ♕xd8) is a blunder.

25 ♖axd1 ♖fd8

26 ♘xf6+ gxf6

Once he became a grandmaster Fischer played remarkably few pure bishops-of-opposite color endings: He won a pawn-up ending with the infamous bishops against Angelo Sandrin in 1957. He drew three equal-material endings of various lengths with Reshevsky early in his career. And he saved one dead-lost ending, two pawns down, against Edgar Walther at Zürich 1959. But after that he avoided the ending or drew quickly as soon as only bishops and pawns were left.

Yet with heavy pieces on the board, the winning chances increase significantly. A pair of rooks or queens add, for example, the wild card factor of a mating threat, as in Game 95. Also, a rook can be used to break the blockade of pawns or even with an Exchange sacrifice to create a passed pawn.

27 ♖xd8+ ♖xd8

28 ♗e7   ♖d4

After 28...♖d2? 29 ♖e3! the mate threat (♖g3+ and ♗xf6) wins a pawn, e.g. 29...h5 30 ♗xf6 ♖xb2 31 a3.

29 ♖e3!   ♗xe4

30 ♗xf6   ♔f8

Or 30...♗d5 31 ♖xe5 ♖d1+ 32 ♔h2.

31 a3   ♗c6

Black had nothing better in view of 32 f3.

32 ♖xe5   ♖d5

33 ♖e3

Of course, 33 ♖xd5? gives away almost all of White's chances. Now he prepares to bring his king to g5, shielded by pawns at f5 and g4. Note that Black has no way of getting his rook to a good square such as e6 that would allow his king to flee the first rank. And 33...♖d6?? loses to 34 ♗e7+.

33 ...   ♖f5?

The rook is clumsy here. Better 33...h5 34 f3 ♔g8 and ...♔h7-g6.

34 ♗e5!   h5

35 f3   a5

36 ♔f2   a4

Black takes the normal precautions on both wings.

37 g4   hxg4
38 hxg4   ♖g5
39 ♗f6!

A powerful move that revives the idea of mate.

39 ...   ♖d5

Not 39...♖g6? 40 g5 and Black must play the rest of the game without king or rook.

40 f4   ♖d2+
41 ♔g3   ♖g2+
42 ♔h4   ♖d2
43 f5   ♗d5
44 ♔g5   ♖d1

Despite a bit of his sloppiness, Black's position looks solid: His pawns are easily protected and 45 ♖h3 (which would have won after 44...♗c4) means nothing after 45...♔e8.

45 ♖c3!

45 ...   ♖e1?

Black also perishes quickly with 45...♗c4? 46 ♖h3 ♔e8 47 ♖h8+ ♔d7 48 ♖d8+ and ♖xd1. But even on 45...♔e8 Black loses a pawn to 46 ♖c5. Then the win isn't easy but

46...♔d7 47 ♖xb5 ♔c6 48 ♖b4 ♗b3 49 ♔h6 followed by ♔g7 and g4-g5-g6 – or an Exchange sacrifice on f7– will suffice.

46 ♖h3!

Not 46 ♖d3 ♗c4 47 ♖d8+ ♖e8.

46 ...   ♔e8
47 ♖d3!   Resigns

The bishop can't move because of 48 ♖d8 mate. Black would also lose after 46...♖h1 47 ♖d3 ♗c6 48 ♖d8+ ♗e8 49 ♖b8 followed by ♗c3-b4+.

62

This game, like the last two, illustrates Fischer's ability to blend the tactical and technical in the endgame. Botvinnik later compared him to his most famous student. "From a combinational point of view, I suggest Kasparov outstripped Fischer," he wrote. "But in the endgame, Fischer was stronger."

Bent Larsen – Fischer
Monte Carlo 1967
King's Indian Defense,
Classical Variation (E97)

1	d4	♘f6
2	c4	g6
3	♘c3	♗g7
4	e4	d6
5	♗e2	0-0
6	♘f3	e5
7	0-0	♘c6
8	♗e3	

Larsen had injected several ideas into the Classical King's Indian. For example, in Benko's line, 8 d5 ♘e7 9 ♘e1 ♘d7 10 f3 f5 11 g4, he showed that what was considered the book refutation – 11...h5 12 g5 h4 13 ♘d3 f4 followed by winning the g-pawn – was actually a strong gambit after 14 ♔h1 ♔f7 15 c5 ♖h8 16 ♕b3!.

8	...	♖e8
9	dxe5	

Black is at least equal after 9 d5 ♘d4! (10 ♘xd4 exd4 11.♗xd4 ♘xe4).

9	...	dxe5
10	♕xd8	♘xd8
11	♘b5	♘e6
12	♘g5	♖e7

White's pressure is strong after 12...♘xg5 13 ♗xg5 ♖e7 14 ♖ad1 ♗e6 15 f4!.

13 ♖fd1

Najdorf, who popularized 8...♖e8, had pronounced 13 ♘xa7 ♘f4! good for Black.

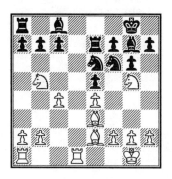

13	...	b6!

Fischer is the first to vary from book (his ninth match game with Reshevsky, which went 13...c6 14 ♘xe6 ♗xe6 15 ♘c3 ♖d7). Larsen had been waiting to test a new idea – 13...c6 14 ♘xa7! ♗d7 15 ♘xe6 ♗xe6 16 f3.

14	c5!	♘xc5!

One point of the pawn sacrifice is 14...bxc5 15 ♘xe6 ♗xe6 16 ♗xc5 ♖d7 17 f3 and Black's pawns are just too weak (17...c6 18 ♖xd7 ♘xd7 19 ♘c7).

15	♖d8+	♗f8

White also has a big edge after 15...♖e8? 16 ♖xe8+ ♘xe8 17 ♗xc5 bxc5 18 ♗c4 (18...♘d6 19 ♘xd6 cxd6 20 ♘xf7 ♔f8 21 ♘xd6).

16	♘xa7	♖xa7
17	♖xc8	♔g7

With this Black anticipates ♗h6 (17...♘cxe4?? 18 ♘xe4 ♘xe4 19 ♗h6 and wins) and declines an invitation into 17...♘b3 18 ♖d1 ♖xa2 19 ♖dd8 ♘d7 20 h4! threatening ♗c4 or ♗b5.

Fischer later said 17...h6 18 ♘f3 ♔g7 19 ♗xc5 bxc5 was a straighter road to equality but even then White is a bit better, e.g. 20 ♗d3 c4 21 ♗xc4 ♘xe4 22 ♖d8. Better is 17...♖e8 18 ♖xe8 ♘xe8 with equality.

18	f3	♘e8
19	a3	

Fischer thought 19 ♗xc5 bxc5 20 ♖b8 was best but there's little if anything after 20...f6 followed by ...♘d6/...♖e8.

19	...	♘d6

Now 20 ♖b8 ♘d7! 21 ♖d8 ♘b7 leads to a repetition of moves.

20	♖d8	h6
21	♘h3	♘e6
22	♖b8	♖e8
23	♖xe8	♘xe8

24 ♗b5

The position is dead even and only Larsen's eternal optimism changes that. He wants to prevent ...♗c5 and considers planting the bishop on c6.

24 ... ♘d6

Now 25 ♗c6? ♘c4 26 ♗c1 ♗c5+ favors Black.

25 ♗f1 ♘b7!

26 ♘f2 ♗c5

27 ♗xc5 ♘bxc5

28 ♖d1 h5

This avoids the complications of 28...♘d4 29 ♘g4 f6 30 f4! – although Black stands perfectly well after 30...♘xe4 31 fxe5 fxe5 32 ♘xe5 c5.

After the text White should acknowledge the way of the world, play 29 ♘d3 and ♔f2 and offer a handshake.

29 ♖d5 ♔f6

30 h4 ♔e7!

Now 31 ♖xe5?? c6 seals the rook's doom (32...f6). White's position slowly deteriorates now.

31 ♗c4 c6

32 ♖d2 ♘d4

33 ♔f1 f5!

34 b4?

In his calculations Larsen missed either Black's 34th or 35th move. Again 34 ♘d3 was better although Black can play for a win after 34...♘xd3 and ...f4.

34 ... b5!

35 ♗g8 fxe4!

Now the e-pawn is a major weakness. Black is also winning after 36 bxc5 e3 37 ♖d3 exf2 38 ♔xf2 (38 f4 ♔f6 39 ♔xf2 ♘f5 is slightly better) ♖a8 39 ♗a2 b4 or 37 ♖xd4 exd4 38 ♘d3 ♖xa3.

36 fxe4 ♘d7

37 ♖d3 ♖a6

38 ♖c3

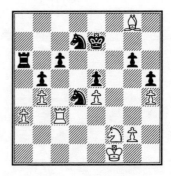

38 ... c5

This is one of Fischer's most famous moves – an echo of Larsen's own pawn sacrifice on the same square, at move 14. But it's an error.

With the more precise 38...♖a8! Black wins quickly, e.g. 39 ♗a2 c5! 40 bxc5 b4. Then 41 ♖g3 ♘xc5 and ...b3 wins. The key point is that 41 ♖c1 ♖xa3 now attacks the bishop – and after 42 ♗d5 ♖c3 43 ♖b1 ♘xc5 44 ♘d1 ♖c2 or 43 ♖xc3 bxc3 44 ♘d3 c2 the game would likely have ended some 10 moves earlier than it did.

39 g4?

A typical time-pressure stab. White could have exploited Black's miscue with 39 bxc5 b4! 40 ♖c1!. Fischer said the outcome is uncertain then (40...♖a8 41 ♗d5; 40...♖xa3 41 c6 or 40...bxa3 41 ♗a2). Closer to a win is 40...♘f6 41 ♗a2 ♖xa3 42 c6 ♔d8.

39	**...**	**c4**
40	**gxh5**	**gxh5**

The crippled a-pawn and the lack of a good square for White's bishop prove decisive.

41	**♗d5**	**♘f6**

White has counterplay after 41...♘b3 42 ♖g3!.

42	**♖g3**	**♘xd5**
43	**exd5**	**♖f6**

Now 44 ♔g1? ♘e2+ or 44 ♔e1 ♖f4.

44	**♔g2**	**♘f5**
45	**♖h3**	**♖g6+**
46	**♔f3**	**♘d4+**
47	**♔e3**	

Fischer pointed out that 47 ♔e4 ♔d6 was *zugzwang*. For example, 48 ♖h2 ♖g3 or 48 a4? bxa4 49 ♖a3 ♖g1 50 ♖xa4?? ♖e1 mate.

47	**...**	**♖g2**

The rest was *kinderspiel*:

48 ♖h1 ♔d6 49 ♘e4+ ♔xd5 50 ♘c3+ ♔e6 51 ♖c1 ♖h2 52 a4 ♖h3+! 53 ♔f2 ♘b3 54 ♔g2 ♘xc1 55 ♔xh3 bxa4 56 ♘xa4 ♘e2 57 b5 c3 58 b6 c2 59 ♘c5+ ♔d5 60 ♘b3 ♔c6 61 ♔g2 ♔xb6 White resigns

63

Fischer's next chess was in the Philippines, where an abortive international tournament was replaced by a series of clocked games, sponsored by the Manila electric company under the theme "Beat Bobby Fischer." The following game was virtually unknown until it appeared, with seven others from the series, in the *British Chess Magazine* in 1980. The real battle only lasts from move 7 to 14 but the exact nature of Fischer's moves, particularly his 10th and 11th, is impressive.

Fischer – Renato Naranja
Philippines 1967
Sicilian Defense (B23)

1	**e4**	**c5**
2	**♘c3**	**♘c6**
3	**♘ge2**	

Fischer began to test this move order in 1967 and later returned to it in the 1992 rematch with Spassky.

3	**...**	**e5**

The principled reply, as the Russians would say. It was unfairly criticized at the time for surrendering d5.

4	**♘d5**	**♘f6**
5	**♘ec3**	

The point. White will develop his bishop on c4.

5	**...**	**♗e7**
6	**♗c4**	**0-0**
7	**d3**	**h6?**

Black wanted to avoid 8 ♘xe7+ and 9 ♗g5 but this puts his king on the endangered species list. Today's grandmasters get close to equality with 7...♘xd5 8 ♗xd5 d6 and a trade of bishops after ...♗g5.

8 f4!

Geller gave 8 0-0 in ECO but White shouldn't abandon the prospect of a kingside pawn storm so early.

8 ... d6?

Black must exchange on f4.

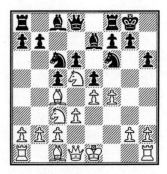

9 f5!

This strategically decides the game. White stops ...♗e6 and sets the stage for a decisive advance of the g-pawn.

9 ... b6

It was too late for 9...♘xd5 10 ♘xd5 ♗g5 because 11 ♕h5! ♗xc1 12 ♖xc1 threatens 13 f6 with a quick mate. (The defense of 12...♕g5 fails to 13 ♕xg5 hxg5 14 h4! since 14...gxh4 15 ♖xh4 leaves Black in a quandary over how to stop ♔f2 and ♖ch1.) But Black should at least eliminate the bishop with 9...♘a5.

10 h4!

A striking move which prepares g4-g5, with or without ♘xe7+ and

♕h5. The key variation is 10...♘xd5 11 ♗xd5! ♗xh4+ and now 12 g3! ♗xg3+ 13 ♔f1, à la a King's Gambit, gives an overwhelming attack.

For example, 13...♗d7 14 ♕g4 ♗f4 and now a bit faster than 15 ♗xf4 exf4 16 ♖xh6 ♘e5 or 16 ♗xc6 ♗xc6 17 ♖xh6 ♕g5 is 15 ♖xh6! threatening 16 ♗xf4 exf4 17 ♕g6 and mates. Black loses the queen after 15...♗xh6 16 ♗xh6 ♕f6 17 ♗g5.

10 ... ♗b7

11 a3!

Another exact move, preserving the bishop against 11...♘a5 and stopping ...♘b4. The significance of this is shown by 11 ♘xf6+ ♗xf6 12 ♕h5? when Black has 12...♘b4! with good chances, e.g. 13 ♗b3 d5 14 g4 c4!.

Black also would have counterplay after 11 ♘xe7+ ♘xe7 12 g4 d5! 13 exd5 ♘fxd5 or 13 g5! dxc4 14 gxf6 ♘xf5!.

11 ... ♖c8

12 ♘xf6+! ♗xf6

13 ♕h5

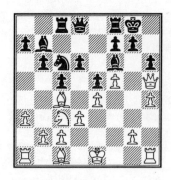

13 ...   ♘e7

Black had to do something about 14 g4 and 15 g5, and this enables him to shoot back with 14 g4 d5. Play could continue 15 g5 g6! 16 fxg6 – not 16 ♕xh6? ♗g7 winning the queen – fxg6 17 ♕g4 dxc4 18 ♕e6+ ♔h7 19 gxf6 ♘c6 and Black is still alive. White does much better with 18 gxf6 ♖xf6 19 ♗xh6! and 20 0-0-0.

14 ♗g5!

Another terrific move, threatening ♗xf6. Of course, 14...hxg5 15 hxg5 is taboo because of mate on the h-file.

14 ...   d5

After 14...♘c6 15 ♗xf6 ♕xf6 16 ♘d5 ♕d8 17 f6 Black can safely stop the clocks.

15 ♗xf6   dxc4

Black cannot recapture on f6 because of mate after ♕xh6 and ♖h3.

16 ♕g4   g6

17 dxc4!

There must have been a huge temptation to try to finish the game off in style – particularly after White saw 17 ♕g5 hxg5?? 18 hxg5 and ♖h8 mate. The temptation could only grow once he found that 17...♘c6 18 ♘d5! or 17...♔h7 18 h5!! also won.

But again ...♘xf5 bursts the bubble: 17 ♕g5? ♘xf5! and now 18 ♗xd8 hxg5 19 ♗xg5 ♘d4 is a roughly equal ending, or 18 exf5 hxg5 19 hxg5 ♕xf6.

17 ...   ♕d6

This acknowledges defeat but 17...♔h7 would have breathed life into 18 ♕g5!!:

(a) 18...♖e8 19 h5! hxg5 20 hxg6+ and ♖h8 mate,

(b) 18...♖c6 19 h5! (the fastest) ♘xf5 20 hxg6+ ♔g8 21 ♘d5!, and

(c) 18...♘g8 19 ♗xd8 hxg5 20 hxg5+ ♔g7 21 f6+ and mates.

18 ♗xe7!

Black's last move was designed to meet 18 ♕g5 with 18...hxg5 19 hxg5 ♕xf6!. So Fischer decides to cash in.

18	...	♕xe7
19	fxg6	fxg6
20	♕xg6+	♕g7
21	♕xg7+	♔xg7
22	♖d1	

The endgame is easy (22...♖c7 23 ♖h3 and ♖g3+/♖d6 etc.) or as the game went:

22 ... ♖cd8 23 ♖xd8 ♖xd8 24 ♘d5 b5 25 cxb5 ♗xd5 26 exd5 c4 27 a4 ♖xd5 28 ♔e2 ♖d4 29 ♖d1! ♖e4+ 30 ♔f3 ♖f4+ 31 ♔e3 c3 32 b3 Resigns

64

The tournament known as Skopje 1967 was held to show how the Macedonian city had recovered after a devastating earthquake four years before. Actually the 17-round invitational was held in a series of cities – Skopje, Kurshevo, Ohrid and finally back to Skopje again. Despite the constant travel and the August heat, Fischer was the only player in the tournament who always played in suit and tie. He hardly got a wrinkle in his shirt before Black resigned in the following game:

Fischer – Peter Dely
Skopje 1967
Sicilian Defense,
Sozin Variation (B88)

1	e4	c5
2	♘f3	♘c6
3	d4	cxd4
4	♘xd4	♘f6
5	♘c3	d6
6	♗c4	e6
7	♗b3	

By the mid-1960s, the Sozin move order was explored in enough depth to distinguish this move, which prepares f2-f4-f5, from 7 ♗e3, which prepares queenside castling à la Velimirović (8 ♕e2 and 9 0-0-0) or by way of 8 f4 and 9 ♕f3.

7	...	a6
8	f4	♕a5

The threat of 9...♘xe4 forestalls the formula mentioned in Game 9, compared with 8...♘a5 9 f5 ♘xb3 10 axb3 ♗e7 11 ♕f3 0-0 12 ♗e3

♗d7 13 g4 as in Fischer – Bielicki, Mar del Plata 1960.

Fischer said that on 8...♕c7 White should play 9 f5 ♘xd4 10 ♕xd4 exf5 11 exf5 ♗xf5 12 0-0, which he regarded as favorable. Yet there hasn't been a serious test of the gambit since he suggested it.

9 0-0! ♘xd4

Fischer considered 9...d5, which threatens 10...♘xd4 11 ♕xd4 ♗c5, as very favorable for him after 10 ♘xc6 bxc6 11 f5.

10 ♕xd4

10 ... d5?

Black makes a major tactical threat (11...♗c5) as well as a very minor positional one (11...dxe4). On other moves – except for the poor ending of 10...♕c5 11 ♕xc5 dxc5 (12 e5 ♘d7 13 ♘e4) – White has a strong f4-f5.

11 ♗e3

Now 11...dxe4 12 ♘xe4 ♗e7 13 ♘d6+ concedes Black's opening is a flop.

11 ... ♘xe4

The main problem with Black's 10th move was that he can't exploit the a7-g1 diagonal as planned, e.g.

11...♘g4 12 ♔h1! ♘xe3 13 ♕xe3 dxe4 14 ♕xe4. Then White threatens 15 f5 and introduces a dangerous idea that will plague Black for the rest of the game, the check on a4.

For example, 14...♕b4 15 ♗a4+! ♗d7 16 ♗xd7+ ♔xd7 17 ♖ad1+ ♔e8 18 ♕d3 or 17...♔c7 18 ♕e5+ puts the black king on the run.

He can also try 14...♗e7 after which 15 ♗a4+ ♔f8 16 ♖ad1 or 15 ♖ae1 and 16 f5 is powerful (e.g. 15 ♖ae1 g6? 16 ♘d5! ♗d8 17 ♕e5 0-0? 18 ♘e7+!).

12 ♘xe4 dxe4

Here 13 ♗a4+ b5 14 ♕xe4 allows Black to recoup a bit after 14...♖b8 15 ♗b3 ♕c7 16 f5 ♗b7.

13 f5!

After 13...exf5 White wins with 14 ♗a4+ b5 15 ♕e5+! ♗e7 16 ♗b3, threatening ♕xg7. For example, 16...♔f8 17 ♖xf5! ♗xf5 18 ♕xf5 ♗f6 19 ♗c5+ ♔g8 20 ♕d7. Or 16...♕d8 17 ♖ad1 ♗d7 18 ♖xf5! 0-0 19 ♖xd7! ♕xd7 20 ♗d4 wins.

13 ... ♕b4

The best chance of surviving to a middlegame was 13...♗e7 14 ♕xg7 ♖f8 – although after 15 ♕xh7 it's a lost middlegame (15...♗c5 16 ♗a4+!, that move again).

14 fxe6 ♗xe6

Black has no time for 14...♕xd4 15 exf7+.

15 ♗xe6 fxe6

Or here 15...♕xd4 16 ♗xf7+.

16 ♖xf8+! ♕xf8

Otherwise the queen hangs.

17 ♕a4+! Resigns

Black was so demoralized he didn't wait to see what White would do after 17...b5 18 ♕xe4 ♖d8 (not 18...♖b8 19 ♕c6+ or 18...♔d7 19 ♕b7+) 19 ♕c6+ ♖d7 20 ♖d1 ♕e7.

Then on 21 ♗c5?? ♕xc5+ Black is not losing and after 21 ♗g5 0-0! he can play a bit further. But 21 ♗b6! would have been the killer.

65

Fischer won Skopje 1967 thanks to this next-to-last-round game. But an ominous sign had appeared six rounds earlier when he insisted on playing in a separate area, without spectators, and using a set in which the distinction between the queen and king was more pronounced. The organizers refused and Fischer forfeited his game. Cooler heads prevailed and Fischer agreed to finish out the tournament and reschedule the forfeit. But for the rest of Fischer's career he became increasingly more inflexible in his demands.

Ratmir Kholmov – Fischer
Skopje 1967
King's Indian Defense,
Fianchetto Variation (A49)

1 d4	♘f6
2 ♘f3	g6
3 g3	♗g7
4 ♗g2	0-0
5 0-0	d6
6 ♘c3	♘bd7

At the Piatigorsky Cup Fischer tried 6...d5, to penalize lvkov for blocking White's c-pawn. That was good enough for equality but no more after 7 ♘e5 c6 8 e4.

7 b3

A unique position already. More common is the Pirc-like 7 e4 e5.

7 ...	e5
8 dxe5	

White's dilemma is that if he plays 8 e4, he creates a target (8...exd4 9 ♘xd4 ♖e8 10 ♗b2 ♘c5 11 ♖e1 ♗g4). But if he doesn't, Black cramps his game with ...e4!.

8 ...	dxe5
9 e4	♖e8
10 ♗a3	

After 10 ♗b2 c6 and ...♕e7 Black has little to fear. But the bishop gets into trouble on a3.

10 ...	c6
11 ♗d6	♕a5

Fischer believed this punished 11 ♗d6. But...

12 ♕d3??

...this was the real error. White can allow 12 a3! ♕xc3 because both players must accept a draw by repetition of moves (13 ♗b4 ♕b2 14 ♖b1 ♕a2 15 ♖a1 ♕b2). This would have been the shortest game Fischer ever played.

Note that if White insists on trapping the queen with 14 ♕e2 a5 15 ♖fb1 the cost is too great (15...♕xa1 16 ♖xa1 axb4).

12 ... ♖e6!

Astonishingly strong. The threats are 13...♘e8, trapping the bishop, and 13...♖xd6 14 ♕xd6 ♕xc3.

Kholmov had counted on 13 ♘g5 (and 13...♖xd6 14 ♕xd6 ♕xc3? 15 ♕e7). But now he saw 14...h6! 15 b4 ♕a3 costs him material.

13 b4	♕a3!
14 ♗c7	♕xb4

Fischer indicated this was much better than 14...♘e8 15 ♗a5 b6 16 ♖ab1! bxa5 17 ♖b3 after which Black's best winning try is the unclear 17...♘c5 18 bxc5 ♕xc5.

But that shortchanges Black, who could win with 16...♖d6! (instead of 16...bxa5) 17 ♕c4 ♗a6 18 ♕xa6

♕xc3 since the bishop remains trapped. The same goes for 17 ♕e3 ♗h6 18 ♕e1 ♗d2! or 18 ♕xh6 ♕xc3.

15 ♖ab1   ♕e7

Black should keep c5 free since White would have serious compensation after 15...♕c5? 16 ♘g5 ♖e8 17 ♘a4 ♕d4 18 ♕b3.

16 ♖fd1

But here Black can meet 16 ♘g5 with 16...♘c5! (17 ♕c4 ♕xc7).

16 ...	**♘e8**
17 ♗a5	**♖d6**
18 ♕e2	**♖xd1+**
19 ♕xd1	**♗f8**

Black again threatens to win the bishop with ...♕a3, and 20 ♗b4 should lose to 20...♕f6 (not 20...c5? 21 ♘d5) 21 ♗xf8 ♘xf8.

20 ♘d2	**♕a3!**
21 ♘c4	**♕c5**
22 ♗f1	**b5**
23 ♘d2	

When the dust settles after 23 ♗b4? ♕d4! White is dead lost.

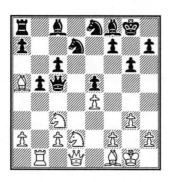

23 ...   ♕a3!

Powerful, for the third time in game. Black wins material.

24 ♘b3   ♘c5!

White now runs out of squares (25 ♗d8 ♘e6 26 ♗a5 ♘d6 or 25 ♕d8 ♗b7).

25 ♗xb5!?   cxb5!

Safer, despite appearances, than 25...♘xb3 26 ♗xc6 ♖b8? 27 ♗d8! or 26...♘xa5 27 ♘b5 ♕c5.

26 ♘xb5   ♕a4

Forced – but more than sufficient (27 ♕d5 ♕xe4).

27 ♘xc5	**♕xa5**
28 ♕d5	**♖b8**
29 a4	**♗h3!**
30 ♕xe5	**♖c8**
31 ♘d3	**♕xa4**

Black wins after 32 ♘f4 ♕xc2 33 ♖e1 ♗b4 34 ♘d4 ♕c5!.

32 ♘e1   a6!

White resigns

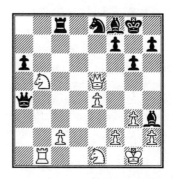

The handwriting on the wall reads 33 ♘d4 ♗g7; 33 ♘c3 ♕c4 and 33 ♘a7!? ♖c7 34 ♖a1 ♕d7 (or 34...♕c4!) 35 ♖xa6 ♖xa7 36 ♖xa7 ♕xa7 37 ♕xe8 ♕a1! and wins.

66

Technically, the next three games didn't happen. They were among ten played by Fischer – seven of them wins – that were wiped off the scoretable after he withdrew from the 1967 Interzonal at the Tunisian resort City of Sousse. Fischer walked out after an escalating dispute over scheduling that created a kind of time pressure crisis in the 22-player tournament's "middlegame."

Fischer – Lhamsuren Miagmasuren
Interzonal, Sousse 1967
King's Indian Reversed (C00)

1	e4	e6
2	d3	d5
3	♘d2	♘f6
4	g3	c5
5	♗g2	♘c6
6	♘gf3	♗e7
7	0-0	0-0
8	e5	♘d7
9	♖e1	b5

In the early 1960s when 2 d3 began to beat the French, Black tried a variety of slow responses (9...♕c7, 9...♖b8, 9...b6) – but not 9...b5 because it was feared that 10 a4 would disrupt his queenside initiative. It took a while before Black realized that open lines (10...bxa4!) were more important than pawn integrity.

10	♘f1	b4
11	h4	a5
12	♗f4	a4

That led to the conviction that the middlegame was a race in which Black tried to open the queenside before White crashed through on the kingside.

13 a3!!

But this move, allowing the opening of the b-file, was a thunderbolt. Kmoch believed Fischer played it after he realized 13 ♘e3 a3 14 b3 would allow 14...f5 15 exf6 ♗xf6, attacking the rook at a1 and gaining a key tempo. Yet when Fischer annotated the game in *Boy's Life* he explained he was thinking in general terms. He just didn't want to create a hole at c3 after 13...a3 14 b3. Chess, he added, is "knowing when to punch and how to duck."

13	...	bxa3
14	bxa3	♘a5?

The knight turns out to be vulnerable here (!). If Black wanted to support ...c5-c4, then 14...♗a6 was better, although 15 ♘e3 ♘d4 16 c4! is a good reply as Gheorghiu showed a year later in a game that went 16...♘b3 17 cxd5! ♘xa1 18 ♕xa1 exd5 19 ♘xd5 ♗xd3 20 e6!.

15 ♘e3

Fischer had considerable experience with the pawn-based attack – that is h4-h5-h6, followed by ♗g5xe7 and the occupation of f6. But here he adopts the piece-based plan of ♕h5, ♘g5 and ♘g4.

15 ...   ♗a6

Kmoch preferred 15...♘b6 or 15...♘c6, conceding that Black's last move was an error. But Black apparently wanted to keep a white knight out of c4 once he played ...d4.

16 ♗h3!

This is the one piece that doesn't seem to fit in with the opening but here it discourages ...f6 or ...f5.

16 ...   d4

17 ♘f1

If White switches to the pawn-based attack, 17 ♘g4 ♘b6 18 h5, Black continues 18...♘d5 19 ♗d2 h6. Then White is more or less committed to a sacrifice on h6 that may or may not work.

17 ...   ♘b6

18 ♘g5   ♘d5

Fischer said 18...h6 19 ♘e4 c4 was superior but didn't go any further. The likely continuation would be 20 ♕h5 cxd3 and now:

(a) 21 ♗xh6 gxh6 22 ♗xe6 offers at most a perpetual check, and

(b) 21 ♗xh6 gxh6 22 ♘f6+ ♗xf6 23 exf6 ♕xf6 24 ♕xa5 ♖fb8 which is fine for Black, but

(c) 21 ♘f6+! gxf6 22 ♗xe6! is more convincing. Then 21...fxe6 22 ♗xh6 ♖f7 is best but White is winning after 23 ♕g6+ ♔h8 24 ♕xf7.

19 ♗d2   ♗xg5

This trashes the kingside dark squares. But what was there to do about the threats such as 20 ♕h5 or 20 ♘xe6 fxe6 21 ♗xe6+ ♔h8 22 ♗xa5 ♕xa5 23 ♗xd5? For example, 19...♘c6 20 ♕g4 or 20 ♕h5 h6 21 ♘e4 is also unpleasant.

20 ♗xg5   ♕d7

21 ♕h5   ♖fc8

Black pins his hopes on protecting the dark squares with ...♕e8-f8. The quickness of White's attack is shown by 21...c4 22 ♗g2! cxd3 and now 23 ♗e4 g6 24 ♕h6 f5 25 exf6 dxc2? 26 ♗xd5! exd5 27 ♖e7 or 23...h6 24 cxd3 and ♘h2-g4xh6+.

22 ♘d2!   ♘c3

In the first edition of this book I wrote: Black loses if the knight gets to stay on e4, e.g. 22...c4 23 ♘e4 cxd3 24 ♗f6!. Computers now show me that after 24...♕e8! White has nothing better than 25 ♗xg7 ♔xg7 26 ♘f6 ♘xf6 27 ♕g5+ ♔h8 28 ♕xf6+ ♔g8 and a draw.

23 ♗f6!

Based on 23...gxf6 24 exf6 ♔h8 25 ♘f3 ♖g8 26 ♘e5! and wins. Or 25...♘d5 26 ♘g5 (also 26 ♕h6 ♖g8 27 ♘e5 ♕e8 28 ♗g2!! ♕f8 29 ♗e4!) ♘xf6 27 ♕h6 ♕e7 28 ♗f5! and ♘xh7.

| 23 | ... | ♕e8 |

24 ♘e4 g6

Played to gain a tempo after 25 ♕h6 ♕f8!. On the immediate 24...♕f8 White has 25 ♘g5 h6 26 ♘xe6 fxe6 27 ♗xe6+ ♔h7 28 ♗f5+ ♔g8 29 ♕g6 and wins.

25 ♕g5! ♘xe4

26 ♖xe4 c4

The attack rolls on after 26...♗b7 27 ♖g4 and 28 h5. For instance, 27...♕f8 28 h5 h6 29 ♕f4 g5 30 ♖xg5+! hxg5 31 ♕xg5+ ♔h7 32 ♗xe6! and ♗f5 mate (or 32...fxe6 33 ♕g6 mate).

27 h5! cxd3

28 ♖h4

White's idea is ♖xh7!, e.g. 28...dxc2 29 hxg6 fxg6 30 ♖xh7! ♔xh7 31 ♕h4+ or 30...c1(♕)+ 31 ♖xc1 ♖xc1+ 32 ♕xc1 ♔xh7 33 ♕c7+! and mates.

28 ... ♖a7

Fischer said 28...♖c7 was better because it would allow Black to meet hxg6 with ...fxg6 and not fear ♖xh7.

29 ♗g2!

Fischer is the best bishop player in history, Robert Byrne once said, and here his handling of the KB is as remarkable as 28 ♗e4!! in Game 84. Computers point out that 29 ♗g4! also wins here because 30 ♕h6 ♕f8 31 ♕xh7+! ♔xh7 32 hxg6+ ♔xg6 33 ♗h5+ ♔h7 34 ♗f3+ mates.

29 ... dxc2

White also wins after 29...♕f8 30 ♗e4 dxc2 31 hxg6 fxg6

32 ♗xg6!, e.g. 32...c1(♕)+ 33 ♖xc1 ♖xc1+ 34 ♔h2! hxg6 35 ♖h8+ ♔f7 36 ♖h7+! ♔e8 37 ♖xa7!.

30 ♕h6 ♕f8

31 ♕xh7+! Resigns

The final reason for 29 ♗g2 is revealed by 31...♕xh7 32 hxg6+ ♔xg6 33 ♗e4 mate.

67

One round after the Miagmasuren game, Fischer showed signs of the strain of playing in his first Interzonal since Stockholm: During his game with the Colombian Miguel Cuéllar he complained about "weak lighting." But the tournament judge refused to do anything, so Fischer and Cuéllar ended up shifting the table. The tournament organizers "are against me," Fischer later said. "They're waiting for me to lose a game."

Miguel Cuéllar – Fischer
Interzonal, Sousse 1967
Modern Benoni Defense (A71)

1	d4	♘f6
2	c4	c5
3	d5	e6
4	♘c3	exd5
5	cxd5	d6
6	♘f3	g6
7	e4	♗g7
8	♗g5	h6
9	♗f4!?	

An attempt to avoid the sharp 9 ♗h4 g5 10 ♗g3 ♘h5 11 ♗b5+.

9 ...   g5!

"I don't believe in psychology," Fischer famously said, "I believe in good moves." The text has elements of both: White either has to lose time with his bishop or admit he was wrong last move and transpose into the previous note with 10 ♗g3. The alternatives are (a) 10 ♗b5+ ♔f8 11 ♗e3 ♘g4 11 ♗d2 a6 12 ♗e2, which offers him little, (b) 10 ♗e3 0-0 followed by ...♘g4/...f5 which offers less, and (c)...

10 ♗c1?

...which overestimates the weakness of Black's kingside pawns.

10 ...   0-0

11 ♘d2

On 11 ♗e2 Black might have continued with 11...b5! 12 ♗xb5 ♘xe4, a common Benoni motif.

Compare that with 8 ♗e2 0-0 9 ♗f4 b5! 10 ♗xb5 ♘xe4 11 ♘xe4 ♕a5+ 12 ♕d2 ♕xb5 13 ♘xd6 ♕xb2, a position well known to theory as roughly equal.

11 ...   ♘bd7

12 ♗e2   ♘e5

Only in the 1970s was it appreciated that ...g5 – even without a gain of tempo – was worthwhile to

secure e5. For example, in the standard Benoni line that runs 8 ♗e2 0-0 9 0-0 ♖e8 10 ♘d2 Black was found to have good play after 10...♘bd7 11 h3 g5!.

13 ♘f1!

Since Black stands excellently after 13 0-0 a6 14 a4 ♖b8, White aims to exploit the f5 and h5 holes with ♘g3 or ♘e3.

13 ...   b5!

This diverts him. Black would hold the initiative after 14 ♘g3 b4 15 ♘b1 c4.

14 ♗xb5   ♕a5

The threat is 15...♘xe4 (and if 15 ♗d3 then 15...♘xd3+ 16 ♕xd3 ♘xe4!).

15 ♘g3   c4

Also thematic is 15...♖b8 16 ♗e2 h5?!, with possibilities such as 17 ♗xg5 ♖xb2 18 ♕c1 ♖xe2+! 19 ♔xe2 (19 ♘xe2?? ♘d3+) ♗a6+ 20 ♔d1 ♘fg4. But White assures himself of an edge with the sensible 17 0-0!.

16 0-0   ♖b8

17 ♕a4!

The bishop looks well placed after 17 ♗c6 and White gets the play he needs after 17...♘xc6 18 dxc6 ♕c5 19 ♕a4!. But Black should ignore it with 17...♘d3! and ...♘g4.

17 ...   ♕xa4

18 ♗xa4   ♘d3

19 ♗b5

A less artificial defense of b2 was 19 ♖b1 ♘d7 20 ♗c2 ♘b4 21 ♗d1 ♘c5 22 ♗e3.

19 ...   ♘g4!

20 ♘ge2

On 20 ♗xc4 ♘xb2 21 ♗xb2 ♖xb2 22 ♖ac1 ♗d4 22 ♘ge2 ♗c5 23 ♘a4! White is clearly better but 22...♗e5 leaves matters uncertain.

20	...	♘xc1
21	♖axc1	♘e5

Black has ample play for a pawn, e.g. 22 ♖c2 f5 23 ♘g3 f4 24 ♘ge2 f3 25 gxf3 ♗h3 or 23 exf5 ♗xf5 24 ♖d2 ♗d3.

22	b3	cxb3
23	axb3	a6
24	♗a4	

The bishops begin to dominate after 24 ♗c4 ♘xc4 25 bxc4 ♖b4 26 ♘d1 f5.

24	...	♘d3
25	♖c2	f5
26	♘g3	

No better was 26 exf5 ♗xf5 27 ♖a2 ♘c5 or 27 ♖d2 ♘c5 (28 ♘d4? ♗d3).

26	...	f4!
27	♘ge2	

After 27 ♘h5 ♗e5 White's knight is a new worry (...♗g4, ...♔h7-g6).

27	...	f3

Now 28 gxf3 ♖xf3 and ...♗h3 is very strong.

28	♘g3	fxg2
29	♔xg2	♗g4!

Among the nice finishes are 30 f3 ♗xf3+ 31 ♖xf3 ♘e1+ and 31 ♔h3 ♘f4 mate.

30	♘f5?	

A blunder that drops a piece. But 30 ♘d1 ♗f3+ 31 ♔g1 h5! followed by ...h4 or ...♘f4 also favors Black.

30	...	♘f4+!

Now 31 ♔h1 ♗f3+ and mate next.

31	♔g3	♗xf5
32	exf5	♗xc3

Since 33 ♖xc3 ♘e2+ leaves Black a rook up, White decides to play a piece down until adjournment. The finish was efficient:

33 ♔f3 ♗e5 34 ♔e4 ♖b4+ 35 ♖c4 ♖fb8 36 f6 ♔f7 37 ♔f5 ♖xc4 38 bxc4 ♘e2 (Now 39 c5 ♖b4!.) **39 ♖e1 ♘d4+ 40 ♔g4 h5+!** (41 ♔xh5 ♖h8+ 42 ♔g4 ♖h4+ 43 ♔xg5 ♘f3+ and mates.) **41 ♔h3 ♔xf6 White resigns**

68

Fischer was justly proud of his 6-hour-12-minute marathon with Leonid Stein. His opponent was both the reigning Soviet champion and the winner of the recent Alekhine Memorial tournament in Moscow – to which Fischer, like other Westerners, was not invited. When Fischer was about to bolt the Interzonal, Bjelica asked him who would be left in the championship eliminations to face Petrosian in 1969 Fischer's replied as if there was no one worthy: "I beat Stein here and Stein was the winner of Moscow tournament. I've proved I'm the best."

Fischer – Leonid Stein
Interzonal, Sousse 1967
Ruy Lopez (C92)

1	e4	e5
2	♘f3	♘c6
3	♗b5	a6
4	♗a4	♘f6
5	0-0	♗e7
6	♖e1	b5
7	♗b3	d6
8	c3	0-0
9	h3	

Stein, a devout Sicilophile, defended the Lopez rarely. Here he uses a new four-move manoeuvre of the problem knight to reinforce e5 and prepare ...d5 or ...c5.

9	...	♗b7
10	d4	♘a5
11	♗c2	♘c4
12	b3	♘b6

Black's pawn is protected because of ...♖d1+ (13 dxe5 dxe5 14 ♕xd8 ♖axd8 15 ♘xe5 ♘xe4!).

13	♘bd2	♘bd7

Stein's idea would work well after 14 ♘f1 ♖e8 15 ♘g3 ♗f8 16 b4 and

now 16...a5! 17 a3 axb4 18 cxb4 d5! with equal chances.

14 b4!

In an extensive study of Fischer's openings, prepared by an elite Soviet team in 1971, this game was cited as a case of how "Fischer metes out punishment for fanciful opening play designed merely to avoid the beaten path." White's move eyes a5 (14...a5 15 ♘b3!) and stops 14...c5 (15 bxc5 dxc5 16 dxe5).

14	...	exd4

More consistent is 14...♖e8 after which 15 a4 ♗f8 16 ♗b2 allows Black a promising pawn sack 16...exd4 17 cxd4 d5 18 e5 ♘e4!.

15	cxd4	a5!
16	bxa5	

White targets the b-pawn (16...♖xa5 17 d5, e.g. 17...♘b6 18 ♘d4 ♕d7 19 ♗d3 ♖fa8 20 ♕c2).

16	...	c5!
17	e5!	dxe5

White's superiority is obvious following 17...♘d5 18 ♘e4 or 18 exd6 ♗xd6 19 ♘e4 (19...♗e7? 20 dxc5 ♘xc5 21 ♘xc5 ♗xc5 22 ♗xh7+!).

18	dxe5	♘d5
19	♘e4	♘b4!

In his notes Fischer disposed of
19...♖xa5 with 20 ♘eg5! h6 21 ♕d3
g6 22 ♘e6! and wins.

20 ♗b1 ♖xa5

21 ♕e2

The tempting 21 e6 fxe6 22 ♘eg5?
is exploded by 22...♗xf3 23 ♘xf3
♗f6!. But 22 ♘fg5! ♖a6 23 ♘xh7!
lunges into obscure after 23...♖f5!.
Kasparov thought a perpetual check
was the proper result after a long line
beginning with 24 ♘c3 ♖e5 but
24...♖d6! is more testing.

21 ... ♘b6

Black never has enough pieces on
the kingside after this. Fischer and
other annotators endorsed 21...♖e8
and ...♘f8, e.g. 22 e6 fxe6 23 ♘eg5
♗xg5 24 ♘xg5 ♘f8.

22 ♘fg5! ♗xe4

White planned to meet 22...h6 with
23 ♘h7!. For instance, 23...♔xh7
24 ♘xc5+ ♔g8 25 ♘xb7 or 23...♖e8
24 ♘hf6+! gxf6 25 ♕g4+ ♔h8
26 ♘d6 ♗xd6 27 ♕f5!.

23 ♕xe4 g6

24 ♕h4 h5

25 ♕g3! ♘c4!

Stein parries well. He can meet
26 ♘e6? with 26...♗h4!! 27 ♘xd8
♗xg3 28 ♘b7 ♖a7 29 ♘xc5? ♗xe5
and wins.

26 ♘f3

Given an exclamation point by
several annotators – and a question
mark by Fischer, who felt 26 e6 f5
27 ♘f3! ♔g7 28 ♕f4 was more
accurate. But Robert Hübner found
an immediate win in 26 ♘xf7! ♖xf7
27 ♗xg6 ♖g7 28 ♗h6 ♕f8 and now
29 a4! so that a white rook enters
the game (29...bxa4 30 ♖e4 and
♖f4).

26 ... ♔g7

Euwe claimed 26...♘d3 27 ♗xd3
(or 27 ♖d1 ♘xc1!) ♕xd3 "could
have stopped White's attack." He
gave 28 ♗g5 ♖a7!.

Stronger is 28 ♗h6 and then
28...♖d8 29 e6, e.g. 29...f6 30 ♖ad1
or 29...♗f6 30 ♕f4 ♕f5 31 ♕c7!
fxe6 32 ♘g5. But Euwe may be right
after all (28...♖e8! 29 e6 ♕f5).

27 ♕f4 ♖h8

28 e6! f5

Fischer thought Black missed a
chance to punish White's 26th move
with 28...♗f6. Then 29 exf7 ♗xa1
30 f8(♕)+ ♕xf8 31 ♕c7+ ♔g8
32 ♗xg6 ♘d5 leads to an endgame
with some survival chances after
33 ♕b7 ♘f6 34 ♗f4 ♖h7 35 ♗xh7+
♘xh7.

However, Keres found an astonishing rejoinder: 33 ♕g3 ♕d6 34 ♕g5!?! (threatening ♖e8+) ♗f6 35 ♗h7+! ♔xh7 36 ♕h6+ ♔g8 37 ♕g6+ ♗g7 38 ♖e8+ ♕f8 39 ♕e6+ ♔h7 40 ♘g5 mate!

Also, 35...♔f8 36 ♕xh5! after which 36...♘ce3 37 ♗xe3 ♘xe3 38 ♖xe3 ♖xh7 leaves White on top after 39 ♖e8+! ♔g7 40 ♕g4+ ♔h6 41 ♘h4!!.

No better is 34...♘e7 35 ♖xe7 ♗f6 because of 36 ♖e8+ ♔g7 37 ♕f5 ♖xe8 38 ♗h6+! ♔xh6 39 ♕xh5+ and mates or 38...♔g8 39 ♗xe8.

29 ♗xf5! ♕f8

White wins easily after 29...gxf5 30 ♕g3+ ♔h7 31 ♘g5+ ♗xg5 32 ♗xg5 ♕e8 33 ♖ad1 or 32...♕d3 33 ♕c7+ ♔g6 34 ♕f7+! ♔xg5 35 ♕g7+ ♔f4 36 ♖ad1.

30 ♗e4?

Faster was 30 ♘h4! as John Littlewood pointed out two months later in *Chess*: 30...gxf5 31 ♕g3+ is a mate and 30...♗xh4 31 ♕xh4 ♕xf5 loses to 32 ♕e7+ ♔g8 33 ♕d8+ ♔g7 34 ♕c7+ ♔g8 35 e7.

30 ...   ♕xf4
31 ♗xf4   ♖e8?

Stein believed 31...♖a6 would have drawn. But 32 a3 offers good winning chances and Fischer's 32 ♖ad1 ♖xe6 33 ♖d7 is convincing (33...♖e8 34 ♘g5 ♖f6 35 ♗f3).

The best defense was 31...♖xa2 although Black still has a long way to go to draw after 32 ♖ad1 ♖a7 33 ♘g5, with the idea of ♖d7.

32 ♖ad1   ♖a6

33 ♖d7   ♖xe6!
34 ♘g5   ♖f6
35 ♗f3!   ♖xf4

There was no way to save material (35...♔f8 36 ♘h7+). Fischer navigated through the final traps:

36 ♘e6+ ♔f6 37 ♘xf4 ♘e5 38 ♖b7 ♗d6 39 ♔f1 ♘c2 40 ♖e4! ♘d4 41 ♖b6! ♖d8 42 ♘d5+ ♔f5 43 ♘e3+ ♔e6 44 ♗e2! ♔d7 45 ♗xb5+ ♘xb5 46 ♖xb5 ♔c6 47 a4 ♗c7 48 ♔e2 g5 49 g3 ♖a8 50 ♖b2 ♖f8 51 f4 gxf4 52 gxf4 ♘f7 53 ♖e6+ ♘d6 54 f5 ♖a8 55 ♖d2! ♖xa4 56 f6 Resigns

69

By early 1968 Fischer had left New York for southern California and his post-Sousse retreat from chess extended to the summer. A proposed match with the teenage grandmaster Enrique Mecking collapsed when Mecking's father said it would take too much time away from his schooling – an excuse Fischer must have wondered at. Instead, Fischer agreed to play in a round-robin commemorating the 20th anniversary of the founding of Israel, another irony considering his evolving beliefs. His most impressive victory at the seaside resort of Netanya was a stunning illustration of the use of superior space.

Fischer – Shimon Kagan
Netanya 1968
Caro-Kann Defense,
Two Knights Variation (B11)

1	e4	c6
2	♘c3	d5
3	♘f3	♗g4
4	h3	♗xf3
5	♕xf3	♘f6
6	d3	e6
7	a3	♘bd7

Black's move was considered a significant improvement over 7...♗e7 8 g4 ♘fd7 9 d4 which had turned out badly for Botvinnik in a 1958 world championship match game.

Much later it was realized that the culprit was Botvinnik's 9...♘f8? – and that Black would stand quite well after 9...♕b6!, e.g. 10 ♕d3 e5! 11 exd5 exd4.

8   g4!

Much better than the book 8 g3 g6 9 ♗g2 ♗g7 10 0-0 0-0 11 ♕e2 ♘e8 and 12...f5. White's move exploits

the black knight's lack of a good retreat, thanks to 7...♘bd7. For example, on 8...g6 9 h4 h5 (not 9...♘e5 10 ♕g3 ♘exg4? 11 e5) 10 g5 ♘g4 White assures himself an edge with 11 d4.

8	...	♗d6
9	g5	♘g8

Black may have been dissuaded from 9...♘e5 by 10 ♕e2 ♘fd7 11 f4. For example, 11...♘g6 12 exd5 cxd5 13 f5 ♘ge5 14 fxe6 fxe6 15 d4.

10	h4	♘e7
11	h5?	

Fischer is reluctant to give Black a queenside target after 11 ♗d2 ♕b6 12 0-0-0 d4 but he is taking too many liberties.

11	...	♕b6
12	♗h3	0-0-0

Now what? On 13 ♕xf7?? ♖hf8, Black wins.

13	a4!	a5

Black's move stopped 14 a5 but ultimately allows the opening of the queenside by b2-b4xa5 that costs Black the game. However, the real blame for his defeat lies elsewhere. So far, his shield of center pawns allowed him to ignore the wings. But at some point the middlegame begins and Black must drop the shield to obtain squares for his pieces. This is difficult to time accurately because, for example, 13...d4 14 ♘e2 ♘e5 will favor White after 15 ♕g2 ♗b4+ 16 ♔d1! c5 17 f4.

14	0-0!	♖hf8
15	♔h1	f5!

Again 15...d4 looks promising but 16 ♘e2 ♕c5 17 c3 ♘e5 18 ♕g3 or

just 16 ♘b1! and ♘a3-c4 favors White.

16 ♕g2! g6

17 h6!

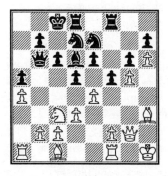

Fischer's thinking becomes more transparent. By seizing control of two thirds of the kingside, he hopes to reduce Black's room for maneuver to a minimum, after which White can open the queenside at leisure.

17 ... ♔b8

18 f4 ♖fe8?

Now was the time for 18...dxe4 19 dxe4 and then 19...e5, or 19...♘c5 or perhaps even 19...♗b4 20 ♘a2 ♗c5 and ...fxe4/...♘f5.

19 e5! ♗c5

20 ♕f3

Even though his QB is "bad" White stops ...♗e3 because Black's piece congestion is becoming suffocating. But Black should be OK now with 20...d4! 21 ♘e2 ♖c8 and ...♘d5.

20 ... ♘c8

21 ♗g2 ♔c7

Hoping to escape to the kingside and/or play ...♘b8-a6-b4.

22 ♘e2 ♘b8

23 c3 ♔d7

On 23...♕b3 White has 24 ♗e3! and ♘d4. For example, 24...♗xe3 25 ♕xe3 ♕xb2?? 26 ♖fb1 ♕c2 27 ♘d4 ♕xc3 28 ♖a2! and 29 ♖b3 traps the queen.

24 ♗d2!

White prepares a crushing b2-b4. There is a rare mating pattern after 24...♕xb2?? 25 ♖ab1! ♕xd2 26 ♖xb7.

24 ... ♘a6

Flight to the kingside (24...♔e7) is grounded by 25 d4, and then 25...♕xb2 26 ♕d3 ♗b6 27 ♖fb1.

25 ♖fb1 ♗f8

And the king can't go back: 25...♔c7 26 b4 axb4 27 d4 ♗f8 28 cxb4 and 29 a5.

26 b4! axb4

27 cxb4

27 ... ♗xb4

If Black spurns the b-pawn, it becomes a battering ram (27...♔e7 28 b5 ♘c5 29 ♗e3 followed by ♖c1, ♕f2 or a4-a5).

Note that 27...♘xb4 also loses, to 28 a5 ♕b5 29 ♗xb4 ♗xb4 30 ♘d4 ♕c5 31 ♖a4!, for example.

28 a5 ♕c5

201

29	d4	♕f8
30	♗xb4	♘xb4
31	♕c3	♘a6
32	♖xb7+	♘c7
33	♘c1	

The knight heads to c5 or b4 for a knockout.

33	...	♖e7
34	a6	**Forfeits**

70

Three months after Netanya, Fischer won another, considerably stronger tournament, in eastern Croatia. The race for first prize was virtually over after a little more than a week, since Fischer began 8½ -1½. His best game was this gem against a little known master in the ninth round.

Emil Nikolić – Fischer
Vinkovci 1968
King's Indian Defense (E61)

1	c4	g6
2	♘c3	♗g7
3	g3	e5
4	♗g2	d6

Black can play his usual King's Indian setup after 5 e3, or meet 5 e4 with 5...f5 and then 6 exf5 gxf5 7 ♕h5+ ♔f8 as Fischer once tried against Donald Byrne.

5	e3	♘f6
6	♘ge2	0-0
7	0-0	c6
8	d4	

Here 8 d3 would transpose into a position Fischer knew well (from the King's Indian Reversed). But instead of 8...d5, which creates the mirror image of Games 56 and 84, Fischer recommended 8...♖e8 9 e4 a6!. If White then stops 10...b5 with 10 a4, Black equalizes by securing control of b4 and c5 with 10...a5!.

8	...	♖e8

Fischer claimed in the *Informant* that 9 ♕c2 ♕e7 10 e4 can be met by 10...exd4 11 ♘xd4 ♘xe4! 12 ♘xe4 ♗xd4 (13 ♖d1 ♗e5 14 f4 ♗g7 15 ♘xd6 ♗g4! with a slight edge).

But sometimes the theoretically best moves simplify so much that they leave few chances to win against a good defender. That explains why when Karl Burger played 10 e4 in the 1965 U.S. Championship, Fischer kept pieces on the board with 10...♘bd7 11 d5 a5 and eventually won by invading along the h-file.

9	♖b1	

Now 9 dxe5 dxe5 10 ♕xd8 ♖xd8 is drawish, although Fischer thought it favored Black.

9	...	e4!
10	b4	♗f5
11	h3	h5

A familiar plan. Bisguier – Fischer, Western Open 1963 – a game best known for Fischer's falling asleep at the board and being woken by his opponent – went 1 d4 ♘f6 2 c4 g6 3 ♘c3 ♗g7 4 ♘f3 0-0 5 e3 d6 6 ♗e2 ♘bd7 7 0-0 e5 8 b4 ♖e8 9 ♗b2 e4 10 ♘d2 ♘f8 11 ♕c2 ♗f5 12 d5 h5 13 ♘b5 h4 with a promising attack.

12	♘f4	♘bd7
13	a4	♘f8

14 c5?

This is a serious misreading of the situation. White may have wanted to avoid 14 b5 c5 but locking the c-file and center fatally slows his counterplay.

14	...	d5
15	b5	♘8h7
16	♗d2	♘g5

White can open one file at will and can try for a second with a4-a5-a6. Black, on the other hand, must rely on sacrifices to open kingside lines. But his chances are far superior for the simple fact that mate ends the game. His options include:

(a) a sacrifice on f3, e.g. 17 a5 ♘f3+! 18 ♗xf3 exf3 etc.,

(b) a sacrifice on d4, that is moving the knight from f6 and playing for ...♗xd4/...e3, or

(c) a sacrifice on g4.

17	♖b2	♕d7
18	♔h2	

Fischer gave 18 h4 ♗g4! as winning after 19 hxg5 ♗xd1 20 gxf6 ♗f3 21 fxg7 and now 21...g5! 22 ♘fe2 ♕g4 23 ♖e1 h4. Or 22 ♘h3 ♕g4 23 ♖fb1 h4.

18	...	♗h6
19	a5	

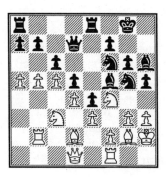

In *Boy's Life* Fischer said he spent a good deal of time weighing the merits of three candidate moves – 19...h4, 19...♘f3+ and 19...♗g4. But the pawn move is not forcing enough. A bit better is 19...♘f3+ 20 ♗xf3 exf3 21 ♕xf3 ♗xf4 22 gxf4 cxb5 – although it is not clear how Black makes progress after 23 ♕g3 a6 (rather than 23 ♘xb5? ♗d3). That leaves...

19 ... ♗g4!!

White will be almost defenceless on the kingside after 20 ♕b3 ♘f3+ 21 ♗xf3 ♗xf3. For example, 22 bxc6 bxc6 23 ♕b7 ♕f5 24 ♕xc6 ♗xf4.

Fischer gave the remarkable finish of 25 gxf4 ♘g4+ 26 ♔g3 h4+ 27 ♔xh4 ♔g7! 28 ♕xd5 ♖h8+ 29 ♔g3 ♖xh3+! 30 ♔xh3 ♘e5+. If, instead, 25 exf4, Black has 25... ♘g4+ 26 ♔g1 ♘xf2!.

20	hxg4	hxg4
21	♖h1	

It should be no surprise that the convoluted defense 21 ♗h1 ♘f3+ 22 ♔g2 fails. One method is 22...♗xf4 23 exf4 ♕f5 and ...♕h5, e.g. 24 ♖g1 ♕h5 25 ♔f1 ♕h2 26 ♗xf3 exf3 27 ♗e3 ♖xe3! (Fischer).

21	...	♘f3+
22	♗xf3	gxf3
23	♔g1	

Most grandmasters would dismiss 23 ♘h3 ♔g7 24 ♔g1 with the note "24...♖h8 and wins." But Fischer added "25 ♕f1 a6!." The main point is that by stopping White's only counterplay – 26 a6 bxa6 27 bxc6 – Black is free to pile up on the h-file, e.g. 26 bxc6 bxc6 27 ♘f4 ♗xf4

28 ♖xh8 ♖xh8 29 exf4 ♕c8 and Black wins as in the game.

23 ... ♗xf4!

Not 23...♔g7 because 24 ♖xh6! ♔xh6 25 a6 gives White chances he doesn't deserve.

24 exf4 ♔g7!

Now 25 a6 is too slow: 25...♖h8 26 ♖xh8 ♖xh8 27 ♕f1 ♕g4 and ...♕h5 wins.

25 f5 ♖h8!

26 ♗h6+

Desperation. Black also wins after 26 ♖xh8 ♖xh8 27 ♗g5 ♕xf5 28 ♗h4 g5.

26 ... ♖xh6

27 ♖xh6 ♔xh6

28 ♕d2+

The queenside operation finally succeeds with 28 a6 ♕xf5 29 axb7 ♖h8 30 bxc6 ♔g7 31 b8(♕). But the patient dies after 31...♖h1+!.

28 ... g5

29 bxc6 ♕xf5!

30 ♘d1 ♕h3

31 ♘e3 ♔g6

White resigns

White has no defense to 32...♖h8.

71

This completes a trilogy begun with Games 68 and 69. In each case Fischer secured an early advantage in space and nursed it into the middle game while his opponent seemed preoccupied. Here the space edge is converted to a winning initiative by move 20.

Fischer – Dragoljub Minić
Vinkovci 1968
Bishop's Gambit (C33)

1	e4	e5
2	f4	exf4
3	♗c4	

The opening books, following musty analysis by Bogolyubov, had maintained for decades that Black gets the edge with 3...♘f6 4 ♘c3 c6 and 5...d5, e.g. 5 ♗b3 d5 6 exd5 cxd5 7 d4 ♗d6 8 ♘ge2 0-0 9 0-0 g5 10 ♘xd5 ♘c6.

But 9 ♗xf4 ♗xf4 10 ♘xf4 ♖e8+ 11 ♘fe2 is the acid test. How this came to light was typically bizarre:

In 1964 Fischer was given carte blanche to write articles for *Chess Life*. He decided to use the opportunity to analyze the forgotten – deservedly so – games of an 1862 match between Steinitz and the obscure Italian master Serafino Dubois.

In one of the games featuring a Bishop's Gambit, Fischer continued the analysis from 11 ♘fe2 with 11...♘g4 12 ♘xd5 ♗e6 13 h3 ♗xd5 14 hxg4 ♗xg2 15 ♖h2 ♗f3 16 ♕d3 – working out to mate in one line – and concluded White was much better. Computers disagree – grandmasters have virtually ignored

9 ♗xf4, so Fischer's analysis remains almost untested after more than 50 years.

| 3 | ... | ♘e7 |

This idea of Steinitz's allows Black to decide later between ...d5 or ...♘g6.

4	♘c3	c6
5	♘f3	d5
6	♗b3!

This drawback to 3...♘e7 is the lack of pressure on e4. On 6...d4 7 ♘e2 c5 8 ♘g5 and Black is lost.

| 6 | ... | dxe4 |
| 7 | ♘xe4 | ♘d5 |

Black could justify his third move with 7...♘g6? – and be crushed by 8 ♘eg5! ♕e7+ 9 ♔f2.

8 ♕e2!

More subtle than 8 c4 ♘f6 9 ♘xf6+ ♕xf6 10 0-0 after which 10...♗d6 or 10...c5 is unclear (and 10...♗e7 11 d4 ♘d7 12 ♕e2 g5? allows 13 ♘xg5! ♕xg5 14 ♗xf4 with a powerful attack).

| 8 | ... | ♗e7 |
| 9 | c4 | ♘c7 |

Putting the knight offsides, 9...♘b4 is playing with fire,

particularly since 10 d4 ♗g4 11 ♗xf4 ♗xf3 12 gxf3 ♕xd4? loses to the pretty 13 ♖d1 ♕b6 14 ♘d6+ ♔f8 15 ♘c8!.

| 10 | d4 | 0-0 |

One of the best things about the King's Gambit is psychological: Defenders look at White's short-term tactical threats and Black's extra pawn – but underestimate White's space edge.

Here Black should fight for operating room with 10...♗g4! and then 11 c5 0-0 12 ♗xf4 ♘e6 13 ♗xe6 fxe6!, e.g. 14 ♗d6 ♗xd6 15 ♘xd6 ♗xf3 16 gxf3 ♕h4+ 17 ♕f2 ♕h6. In this, and other unplayed variations, Minić fails to appreciate how safe Black is after ...fxe6.

| 11 | ♗xf4 | ♘e6 |
| 12 | ♗e3 |

Black can minimize the damage with 12...♘d7 and 13...♘f6 but White's advantage is distinct after 13 0-0 ♘f6 14 ♘xf6+ (or 14 ♘g3 and ♘f5) ♗xf6 15 d5!.

| 12 | ... | ♗b4+ |
| 13 | ♔f2!? |

White wants to embarrass the bishop with c4-c5 and ♕c4.

13	...	♘d7
14	c5!	♘f6
15	♘xf6+	♕xf6
16	♖hf1	♘f4!

Much better than 16...♖e8 17 ♕c4! ♗a5 18 ♔g1.

| 17 | ♗xf4 | ♕xf4 |

18 g3!

The only bid for a middlegame advantage. For example, 18 ♔g1 ♗g4! (intending ...♗xf3 or ...♖ae8) 19 ♕e5 ♕xe5 20 ♘xe5 ♗e6 is roughly equal.

18 ...   ♕h6

White carries out his idea after 18...♕f6 19 ♔g2 ♗g4 20 ♕c4!, threatening ♘e5 as well as ♕xb4. Black can avoid material loss with 20...♕e6! but is worse (21 ♕xb4 ♕e2+ 22 ♖f2 ♗xf3+ 23 ♔g1 ♕e4 24 ♖e1).

19 ♔g1

The idea of an Exchange sacrifice must have occurred to White when he examined 19 ♕e7 ♗h3 and saw that 20 ♔g1! ♗xf1 21 ♖xf1 ♕f6 22 ♕xb7 gives him great compensation. But on further reflection, 19 ♕e7 disappoints since White's edge is relatively minor after 19...♕f6! 20 ♕xf6 gxf6 21 a3 ♗a5 22 d5!.

19 ...   ♗h3?

Missing the point of White's move, just as 19...♗g4 20 ♕e7 ♖ae8? 21 ♗xf7+ would.

Black might have tried to neutralize the diagonal with 19...♗e6, since 20 ♗xe6 ♕xe6

21 ♕xe6 fxe6 22 a3 ♗a5 23 ♘g5 ♖fe8 or 20...fxe6 21 ♘e5 ♕d2 is only a slight edge for White.

20 ♘e5!

Now it's too late to clog the b3-f7 line – 20...♗e6 21 ♘xf7! ♗xf7 22 ♖xf7 ♖xf7 23 ♖f1 or 20...♗d2 21 ♘xf7 ♕e3+ 22 ♖f2! and wins.

20 ...   ♗xf1

21 ♖xf1   ♗d2!

The best try. Black is lost after:

(a) 21...♕d2 (better a move earlier) 22 ♕e4 ♔h8 23 ♘xf7+ ♖xf7 24 ♖xf7 ♖d8 25 ♕e5 ♖g8 26 ♕xg7+! or 25...♕e1+ 26 ♕xe1 ♗xe1 27 ♖xb7 ♗d2 28 ♔f2 g6 29 d5!, or

(b) 21...g6 22 ♘xf7 ♕g7 23 ♘d8+! ♔h8 24 ♖xf8+ followed by mating checks at e5 and e8.

22 ♖f3!

Black weathers the worst after 22 ♘xf7? ♕e3+ 23 ♖f2 ♕xe2 24 ♖xe2 ♗c1 – although White can still play for a win with 25 ♘e5+ ♔h8 26 d5.

22 ...   ♖ad8?

Again Black is mated on 22...g6 23 ♘xf7 ♕g7 24 ♘d8+!. A superior defense is 22...♔h8! and now 23 ♖xf7 ♕e3+ and 23 ♗xf7 ♗c1

206

don't convince. But White is close to a win after 23 ♘xf7+! ♖xf7 24 ♗xf7, threatening 25 ♗e8!, and 24...♗g5 is met by 25 d5!.

23 ♘xf7   ♖xf7

24 ♕e7!   Resigns

It's hopeless after 24...♖f8 25 ♗xf7+ or 25 ♖xf7 ♕e3+ 26 ♖f2+.

72

Of all the gaps in the early collections of Fischer "complete" games, the most glaring is the three final games from his 1958 match with Milan Matulović. Fischer, preparing for the Interzonal at Portorož, had arranged matches with Dragoljub Janosević (two games, both drawn) and Matulović. But only one of the Matulović games, a 41-move Fischer loss with Black, has surfaced. The scores of Fischer's two wins and the drawn fourth game have disappeared. By 1968 Matulović was one of the world's elite GMs.

Milan Matulović – Fischer
Vinkovci 1968
*Sicilian Defense,
Najdorf Variation 6 g3 (B91)*

1	e4	c5
2	♘f3	d6
3	d4	cxd4
4	♘xd4	♘f6
5	♘c3	a6
6	g3	e5
7	♘de2	♗e7
8	♗g5	

A logical move designed to reinforce control of d5. The idea

fails in similar positions because of the ...♘xe4 *desperado*. For example, 6 ♗e2 e5 7 ♘b3 ♗e7 8 ♗g5 0-0 and now, 9 ♘d2 ♘xe4! 10 ♗xe7 ♘xc3 was equal in Fischer – Ghitescu, Leipzig 1960.

8 ...   ♘bd7

Black can still play 8...♘xe4 but 9 ♘xe4 ♗xg5 10 ♘xd6+ ♔e7 favors White after 11 ♘e4 or 11 ♘xc8+ ♕xc8 12 ♖d1.

9 ♗h3

Matulović had some success exploiting the good-♘-versus-bad-♗ after 9...♘b6 10 ♗xc8 ♖xc8 11 ♗xf6 ♗xf6 12 a4!.

9 ...   b5!

A novelty. Now 10 ♗xf6 ♘xf6 11 ♗xc8 ♖xc8 gives quick black queenside pressure that more than makes up for his bishop.

10 a4?

White falls into a psychological trap of his own making. He went into the game thinking 9 ♗h3 was good, then saw that passive moves such as 10 a3 would give Black a comfortable game. Therefore, the position seemed to call for a vigorous response to 9...b5.

10 ...   b4

11 ♘d5

The positional recipe of 11 ♗xd7+ followed by 12 ♗xf6 and 13 ♘d5 turns out badly after 11...♕xd7! 12 ♗xf6 bxc3!. For instance, 13 ♗xg7 ♖g8 14 ♗h6 ♕h3! (15 ♗c1 ♕g2 or 15 ♗e3 cxb2 16 ♖b1 ♕g2 with advantage).

11 ...   ♘xd5

12 ♕xd5   ♖b8!

Black's edge after 12...♘b6 13 ♕c6+ ♗d7 14 ♗xd7+ ♘xd7 15 ♗xe7 ♔xe7 is not nearly as great as in the game.

13 ♗xe7   ♔xe7!!

By providing extra protection to d6 Black is ready to start punching back with 14...♘f6. In contrast, 13...♕xe7 14 0-0-0 ♖b6 15 a5 ♖b5 16 ♕xd6 ♕xd6 17 ♖xd6 can only favor White.

14 ♕d2   ♘f6

15 ♗g2?

Black has a slight edge due to his dominance of dark squares after 15 ♗xc8 ♕xc8 16 f3 ♕c5.

15 ...   ♗b7

Better was 15...♕b6!, seizing the board's best diagonal...

16 ♕d3

...which is why White should have played 16 ♕e3!.

16 ...   ♕b6!

17 0-0   a5!

Had White anticipated this with 17 a5 ♕c5 18 0-0 Black would still hold an edge, but not as great, following 18...♖hc8 and ...♗c6.

18 ♖fd1   ♗a6

19 ♕d2   ♖hc8

20 h3

A grandmaster's instinct tells him 20...♖c4, followed by overwhelming the c-file, should be strong (21 b3 ♘xe4!).

20 ...   h5!

But it was more important to stop 21 g4 and ♘g3. For example, 20...♖c4 21 g4! ♘xe4? 22 ♘xe4 ♖xe4 23 ♘g3 with compensation.

The point is that White's position is so bad that he doesn't deserve chances like that, or 20...♕c6? 21 ♘d4!, which Fischer claimed was equal (presumably because of complications such as 21...exd4 22 e5 ♘e4 23 exd6+ and now 23...♔f8 24 ♕f4 ♗b7 25 ♖xd4 ♕xc2 26 d7).

21 b3?

White should insist on 21 g4! and then 21...hxg4 22 ♘g3 gxh3 23 ♗xh3 ♖c4 24 ♕g5 with ideas such as 24...♔f8 25 ♖xd6! ♕xd6 26 ♘f5 (and not 25 ♘f5? ♕xf2+!). Black may still be winning – but he can retain his huge positional edge without risk by means of 21...h4!.

21 ...   ♗xe2

22 ♕xe2   ♖c3!

White can't save all the children –

23 ♔h2 ♖bc8 24 ♖d2 ♕c5 25 ♖c1?
♖xb3 or 25 ♖a2 g6 as in the game –
and 25 ♖ad1 ♖xc2 26 f4 h4 leads
nowhere.

23 ♖d3   ♖bc8

24 ♖xc3

Another desperate lunge was
24 ♖ad1 ♖xc2 25 ♕f3 ♖8c3 26 g4.
Then Black can win through caution
(26...hxg4 27 hxg4 g6) or by hunting
down more pawns (26...♖b2 or
26...♖xd3 27 ♖xd3 ♖c1+ 28 ♔h2
♖e1).

24 ...   ♖xc3

"White can almost resign on the
spot," wrote Gligorić. The threat of
25...♖xg3 denies him time to
activate his rook

25 ♔h2   ♕c5!

26 ♖a2

Not 26 ♖c1 ♖xb3.

26 ...   g6!

Another high-class safety move
that grants Black time for ...♘d7-b8-
c6-d4, among other winning ideas.

21 ♗f1   ♕d4

28 f3?

Feeble surrender of e3. But after
28 ♗g2 h4 Black wins by exploiting
f4, e.g. 29 gxh4 ♘h5 or 29 g4 ♘h7
and ...♘g5-e6-f4.

28 ...   ♖e3!

The game would be shortened now
by 29 ♕f2 ♖xe4 or 29...h4! 30 gxh4
♘xe4! (31 fxe4 ♖xh3+).

29 ♕g2   ♕d1!

30 ♗c4

On 30 ♗d3 Black should insert
30...h4! 31 gxh4 before 31...♕xf3
32 ♕xf3 ♖xf3 because then the
e-pawn is doomed.

30 ...   ♕xf3

31 ♕xf3   ♖xf3

White played to adjournment –
**32 ♔g2 ♖e3 33 ♗d3 ♘xe4 34 ♗xe4
♖xe4 35 ♔f2 d5 36 ♖a1 d4 37 ♖d1
♖e3 38 h4 ♖c3 39 ♖d2 ♔e6 40 ♔g2
f5** – then waited a few days before
resigning.

After Vinkovci, Fischer travelled
in Europe before arriving at Lugano
a day before the opening ceremony
of the Olympiad. Although he hadn't
played in a FIDE event since Sousse,
there was hope that his goal of
finally taking home a gold medal –
as well as a $3,000 fee – would
overcome any difficulties. But after
examining the tournament site he
insisted on playing his games in a
separate room. When that was
refused, he stormed out. The
respected Belgian GM Alberic
O'Kelly predicted: "If Fischer's
conduct doesn't change radically, it s
clear he will disappear from the
chess arena in a few years because
his excellent play will not make up
for the trouble and torment he
requires of tournament organizers."

73

Fischer played only one game in the 18 months after Vinkovci, one of the longest absences from chess of a world-class player since Emanuel Lasker. Efforts to bring him out of hibernation seemed snakebitten. One grand idea called for three teams – Fischer and Reshevsky of the U.S., Botvinnik and Tal of the Soviet Union, and Najdorf and Oscar Panno of Argentina – to play a roving match-tournament with rounds in New York, Moscow and Buenos Aires. When that failed, Fischer agreed to enter the Milan Vidmar Memorial tournament at Ljubljana in June 1969. But after some of the Yugoslav invitees learned of Fischer's $2,000 fee they asked for the same amount. Embarrassed, the organizers rescinded their offer to Fischer.

The one game Fischer played in this period was in a team match at the Manhattan Chess Club. New York's Metropolitan League was dwindling down after more than 70 years as the premier team event in the U.S. but in its place what was supposed to be an annual eight-board match between the rival Manhattan and Marshall clubs was organized. Only one such match was held, in November 1968, and Fischer led the Manhattan team to an easy victory.

Anthony Saidy – Fischer
Marshall – Manhattan Match,
New York 1968
English Opening (A25)

1	c4	e5
2	♘c3	♘c6

3	g3	f5
4	♗g2	♘f6
5	d3	♗c5
6	e3	f4!?

A new move, even though it is common with colors reversed – 1 e4 c5 2 ♘c3 ♘c6 3 f4 g6 4 ♘f3 ♗g7 5 ♗c4 e6 6 f5. Then the pawn offer is usually refused by 6...♘ge7.

7	exf4	0-0
8	♘ge2?	

But here with a tempo less, the gambit is dubious: 8 fxe5 ♖e8 (8...♘xe5? 9 d4) 9 f4 d6 10 ♗xc6! bxc6 11 d4!. "It would be interesting to know what Fischer intended on 8 fxe5," wrote Lev Aronin with typical Soviet understatement in *Shakhmaty v SSSR*.

8	...	♕e8
9	0-0	

But here 9 fxe5 ♘g4 is risky.

9	...	d6

Black gets some play now with 10 ♘e4 ♘xe4 11 dxe4 ♕h5 e.g. 12 ♗e3 ♗g4 13 ♕d5+ ♔h8 14 ♘c3 ♘d4.

10	♘a4	

The *Informant* gave 10 ♗e3 ♗xe3 11 fxe3 exf4 12 exf4 ♕e3+ 13 ♔h1 ♘g4 14 ♗d5+ ♔h8 15 ♔g2 ♕e8!

as strong for Black. But White improves with 14 ♘e4 ♗f5 15 ♘2c3.

10	...	♗d4
11	♘xd4	exd4!
12	h3	h5
13	a3	a5!
14	b3	♕g6
15	♘b2	♗f5

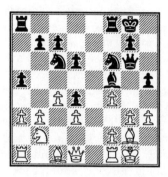

This is the most Nimzovichian of Fischer's games, with elements of restraint, blockade, prophylaxis and a simultaneous attack on two wings that is reminiscent of John – Nimzovich, Dresden 1926. Black has stopped two freeing advances (g3-g4 and b3-b4) and now maneuvers against the targets at b3 and d3.

16	♕c2	♘d7
17	♖e1	♘c5
18	♗f1	♖a6!
19	♗d2	♖b6

White would love to break out of the bind, and the pawn sacrifice 20 b4 axb4 21 axb4 ♘xb4 22 ♗xb4 ♖xb4 23 ♖e7 seems to do the job. But Black has a clever defense, 23...♕f6, since the rook is trapped after 24 ♖xc7 ♕d8! or 24 ♖ae1 ♘e6!.

20 ♗xa5!

This temporary sacrifice (20...♘xa5 21 b4 ♘ab3 22 ♖ab1) deserves a better fate.

20	...	♖xb3!
21	♗d2	♖a8
22	a4	♖a6!
23	a5	♔h7!?

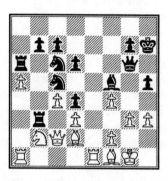

The 6...f4 gambit was virtually forgotten after this game – but one striking exception occurred four years later, when Karpov – Bellon, Madrid 1973 reached this far. Black varied with 23...♘b4? 24 ♗xb4 ♖xb4. White got the upper hand after 25 ♖a3 b6 26 ♖ea1.

Fischer wants to play ...b6 but was apparently concerned about 23...b6 24 axb6 ♖axb6 25 ♖a8+ because 25...♔h7 26 ♖ee8? threatens mate on h8. However, that loses to 26...♘b8!. But White can also play 24 ♘a4!, e.g. 24...♘xa4? 25 ♕xb3 or 24...♗xd3 25 ♕d1 ♗c2 26 ♕e2 bxa5 27 ♗g2! with serious counterplay.

24 ♖ed1 b6

Now 25 axb6 ♖axb6 leaves White without any tactical ideas. He is lost after 26 ♖a2 ♘xd3 and in bad shape after 26 ♗c1 ♘b4.

211

25 ♗e1   bxa5

26 ♘a4   ♖xd3!

Threatening ...♖xg3+ and far superior to 26...♖b8 27 ♘xc5.

27 ♗xd3   ♗xd3

28 ♕a2   ♘b4

After 28...♘xa4? 29 ♕xa4 ♗c2 White can fight with 30 ♕b5 ♖b6 31 ♕d5.

29 ♕a3

Of course, 29 ♗xb4 axb4 is lost. More difficult is 29 ♕b2 ♘xa4 30 ♖xa4 ♗c2 31 ♖xa5! ♗xd1! 32 ♗xb4 ♖xa5 33 ♗xa5 c5. Despite the opposite color bishops, Black wins because of mate threats (34 ♗c7 ♗f3 35 ♔h2 ♕e4).

But White might have tried to confuse matters with 29 ♘xc5!? ♘xa2 30 ♘xa6. Black should win after 30...♘c3 31 ♗xc3 dxc3 32 ♘xc7 c2.

29 ...   ♘c2

30 ♕b2   ♘xa1

31 ♖xa1   ♘xa4

32 ♖xa4   ♕e4!

Black's attack prevails after, say, 33 ♕d2 ♖b6; 33 ♗d2 ♖b6 and 33 ♖a1 ♗xc4 and ...♗d5.

33 ♗xa5?

A time pressure blunder.

33 ...   ♖xa5!

34 ♖xa5   ♕e1+

35 ♔h2   ♕xa5

White resigns

This was the last serious game Fischer played in the United States.

74

As 1970 began Fischer was living in a one-room $75-a-month apartment in Los Angeles and seemed as far from the chess world as possible. He'd played in only one grandmaster-level event in three years. Another attempt to get him back into the international arena collapsed when he changed his mind about a match with Botvinnik in Holland and insisted on conditions that couldn't be accepted. But then in a surprise, Fischer agreed to play first board in a "U.S.S.R. versus the Rest of the World" match beginning in March. Bent Larsen, like almost every else, didn't expect Fischer to abandon his 23 conditions, and he agreed to play second board, assuming Fischer would back out. When Fischer materialized in Belgrade, Larsen insisted on taking the top board. Fischer accepted the demotion to second board and "castled" with Larsen, as Tal put it.

Fischer – Tigran Petrosian
U.S.S.R – Rest of the World match,
First Round, Belgrade 1970
Caro-Kann Defense (B13)

1 e4   c6

2 d4   d5

3 exd5   cxd5

4 ♗d3   ♘c6

5 c3

Later in the year Fischer played 1 e4 c6 2 d3 d5 3 ♘d2 ♘d7 4 ♘gf3 ♕c7 5 exd5! against Marovic at Rovinj-Zagreb. The pawn structure was similar to this game's but Black's minor pieces were misplaced after 5...cxd5 6 d4 g6

7 ♗d3. He was positionally lost soon after 7...♗g7 8 0-0 e6 9 ♖e1 ♘e7 10 ♘f1 ♘c6 11 c3 0-0 12 ♗g5 e5? 13 ♘e3! ♘b6 14 dxe5 ♘xe5 15 ♗f4!.

5	...	♘f6
6	♗f4	♗g4
7	♕b3	♘a5

"Simpler is 7...♕c8," said the Russian book on the match and Fischer gave that move an exclamation point. On c8 the queen doesn't run into ♘e5 the way it does after 7...♕d7 8 ♘d2 e6 9 ♘gf3.

8 ♕a4+

Theory endorsed 8 ♕c2 e6 9 ♘d2 ♗d6 or 9...a6, followed in both cases by ...♗h5-g6. Fischer's finesse diverts the bishop to d7.

| 8 | ... | ♗d7 |
| 9 | ♕c2 | |

Most books at the time cited a 1926 Maróczy – Capablanca game equalizing after 9...♕b6 10 ♘d2 e6 11 ♘gf3 ♗b5. But 11 a4! is better, as in this game.

| 9 | ... | e6 |
| 10 | ♘f3 | ♕b6 |

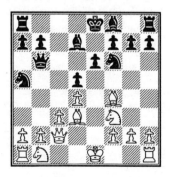

11 a4!

This is the kind of anticipation move that Petrosian was known for playing himself. On 11...♘b3 12 ♖a2

♖c8 White untangles with 0-0 and ♘d2.

Fischer pointed out that 11...♕b3 can be met by 12 ♕e2 since 12...♗xa4? 13 ♖xa4 ♕xa4? 14 ♗b5+ hangs the queen. However, Black can try 12...♘c4 13 ♗c1 ♘e4 – not ...♗d6 14 a5! and White threatens to catch the queen – 14 ♗xe4 dxe4 15 ♕xe4 ♗c6 with good play for a pawn.

11	...	♖c8
12	♘bd2	♘c6
13	♕b1	

Another Petrosianesque move, to stop 13...♘b4 and provoke a kingside weakness.

| 13 | ... | ♘h5? |

Tairnanov recalled how Fischer arrived half an hour late for the game and was "pale as a ghost." The course of the game radically changed his demeanor. "Somehow just looking at Petrosian's face was reassuring," he told Evans. "He looked scared."

| 14 | ♗e3 | h6? |

After 13...♘h5 Black had to accept some risk – but didn't like 14...f5, because of 15 g4! fxg4 16 ♘g5 ♗d6 17 ♗xh7. But 17...♘e7 is OK.

Yet 14...♗d6 was safe (15 ♗xh7 g6 16 ♗xg6 fxg6 17 ♕xg6+ ♔d8 and ...♔c7). White gets his piece back with 18 g4, e.g. 18...♘e7 (not 18...♘f4? 19 ♗xf4 ♗xf4 20 ♕f6+) 19 ♕g5. But then 19...♕xb2 or 19...♔c7 20 c4 dxc4 would be fine for Black.

15 ♘e5!

The threats begin with 16 ♘xf7 ♔xf7 17 ♗g6+ or just 16 ♗g6.

15 ...   ♘f6

This was condemned by annotators who preferred 15...♘xe5 16 dxe5 ♗c5 17 a5 ♕c7. Would Fischer, in his first serious game in more than a year, have trusted 18 g4!? ♗xe3 19 fxe3 ♕xe5 20 gxh5 ♕xe3+ 21 ♔d1 ? Probably not, because he gave 18 ♘f3! in the *Informant*, with advantage to White after 18...♗xe3 19 fxe3 g6 (19...f5!) 20 0-0 and e3-e4.

16 h3   ♗d6

17 0-0   ♔f8

Curiously defeatist. After 17...0-0 18 f4 or 18 ♘2f3 and ♕c1 White has a strong attack (♗xh6). But Black is not without resources (18 ♘2f3 ♔h8 and ...♘g8).

18 f4   ♗e8

Of course, 18...♘xe5 19 fxe5 ♗xe5 loses to 20 a5.

19 ♗f2!

The bishop heads for h4, e.g. 19...g6 20 f5! gxf5 21 ♗xf5 exf5 22 ♕xf5 ♕d8 23 ♗h4 or 21...♖c7 22 ♗xe6 fxe6 23 ♘xc6 and ♗h4 wins.

19 ...   ♕c7

20 ♗h4   ♘g8

21 f5!

White makes the rest of the game look simple but the basis for the attack's success was discouraging ...♗b5 and ...0-0 earlier, and stopping ...g6 and ...♔g7 now.

21 ...   ♘xe5

Black can't hold out long after 21...♗xe5 22 dxe5 ♘xe5 23 fxe6 f6 24 ♘f3 or 22...♕xe5 23 fxe6 f6 (23...♕xe6 24 ♗f5 ♕e3+ 25 ♗f2) 24 ♘f3 ♕d6 25 ♕e1 and ♗g3.

22 dxe5   ♗xe5

23 fxe6   ♗f6

24 exf7   ♗xf7

25 ♘f3!

Now 25...g5 26 ♗f2 and ♗d4 is powerful, e.g. 26...♘e7 27 ♗d4 ♗xd4+ 28 ♘xd4 ♔g7 29 ♕e1 and ♕f2.

25 ...   ♗xh4

26 ♘xh4   ♘f6

27 ♘g6+!   ♗xg6

28 ♗xg6   ♔e7!!

This was Fischer's punctuation: if Black doesn't connect rooks, White carries out the execution with ♕f5 and ♖ae1-e6xf6+.

29 ♕f5   ♔d8

On 29...♖cf8 Black can defend against 30 ♖ae1+ ♔d8 31 ♖e6? ♕c5+. But 30 c4! cracks the defense. For example, 30...♕xc4 31 ♕e5+ ♔d8 32 ♖ac1 and wins.

30 ♖ae1   ♕c5+

31 ♔h1   ♖f8

On 31...♖c6 the widely recommended 32 ♕e5 is not

convincing (32...♕d6). But on 32 b4! Black's queen doesn't have a good square (32...♕xc3 33 b5 ♖c7 34 ♕e6 or 32...♕d6 33 b5 ♖xc3 34 ♖e6).

32 ♕e5   ♖c7

After 32...♕c7 White can choose between 33 ♖xf6! gxf6 34 ♕xd5+ and the prettier 33 ♕xd5+! ♘xd5 34 ♖xf8+ ♔d7 35 ♗f5+.

33 b4!   ♕c6

Losing quickly were 33...♕xc3 34 ♕d6+ and 33...♕e7 34 ♕d4.

34 c4!

Now 34...♕xc4?? 35 ♕d6+ ♖d7 36 ♕xf8+.

34 ...   dxc4

35 ♗f5!

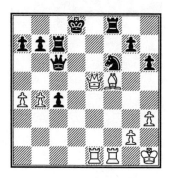

The prisoner's escape is thwarted and he is condemned to ♖d1+.

35 ...   ♖ff7

36 ♖d1+   ♖fd7

Black can resign after 36...♘d7 37 ♖fe1!.

37 ♗xd7   ♖xd7

38 ♕b8+   ♔e7

Or 38...♕c8 39 ♖xd7+ ♘xd7 40 ♕d6!, threatening ♖f8 mate.

39 ♖de1+   Resigns

Because 39...♔f7 40 ♕e8 is mate.

75

Fischer disclosed more of his broad, new repertoire in a five-minute tournament at Herceg-Novi, right after Belgrade on April 8. Dubbed by journalists the "world blitz championship," the double-round event was a splendid success for Fischer, who seemed able to win easily regardless of opening move. He beat Petrosian with 1 e4, Tal with 1 g3, Smyslov with 1 f4, and Hort with 1 d4 (He had told friends he prepared 1 d4 specifically for Spassky when it appeared they would meet on first board in Belgrade.) At the risk of violating Nezhmetdinov's Law ("He who analyzes blitz games is stupid"), here is his most sparkling game.

Fischer – Milan Matulović
Blitz tournament,
Herceg-Novi 1970
Ruy Lopez,
Schliemann Defense (C63)

1	e4	e5
2	♘f3	♘c6
3	♗b5	f5

Fischer wrote that he was surprised at Black's choice of the Schliemann because "I know this variation very well." In fact, he never played it in another serious game that we know of.

4	♘c3	fxe4
5	♘xe4	d5
6	♘xe5	dxe4
7	♘xc6	♕g5

8 ♕e2   ♘f6

9 f4   ♕xf4!

When this was played, the standard authorities believed 9...♕h4+ was forced (although better for White). The capture on f4 was supposed to be worse because of 10 ♘e5+ c6 11 d4 exd3 12 ♗xd3 ♕b4+ 13 ♗d2 ♕e7 14 0-0-0. But later 11...♕h4+ 12 g3 ♕h3 was found to be better than its reputation, raising doubts about 10 ♘e5+.

The theory of 1970 also regarded 10 ♘xa7+ ♔d8 11 ♘xc8 ♔xc8 12 d4 as quite good for White. But that underestimated 10...♗d7 11 ♗xd7+ ♔xd7 12 ♕b5+ ♔e6!.

10 d4   ♕h4+?!

11 g3   ♕h3

Fischer felt he won this game two years before: One night at Vinkovci 1968 he analyzed the variation in depth with Robatsch and Gheorghiu (the latter had failed to gain an edge at Skopje 1968 with the theory-endorsed 12 ♘a7+ ♗d7 13 ♗xd7+ ♕xd7 14 ♘b5 and now 14...c6 15 ♘c3 ♗b4!). The three men stayed up all night and found:

12 ♗g5!   a6

13 ♗a4   ♗d7

Attempts to improve on Black's play start here. They include:

(a) 13...b5 14 ♗xf6 bxa4 and now 15 ♕xe4+ ♕e6 16 ♕xe6+? ♗xe6 17 ♗e5 ♗d5 is lost. But 15 ♗e5 or 15 ♕xe4+ ♕e6 16 ♗e5 ♗b7 17 d5 favors White.

(b) 13...♕h5 14 ♕xh5+ ♘xh5 15 ♘e5+ c6 16 ♗b3 ♘f6 17 ♘f7! costs material.

(c) 13...♗d6 14 ♗xf6 favors White.

14 ♗xf6   gxf6

15 ♕xe4+

White is clearly better after 15...♕e6 16 ♕xe6+ ♗xe6 17 0-0 (17...♗d7 18 ♖ae1+ ♔f7 19 ♘e5+).

15 ...   ♔f7

16 ♘e5+!   fxe5

17 ♖f1+

Now 17...♔g8 18 ♖f6!! is strong. For example, 18...♗xa4 19 ♕d5+ and mates. Or 18...♖e8 19 ♗b3+ ♔g7 (19...♗e6 20 ♗xe6+ ♖xe6 21 ♕d5) 20 ♖f7+ ♔h6 21 dxe5.

The best practical chances lie in 18...♗b4+ 19 c3 ♖f8! and then 20 ♕d5+ ♔g7 21 ♗xd7 ♕xh2 22 ♖xf8 ♖xf8 23 0-0-0.

17 ...   ♔e7!

Black has enough pieces for the queen after 17...♕xf1+ 18 ♔xf1 ♗xa4 but not enough pawns (19 ♕f5+ ♔g8 20 ♕e6+ ♔g7 21 ♕xe5+ and 22 ♕xc7).

18 ♗xd7!

Black is the one playing to win after 18 ♕xe5+ ♕e6 19 ♖f7+! ♔xf7 20 ♗b3 ♖e8!.

18 ... ♔xd7!

On 18...♕xd7 19 0-0-0 ♕e6 20 ♕xb7 White has good chances.

19 ♖f7+?

Not 19 ♕xb7 ♕e6! 20 0-0-0 (20 ♕xa8? ♗b4+) e4!. But 19 0-0-0 keeps the balance.

19 ... ♔e8?

On 19...♗e7!! 20 ♕xe5 ♖ae8 or 20 0-0-0 ♕e6 Black is the one playing for a win.

20 ♖xc7 ♗d6?

In a speed game, Fischer would probably have answered 20...♗b4+ 21 c3 ♖f8 with 22 0-0-0!, rather than 22 cxb4 – and his instinct would be borne out by 22 cxb4? ♕f1+ 23 ♔d2 ♖f2+ 24 ♔c3 ♖f3+ with a winning counterattack after 25 ♔d2 ♕f2+.

But 20...♕e6 21 0-0-0 ♗e7 would have limited White's superiority.

21 ♖xb7!

After 21 ♕xb7 ♗xc7 22 ♕xa8+ ♗d8 Black is still hanging on.

21 ... ♖c8

Black cannot allow 22 ♕c6+, and 21...♕e6 22 ♖xh7 ♖xh7 23 ♕xa8+ should lose.

22 0-0-0 ♕xh2?

23 dxe5 ♗e7

24 ♖xe7+!

Widely praised at the time because it forces mate. But 24 ♕a4+! ♔f7 25 ♖f1+ ♔g6 26 ♖b6+ also mates.

24 ... ♔xe7

25 ♕b7+ ♔e6

26 ♕d7+ ♔xe5

27 ♕d5+

Here 27 ♖d5+ saves a few moves.

27 ... ♔f6

28 ♖f1+ ♔g6

29 ♕f5+

Also 29 ♕f7+!.

The game ended with: **29 ... ♔h6 30 ♕e6+ ♔h5 31 ♖f5+ ♔g4 32 ♖f4+ ♔xg3 33 ♕g4 mate**

76

Fischer believed he suffered from lack of practice at Belgrade and decided to play himself into shape in 1970. He stayed in Yugoslavia for a "Tournament of Peace" that began on Katerina Island, reportedly setting 41 conditions for his participation. All were met but he didn't decide to play until an hour and a half before the first round.

Teodor Ghitescu – Fischer
Rovinj-Zagreb 1970
King's Indian Defense,
Sämisch Variation (E82)

1	d4	♘f6
2	c4	g6
3	♘c3	♗g7
4	e4	d6
5	f3	0-0
6	♗e3	b6
7	♗d3	♗b7

A trap, well-known at the time, goes 7...c5? 8 e5! and wins.

8 ♘ge2 c5

Now 9 ♕d2 ♘c6!, so that 10 0-0 ♘g4! 11 fxg4 cxd4, is fine for Black (or 10 d5 ♘e5 11 ♘c1 e6 12 ♗e2 ♗a6).

9	d5	e6
10	0-0	exd5
11	exd5	

An unassuming alternative to 11 cxd5 ♗a6. White hopes to get an improved version of Szabó's setup in Game 20 – improved because ...b6/...♗b7 is marginally useful.

| 11 | ... | ♘bd7 |

12 ♗g5!

Black is not allowed to set up the cohesive formation of ...♘e8, ...f5, ...♘e5, ...♕e7, ...♘f6 and ...♖ae8.

12	...	h6
13	♗h4	♘e5
14	f4	♘xd3
15	♕xd3	

Here 15...♗c8 is natural but Fischer may not have trusted 16 ♘e4 g5 or 16...♗f5 17 ♘2g3 ♗xe4 18 ♘xe4 g5 to get out of the pin.

| 15 | ... | ♕d7 |

Now 16 f5 g5 17 ♗f2 ♘g4 or 17 ♗g3 ♘h5 18 ♗f2 ♗e5 is fairly balanced despite Black's holes.

16 ♗xf6

White eliminates the most annoying enemy piece – at the expense of turning the dark-squared bishop into Black's best piece.

| 16 | ... | ♗xf6 |
| 17 | f5 | |

White appears to have a promising game, e.g. 17...gxf5 18 ♖xf5 ♗g7 19 ♖af1 or 17...♔g7? 18 fxg6 fxg6 19 ♘f4! and wins.

| 17 | ... | g5 |
| 18 | ♕h3 | |

Of the three candidate moves, 18 ♘e4 promises good chances after 18...♗xb2 19 ♘2c3! and 18...♗e5 19 ♕h3.

Or 18 ♘g3, e.g. 18...♗d4+ 19 ♔h1 ♖ae8 20 f6 followed by ♘f5 or ♘ce4. Also 19...f6 20 ♖ae1 ♗e5 21 ♘h5.

Ghitescu picks door number three, after seeing 18...♔h7? 19 ♘e4! ♕e7 20 ♘2c3.

18 ...   ♗e5!

19 ♕xh6   f6

20 ♖f3

Trying for a middlegame kill with 20 h4 ♖f7 21 hxg5 turns in Black's favour after 21...♖h7 22 ♕g6+ ♖g7 23 ♕h5 ♖xg5 24 ♕f3 ♕h7. For example, 25 g3 ♗c8 and ...♖xf5 or 25 ♘e4 ♗h2+! 26 ♔f2 ♖xf5 27 ♘xf6+ ♖xf6 28 ♕xf6 ♖f8.

20 ...   ♕h7!

White's task is easier after two sets of heavy pieces are traded (20...♖f7 21 ♖h3 ♖h7).

21 ♕xh7+   ♔xh7

22 h4?

Suddenly White must choose between active and passive defense. The energetic text is based on 22...gxh4 23 ♖h3 but 22...g4 leaves White with two very weak kingside pawns. Better was 22 h3 and ♔f1.

22 ...   g4

23 ♖d3

White's rooks are a tactical problem which he should begin

solving with 23 ♖e3 and ♖e4. On 23...♖ae8 24 ♖e4 (24 ♔f2? ♗c8) ♗c8 25 ♖f1! (not 25 ♖xg4 ♗xf5, trapping the rook) ♖g8 he has fair chances.

23 ...   ♖ae8

Black's pressure is so strong he should wait on the ...b5 idea, since 23...♗a6 24 b3 b5 25 cxb5 ♗xb5 26 ♘xb5! will favor White after ...♗xa1 27 ♘xd6 ♗e5 28 ♘c4 and d5-d6.

24 ♘g3?

Necessary was 24 ♖f1 with the idea of ♘f4-e6.

24 ...   ♗a6!

Now 25 ♘b5 ♗xb2 26 ♖b1 ♗xb5 27 cxb5 ♗d4+ and ...♖e5.

25 b3   b5

26 cxb5   ♗xb5

27 ♘xb5

Forced (27 ♖e3?? ♗d4).

27 ...   ♗xa1

28 ♘xd6   ♗d4+!

The rook is too much for the king and knight after 26 ♖xd4? cxd4 27 ♘xe8 ♖xe8 28 ♔f2 d3.

29 ♔f1   ♖e5

30 ♘c4   ♖xd5

| 31 | ♘e3 | ♖d7 |
| 32 | ♘xg4 | ♖g7 |

Material is relatively equal but Black prevails if he can win a pawn and/or break the coordination of the knights.

| 33 | ♘f2 | ♖fg8 |

Now 34 ♘ge4? ♖xg2 35 ♘g5+ loses (35...♖8xg5 36 hxg5 ♖xf2+).

34 ♘fe4

The rule of thumb – that a player who is down the Exchange does not want to trade rooks – is supported by 34 ♘h5 ♖xg2 35 ♖xd4 cxd4 36 ♘xf6+ ♔h6 37 ♘xg8+ ♖xg8 38 ♔e2 (38 ♘e4 ♖g4) ♖g3.

| 34 | ... | ♔h6! |

This takes the check out of ♘xf6 and creates the possibility of another winning plan, a last-rank mate (35 ♘e2 ♖xg2 36 ♘xd4 cxd4 37 ♘xf6 ♖8g3! 38 ♖xd4 ♖xa2 and ...♖xb3-b1+). But 38 ♖xg3 ♖xg3 39 ♔e2 lasts longer.

| 35 | h5 | ♖g4 |
| 36 | ♔e2 | |

White has no counterplay (36 b4? ♗e5! 37 ♔f2 cxb4).

36	...	♗e5
37	♔f2	♖4g7
38	♖f3	♖g4
39	♖d3	a6

Black seems to be taking his time so he can adjourn. But by the time White sealed his 44th move Black had broken through.

40	♖f3	♗d4+
41	♔f1	♗e5
42	♔f2	

| 42 | ... | a5! |

Black wins with 43...a4. For example, 43 ♖d3 a4! 44 bxa4 c4 wins quickly (45 ♖a3 or 45 ♖f3 allow 45...c3!).

After 44 ♖f3 axb3 45 axb3 ♖a8 the rook decides, e.g. 46 ♖d3 ♖a2+ 47 ♔f3 (47 ♔f1 ♖f4+ 48 ♔g1 ♗d4+ 49 ♔h2 ♖h4 mate) ♖f4+ 48 ♔e3 ♖xg2.

| 43 | a4 | ♖d8! |

Also winning are 43...♖b8 and 43...c4 44 bxc4 ♗xg3+ 45 ♘xg3 ♖xc4. But Fischer liked his bishop.

44	♔e3	♖b8
45	♔f2	c4!
46	bxc4	♖b2+

Now 47 ♔e3 ♖a2 does the trick: 48 c5 ♖a3+ 49 ♔e2 ♖xa4.

| 47 | ♔f1 | ♖b4 |

White resigns

The a-pawn promotes.

77

At Rovinj-Zagreb Fischer was in trouble as White against Korchnoi and needed miraculous escapes against Borislav Ivkov and Walter Browne. Nevertheless, he managed to exact some revenge. Ten years before Wolfgang Uhlmann had defeated him impressively in a Winawer French. They met again two years later, and drew in a difficult Winawer. But Fischer won easily in a third Winawer at Herceg-Novi, and this was their fourth.

Fischer – Wolfgang Uhlmann
Rovinj-Zagreb 1970
French Defense,
Winawer Variation (C15)

1	e4	e6
2	♘c3	

The chief virtue of this transpositional trick is to avoid 2 d4 c5, a favorite move order of Bent Larsen's.

2	...	d5
3	d4	♗b4
4	a3	♗xc3+
5	bxc3	dxe4
6	♕g4	

Another suspect line, like the Two Knights Variation of the Caro-Kann, that Fischer seemed attracted to on general principles (♗-vs.-♘) despite his below expectation results with it.

6	...	♘f6
7	♕xg7	♖g8
8	♕h6	♖g6
9	♕e3	♘c6
10	♗b2	

At Herceg-Novi, Uhlmann tried 10...b6 11 0-0-0 ♗b7 but Fischer expanded effortlessly and won after 12 h3 h5 13 c4 ♕d6 14 ♘e2 0-0-0 15 ♘f4 ♖gg8 16 ♗e2 ♕e7 17 d5!.

10	...	♕d6

A new move which disappeared after this game. Black prepares quick queenside castling but allows White's next move (compared with 10...♘e7 11 f3 ♘ed5! and 12...e3).

11	f3!	exf3

The *Informant* recommended 11...e5, and gave 12 fxe4 exd4 13 cxd4 ♘xe4! 14 0-0-0 f5 as equalizing.

But 12 0-0-0, threatening 13 fxe4 is more in keeping with the spirit of the opening, e.g. 12...♘d5 13 ♕e1 exd4 14 cxd4 or 12...exf3 13 ♘xf3 e4 14 c4.

12	♘xf3	♗d7
13	0-0-0	0-0-0

A tempting alternative was 13...b5, to secure control of c4. After 14 ♗xb5 ♖xg2 15 ♘e5 or 14...♖b8 15 c4 White's edge is evident. But 14...♘a5 may offer enough compensation.

14	c4!	

Now it becomes easy to see why Fischer was fond of this variation: White's bishops come alive, and he can change the pawn structure favorably, with a timely d4-d5 or h2-h3 and g2-g4. Most of the tactics favor him. For example, if Black tries to get off the hot file with 14...♕f8 and 15...♕h6 he invites 15 d5! (15...exd5 16 cxd5 ♖e8 17 ♕g1 ♗g4? 18 dxc6 ♗xf3 19 ♕xa7 and wins).

14 ... ♘g4
15 ♕d2 f5

Unpalatable, but safer was 15...♔b8 16 h3 ♘f6 17 g4.

16 d5! ♘b8

Black is losing after 16...♘ce5 17 ♘xe5 ♘xe5 18 ♕d4 or 16...exd5 17 cxd5 ♘e7 18 ♕d4 ♔b8 19 h3 ♘f6 20 ♘e5 ♖g7 21 ♘c4 but in the last line 19...♘h6 20 ♘e5 ♖gg8 holds out hope.

17 h3 ♘f6
18 ♘e5

Now on 18...♖g7 White wins with 19 ♕h6!, e.g. 19...♕f8 20 ♘xd7 ♘bxd7 21 dxe6 and 19...♘e8 20 c5! ♕xc5 21 dxe6 or 20...♕e7 21 c6.

18 ... ♘e4
19 ♕d4

Also good was 19 ♕a5 since 19...♘f2 is crushed by 20 c5 ♕f8 21 ♘xg6 hxg6 22 ♗e5.

19 ... ♖g3?

The rook lands in trouble here. After 19...♖gg8 20 ♕xa7 ♕e7

White is close to a win but not quite there yet (but not 20...♘g3? 21 c5 ♕-moves 22 c6!).

20 ♘f7! ♕f4+
21 ♔b1

White's primary idea is last-rank mate: 21...♖e8? 22 dxe6 ♗xe6 23 ♕d8+! or 22...♖xe6 23 ♕h8+ ♖e8 24 ♕xe8+!.

21 ... c5
22 ♕e5!

Most all of Black's army will be hanging now.

22 ... ♕xe5
23 ♗xe5 ♖dg8

Hoping for 24 ♗xg3 ♖xg3 with some survival chances.

24 ♗d3!

The win will be clear after ♗xe4 and ♘d6+, e.g. 24...♘f2 25 ♘d6+ ♔d8 26 ♘xb7+ ♔e7 27 dxe6 ♗xe6 28 ♗xg3 ♖xg3 29 ♖de1.

24 ... ♖xg2
25 ♗xe4 fxe4
26 ♘d6+ ♔c7

After 26...♔d8 27 ♘xb7+ ♔e7 28 d6+ ♔e8 29 ♘xc5 the win is straightforward.

27 ♘xe4+ ♔b6

28	♘f6	♗a4

Or 28...♖f8 29 dxe6 ♗xe6 30 ♖d6+ and 29...♗a4 30 ♖d6+.

29	♘xg8	♗xc2+
30	♔c1	♘d7

And 30...♗xd1 31 ♘f6 wins a piece.

31	♖dg1	**Resigns**

White walks away with a full rook.

78

Fischer's skill with heavy pieces became more pronounced in his later years. His powerful use of rooks against Geller at Palma 1970 and queen and rooks against Matulović at Skopje 1967 and against Petrosian in the eighth game of the 1971 match are testimony to that. In the following game he converts routine pressure against an isolated d-pawn into a fine demonstration of winning technique.

Fischer – Risto Nicevski
Rovinj-Zagreb 1970
Sicilian Defense,
Taimanov Variation (B47)

1	e4	e6
2	d4	c5
3	♘f3	cxd4
4	♘xd4	a6
5	♘c3	♕c7
6	g3	♘f6
7	♗g2	♘c6
8	0-0	d6
9	♖e1	♗d7

Both 9...♗e7 and 9...♖b8 allow White to isolate the enemy pawns by tactical means with 10 ♘xc6 bxc6 11 e5 dxe5 12 ♖xe5!.

10	♘xc6!	

But without tactics to support it, 10 ♘xc6 was considered by Sicilian canon of the 1960s to be a positional error that strengthened Black's center (...bxc6) or helped his development (....♗xc6).

10	...	bxc6
11	b3	♗e7

In the only previous international game with this line, Black stopped White's next move with 11...e5. But then ♘a4 and c2-c4 is good, e.g. 12 ♘a4 ♗e7 13 c4 c5 (else 14 c5!) 14 ♘c3 ♗c6 15 ♗g5.

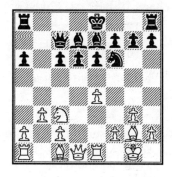

12	e5!	

A temporary pawn sacrifice – temporary because Black's ninth denies him ...♘d7. Also good is 12 ♘a4 because of 12...c5? 13 e5! and 12...♖b8 13 e5! dxe5 14 ♗b2.

12	...	dxe5
13	♗b2	0-0
14	♕e2	♘d5

This threatens 15...f6 and seems to solve Black's opening problems. But it actually trades an isolated c-pawn for an isolated d-pawn.

The extra pawn couldn't be held (14...♗d6 15 ♘a4 or 14...♗c5 15 ♘a4 ♗d4 16 ♖ad1 ♗xb2 17 ♘xb2 e4 18 ♗xe4 ♘xe4 19 ♕xe4 and ♕e5).

15 ♘xd5

Not 15 ♕xe5? ♕xe5 16 ♖xe5 ♗f6.

15 ...   exd5

No better was 15...cxd5 16 ♗xe5 ♗d6 (or 16...♕a5 17 c4) 16 ♗xd6 ♕xd6 17 c4.

16 ♗xe5   ♗d6

Now this was forced (16...♕a5? 17 ♗xg7).

17 ♗xd6   ♕xd6
18 c4   ♗e6

Black is still fairly well off after 18...♖ae8 19 ♕d2 d4! (20 b4 c5).

19 ♖ad1   a5

It was too late for 19...d4 20 ♕e5!, e.g. 20...♖ad8 21 ♕xd6 ♖xd6 22 c5. So Black tries to liquidate the queenside.

20 cxd5   cxd5

· Ridding himself of the bishop – 20...♗xd5 – actually makes it harder for Black to defend d5, e.g. 21 ♖d4 and ♕d3.

21 ♖d4

21 ...   a4?

Tactically sound (22 bxa4 ♖a5 and ...♖fa8) but positionally awful. White now gets an easily protected passed b-pawn and a second weak pawn to attack. Better was 21...♖fc8! and ...♖c5. For example, 22 ♕d3 ♖c5 23 ♖d1 ♖d8 and ...♕e5.

22 b4!   a3

Otherwise 23 a3 and White just piles up on d5 and watches for the right time to push the b-pawn.

23 ♕d2!   ♖ab8

If the other rook goes to b8 White has 24 ♗xd5 ♗xd5 25 ♖xd5 ♕xb4? 26 ♖d8+. And if 23...♖a4 White makes progress with 24 ♖b1 ♖d8 25 ♖b3 and 26 b5.

24 ♖e3!

24 ...   ♖fc8

A counterattack on b4 (24...♖b5) is repulsed by 25 ♖xa3 ♖fb8 26 ♖b3.

25 ♖xa3   ♕e5?

Better was 25...♕b6 26 ♖b3 ♖c4 or 26...♖c1+ 27 ♕xc1 ♕xd4.

26 ♖ad3   h6

Luft is late (26...♖b5 27 ♗xd5 ♗xd5 28 ♖xd5 ♖xd5 29 ♖xd5 ♖c1+? 30 ♕xc1 ♕xd5 31 ♕c8+).

Black's 25th move may have been based on 26...♗f5 27 ♖xd5 ♕a1+ –

but then 28 ♕d1 ♖c1? fails to 29 ♖d8+.

27	♗xd5	♗xd5
28	♖xd5	♕a1+
29	♔g2	

29	...	♔h7

After 29...♖c1 White can approximate the game with 30 ♖d8+ ♖xd8 31 ♖xd8+ ♔h7 32 ♕d3+ g6 and now 33 ♕d4! ♕xd4 34 ♖xd4 ♖a1 35 b5! (rather than 35 ♖d2? ♖b1 36 a3 ♖b3).

Then the b-pawn scores: 35...♖xa2 36 ♖b4 ♔g7 37 b6 ♖a8 38 ♔f3 ♔f6 39 ♔e4 ♔e6 40 b7 ♖b8 41 ♖b6+ and ♔e5.

30	♖3d4	♖c1
31	♕d3+!	

This was not designed to stop ...♖g1+ and ...♕f1+ because White's king would be safe if driven to ♔h4.

His idea was rather to probe the kingside before resorting to pushing his passed pawns.

31	...	g6

Now 32 a3? ♖c3 or 32 ♕e2 ♖e1 is negative progress.

32	♖d7	♖g1+
33	♔h3	♕xa2

Annotators said White wins slowly after 33...♔g7 34 ♖f4 ♖f8 35 b5.

But mate is preferable – 34 ♖xf7+! ♔xf7 35 ♕c4+, e.g. 35...♔f8 (35...♔g7 36 ♕c7+ ♔f6 37 ♖d6+) 36 ♕c5+ ♔g8 37 ♕d5+ ♔h8 38 ♕e5+ ♔h7 39 ♖d7+.

34	♖4d6!	Resigns

The threat is 35 ♕xg6+, and 34...♖g8 35 ♖f6 ♖g7 36 b5 is convincing.

79

When Miguel Najdorf escaped from a lost endgame at the Leipzig Olympiad in 1960, Bobby angily knocked over the pieces according to the Argentine. "You'll never play again in South America," Najdorf told him. But in July 1970 Fischer's exile ended when he – and Miguel – played at an international in Buenos Aires.

Najdorf recalled how much Fischer had changed in a decade. At Buenos Aires 1960 Fischer habitually appeared at the board in a sweater and slacks. He noticed how Najdorf, a wealthy insurance company executive, changed suits each day and asked how many he owned. Not taking the question seriously, Najdorf replied 150. At Buenos Aires 1970 Fischer approached Najdorf and said, "1 broke your record. I have 187 suits." "Bravissimo. I congratulate you" said Najdorf. "But I have to confess I never had more than 30."

Suits or not, the 27-year-old Fischer was a much more mature player in 1970. He allowed only four draws at Buenos Aires, pointedly refusing draws in positions he might have accepted ten years before:

László Szabó – Fischer
Buenos Aires 1970
King's Indian Defense,
Fianchetto Variation (E61)

1	c4	g6
2	g3	♗g7
3	♗g2	c5
4	♘c3	♘c6
5	e3	♘f6
6	d4	0-0
7	♘ge2	d6
8	0-0	♗f5

This provocative move is designed to draw White's pawns forward. For example, 9 e4 ♗d7 10 ♗e3? ♘g4 or 10 h3? cxd4 11 ♘xd4 ♘xd4 12 ♕xd4 ♕c8! wins a pawn (13 ♔h2? ♘g4+).

9	d5	♘a5
10	e4	♗d7
11	b3	

11	...	a6!

This shows Black has won the battle of the opening since after the natural 12 ♗b2 b5 13 ♕d3 ♖b8 14 ♖ab1 he wins a pawn with 14...bxc4 15 bxc4 ♖b4 16 ♘d1 ♖xc4 but even better is the pinning pressure of 16...♕b6. Szabó prepares to dissolve the queenside.

12	♖b1	b5
13	cxb5	axb5
14	b4	cxb4
15	♖xb4	

The b-pawn is as weak as the a-pawn and White will stand well after 15...♖b8 16 ♘d4.

15	...	♕c7!
16	♘xb5	

Black would have good winning prospects after 16 ♗e3 ♘c4 17 ♗d4 ♕a5. Szabó is looking for complications...

16	...	♕c5!

...and would find them after 16...♗xb5 17 ♖xb5 ♕c4 with 18 a4 ♘xe4 19 ♕e1!, threatening ♖b4 or ♖xa5.

Then 19...♘c3 20 ♘xc3 ♗xc3 21 ♕xe7 ♕xa4 22 ♖b1 or 19...♗c3 20 ♕d1 offers chances to both sides. Fischer plays for more.

17 ♕d4

17 ...   ♘xd5!

This was not very difficult to calculate. What was hard was deciding whether to pull the tactical trigger here or try to improve Black's chances with preliminary moves:

(a) After 17...♖fb8 White has nothing better than 18 a4, and Black can't improve on 18...♘xd5 19 ♕xc5 dxc5 20 ♖b1 ♘b4. But White has better drawing chances than in the game after 21 ♗e3!! ♗xb5 22 axb5 ♖xb5 23 ♗xc5.

(b) Similar is 17...♖ab8 18 a4 ♘xd5 19 ♕xc5 dxc5 20 ♖b1. There is a slight difference between this position and (a) because 20...♘b6 (rather than 20...♘b4) cannot be met by 21 ♘c7 as in (a). The difference favors Black after 21 ♘ec3 ♘xa4! or 21 ♗f4 e5 22 ♗e3 ♘xa4.

18 ♕xe5   dxc5

Around here Szabó offered a draw, explaining later that Fischer had rejected "many rather complicated continuations" and seemed "agreeable to a draw." "But when I offered peace he shook his head indignantly."

19 ♖b1   ♘b4
20 ♘c7!

The shots continue. On 20 ♘bc3 ♘c4 Black keeps improving his position (21 ♖a1 ♘c2 22 ♖b1 ♘d4). Worse is 20 ♘ec3 ♘c4 21 a3 because of 21...♘xa3 22 ♗xa3 ♗xc3.

White can try to transpose into the note (a) to move 17 with 20 a4 but instead of 20...♖fb8 Black has 20...♗e6, threatening 21...♗a2 but also 21...♗c4!.

20 ...   ♖a7
21 a3!

White's rook is embarrassed after 21 ♘d5 ♘xd5 22 exd5 ♗f5 (23 ♖b6 ♘c4).

21 ...   ♖xc7
22 axb4   cxb4!?

This shows astonishing faith in his ability to win an endgame in which there will only be kingside pawns. The alternative, 22...♖b7 23 ♗g5 ♖xb4, favours Black more (24 ♗xe7 ♖fb8 25 ♖bd1 ♗b5 26 ♖fe1 ♖b2 21 ♗f3 ♘b3). Fischer misjudged the strength of his next move.

23 ♖xb4   ♖c2

24 ♘d4

This was unfairly called the losing move, when in fact it only makes a shaky position more precarious.

White's disadvantage is also manageable after 24 ♘f4, e.g. 24...♖fc8 25 ♗e3.

24 ...   ♗xd4!

25 ♖xd4   ♗b5

Annotators were quick to claim that 26 ♖fd1 loses to 26...♗e2. Actually, the win is not certain after 27 ♗h6! ♘c6 28 ♖d5 ♗xd1 29 ♗xf8 ♖c1 30 ♗h6 ♖b1! 31 ♖c5! ♗c2+ 32 ♗f1 ♗xe4.

Also muddy is 26...♘b3 (instead of 26...♗e2) 27 ♖b4 ♘xc1 28 ♖xb5 ♘e2+ 29 ♔h1!.

26 ♖e1   ♘b3

27 ♖b4   ♘xc1!

28 ♖xb5   ♘e2+

29 ♔f1?

This allows the f-pawn to be captured with check in key lines. Correct was 29 ♔h1! ♘c3 30 ♖c5 ♖d8 31 ♗f3!, which leaves Black with slim winning chances and nothing convincing after 31...♖dd2 32 ♖f1 or 31...♖d3 32 ♔g2.

29 ...   ♘c3

30 ♖c5?

Soviet analysis vaguely said 30 ♖b7 "held out some chances," and that "some" is right (30...♖d8 31 ♔g1! ♖dd2 32 ♖f1).

30 ...   ♖d8

White is on the cusp of losing now, e.g. 31 ♗f3 ♖dd2 32 ♗e2 ♘xe2 (or 32...e5, seeking *zugzwang*) 33 ♖xc2 ♘xg3+ or 31 f4? ♖dd2 32 ♖c8+ ♔g7 33 ♖e3 ♖f2+.

But at least the rook endgames require some technique. Szabó's next move shortens the game considerably.

31 ♗h3?   ♖dd2

32 ♖c8+   ♔g7

33 ♖e3

33 ...   ♘d1!

34 ♖f3

Also lost was 34 ♖xc2 ♘xe3+, 34 ♖e1 ♖b2 and 34 ♖d3! ♘xf2!.

34 ...   ♖xf2+

35 ♖xf2   ♖xf2+

36 ♔g1

Or 36 ♔e1 ♖xh2 and wins.

36 ...   ♖e2

Ditto 37 ♗g2 ♖e1+ 38 ♗f1 ♖xe4.

37 ♗g4   ♖xe4!

White resigns

This rook endgame (38 ♗xd1 ♖e1+) isn't difficult.

80

If the moves of the following game had been jumbled a bit – and began, say, with 1 e4 c5 2 ♘f3 d6 3 ♘c3 e6 4 ♗e2 a6 5 0-0 b6 6 d4 cxd4 7 ♕xd4 ♘c6 8 ♕d3 ♗b7 9 ♗f4 ♕c7 10 ♖ad1 ♖d8 – it would be easy to explain White's loss. He simply didn't know how to play an open Sicilian, the annotators would say. Certainly not with moves like 11 h3, 12 ♕e3, 13 ♘d2 and 14 ♔h1, they would add.

But in the real move order, with colors reversed, the game makes quite a different impression. Vladimir Tukmakov was simply outplayed in an opening that seemed only months old. At the time Tukmakov was regarded as a potential new Soviet superstar. A year later he played first board on the Soviet student team while Anatoly Karpov was relegated to third board.

Fischer – Vladimir Tukmakov
Buenos Aires 1970
Nimzo-Larsen Opening (A01)

1	b3!	e5
2	♗b2	♘c6

One of the standard opening references of the time, Euwe's 12-volume *Theorie der Schacheröffnungen*, devoted only a quarter of a page to 1 b3 and stopped its analysis here with the comment "Black stands very satisfactorily."

3	c4	♘f6
4	e3	♗e7
5	a3!	0-0

6	d3	d5
7	cxd5	♕xd5

The more natural 7...♘xd5 leaves Black with a problem of defending his e-pawn, as Game 87 shows.

8	♘c3	♕d6
9	♘f3	♗f5

There were two ways of using pressure on d3 but the right way was 9...♗g4 10 ♗e2 ♖ad8, e.g. 11 0-0 ♗xf3 12 gxf3 ♕e6 and ...♘d5/...f5.

10	♕c2	♖fd8
11	♖d1	h6

The psychology begins to work against Tukmakov. Of course, he is Black, facing a much stronger player and should be content with rough equality. There was no threat (12 ♘b5 ♕d7 13 ♘xe5? ♘xe5 14 ♗xe5 ♕xb5) and solid moves as 11...♖ac8 and 12...♗f8 were appropriate.

Yet the position on the board tells Tukmakov he is really White in a Sicilian Defense, and as in any Sicilian he is virtually required to strive for the initiative. This explains why he chose 6...d5 instead of a solid 6...d6 followed by ...♘d7-c5 and ...f5. Here he eyes ...♕e6 and ...e4 (but wants to avoid 11...♕e6 12 ♘g5).

12 h3!

Black may have expected 12 ♗e2 ♕e6 13 ♘d2 ♗g4!, putting the d-pawn in his gunsights.

12 ...   ♕e6

13 ♘d2

Not 13 ♗e2 e4! with advantage.

13 ...   ♘d7

On 13...♖d7 14 ♗e2 ♖fd8 White has a comfortable game with 15 ♘de4.

14 ♗e2   ♔h8

Black rejected 14...♘c5 15 ♘ce4 and didn't want to give up b5 after 14...a5. But the consistent idea was 14...♕g6 and if 15 ♘d5 then 15...♗d6 and ...♘b6.

15 0-0   ♗g6

16 b4   a6

Black loses this game because he never figures out how to defend his queenside. After 16...f5 White has a promising game from 17 ♘b5, 17 ♗f3 or 17 b5.

17 ♖c1!   ♖ac8

18 ♖fd1   f5

A reasonable alternative was 18...♘b6 to discourage ♘a4 or ♘c4.

19 ♘a4   ♘a7?

Bad but White would have a nice queenside initiative percolating after the superior 19...♘f6 20 ♘b3 and ♘ac5. Also, 19...f4 invites 20 ♗g4 ♗f5 21 ♗xf5 ♕xf5 21 e4! followed by ♘f3 and pressure on the e-pawn with ♕b1-a1. Better was 19...♘b6 and 20 ♘c5 ♗xc5 21 ♕xc5 ♘a4.

20 ♘b3   b6

There was no relief from 20...c6 21 ♘a5 and 22 d4.

21 d4!

21 ...   f4

The *Informant* notes said Black is only slightly worse after 21...♘b5, probably with 22 ♗c4 ♕c6 23 dxe5 ♘xa3 in mind (24 ♗xa3 ♕xa4 25 ♖a1 ♘b8).

22 e4!

White has a big edge and would win outright after 22...exd4 23 ♘xd4 ♕xe4 24 ♗d3 because 24...♕xd3!? 25 ♖xd3 ♘e5 is refuted by the sparkling 27 ♘f5! ♘xd3 28 ♘xe7!. White has a simpler win after 23...♕xe4 in the form of 24 ♕xe4 and 25 ♘e6.

22 ...   ♘b5

Black was probably counting on 22...♗xe4 23 ♕xe4 ♕xb3 but now saw that 24 ♗xa6 ♕xa4 25 ♗xc8 ♖xc8 26 dxe5 would win easily. Nevertheless, that was the best practical try, with 25...♘f6.

23 ♗g4!   ♕f6?

24 dxe5   ♘xe5

25 ♗xc8   ♖xc8

26 ♖d5!   Resigns

Because of 26...♗d6 27 ♘xb6!.

81

Two of Fischer's games at Buenos Aires exasperated annotators. In his tactical brawl with Quinteros (Game 83) they went to extraordinary efforts to prove he was lost at some point or other. In the following game, it was a single move, 18 ♖g3, that provoked them. It was variously described as an unworthy trap, a profound waiting move, a wasted tempo, and a clever case of prophylaxis. Perhaps Boris Gulko, who reanalyzed the game in 2002, came closest when he praised it – and yet called it "one of the most bizarre and inexplicably 'stupid' moves of all time."

Fischer – Samuel Schweber
Buenos Aires 1970
French Defense (C19)

1	e4	e6
2	d4	d5
3	♘c3	♗b4
4	e5	c5
5	a3	♗xc3+
6	bxc3	♕c7
7	♘f3	♘c6
8	♗e2	

Fischer was virtually alone in preferring this order to 8 a4 ♗d7 9 ♗d2. Perhaps he was afraid of 8 a4 cxd4 9 cxd4 ♘b4, when White has to try 10 ♖b1 ♘xc2+ 11 ♔d2 or gambit the pawn (10 ♗b5+ ♗d7 11 ♗xd7+ ♔xd7 12 0-0 ♕xc2 13 ♕e1).

8	...	♗d7
9	0-0	♘ge7

| 10 | a4 | ♘a5? |

This is premature before White has provided a target for the knight with ♗a3. Standard moves are 10...f6 and 10...b6 (and if 11 ♗a3, then 11...♘a5).

11	♖e1	cxd4
12	cxd4	♘c4

| 13 | ♗d3! | |

White sets the table for the ancient sacrifice: 13...0-0 14 ♗xh7+! ♔xh7 15 ♘g5+ ♔g6! and now 16 ♕g4 f5 17 exf6 e5 18 ♘e6+ ♔xf6 19 dxe5+. White wins material after 19...♘xe5 20 ♘xc7 and wields a killing initiative after 19...♔f7 20 ♕xg7+! ♔xe6 21 ♕h6+.

13	...	h6
14	♘d2!	

White prepares ♕g4 or ♕e2 as well as ♗xc4 followed by invasion of d6 via ♘e4.

| 14 | ... | ♘xd2 |

Black doesn't stand badly after 14...0-0-0 15 ♗xc4? dxc4 16 ♗a3 ♘f5 but 15 ♕g4 g6 16 ♕e2 leaves him seriously weak on both wings.

15	♗xd2	♘c6
16	♕g4	g6
17	♖e3	

Botvinnik, in his preparation for the unplayed 1970 match, pointed out how much Fischer liked to shift rooks along the third rank. There's a tactical explanation here: 17 ♗xg6 is handled by 17...♖g8!, rather than 17...fxg6 18 ♕xg6+ ♔e7 19 ♕g7+ or 18...♔f8 19 ♗xh6+. The text threatens 18 ♗xg6 ♖g8 19 ♗xf7+! ♔xf7 20 ♖f3+.

17 ...   0-0-0

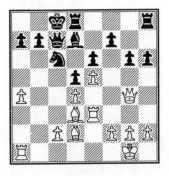

18 ♖g3!

White would love to paralyze the kingside by planting a heavy piece on f6. But 18 ♕f4? allows 18...f5! with a fine game. Trifunovic, in the *Informant*, claimed 18 ♖f3 was best. However, Black has 18...f5!, since 19 ♕xg6 ♘xd4 and 19 exf6 e5 20 ♕xg6 e4 yield smaller edges.

Instead, 18 ♖g3 – which Euwe said "does not accomplish anything" – prepares ♕f4-f6 while stopping 18...f5 with 19 ♕xg6 ♖dg8 20 ♕xg8+. Another point is that on 18...♘e7 19 ♕f3 ♘f5 White's rook penetrates via 20 ♗xf5 gxf5 21 ♖g7.

18 ...   ♔b8

This clears c8 for a rook or a bishop and avoids 18...♘a5 19 ♕f4!. since 19...♖df8? is met by 20 ♗b4. But by evacuating his king from a potentially hot file Black puts it on a closed – yet ultimately hotter – diagonal.

19 ♖f3!   f5

White would rule the kingside after 19...♗e8 (or 19...♖df8) 20 ♖f6!. But Black's combination has a dramatic flaw.

20 exf6   e5

21 ♕g3!

Black's wildest dreams are realized by 21 ♕xg6 ♖dg8 22 ♕h5 ♗g4 or 22 ♕f7 ♖xg2+! 23 ♔xg2? ♗h3+. Or even 22 ♕xg8+ ♖xg8 23 f7 ♖f8 24 ♗xh6 ♕d6.

21 ...   ♘xd4

Not 21...e4?? 22 ♗f4.

22 ♖e3   e4

Or 22...♘f5 23 ♗xf5 and ♕xe5.

23 ♖xe4!

Black has excellent survival chances after 23 ♕xc7+ ♔xc7 24 ♗f1 ♗c6 or 24...♘f5. But now the threat of 24 ♗f4 drags him into a lost endgame via what Gulko called "a very brilliant point."

23 ...   ♕xg3

24 ♖xd4!!

Black's queen is trapped (24... ♕c7 25 ♗f4) thanks to 18...♔b8.

24	...	♛g4
25	♖xg4	♝xg4

White must regain the Exchange, leaving him a winning pawn ahead.

| 26 | ♝xg6 | ♖hg8 |

The rooks prove extremely awkward. After 26...♖df8 27 f7 there is no defense to ♝f4+-e5, for example.

| 27 | ♝h7! |

A bit simpler than 27 ♝d3 ♖df8 28 ♝c3 ♝f3 29 ♝e5+ which should also win.

| 27 | ... | ♖h8 |

Or 27...♖gf8 28 ♝xh6 ♖xf6 29 ♝g5.

The remainder was mop-up:

28 ♝d3 ♖de8 29 f7 ♖e7 30 f8(♛)+! ♖xf8 31 ♝b4 ♖ff7 32 ♝xe7 ♖xe7 33 f3 ♝d7 34 a5! ♚c7 35 ♚f2 ♖f7 36 ♚e3 ♚d6 37 g3 ♚c5 38 f4 ♝g4 39 ♖b1 ♖e7+ 40 ♚d2 b6 41 axb6 axb6 42 h3! ♝d7 43 g4 d4 44 f5 ♖e3 45 f6! ♖f3 (Or 45...♖xh3 46 f7 ♖f3 47 ♝f5! and queens) **46 ♖f1 ♖xf1 47 ♝xf1 ♝e6 and Black resigned**

82

The outcome of this game seems routine, unless you know of the other meetings between the two players. Florin Gheorghiu was a promising Rumanian who had ended Fischer's six-year run as the world's youngest GM when he earned the title in 1964. Two of their four games were drawn and in the third, Gheorghiu took only 55 minutes to beat Fischer in 50 moves.

Fischer – Florin Gheorghiu
Buenos Aires 1970
Petroff Defense (C42)

1	e4	e5
2	♘f3	♘f6
3	♘xe5	d6
4	♘f3	♘xe4
5	d4	♝e7!?
6	♝d3	♘f6
7	h3	

Black's super-conservative play (in place of 5...d5) suggests White will have an easy time getting a substantial edge. Yet the position soon resembles an Alekhine's variation that goes 1 e4 ♘f6 2 e5 ♘d5 3 c4 ♘b6 4 d4 d6 5 exd6 exd6 6 ♘c3 ♝e7 7 ♘f3 0-0 8 h3 and is considered only slightly better for White. (In this game Black should be better off than that because his knight stands on f6, not b6.)

7	...	0-0
8	0-0	♖e8
9	c4!	

Now 9...c5 10 d5 ♝f8 11 ♘c3 a6 12 a4 fails to equalize as did the slower approach, ...♘bd7-f8-g6 and ...♝f8, in early 20th Century tests.

| 9 | ... | ♘c6 |

233

Petrosian revealed how much he had studied Fischer's games when he improved against Fischer in their Candidates match with 9...c6 10 ♘c3 ♘bd7 11 ♖e1 ♘f8 12 ♗f4 a6 13 ♕b3 and now 13...♘e6 14 ♗h2 ♗f8 15 ♖e2 b5!.

10 ♘c3   h6
11 ♖e1   ♗f8

Black's only real problem is the log jam of pieces on his first two ranks. He needs to develop his QB, followed by ...♕d7.

12 ♖xe8   ♕xe8
13 ♗f4   ♗d7

On 13...♘b4 14 d5 ♘xd3 15 ♕xd3 g6 Black can untangle – but not after 14 ♗b1!.

14 ♕d2

Annotators were quick to sacrifice White's pieces with 14...g5 15 ♗xg5 hxg5 16 ♕xg5+ although the compensation is barely visible after 16...♗g7 17 ♖e1 ♕d8 18 ♖e3 ♖e8. Better is 15 ♖e1 ♕d8 16 ♘xg5!.

14 ...   ♕c8

Black expected to play ...♗f5xd3 since 15 g4? allows 15...♗xg4.

15 d5!   ♘b4
16 ♘e4!

This is what Black missed (16...♘xd3 17 ♘xf6+).

16 ...   ♘xe4
17 ♗xe4   ♘a6

Now he can solve the QB-problem with 17...a5 18 a3 ♘a6 19 ♕xa5 ♘c5 but that isn't worth a pawn.

18 ♘d4

A younger Fischer might have sought a queenside bind with 18 b4 (18...b5 19 cxb5 ♗xb5 20 ♘d4 ♗d7 21 ♖c1) rather than kingside attack.

18 ...   ♘c5
19 ♗c2   a5
20 ♖e1   ♕d8

Again the annotators liked 20...g5 21 ♗xg5? hxg5 22 ♕xg5+ ♗g7 23 ♖e7 but that's refuted by 21...♕d8! and 22...♔f8.

21 ♖e3

21 ...   b6

Here Black overlooks White's reorganizing idea (♘f3/♗e3-d4). Emanuel Lasker would have tried 21...g5 22 ♖g3 ♗g7. The black kingside is remarkably resilient. For example, 23 ♗e3 ♕e7 24 h4 ♘e4 25 ♗xe4 ♕xe4 26 hxg5 h5. Or 23 f4 ♘e4! 24 ♗xe4 ♕xe4 25 hxg5 ♗e5.

22	罝g3	含h8
23	匄f3!	豐e7

Not 23...豐f6 24 兔e3! and 兔d4.

| 24 | 豐d4! |

| 24 | ... | 豐f6 |

White wins after 24...f6 25 匄h4
豐e2 26 匄g6+ 含g8 27 兔xh6! 豐xc2
28 匄xf8 罝xf8 29 罝xg7+ and
30 罝e7.

25	豐xf6	gxf6
26	匄d4!	罝e8
27	罝e3	罝b8

After a trade of rooks White's
fastest win is 兔f5.

| 28 | b3 | b5 |

Losing a pawn but 28...兔e8
29 匄f5 h5 30 匄g3 h4 shouldn't
prolong Black's life much, e.g.
31 匄f5 b5 32 匄xh4 bxc4 33 bxc4.

29	cxb5	兔xb5
30	匄f5	兔d7
31	匄xh6	罝b4
32	罝g3!	兔xh6

The threat was 33 罝g8 mate, and
32...含g7 33 匄xf7+ 含g8 34 匄h6+
含f8 35 兔e3 was of little help.

| 33 | 兔xh6 | 匄e4 |

| 34 | 兔g7+ | 含h7 |

Or 34...含g8 35 兔xe4 罝xe4
36 兔xf6+ 含f8 37 罝c3.

| 35 | f3 | **Resigns** |

83

Miguel Quinteros, a close friend of
Fischer's, liked to grab material and
hold onto it with both hands. But in
the following game, the Argentine
GM is forced to attack, and responds
by offering the most audacious
sacrifice ever played against Fischer.
Even though the battle is lost by
move 27, it has more spectacular
might-have-beens than any other
Fischer game.

Miguel Quinteros – Fischer
Buenos Aires 1970
English Opening (A35)

1	c4	g6
2	匄c3	兔g7
3	匄f3	c5
4	d4	cxd4
5	匄xd4	匄c6

Black attacks d4 before White gets
his Maróczy house in order. For
example, 6 匄b3 d6 7 e4 b6 8 兔e2
兔xc3+ 9 bxc3 匄f6 and ...兔a6.

6	♘c2	♝xc3+
7	bxc3	♘f6

8 f3

In the long run, Black should prevail on the queenside after ...♛a5, ...♝a6, ...♜c8 and ...♘d7-c5. But in the short run he may be mated. White will play 9 e4, shift the knight to d5 via e3 and watch for the right time to push his f-pawn.

8	...	d6
9	e4	♝e6
10	♝e2	♜c8
11	♘e3	♛a5
12	♝d2	♘e5
13	♛b3	♘fd7!

This dooms the c-pawn (...♘c5 and ...♛a4). Note that 14 ♛xb7? is refuted by 14...♜b8.

14 f4

After 14 0-0 White can meet 14...♘c5 with 15 ♛b4. But Black does better with 14...♛c5!, threatening ...♝xc4 as well as ...♘b6, e.g. 15 ♛xb7 ♝xc4!.

14	...	♘c5
15	♛c2	

And here 15 ♛b5+? ♛xb5 16 cxb5 ♘ed3+ drops material.

15	...	♘c6

16	0-0	♛a4!

White pawns fall in any endgame, e.g. 17 ♛xa4 ♘xa4 18 ♜ab1 ♘c5. But 18 f5 ♝d7 19 f6 offers compensation (19...e6 20 ♜fd1).

17	♛b1	♘a5

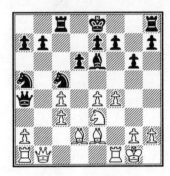

If there were no kings, Black should win. e.g. 18 ♝d1 ♛a3 19 ♝b3 ♘axb3 20 axb3 ♛xb3 21 ♜xa7 ♛xb1 22 ♜xb1 ♘xe4.

18 e5!

The position demands open lines but 18 f5 ♝xc4 19 ♘xc4 ♘xc4 20 ♝g5 promises little after 20...f6.

18	...	dxe5
19	fxe5	0-0

After 19...♘xc4 20 ♘xc4 ♝xc4 White has 21 ♜f4! b5 22 ♝xc4 bxc4 23 ♝e3 0-0 24 ♛f1 ♘d7 25 ♝d4 followed by ♜b1 or ♜h4 with some tactical opportunities.

20	♜f4	♘d7

Better was 20...♛d7 with threats of ...♛xd2 and ...♛c7xe5 but there is no Black win, as annotators claimed, after 21 ♜d4!, e.g. 21...♛c7 22 ♛b4 b6 23 ♘d5 ♝xd5 24 cxd5 ♛xe5 25 ♝g4.

21	♘d5!	♜fe8
22	♛e4	b5!

In his introduction to the Russian edition of *My 60 Memorable Games*, Alexey Suetin recommended 22...♘f8, and gave 23 ♖h4 b5 24 ♗g5 ♗xd5 25 cxd5 ♕xe4 26 ♖xe4 a6 as proof that Black is holding.

Holding, perhaps. But 22...b5 goes for the win. White would be lost after, say, 23 ♗e3 ♘xc4 24 ♗d4 ♘c5.

23 ♖xf7‼

A terrific shot, based on variations such as 23...♗xf7 24 e6 ♘f6 25 ♘xf6+ exf6 26 exf7+ ♔xf7 27 ♕d5+ ♔g7 28 ♕d7+ ♔h8 29 ♗h6 ♖g8 and now 30 ♕f7 ♖c6 31 ♗f3‼ is faster than the 30 ♗g7+ endgame.

The key to many of the lines that follow is ♗g4. For example, 24...bxc4 (instead of 24...♘f6) allows 25 ♗g4 ♖cd8? 26 exf7+ ♔xf7 27 ♖f1+ ♘f6 28 ♕e6+ ♔g7 29 ♘xf6 ♖xd2 30 ♘h5+! and mates. (Actually, 25 ♖f1! is stronger.)

23 ... ♔xf7

Black can try to upset White's calculations by inserting 23...♘c5. Suetin gave 24 ♕h4 ♗xf7 25 ♘xe7+ ♖xe7 26 ♕xe7 as a crucial position.

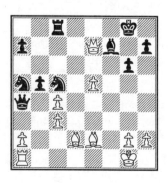

There are convincing wins after, for example, 26...♗xc4 27 ♗h6 ♗f7 28 ♖f1 ♕xa2 29 ♕f6.

Adrian Mikhalchishin, in *Shakhmaty v SSSR*, offered a third idea, 26...bxc4. He analyzed 27 ♗g4! ♕e8 28 ♕xa7 ♖a8 29 ♕xc5 ♘b3 30 ♕d6! and wins, e.g. 30...♖d8 31 ♕f6 and 32 e6 or 30...♘xa1 31 e6! ♖d8 32 exf7+ ♔xf7 33 ♗e6+. But 27...♕e8 is unclear.

Mark Dvoretsky claimed a fourth idea, 26...♘e6 27 ♖f1 ♖c7! was equal.

There's a fifth option, 26...♘xc4!. Black is winning after 27 ♗g4 ♖e8 28 ♕xc5 ♘xd2 or 27 ♗h6 ♘e6 28 ♗g4 ♖e8. White can improve with 27 ♖f1 ♘xe5 28 ♕xe5 after which 28...♕e4! 29 ♕f6! should only favor him slightly.

24 ♕h4! ♔g7!

It should be no surprise Black can't allow a capture on h7, e.g, 24...♗xd5 25 ♕xh7+ ♔e6 26 ♕xg6+ ♔xe5 27 ♗f4+! and mates.

But what about 24...♘f8 ? There are some pretty lines, such as 25 ♖f1+ ♗f5 26 ♖xf5+ gxf5 27 ♗h5+ ♔e6 28 ♕d4‼ ♘g6 29 ♘c7+ and mates. But 27...♘g6 puts the line under a cloud.

To justify his sacrifice after 24...♘f8 25 ♖f1+ ♗f5, White may have to plunge into 26 g4 ♘xc4 27 gxf5! (not 27 ♗f4 ♕a3! when ...♕c5+ wins for Black).

Then on 27...♘xd2 White has 28 fxg6+ ♔e6 29 ♖f4! and wins. For example, 29...♕xa2 30 ♗xe7, threatening 31 ♕f6+ and mates, e.g. 30...♔d7 31 ♖f7 with a killing attack.

25 ♘xe7!

White's threats include 26 ♕h6+ ♔h8 27 ♗g5 and ♗f6+ or 27 ♘xg6+ ♔g8 28 ♗d3!. After

25...♘c6 he can finish off neatly with 26 ♗h6+ ♔h8 27 ♘xc8 ♖xc8 28 ♖d1! (threat: ♖xd7) g5 29 ♕f2 ♘cxe5 30 ♖xd7! ♘xd7 31 ♕d4+ and mates.

25 ...   ♕c2!!

One of the many difficult variations, cited by Mikhalchishin runs 25...♖xc4 26 ♕h6+! ♔h8 27 ♘xg6+ ♔g8 28 ♗d3 ♖c7 29 ♖f1!! with the idea of 29...♘c4 30 ♘e7+! ♖xe7 31 ♗xh7+ ♖xh7 32 ♕xe6+ ♔h8 32 ♕e8+.

The prettiest line runs 29...♘c6 30 ♘f4 ♘f8 31 ♘xe6 ♘xe6 32 ♗xh7+! ♖xh7 33 ♕g6+ ♘g7 34 ♕f7+ ♔h8 35 ♕f8+! and mates.

26 ♕h6+?

The *Informant* claimed White missed a simple win with 26 ♘xc8 ♕xd2 (Or 26...♖xc8 27 ♕e7+ ♔h8 28 ♗h6 ♖g8 29 ♕xe6 ♕e2 30 ♕xd7) 27 ♘d6. But then 27...♖f8 28 ♕e7+ ♔h8 29 ♕xe6 ♕e3+ 30 ♔h1 ♕xe2 can only favor Black.

Yet White does have better than 26 ♕h6+. The most promising try is 26 ♗h6+ ♔h8 27 ♘xc8! as suggested by Herman Pilnik in *64 –* 27...♕xe2 28 ♘d6 g5 29 ♗xg5 ♖g8 30 ♗f6+ ♘xf6 31 ♕xf6+ ♖g7 32 g3 ♗g8? 33 ♘f5.

Black can improve with 32...♘xc4 – or earlier with 28...♖g8. And White can improve after 28...g5 29 ♗g7+!. But the final verdict on 23 ♖xf7 seems clear: With best play White has at least a draw.

26 ...   ♔h8
27 ♖c1   ♕xc1+!

Simplest. Two rooks and a knight beat a queen.

28 ♗xc1   ♖xe7
29 cxb5   ♘c4
30 ♕h4

White has no way of impeding Black's progress after 30 ♗g5 ♖f7 and ...♘cxe5. He tries to create a passed b-pawn.

30 ...   ♖f7
31 ♕d4   ♔g8
32 ♗f4   ♖c5!

The main threat was 33...♖d5! (33 ♕xc4 ♖d1+). The pieces swarmed during the remainder:

33 ♗f3 ♖xb5 34 h3 ♘cxe5 35 ♗a8 ♖f8 36 ♗xe5 ♘xe5 37 ♕xa7 ♗d5! 38 ♗xd5+ ♖xd5 39 ♕e3 ♖a5 40 ♕e2 ♖fa8 41 a4 ♘f7 42 h4 ♖xa4 White resigns

84

Fischer played hypermodern openings, like the King's Indian Defense and King's Indian Reversed, with a classical sensibility. He would concede the center if it meant sharpening the position. But if his opponent relinquished the opportunities that the opening granted him, Fischer filled the vacuum. Then it became a simple matter: the player with more space wins, just as in a Capablanca game. Or in this:

Fischer – Oscar Panno
Buenos Aires 1970
King's Indian Reversed (C00)

1	e4	c5
2	♘f3	e6
3	d3	♘c6
4	g3	g6
5	♗g2	♗g7
6	0-0	♘ge7
7	♖e1	d6
8	c3	0-0
9	d4	cxd4
10	cxd4	

The natural policy for Black is an attack on d4 with 10...♕b6 since White can't reinforce his center and has to take his chances in lines such as 11 d5 ♗xb2 (or 11...♘d4) 12 ♗xb2 ♕xb2 13 dxc6 ♕xa1 14 ♕b3 ♘xc6 15 ♘c3 ♘d4 or 14 cxb7 ♗xb7 15 ♕b3 ♗d5.

10	...	d5
11	e5	

Now 11...♕b6 12 ♘c3 ♘f5 is thwarted by 13 ♘a4.

11	...	♗d7
12	♘c3	♖c8

The space edge is obvious after 12...♘f5 13 h4 f6 14 ♗f4 and then 14...fxe5 15 ♗xe5 ♘xe5 16 ♘xe5.

13	♗f4	♘a5
14	♖c1	b5

Euwe preferred doubling rooks on the file (14...♕b6 15 b3 ♖c7 and ...♖fc8/...♕b4). But 15 ♖c2 ♖c7 15 h4 ♘c4 16 ♗c1 leaves White free to pursue his attack.

15 b3!

White can afford to weaken c3 because ...♕a5 is not in the picture.

15	...	b4
16	♘e2	♗b5!

Trading rooks (16...♖xc1 17 ♘xc1! ♗b5) offers little after 18 ♕d2 (not 18 ♘d3 ♗xd3 19 ♕xd3 ♕b6) ♘ac6 19 g4.

| 17 | ♕d2 | ♘ac6? |

Here (or on the next move) 17...♗xe2 18 ♕xe2 ♕b6 was helpful.

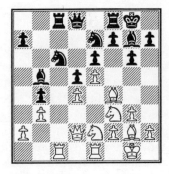

18 g4!

This clears g3 for a knight and makes sure h2-h4-h5 won't stopped by ...h5.

18 ... a5

Also bad was 18...f6 19 exf6 ♗xf6 20 ♗h6, e.g. 20...♗xe2 21 ♖xe2 ♘xd4? 22 ♘xd4 ♖xc1+ 23 ♕xc1 ♗xd4 24 ♗xf8 ♕xf8 25 ♕d2.

19 ♘g3 ♕b6

Black can continue his wing attack with 19...a4 20 h4 axb3 21 axb3 ♖a8 22 h5 ♖a3 23 ♖b1 ♕b6 24 ♗h6 ♖fa8. But the kingside counts more after 25 ♗xg7 ♔xg7 26 ♕f4.

20 h4 ♘b8
21 ♗h6

The serious threats will begin with 22 ♕g5 followed by ♗xg7 and ♘h5+ (but not 22 ♗xg7 ♔xg7 23 ♕g5 ♘g8!).

21 ... ♘d7
22 ♕g5! ♖xc1
23 ♖xc1 ♗xh6

Again Black rejects ...f6, which would end the mating ideas based on sacrifice on g6 but give White a marked positional edge after 24 exf6 ♗xf6 25 ♕e3.

24 ♕xh6 ♖c8
25 ♖xc8+ ♘xc8

26 h5!

Black may have assumed there was too little material on the board for a mate – and he'd be right after 26 ♘g5 ♘f8 27 ♘3e4 dxe4 28 ♘xe4 ♕d8.

26 ... ♕d8?

Black should anticipate White's next move with 26...♘f8, since then 27 ♘g5? ♕xd4 is unsound (28 ♘xh7 ♘xh7 29 hxg6 ♘f8!). White's best winning plan then is 27 ♕g5 followed by ♗f1 and invading on the queenside with ♕c1!.

27 ♘g5 ♘f8

28 ♗e4!!

Improbably, White finds a way to add his last piece to the attack. This is much cleaner than 28 ♘xh7 ♘xh7 29 hxg6 fxg6 30 ♕xg6+ ♔h8 31 ♕xe6 ♘e7 32 ♘f5.

28 ... ♕e7

Not 28...dxe4 29 ♘3xe4 followed by ♘f6+ and ♘gxh7, mating.

The real alternative to 28...♕e7 is 28...♗e8 29 hxg6 hxg6 (not 29...fxg6? 30 ♕xf8+!). Then after 30 ♘h5! gxh5 there are at least three wins – two beginning with 31 ♗h7+ ♘xh7 32 ♘xh7, and a third starring

the h-pawn after 31 ♘h7 ♘xh7
32 ♗xh7+ ♔h8 33 ♗d3+ ♔g8
34 ♕h7+ ♔f8 35 ♕h8+ ♔e7
36 ♕f6+ ♔d7 37 gxh5!.

29 ♘xh7! ♘xh7

30 hxg6 fxg6

White wins immediately on
30...♘f8 31 g7.

31 ♗xg6!

The 31 ♕xg6+ and ♕xh7+
endgame may be won but this threat
of ♘f6+/♗h7+ shortens the game
considerably.

31 ... ♘g5

No better is 31...♗e8 32 ♗xh7+
♕xh7 33 ♕xe6+ or 31...♘f8
32 ♘h5. Also, 31...♕g7 32 ♗xh7+
♔h8 gives White a choice between a
two-pawn-up ending or finishing
Black off in the middlegame with
33 ♕xe6 ♗d7 34 ♕xd5.

32 ♘h5 ♘f3+

33 ♔g2 ♘h4+

34 ♔g3 ♘xg6

35 ♘f6+ ♔f7

36 ♕h7+ Resigns

It's mate on 36...♔f8 37 ♕g8.

85

Fischer often compared chess with
basketball. In both games you have
to maneuver around your main
target. "Sometimes you have to spin
near the basket in order to get a
favorable position to shoot," he told
Dragoljub Cirić, as Cirić recalled in
the newspaper *NIN*. But this takes
patience such as in the following.
Clearly d4 is the basket but Black
must spin a lot before he can shoot.

José Agdamus – Fischer
Buenos Aires 1970
Queen's Indian Defense (A50)

1 d4 ♘f6

2 c4 b6

A remarkable choice considering
Fischer never played the normal
(2...e6 3 ♘f3 b6) Queen's Indian
Defense. What, one wonders, did he
have in mind against 2...b6 3 f3 ?

3 ♘c3 ♗b7

4 f3 d5

5 cxd5 ♘xd5

6 ♘xd5

More natural is 6 e4 ♘xc3 7 bxc3
g6, as in a Grünfeld. Black can also
treat the position more sharply, with
7...e5 (8 dxe5 ♕h4+).

6 ... ♕xd5

7 e4 ♕d7

8 ♗c4 g6

More enterprising than 8...e6.
Now on 9 ♘h3 ♗g7 10 ♘g5 0-0
11 ♕b3 Black can play 11...♕e8
(not 11...e6 12 ♘xe6) 12 ♗e3 ♘c6
threatening ...♘xd4 or ...♘a5.

9 ♕b3?

White doesn't have the freedom to pursue exotic ideas such as 9 h4 because Black quickly pounds d4 with ...♗g7, ...♘c6 and ...♖d8. But the text misplaces the queen, and 9 ♘e2 and 10 ♗e3 was preferable.

9	...	e6
10	♘e2	♗g7
11	♗e3	♘c6
12	♖d1	

White threatens 13 d5 ♘a5? 14 dxe6. But 12 ♕d3 would have stayed in the middlegame.

12	...	♘a5
13	♕c2	♕c6!?

A rare case when Fischer passes up the two bishops (13...♘xc4 14 ♕xc4 0-0 15 0-0 ♖ad8 16 ♘f4 ♗c6 and 16...♗b5). Instead, he forces a queenless middlegame in which his knight becomes the most versatile piece on the board.

14	♗d3	♕xc2
15	♗xc2	0-0-0
16	♔f2	♖d6!

Even though this gives White tempo-gainers such as ♗f4 and e4-e5 this is better than 16...♖d7 because the rook may be needed for ...♖c6-c2.

17 b3

Necessary in view of ...♘c4, e.g. 17 ♕d3 ♗a6 18 ♖d2 ♘c4.

17	...	♘c6
18	♖d2	♖hd8
19	♖hd1	

19	...	♘b4!

Both sides have committed maximum force to d4 but Black, who can favorably change the pawn structure with ...f5, has much greater winning chances. He needs to spin a bit since 19...f5 20 e5 ♖6d7 21 ♘f4 is not convincing.

20	♗b1	♗a6
21	a3?	

White wants to trade his passive bishop for an active one but this weakening of b3 comes back to haunt him. True his options are limited (21 ♘c3? c5 22 e5 cxd4! 23 exd6 dxc3 24 ♖c1 ♔f7).

But there was no immediate threat, since 21...♗xe2 22 ♔xe2 ♘c6 is ably handled by 23 e5 and 24 ♗e4. Moreover, White had a good pass in 21 ♗g5, e.g. 21...♖8d7 22 e5 ♖d5 23 ♘c3 ♖a5 24 ♘e4.

21	...	♘c6
22	♗d3	♗xd3

23 ♖xd3   f5

Now is the time for this break. Black doesn't threaten anything yet (24...fxe4 25 fxe4 ♘e5, e.g. 26 ♖c3 ♘g4+ 27 ♔f3 h5! 28 h3 ♘xe3 29 ♔xe3) but he may in a move or two.

24 ♖3d2   ♘a5

On 25 ♘c1 Black justifies his 16th move with 25...♖c6, threatening 26...♖c3 with mounting pressure after 26 ♖d3 ♖c2+ 27 ♔f1 fxe4 28 fxe4 ♗f8.

25 e5?

Another serious concession that grants White only a few tactical chances, such as the pin after 25...♖c6?! 26 b4 ♘c4 27 ♖c1.

25 ...   ♖6d7

26 ♘c1

Or 26 ♖d3 ♗xe5 and 26 b4 ♘c4 27 ♖d3 ♘b2.

26 ...   ♗f8!

27 b4?

The center would also collapse after 27 ♖a2 c5! (28 ♗g5 ♖xd4). But White wrongly rejected 27 a4, apparently believing 27...♗a3 28 ♘e2 ♘xb3 would win – but overlooking 29 ♖d3. Instead, Black can increase his edge with 27...♗e7

and 28...g5. He would also have a long but favorable endgame ahead of him after 27 ♗g5 ♖e8 28 a4 h6 29 ♗f6 ♗a3.

27 ...   ♘c4

28 ♖a2

Black can beat 28 ♖c2 with 28...♘xa3 29 ♖c6 f4 or just 28...♘xe5.

28 ...   ♘xe5

29 ♖c2   b5!

30 ♘e2   ♘c4

31 ♖c3?

This allows a much quicker finish than 31 ♖a1.

31 ...   e5

Threatening, among other things, 32...c5!.

32 f4   exd4

Now 33 ♗xd4 c5 or 33...♗g7 34 ♖cd3 ♘xa3.

33 ♖xd4   ♘xe3

And since 34 ♖xd7 ♘g4+ costs a piece, White played:

34 ♔xe3   ♖xd4

35 ♘xd4   ♖xd4

White resigns

The pawn endgame (36 ♕xd4 ♗g7+) is hopeless.

86

Perhaps Fischer's most important legacy was a comment he made in typical Bobby-speak: "To get squares, ya gotta give squares." Translated, this means that in order to make progress in the middlegame, you often have to concede control of certain key points on the board. In Game 92, we will see how ...f4, a heretical move in the King's Indian because it gives up e4, was a strategic killer. In the following game, he employs a similar version with 11 f5!.

Fischer – Wolfgang Unzicker
Olympiad, Siegen 1970
Ruy Lopez (C69)

1	e4	e5
2	♘f3	♘c6
3	♗b5	a6
4	♗xc6	dxc6
5	0-0	f6
6	d4	exd4
7	♘xd4	♘e7

This flexible move neutralizes White's piece play after 8 ♗f4 ♘g6 9 ♗g3 ♗c5 10 ♘b3 ♗d6!.

8	♗e3	♘g6
9	♘d2	♗d6
10	♘c4	0-0

Black's defensive setup received high marks after a Portisch game that continued 11 ♘xd6? cxd6 12 ♕d2 ♖e8 13 f3 ♘e5 14 ♗f2 d5 with an edge.

11 ♕d3! ♘e5

But White has spotted a fundamental problem: Black lacks space and will be in trouble if he has to settle for ...♗d7, e.g. 11...♔h8 (11...♗d7 12 ♕b3!) 12 ♖ad1 ♕e7 13 f4 ♗d7 (or 13...♗g4) 14 ♘f5!.

12 ♘xe5 ♗xe5

Both 12...fxe5 13 ♕b3+ ♔h8 14 ♘e6 and 13...♖f7 14 ♘f3 h6 15 ♘d2 favor White.

13 f4! ♗d6

Black might draw an ending after 13...♗xd4 14 ♗xd4 ♗e6. But in the

middlegame, the bishops of opposite color aid the player with the attack – that is, White after 15 ♖f3.

14 f5!

This introduces a theme made famous in Lasker – Capablanca, St. Petersburg 1914. White makes his e-pawn a backward target on a half-open file but also mobilizes his kingside majority with the goal of e4-e5!.

14 ... ♕e7

Once Black connects his heavy pieces, he hopes to start shoving White back with ...c5 (which doesn't work here because of 14...c5 15 ♘b3 b6?? 16 ♕d5+).

He can also prepare with 14...♔h8 and 15 ♗f4 ♖e8 (better than 15...♗xf4 16 ♖xf4 c5 17 ♘e2!).

15 ♗f4! ♗xf4

Unzicker didn't want to repeat Capablanca's mistake of creating a weak d6 pawn after ♗xd6/...cxd6. And on 15...♗d7 16 ♕b3+ ♔h8 17 ♗xd6 ♕xd6 18 ♖ad1 White's edge is growing.

But more resourceful is 15...♗c5 16 ♔h1 ♖e8 with the trap of 17 ♖ae1? ♗xd4 18 ♕xd4 ♗xf5.

16 ♖xf4 ♗d7

17 ♖e1   ♕c5

It's still not the right moment for ...c5 – 17...c5 18 ♘f3 ♗c6 19 ♕c4+ ♔h8 and now 20 ♘h4! threatens 21 ♘g6+!. White is better after 20...♗e8 21 e5 fxe5 22 ♘f3.

18 c3   ♖ae8

19 g4!

A daring move to make when your opponent has the only light-squared bishop. But by safeguarding f5 White sets the stage for e4-e5 and also creates the possibility of another winning break, g4-g5.

19 ...   ♕d6

20 ♕g3   ♖e7

Slightly better than the game was 20...c5 21 ♘f3 ♗c6 (22 g5 ♔h8 23 ♘h4).

21 ♘f3   c5

22 e5!

Otherwise 22...♗c6 turns the e-pawn into a target.

22 ...   fxe5

23 ♖fe4   ♗c6

Black's best chance of derailing the kingside majority is a timely ...h5 but here 23...h5 24 ♘h4! and ♘g6 helps White.

24 ♖xe5   ♖fe8

25 ♖xe7   ♖xe7

26 ♘e5!

Now White seeks a queen endgame with, in effect, an extra pawn (26...♕d5 27 ♘xc6 ♖xe1+ 28 ♕xe1 ♕xc6 29 ♕e7 h6 30 ♔f2! ♕d5 31 ♔e3!). But Black can stop the White kingside pawns before they advance with, say, 26...g6 (27 ♔f2 ♕f6 28 ♘xc6? ♖xe1 29 ♔xe1 ♕xc6 with a likely draw).

26 ...   h6

27 h4   ♗d7

Black's passive play makes a poor impression, and critics recommended 27...♕d5 28 ♘xc6 ♖xe1+ 29 ♕xe1 ♕xc6 30 ♕e3 ♕d5! e.g. 31 b3? ♕d1+ 32 ♔h2 ♕xg4 or 31 f6 gxf6 32 ♕xh6 ♕d1+.

However, White maintains his edge in either case with 28 g5!, e.g. 28...hxg5 29 hxg5 ♕d2 30 f6.

28 ♕f4   ♕f6

29 ♖e2!

A splendid "little" move that prepares ♘g6 and stops 29...♕xh4 (30 ♘g6) as well as 29...h5, which loses to 30 ♕c4+ ♔h7 31 g5! ♕xf5 32 g6+ and ♘f7+.

29 ...   ♗c8

30 ♕c4+   ♔h7

31	♘g6	♖xe2
32	♕xe2	♗d7?

Black would still be holding after 32...♕d6 because the white king has no place to hide (33 ♕e8 ♕d1+ 34 ♔f2 ♕c2+ 35 ♔f3 ♕d3+).

33 ♕e7!

After 33 ♕e5 ♕xe5 34 ♘xe5 ♗c8 Black seems to have a chance with 35...h5. For example, 35 h5 ♔g8 36 ♔f2 ♔f8 and ...♔e7-f6. But White wins anyway with 35 ♘g6! h5 36 ♘e7 ♗d7 37 g5.

33	...	♕xe7
34	♘xe7	g5!

Allowing g4-g5 is quite lost.

35 hxg5!

On 35 fxg6+? ♔g7 Black may survive (36 g5 hxg5 37 hxg5 ♗e6 threatening ...♔f8, or 36 ♘f5+ ♔xg6 37 ♘e3 ♗e6 38 a3 ♔f6 and ...♔e5).

35	...	hxg5
36	♘d5!	♗c6

The king is no help: 36...♔g7 37 ♘xc7 ♔f6 38 ♔f2 ♔e5 39 c4 ♔d4 40 f6.

37	♘xc7	♗f3
38	♘e8!	♔h6
39	♘f6	♔g7
40	♔f2!	♗d1
41	♘d7!	

Now 41...♗xg4 42 f6+ and 43 f7 costs a bishop.

41	...	c4
42	♔g3 (sealed)	
42	...	**Resigns**

87

Before leaving Siegen, Fischer agreed to play an exhibition game, arranged by the Swedish newspaper *Expressen*, with the teenage star Ulf Andersson. This, along with Browne – Fischer from Rovinj-Zagreb, his two encounters with Mecking and Fischer – Hübner from the Palma Interzonal are among the few glimpses of how Fischer would have played against the next generation.

Fischer – Ulf Andersson
Exhibition game,
Siegen 1970
Nimzo-Larsen Opening (A01)

1	b3	e5
2	♗b2	♘c6
3	c4	♘f6
4	e3	♗e7
5	a3	0-0
6	♕c2	♖e8

Black could have opened the center immediately with 6...d5 7 cxd5 ♘xd5 8 ♘f3 ♗f6 9 d3 and then 9...a5 or 9...g5. But he can get into quick trouble if he allows White pressure on e5 or a free hand on the queenside, as in 9...g6 10 ♘bd2 ♗g7 11 ♖c1 g5 12 ♘c4 ♕e7 13 b4! (Petrosian – Sosonko, Tilburg 1981).

7	d3	♗f8
8	♘f3	a5

9 &e2   d5
10 cxd5   ♞xd5
11 ♞bd2

Now on 11...g6 (or 11...g5) 12 ♞c4 &g7, White can continue his pressure on e5 eventually by way of the Réti maneuver, &c1 followed by ♛b1-a1!. He should avoid 12 d4 exd4 13 ♞xd4 ♞xd4 14 &xd4 because of 14...♞f4!.

11 ...   f6?

This solves the e5 problem and prepares ...&e6 and ...♛d7. But it is quite passive, as a comparison with the comparable Sicilian position shows.

12 0-0   &e6
13 ♔h1!!

White's grand plan is &g1, ♞e4, and g2-g4-g5. Like the Tukmakov game, it seems like Fischer is taking luxuries against a less experienced opponent. But in fact his plan is the best available and can be compared with Soruco – Fischer, Havana 1966: 1 e4 c5 2 ♞f3 d6 3 d4 cxd4 4 ♞xd4 ♞f6 5 ♞c3 a6 6 &c4 e6 7 &b3 b5 8 a3 &e7 9 &e3 0-0 10 0-0 &b7 11 f3 ♞bd7 12 ♛d2 ♞e5 13 ♛f2 ♛c7 14 &c1 and Black can trade into an even ending with a timely ...d5.

But White's 11th move not only made the equalizing ...d5 possible, it also gave Black an aggressive plan of 14...♔h8! 15 ♞ce2 &g8 16 ♔h1 g5! 17 h3 &g6 18 ♞g3 &ag8. White's concern about ...h5 and ...g4, prompted him to try 19 ♞xe6?? fxe6 20 &xe6 but after 20...♞xe4! 21 ♞xe4 &xe6 he resigned.

Back to Siegen:

13 ...   ♛d7
14 &g1!   &ad8
15 ♞e4   ♛f7

16 g4!   g6

In the short run, this was a good way to keep the g-file closed (since 17 g5? is rebuffed by 17...f5 18 ♞c5 &c8, e.g. 19 d4? exd4 20 ♞xd4 ♞xd4 21 &xd4 b6 22 ♞d3 c5 and ...&b7 with advantage to Black).

Nevertheless, now would be the right time for 16...♞b6, attacking b3. White can continue 17 ♞ed2 and ♞c4 but then he's given up on ♞c5.

17 &g3   &g7
18 &ag1

From now on Black has to watch out for the knight sacrifice ♞h4-f5!.

18 ...   ♞b6

A better try was the immediate 18...&c8, which allows Black to

answer 19 ♘c5 with 19...b6! 20 ♘e4
♘de7 and...♗b7.

19 ♘c5 ♗c8

20 ♘h4 ♘d7

Common sense says the knight
belongs on the kingside but it just
ends up in the way on f8. Better was
20...♗f8 21 ♘e4 ♘d5.

21 ♘e4 ♘f8?

On 21...♘b6 White has 22 g5! f5
23 ♘f6+ ♗xf6 24 gxf6 with a killing
♘xg6 sacrifice coming up.

22 ♘f5!

Fischer's fondness for giving up
rooks for the queen is evident again
22...gxf5 23 gxf5 ♔h8 (23...♗xf5?
24 ♖xg7+ ♕xg7 25 ♘xf6+ and
23...♘d7 24 d4! are lost) 24 ♖xg7
♕xg7 25 ♖xg7 ♔xg7 26 ♗h5 or
26 ♘g3, with a win.

White is also winning after
22...♗xf5 23 gxf5 ♘e7 (23...g5
24 ♘xg5!) 24 fxg6 hxg6 25 d4 with
26 ♗c4 in store.

22 ... ♗e6

Also lost is 22...h6 23 f4!.

23 ♘c5 ♘e7

24 ♘xg7 ♔xg7

25 g5!

The fastest win after 25...fxg5
26 ♗xe5+ ♔g8 is 27 ♘e4.

25 ... ♘f5

26 ♖f3 b6

27 gxf6+ ♔h8

27...♕xf6 (27...♔xf6 28 ♘e4+)
28 ♘e4 ♕e7 29 ♗xe5+ ♔f7 30 ♗xc7.

28 ♘xe6 ♖xe6

Worse is 28...♕xe6 29 d4! exd4
30 ♗c4 ♕c6 31 ♕xf5! or 30...♖d5
31 f7 ♕xf7 32 ♖xf5! ♕xf5 33 ♗xd4+.

29 d4! exd4

30 ♗c4 d3

31 ♗xd3 ♖xd3

The counterattacking 31...♖ed6
32 ♗xf5 ♖d2 allows 33 ♕c3 gxf5
34 ♖g7 ♖d1+ 35 ♔g2 ♕d5 36 f7,
winning.

32 ♕xd3 ♖d6

33 ♕c4 ♘e6

34 ♗e5

After the game it was pointed out
that White missed a chance for a
Morphy finish, with 34 ♖xf5 gxf5
35 ♖g7 ♕f8 36 ♕xe6!! ♖xe6 37 f7!
and wins or 36...♕a8+ 37 e4 ♖xe6
38 f7 ♕xe4+ 39 ♖g2+.

But Black is being too cooperative
in that line. With 35...♖d1+ 36 ♔g2
♕e8! there are extraordinary tactics
such as 37 f7 ♕a8+. Then 38 ♕c6

♕xc6+ 39 ♔h3 appears to win – but loses to 39...♘f4+.

However, 38 ♕d5!! ♕xd5+ 39 ♔h3 puts the onus on Black. Then 39...h6! and it is White who has to find 40 f8(♕)+ ♘xf8 41 ♖d7+!, drawing.

Yet there are two final twists: White wins after all with 37 ♖g3 ♕f7 38 ♕xe6! or 37 f3! ♖d2+ 38 ♔g3 ♖xb2 39 f7.

| 34 | ... | ♖d8 |

| 35 | h4 | |

The remainder was a massacre:

35 ... ♘d6 36 ♕g4 ♘f8 37 h5 ♘e8 38 e4 ♖d2 39 ♖h3 ♔g8 40 hxg6 ♘xg6 41 f4! ♔f8 42 ♕g5 ♘d6 43 ♗xd6+ Resigns

88

Fischer began 1970 predicting that Korchnoi or Larsen had the best chance of becoming Spassky's challenger in the 1972 world championship match. That scenario changed after Pal Benko agreed to give up the third U.S. spot in the 1970 Interzonal. Benko was paid $2,000 "for stepping down and making room" for Fischer, USCF executive director Ed Edmondson told Bobby in a letter just before Palma. Fischer nevertheless was undecided. He was making last minute demands and threatening not to play until just before he left for the Balearic island. After a first-round hiccup, when he blundered a piece but managed to draw against Hübner, he settled down with the following win.

Vasily Smyslov – Fischer
Interzonal,
Palma de Mallorca 1970
English Opening (A36)

1	c4	g6
2	♘c3	♗g7
3	g3	c5
4	♗g2	♘c6
5	b3	

At Belgrade, Petrosian played 5 ♘f3 but ended up with the worst of it after Fischer seized the center with 5...e6 6 0-0 ♘ge7 7 d3 0-0 8 ♗d2 d5 (like Game 79, but with colors reversed) and then 9 a3 b6 10 ♖b1 ♗b7 11 b4 cxb4 12 axb4 dxc4 13 dxc4 ♖c8.

5	...	e6
6	♗b2	♘ge7
7	♘a4	

This improves on 7 ♘f3 0-0 8 ♘a4 e5!, which would transpose into Smyslov – Fischer from Buenos Aires, four months before. Since 9 ♘xc5? e4! is dubious, White had to accept a passive setup. It was in that game that Fischer rejected a draw by saying "I don't take draws in under 40 moves!"

7	...	♗xb2
8	♘xb2	0-0
9	e3	d5
10	cxd5	

Smyslov is also trying to improve over his celebrated loss to Tal six years before which went 10 ♘f3 ♘f5. On 10 ♘e2 d4! Black has too much of the center.

| 10 | ... | ♘xd5 |
| 11 | ♘e2 | b6 |

12 d4

Soviet annotators said 12 0-0 ♗a6 13 d3 was necessary, although Black can set up a good version of the Maróczy-Bind center with 13...e5. The text will give Black a fine game after 12...cxd4 13 exd4 ♗a6 14 ♘c4 ♕f6 or 13 ♘xd4 ♘xd4 14 ♕xd4 ♗a6 15 ♘c4 ♖c8. But he has better.

12 ...   ♗a6!

"A brillant positional sacrifice in the style of the young ... Smyslov!," wrote Vasily Panov. White has problems now (13 ♘c4 b5).

13 dxc5   ♕f6!

Now 14 ♘d4 bxc5 15 ♘xc6 ♕xb2 16 ♖b1! (not 16 ♖c1 ♘xe3) ♕f6 with a threat of ...♘c3 increases pressure.

14 ♘c4   ♘c3!

Black's attack is overwhelming following 15 ♕c1 ♘xe2 16 ♔xe2 ♖ac8 17 cxb6? ♘e5! 18 bxa7 ♘xc4 19 a8(♕) ♖xa8 20 bxc4 ♖ac8 or 20 ♗xa8 ♘b2+.

15 ♘xc3   ♕xc3+

16 ♔f1   ♖fd8

17 ♕c1

White has less chance of relief in 17 ♕e1 ♗xc4+ 18 bxc4 ♕xc4+ 19 ♔g1 ♖ac8 20 ♖c1 ♕a4.

17 ...   ♗xc4+

18 bxc3   ♕d3+

19 ♔g1   ♖ac8

The c-pawn is doomed by ...♘e5 or ...♘a5.

20 cxb6   axb6

21 ♕b2   ♘a5

Also good is 21...♕xc4 22 ♕xb6 ♖d2 and ...♘e5.

22 h4!?

White's king problem becomes serious after 22 ♕xb6 ♘xc4 23 ♕b3 ♕d2 24 a4 ♘b2 and ...♘d3 or 23 ♕b5 ♖b8 24 ♕c5 (24 ♗b7 ♕e2) ♖b1+.

Some annotators preferred 22 ♗f1 ♘xc4 23 ♕f6, after which ...♕d5 24 ♗xc4 ♖xc4 25 h4! would threaten h5-h6. If Black stops that with 25...h5 White plays 26 ♔h2 and puts up some middlegame resistance.

22 ...   ♘xc4

23 ♕f6

23 ...   ♕f5

White's only active piece is exchanged. Unsound was 23...♘xe3 24 fxe3 ♖c2 25 ♔h2 or 25 ♕f3.

24 ♕xf5   gxf5

25 h5

250

Or 25 ♔h2 ♖d2 26 ♖hf1 ♘e5
27 ♔g1 ♖cc2 28 a4 ♘g4 and wins.

25 ...   ♖d2

26 ♖c1

Greater resistance comes from
26 h4 ♘e5 27 e4 ♖cc2 28 exf5 ♖xf2
29 ♗e4.

26 ...   ♖c5!

Black has a passed c-pawn in
mind. This is faster than 26...♖xa2
27 ♖h4 b5 28 ♗f1 ♖a4 29 ♖d4.

27 ♖h4   ♘e5

Not 27...b5? 28 a4! bxa4 29 ♗f1,
winning a piece.

28 ♖xc5   bxc5

29 ♖a4   c4

30 h6   ♔f8

Now 31 f4 ♘g4 32 ♖xc4? ♖xg2+.

31 ♖a8+   ♔e7

The threat of ...c3-c2 wins a pawn.

32 ♖c8   ♖xa2

33 ♗f1   ♖c2

34 ♔g2?

White can prolong matters with
34 ♖c7+ (but not 34 ♖h8 c3 35 ♖xh7
♖xf2! and ...c2).

34 ...   ♘g4

35 ♔g1   ♖xf2

36 ♗xc4   ♖f3

Also winning is 36...♔f6 and
....♔g6, e.g. 37 ♖h8 ♖d2 38 ♗b5
♔g6. The technical phase is crowned
by a cute finish:

37 ♔g2   ♖xe3

38 ♖h8   ♘xh6

39 ♖xh7   ♘g4

40 ♗b5   ♖b3

41 ♗c6   ♖b2+

42 ♔g1   ♘e5!

43 ♗a8   ♖b8!

The bishop has no good square,
e.g. 44 ♗g2 ♖b3 45 ♔h2 f4! 46 gxf4
♘g4+ 47 ♔g1 ♖b1+ 48 ♗f1 ♘e3
and wins.

44 ♗h1 and White resigns

After 44...♖b1+ 45 ♔g2 ♘g4 the
e-pawn marches to victory.

89

"There are no longer any surprises,
any departures from book, any 19th
century gambits," Fischer said in
1971 . "Whatever position you've
got, it's been played before."
Whether he believed this is doubtful.
In fact, Fischer's results at Palma,
good and bad, were influenced by
surprise. He lost to Larsen with the
Velimirović Attack, and he drew
against Polugayevsky with 1 c4. As
Black, Fischer caught Uhlmann in a
known Benoni trap and scored
2½-1½ with the Alekhine's Defense.
The following game was one of his
seven straight wins to finish the
tournament. It brought his record
from four Interzonals to 41 wins, 31
draws and only three losses – a 75.3
percent score.

Duncan Suttles – Fischer
Interzonal,
Palma de Mallorca 1970
Alekhine's Defence (B03)

1	e4	♘f6
2	e5	♘d5
3	d4	d6
4	c4	♘b6
5	exd6	cxd6
6	♗e3	g6

Fischer had played 5...cxd6 and 6...g6 six rounds before against Minić. The night before this game Suttles worked out a new idea based on trading off bishops via d4.

7	d5!?	♗g7
8	♗d4	♗xd4
9	♕xd4	0-0
10	♘c3	

10 ...   e5!

Black transforms his e-pawn from a liability to an asset. The basis is 11 dxe6 ♘c6! 12 exf7+ ♖xf7 and 13...♖e7+ or 12 ♕d2 ♗xe6, with good play in either case.

11	♕d2	f5
12	♘f3	

Wade recommended 12 h4 ♘8d7 13 h5 g5 14 h6 in the tournament book, perhaps with the idea of 14...♕f6 15 0-0-0 ♘c5 16 ♘f3 g4 17 ♕g5+! with an uncertain endgame. But White misjudges his middlegame chances.

12 ...   ♘8d7

13 0-0-0

White has little play after 13 ♗e2 ♕f6 14 0-0 a5 and ...♘c5. The adventurous alternative is 13 ♕h6 ♕e7 14 ♘g5, after which 14...e4! tempts White to overextend himself (15 ♘e6 ♖f6 16 ♘b5 ♘e5 17 ♘bc7 ♖b8 18 c5! – otherwise 18...♘a8! with advantage).

13	...	♕f6
14	♕h6	♕e7
15	♖e1	e4!

Both 16 ♘d4 ♘e5 17 f3 and 17 b3 a5 are unpleasant.

16	♘d2	♘e5
17	h3?	

Evans called this game typical "of how Fischer's opponents seem to fall into a hypnotic trance." The best White could get was double-edged positions such as 17 ♗e2 ♘bd7 18 f4! exf3 19 ♘xf3 ♘g4 and 17...♗d7 18 f4! exf3 19 ♘xf3 f4.

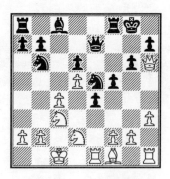

17 ...   ♘bd7!

Suttles had counted on 17...♕c7 after which 18 f3! ♘bxc4 19 ♘xc4 ♘xc4 20 ♗xc4 ♕xc4 21 h4 leads to promising chances, e.g. 21...b5? 22 h5! or 21...♗d7 22 h5 ♗e8 23 g4 fxg4 24 ♖xe4.

After the text, White has to worry about ...♘c5-d3, e.g. 18 g4 ♘c5 19 ♔b1 fxg4 and ...♗f5. But he still needs center play, 18 f3! ♘c5 19 ♔b1.

18	♕e3	♕h4

The threat is 19...♘g4, e.g. 19 f4 ♘g4 20 hxg4 ♕xh1 21 ♘b5 ♘f6!.

19	g3	♕f6
20	♔b1	♘c5
21	f4	exf3
22	♘xf3	f4!

Well timed. Black gets control of the two open files and the b1-f5 diagonal.

23	gxf4	♘xf3
24	♕xf3	♕h4!

Fischer handles the next stage with precision. By attacking the rook he makes ...♖xf4 stronger (25 ♗g2 ♖xf4 26 ♕e3 ♗f5+ 27 ♔a1 ♖xc4).

25	♗e2	♗f5+
26	♔a1	♖ae8
27	♖c1	

On 27 ♖ef1 ♘e4! Black has the upper hand. But 27 ♖d1 ♗e4 28 ♘xe4 ♘xe4 29 ♖d4 held out greater hope for White (29...♖xf4 30 ♕e3 ♕f2 31 ♕xf2 ♖xf2 32 ♗d3).

27	...	♗e4!
28	♘xe4	♖xe4
29	♖h2	♖fxf4
30	♕c3	♕e7
31	♗f1	

31	...	♖e3
32	♕d2	♖ef3!
33	♖e2	

Or 33 ♗e2 ♖f2 34 ♖xf2 ♖xf2 35 ♖e1 ♕e5 and White cannot last long.

33	...	♕f6
34	♗g2	♖f2

The prettier bid to win begins with 34...♖g3, threatening 35...♘d3. For example, 35 ♖b1 ♖a3! threatens smothered mate. There are other neat finishes but 35 ♕e1 ♘d3? 36 ♕xg3 ♘xc1 37 ♖e8+ ♔f7 38 ♖b8 or 37...♔g7 38 ♕e3 defends.

35	♖ce1	♖xe2
36	♖xe2	

Also 36 ♕xe2 ♖f2 37 ♕e8+ ♔g7 and the threats of mate and ...♖xg2 lead to 38 ♕e7+ ♕xe7 39 ♖xe7+ ♔f6 and wins.

36	...	♖xc4

There's no relief now from 37 ♖e8+ ♔f7 38 ♖e1 ♖f4.

37	♕e3	♕e5!

The rest was predictable:

38 ♔b1 ♕xe3 39 ♖xe3 ♖f4 40 ♗f3 h5 41 ♔c2 ♔f7 42 ♔d2 ♖b4 43 ♔c3 ♖h4 44 b4 ♘d7 45 ♗e2

♘f6 46 ♖f3 ♔g7 47 ♖d3 g5 48 a3 g4 49 ♗f1 ♘e4+ 50 ♔c2 ♘f2 51 ♖e3 gxh3 52 ♖e7+ ♔f8 **White resigns**

90

Yuri Balashov was 22 in 1971 but had become the Soviet expert on Fischer's play after writing a dissertation about him while attending the Institute of Physical Culture. He was included in the small support group for Taimanov in the 1971 Candidates match. It was Balashov who exclaimed "Fischer never has any bad pieces!" – because he always managed to exchange his poorly placed pieces and leave his opponent with bad ones. In the following, perhaps Fischer's most famous endgame, Black's knight can't be called bad. It just never equals White's bishop.

Fischer – Mark Taimanov
Fourth game, Candidates
Quarterfinals
Vancouver 1971
*Sicilian Defense,
Taimanov Variation (B47)*

1	e4	c5
2	♘f3	♘c6
3	d4	cxd4
4	♘xd4	♕c7
5	♘c3	e6
6	g3	a6
7	♗g2	♘f6
8	0-0	♘xd4
9	♕xd4	♗c5
10	♗f4!	

Taimanov used this finesse himself in a very early testing of this variation. He drew soon after 10...♗xd4 11 ♗xc7 ♗xc3 12 bxc3 d5 13 exd5 ♘xd5 14 ♗e5 f6 although 15 c4! gives White a definite edge, e.g. 15...♘b4 16 ♗d6 ♘xc2 17 ♖ab1.

10	...	d6
11	♕d2	h6

One of the benefits of 11 ♕d2 over 11 ♕d1 is revealed by 11...♘d7 12 ♖ad1 ♘e5 13 ♘a4 0-0 14 ♕c3! with a big edge.

12	♖ad1	e5
13	♗e3	

Once the dark-squared bishops are exchanged, Black will have problems defending d6, whether or not there is still a pawn there. For example, 13...♗xe3 14 fxe3! (14...♔e7? 15 ♖xf6!) or 13...0-0 14 ♗xc5 dxc5 15 ♕d6!.

13	...	♗g4

14	♗xc5!	

The point of Black's 13th move was that 14 f3? ♗xe3+ equalizes (no fxe3). Now, however, 14...♕xc5? 15 ♕xd6 or 14...♗xd1? 15 ♗xd6 are bad.

14	...	dxc5
15	f3	♗e6

16 f4   ♖d8

Taimanov later claimed 16...0-0 17 ♘d5 ♗xd5 18 exd5 ♕d6 holds White's edge to a minimum.

17 ♘d5   ♗xd5

18 exd5   e4!

Not 18...exf4 19 ♖de1+ or 18...0-0 19 d6 ♕b6 20 fxe5.

19 ♖fe1?!

Fischer was highly praised for rejecting 19 d6 ♕b6!, e.g. 20 ♖fe1 0-0 21 ♗xe4 c4+ and now 22 ♔f1!? ♘xe4 23 ♖xe4 ♕c6! 24 ♕d5 ♖xd6, as pointed out by Boleslavsky. But 24 ♖e5 ♕h1+ 25 ♔f2 ♕xh2 26 ♔f3 is playable.

But, it's hard to explain why he passed up 19 c4!. After 19...0-0 20 ♖fe1 ♖fe8 21 ♖e2 b5 22 b3 ♖d6 23 ♖de1 ♕c7 he would have jumped at the chance to trade rooks for the queen – 24 ♗xe4! ♘xe4 25 ♖xe4 ♕xe4 26 ♖xe4 ♖xe4 27 ♕a5. And if Black tries to secure the e-pawn with 22...♕d7 23 ♖de1 ♕f5 he allows the 24 ♕a5 raid.

19 ...   ♖xd5

20 ♖e4+   ♔d8

White has an easier time after 20...♔f8 21 ♖e8+!. But now 20...♔d8 21 ♖e8+ ♖xe8 22 ♗xd5 ♘xd5 23 ♕xd5+ ♔c8 gives Black counterplay (24 ♕f5+ ♔b8 25 ♖d7 ♕c6 26 ♕xf7 ♖e2).

21 ♕e2!

The flashy 21 ♕xd5+ ♘xd5 22 ♖xd5+ ♔c8 23 ♖ee5 is good after 23...b6 24 ♗h3+ ♔b8 25 ♖d7 and ♖ee7 – but should lose after 23...♔b8! 24 ♖xc5 ♕b6.

Two men, two different views: Taimanov saw a knight-versus-bishop middlegame becoming a drawish endgame. "It seemed more or less problem-free for Black," he wrote. Fischer visualized the same ending but saw opportunities on both wings.

21 ...   ♖xd1+

22 ♕xd1+   ♕d7

23 ♕xd7+   ♔xd7

24 ♖e5!   b6

On 24...♔d6 25 a4 (25 ♗xb7 ♖b8) b5 26 a5 Black's queenside becomes highly vulnerable. But Kasparov believed it was tenable.

25 ♗f1   a5

This weakness proves fatal 30-plus moves later (57 ♔a6!). But otherwise Black loses a pawn immediately (25...♖a8 26 ♗c4 ♘g4 27 ♖e2).

26 ♗c4   ♖f8

27 ♔g2   ♔d6

28 ♔f3   ♘d7

29 ♖e3   ♘b8

30 ♖d3+   ♔c7

On 30...♔e7 31 ♗b5! Black's knight lacks moves – so much so that 31...♖d8? 32 ♖xd8 ♔xd8 33 ♔e4 must lead to a winning pawn ending. (Fischer missed the same method of stalemating a knight in his match with Reshevsky and only drew.)

31	c3!	♞c6
32	♖e3	♚d6
33	a4	♞e7
34	h3	♞c6
35	h4	h5

The first major kingside concession, which was blamed, like other Taimanov errors in this match, on "fifth-hour fatigue." Black soon has all three kingside pawns on light squares and subject to ♗f7xg6. Taimanov knew the danger but had to meet a more direct threat of White pushing his pawns to h5 and g4 followed by king to h4 and a breakthrough with g4-g5.

36	♖d3+	♚c7
37	♖d5	f5

After 37...g6 White plays 38 ♗b5 and 39 f5 (not 38 f5? ♞e7!).

38	♖d2	♖f6
39	♖e2	♚d7
40	♖e3	g6
41	♗b5	♖d6

This sealed move leads to an unfavorable exchange of rooks but

41...♚d8 42 ♚e2 ♞b8 43 ♚d3 ♚c7 44 ♚c4 is worse.

42 ♚e2!

White gets his king closer to the target area before swapping. 42 ♖d3 ♖xd3+ 43 ♗xd3 ♞d8! Black can blockade with ...♞f7-d6.

42 ...	♚d8

Both sides have to keep in mind what happens if pieces are traded:

(a) White will win many bishop-versus-knight endings but his chances depend on the king positions.

(b) He will win most pawn endings, such as 42...♚c7 43 ♖d3 ♖xd3? 44 ♚xd3 ♚d6? 45 ♗xc6! ♚xc6 46 ♚c4 ♚c7! 47 ♚b5 ♚b7 48 c4 ♚c7 49 ♚a6 ♚c6 50 ♚a7 ♚c7 51 b3! ♚c6 52 ♚b8 and 53 ♚b7.

(c) It is only the rook endings that tend to be drawn. Finally, White is close to winning if his rook penetrates, e.g. 42...♖f6 43 ♚d3 ♚d8 44 ♚c4 ♚c7? 45 ♖e8. But even then there is no knockout in sight (45...♖d6 46 ♖g8 ♞e7 47 ♖g7 ♚d8).

43	♖d3!	♚c7
44	♖xd6	♚xd6
45	♚d3	

This threatens to win with 46 ♗xc6. The immediate 45 ♗xc6?? ♚xc6 46 ♚d3 ♚d5 is dead drawn.

45	...	♘e7
46	♗e8!	♚d5
47	♗f7+	♚d6
48	♚c4	♚c6
49	♗e8+	♚b7
50	♚b5	♘c8!

With a cute threat of 51...♘d6 mate.

51	♗c6+	♚c7

52	♗d5!	♘e7

If it becomes passed h-pawn versus passed f-pawn, the bishop decides (52...♘d6+ 53 ♚a6 ♘e4 54 ♗f7 ♘xg3 55 ♗xg6 ♘e2 56 ♗xh5! ♘xf4 57 ♗f7! ♚c6 58 h5 or 57...♘d3 58 ♗g6).

53	♗f7!	♚b7
54	♗b3	♚a7

Black can only shift back and forth to avoid *zugzwangs*. Taimanov later confessed he "felt like Dr. Watson, who could only play along and admire the resourcefulness and imagination of the great Sherlock Holmes!"

55	♗d1	♚b7
56	♗f3+	♚c7

One of the *zugzwangs* was 56...♚a7 57 ♗g2.

57	♚a6	♘g8
58	♗d5	♘e7

And another version of both *zugzwang* and the lost pawn race is 58...♘f6 59 ♗f7 ♘e4 60 ♗xg6 ♘xg3 61 c4! ♚c6 62 ♚a7 ♚c7 63 ♗f7! ♘e2 64 ♗xh5 ♘xf4 67 ♗f7 and 68 h5.

59	♗c4	♘c6
60	♗f7	♘e7

61	♗e8!

This is the position White had been seeking since move 46. There is no hope in 61...♘c8 62 ♗xg6 or 61...♚d6 62 ♚xb6, so...

61	...	♚d8
62	♗xg6!	♘xg6
63	♚xb6	♚d7
64	♚xc5	♘e7
65	b4!	

Not even a flicker of counterplay (65 ♚b5 ♘d5 66 ♚xa5 ♚c7 67 ♚b5 ♘e3 68 c4 ♘f1 69 b4 ♘xg3 70 a5 ♘e2) is allowed.

65	...	axb4
66	cxb4	♘c8
67	a5	♘d6
68	b5	♘e4+

69	♔b6	♚c8
70	♔c6!	♚b8

Black resigned, not waiting to try the stalemate trick of 71 b6 ♘c3 72 a6 ♚a8 73 a7 ♘a4 74 ♔c7?? ♘xb6! (since 74 b7+ ♚xa7 75 ♔c7 wins).

91

In 1970, when Fischer was looking for competition, he suggested to Larsen that they play a private match, according to Fischer's then-favorite ground rules: draws would not count, victory goes to the first to win six games. But Larsen didn't have spare time. There was irony when they met in a Semifinal Candidates match in Denver in July 1971. It was a best-of-ten-game affair. But draws didn't count – because there weren't any. Fischer won all six games played.

Fischer – Bent Larsen
First game, Candidates Semifinals,
Denver 1971
*French Defense, Winawer Variation
(C19)*

1	e4	e6
2	d4	d5

This was generally praised as a good choice. As Botvinnik had written, "Fischer does not like pawn chains. He needs 'room' for his pieces."

3	♘c3	♗b4
4	e5	

Fischer, on the other hand, believed the Winawer was "antipositional and weakens the kingside."

4	...	♘e7
5	a3	♗xc3+
6	bxc3	c5
7	a4	♘bc6
8	♘f3	♗d7
9	♗d3	♛c7

Larsen employs a system, aiming to liquidate e5 with ...f6 that Mednis used to upset Fischer in the first round of the 1962-63 U.S. Championship.

10	0-0	c4
11	♗e2	f6

12 ♖e1!

In the Mednis game, White played 12 ♗a3 0-0 13 ♖e1 but Black stood well after 13...♖f7! 14 exf6 gxf6 15 ♗f1 ♖e8 16 ♘h4 ♘g6 and ...♖g7. Fischer's move here preserves the possibility of ♗g5 or ♗h6.

12 ... ♘g6

If White resolves the pawn tension with exf6, Black can safely castle on either wing. But here Black must choose between passes, such as the text, and the slight inferiority of 12...0-0-0 13 ♗a3 or 12...0-0 13 exf6!, now that 13...gxf6 can be met by 14 ♗h6 and 13...♖xf6 by 14 ♗g5.

258

13 ♗a3!

With no ...♘f5 to worry about White eyes ♗d6.

13 ...   fxe5

Castling was both risky (13...0-0-0 14 a5 and/or ♗d6) and an admission that White had called his bluff.

14 dxe5

The tempting 14 ♘g5? allows 14...h6! 15 ♗h5 hxg5 16 ♗xg6+ ♔d8 and Black is better.

14 ...   ♘cxe5
15 ♘xe5   ♘xe5

On 15...♕xe5, both discovered attacks are excellent – 16 ♗g4 ♕xc3 17 ♗xe6 0-0-0 18 ♕xd5 and 16 ♗xc4 ♕xc3 17 ♗xd5 0-0-0 18 ♗b3.

16 ♕d4!

There were two alternatives, one poor – 16 f4? ♘c6 17 ♗g4 0-0-0! with advantage to Black – and one that held promise, 16 ♗h5+, e.g. 16...g6 17 ♕d4! gxh5 18 ♖xe5 or 16...♘f7 17 ♕f3! g6 18 ♕f6.

16 ...   ♘g6

Black loses immediately after 16...♘c6? 17 ♗h5+, while 16...0-0-0 hangs the a-pawn. Jan Timman pointed out that 16...h5, stopping the check and preparing 17...♘c6, is met strongly by 17 ♕h4!.

17 ♗h5!   ♔f7!

A lesser grandmaster might have doomed himself to trying to draw the endgame after 17...0-0-0 18 ♕xa7 b6 (18...♕b8 19 ♕d4 and ♗g4/♗c5) 19 ♕a8+ ♕b8 20 ♕xb8+ ♔xb8 21 a5! ♔c7 (better than 21...bxa5 22 ♗d6+ or 21...b5 22 ♗c5 and 23 a6).

18 f4!

For once, Fischer passes up a rook lift, 18 ♖e3 – which grants Black fine chances after 18...♖fe8 19 ♖g3 ♗xa4! – and takes a more dynamic approach. His threat is 19 f5 exf5 20 ♖e7+.

18 ...   ♖he8!
19 f5   exf5
20 ♕xd5+   ♔f6

Forced because 20...♖e6 allows 21 ♕xf5+ ♖f6 22 ♖e7+ and 20...♗e6 invites 21 ♖xe6! ♖xe6 22 ♕xf5+ ♖f6 23 ♕d5+ ♖e6 24 ♗g4 or 24 ♖f1+.

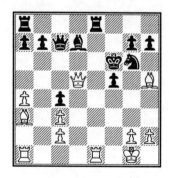

21 ♗f3!?

Timman concluded that 21 g4 would give Black good chances after 21...♕b6+ 22 ♗c5 ♕c6 23 ♕d4+ ♔g5 24 h4+ ♔xh4 25 gxf5+ ♔xh5. But this analysis hangs on a slender thread, and White wins with 25 ♗xg6 hxg6 26 ♗e7+.

That suggests that White's best may be 21 ♗d6!, e.g. 21...♕c6 22 ♕d4+ and now 22...♔f7 23 ♗f3 ♕b6 24 ♗c5 ♕c7 25 ♗d5+ wins.

Better is 22...♔g5 but after 23 ♗f3! ♕b6 24 ♗c5 ♕c7 the same ♗e7+ idea wins – 25 ♗e7+! ♖xe7 26 ♖xe7 ♘xe7 27 ♕xg7+ ♘g6 28 h4+! or 25...♔h6 26 ♕d2+ f4 27 ♕d5!).

And if 21...♕c8 White replies 22 g4! as in the Timman line (22...♕c6 23 ♕d4+ ♔g5 24 h4+ ♔xh4 25 ♗xg6 hxg6 26 ♗e7+).

| 21 | ... | ♘e5 |
| 22 | ♕d4 | ♔g6! |

Black is willng to give up two minor pieces for a rook in order to coordinate his heavy wood. It was clock-stopping time after 22...♖ad8? 23 ♗d6 ♕a5 24 ♗d5!.

23 ♖xe5!!

Accepting the challenge. The alternative, 23 ♗d6 ♘xf3+ 24 gxf3 ♕c6, is nothing Neither is 23 ♔h1 h6.

| 23 | ... | ♕xe5 |

Not 23...♖xe5 24 ♗d6.

| 24 | ♕xd7 | ♖ad8 |

A quick finish follows 24...♕xc3?? 25 ♕d6+ ♔g5 26 h4+! (26...♔xh4 27 ♕f4 mate).

25 ♕xb7 ♕e3+

A tsunami of criticism greeted this move after the game and 25...♕xc3 was recommended. There are two key lines.

The one that first drew the attention of analysts was 26 ♕b1 ♖d2 27 ♗b4 but 27 ♗c5! and now 27...♕d4+ 28 ♔h1 c3 is OK.

More pertinent is the second line, 26 ♕c6+ ♔g5! and then 27 ♗c1+ f4 28 h4+ ♔f5!. Black appears to have survived but Igor Zaitsev found 29 g4+ fxg3 30 ♔g2!!. Then 30...♕xa1 loses brilliantly to 31 ♗g4+! ♔xg4 32 ♕f3+ or 31...♔e5 32 ♕b5+ ♔d6 33 ♕b4+ ♔d5 34 ♗b2! (Kasparov). So Black must settle for 30...♕d4 31 ♔xg3 ♕xa1 and White only has perpetual check.

| 26 | ♔f1 | ♖d2 |
| 27 | ♕c6+! | ♖e6 |

This appears to win the Exchange (28 ♕c5 ♖f2+ 29 ♔g1 ♖xf3+).

28 ♗c5!!

What makes this move impressive is that White probably saw it when he chose 23 ♖xe5 and perhaps two moves earlier. Since 28...♕e5 29 ♗d4!! is hopeless, Black must accept the queen sacrifice.

28	...	♖f2+
29	♔g1	♖xg2+

Or 29...♖xf3+ 30 ♗xe3 ♖xc6 31 gxf3 and wins.

30	♔xg2	♕d2+
31	♔h1	♖xc6
32	♗xc6	♕xc3

Black thought 30 minutes over this, leading spectators to recall how Taimanov spent 72 minutes over a losing move in Fischer's previous match. Larsen felt his chances would improve greatly if he'd played 32...a5 33 ♖g1+ ♔f7 34 ♗d4 g5! 35 ♗d5+ ♔g6 36 ♗xc4 ♕xc2.

Timman, meanwhile, liked White's chances after 33 ♗d4 (instead of 33 ♖g1+) ♔h6 34 ♖f1! f4 35 h4.

33	♖g1+	♔f6
34	♗xa7	f4
35	♗b6	♕xc2
36	a5	♕b2
37	♗d8+	♔e6
38	a6	♕a3
39	♗b7	♕c5

Both sides promote after 39...c3 40 ♗b6 c2 41 a7 but White gets to keep his queen after 41...c1(♕) 42 ♖xc1 ♕xc1+ 43 ♗g1.

40	♖b1	c3
41	**♗b6!**	**Resigns**

The outcome is unavoidable after 41...c2 42 ♖e1+ ♕e5 43 ♖xe5+ ♔xe5 44 a7 c1(♕)+ 45 ♗g1. "One of the best games of my life," said Fischer.

92

Soviet critics were able to explain Fischer's quarterfinals match as a case of a big age difference (Fischer 28, Taimanov 45), of Taimanov's over-optimism and his carelessness when he fell behind. But when Fischer began to beat Larsen by the same 6-0 score there were no easy answers. Botvinnik, who for years had expressed doubts about him, wrote: "It's a marvel. One can explain how Fischer won each game individually. But how can you explain the result in total?"

Bent Larsen – Fischer
Fourth game,
Candidates Semifinals,
Denver 1971
*King's Indian Defense,
Classical Variation (E97)*

1	c4	g6
2	♘f3	♗g7
3	d4	♘f6
4	♘c3	0-0
5	e4	d6
6	♗e2	e5
7	0-0	♘c6
8	d5	♘e7
9	♘d2	

Before 1970 this was considered inferior to 9 ♘e1 because Black can trade his "bad" king's bishop with 9...♗h6. But about the time this game was played it was realized that White can break favorably on the queenside after 10 b4 and 11 c5, when the knight has a much better outpost at c4 than it would at d3.

9	...	c5!?

This "logical move," as Fischer put it, had only been played a few times before he used it against Korchnoi at Herceg-Novi. King's Indian dogma held that in a closed center Black must direct his attention to the kingside and make as few pawn moves on his right as possible.

10 ♖b1

Korchnoi played 10 a3, again following conventional wisdom that said once White plays b2-b4, he must be able to answer ...cxb4 with axb4, to preserve pawn control of c5. But later experience showed that c5 was overrated. After 10 a3 ♘e8 11 b4 b6 12 ♖b1 f5 13 f3 f4 14 a4 Korchnoi was a tempo behind the Larsen game and losing soon after 14...g5 15 a5 ♖f6! 16 bxc5? bxc5 17 ♘b3 ♖g6 18 ♗d2 ♘f6 19 ♔h1 g4.

10 ... ♘e8

11 b4 b6

Every defensive step Black takes opens new windows for White. This one allows White to open two files by way of a4-a5. The alternative strategy was 11...cxb4 12 ♖xb4 b6. But after 13 a4 ♘c7 14 ♘b5 ♘a6 15 ♖b1 ♘c5 16 ♗a3 Black must

decide whether to create yet another weakness and stop a4-a5 with ...a5.

12 a4

White's access to the b-file is balanced by Black's kingside attack after 12 bxc5 bxc5 13 ♘b3 f5 14 f3 ♔h8 and ...♘g8-f6-h5. But a two-wing policy, such as 14 ♗g5 and exf5/f2-f4, may be best.

12 ... f5

Here 12...a5? is one precaution too many: 13 bxc5 bxc5 14 ♘b3 followed by ♗d2 and ♘b5 leaves Black with a weak a-pawn and no...a6 to oust the knight.

13 a5 ♘f6

A promising plan now is 14 axb6 axb6 15 f3 ♗h6 16 ♘b3 ♗xc1 17 ♘xc1! followed by ♘d3 and ♕b3.

14 ♕a4 ♗d7

Now 15 b5 bxa5 16 ♖a1 liquidates the queenside to a draw.

15 ♕a3 ♗h6!

16 ♗d3

More in keeping with the nature of the position was 16 bxc5 bxc5 17 a6 after which 17...♗xd2 is very risky (18 ♗xd2 ♘xe4 19 ♘xe4 fxe4 20 ♗g5).

Instead, Black can challenge the file with 17...♖b8 18 ♖xb8 (18 ♖b7) ♕xb8. After 19 ♘f3 ♗xc1 20 ♖xc1 ♕c7 and ...♖b8 White's advantage is microscopic. (Not 20...♕b4 21 ♕a1! ♘xe4 22 ♘xe4 fxe4 23 ♖b1 ♕a4 24 ♕xa4 and ♘g5 with advantage because of ♖b7.)

Trailing 0-3, Larsen is struggling to find a way to avoid a balanced middlegame.

16 ... ♕c7

17 bxc5 bxc5

Now Black has time to demilitarize the file (18 a6 ♖ab8).

18 exf5

This exchange is useful in King's Indian positions when f5 is significantly weakened or White wins control of e4. Neither condition applies here and the capture is inferior to 18 ♘f3.

18 ... gxf5

Not quite equal is 18...♘xf5 19 ♘de4 ♗xc1 20 ♘xf6+ ♖xf6 21 ♖fxc1.

19 ♗c2?

White misses his chance for 19 ♘b5 – perhaps believing Fischer's next move was too much of a concession. After 19 ♘b5 ♗xb5 20 ♖xb5 a6 21 ♖b6 ♘d7 the chances are in rough balance.

But Larsen wants to set up 20 ♘de4, e.g. 19...♖ab8 20 ♘de4 ♖xb1 21 ♘xf6+ with a double-edged game. (This couldn't be played immediately because of 19 ♘de4 fxe4 20 ♗xh6 exd3!.)

19 ... a6!

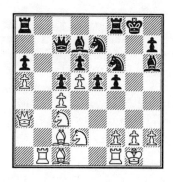

Black can give up b6 and even allow an invasion of c6, in order to control the more important b5.

20 ♘de4 ♗xc1

21 ♘xf6+ ♖xf6

22 ♖fxc1 ♖af8!

23 ♖b6

Necessary was 23 ♕b3 and ♕b7. White has increased chances after 23...♕xa5 24 ♖a1 ♕c7 25 ♖xa6 ♖b8 26 ♕a2 ♘c8 27 ♖b1.

23 ... ♗c8

24 ♘e2

Better was 24 f4 e4 25 ♘e2 ♘g6. Black's impending ...♘h4 always packs a punch, e.g. 24 ♖cb1 ♘g6 25 ♖c6 ♕g7 26 ♖b8? ♘h4 and wins, e.g. 27 g3 ♘f3+ 28 ♔g2 ♘e1+ or 28 ♔f1 ♗b7.

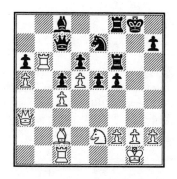

24 ... f4!

Giving up another choice square to keep the knight from the kingside. Swallowing his pride now with 25 ♘c3 ♘f5 26 ♘e4 wouldn't save White (26...♖g6 27 ♖cb1 ♘d4 28 ♗d3 ♕g7 and the attack rolls on).

25 ♗e4 ♘f5

26 ♖c6

This offers slim hope of slowing the kingside attack with ♖xc8.

26 ... ♕g7

27 ♖b1

Still overly optimistic. After 27 ♔h1 ♘h4 (27...♖h6? 28 ♖xc8) 28 ♖g1 ♖h6 White loses at once with 29 g3 ♘f3! 30 ♗xf3 ♖xh2+ but a neutral move such as 29 ♖b6 keeps the issue in doubt.

27 ... ♘h4!

28 ♕d3

White may have counted on 28 ♖xc8 ♖xc8 29 ♕h3 – but the double attack fails to 29...♖cf8 30 ♕xh4 ♖h6, trapping the queen. Failing that, there was no satisfactory way of meeting 28...♗f5. For instance, 28 ♖bb6 ♗f5! 29 ♕d3 ♕xg2+ or 29...♘xg2.

28 ... ♗f5!

29 ♔h1 f3!

Much faster than 29...♕xg2+.

30 ♘g3

Another wipeout is 30 g3 fxe2 31 gxh4 ♗xe4+ 32 ♕xe4 ♖xf2.

30 ... fxg2+

31 ♔g1 ♗xe4

32 ♕xe4 ♘f3+

33 ♔xg2 ♘d2

White resigns

93

Fischer never changed his attitude about 6 ♗c4 in the Sicilian Defence as Hans Ree's encounter with him at Netanya 1968 will attest. Ree asked Fischer about the infamous story how Steinitz believed he could give odds to God. Fischer, whose interest in Steinitiziana was well known replied that no one could give odds to the Almighty. He added: But with White I should be able to draw against Him. I play 1 e4 and if we have a Ruy, the position would balanced. I could never lose."

Then Fischer became concerned – what if God played 1...c5 ? He soon brightened up. "No, then I play ♗c4 and I'm better, he said. "So what can He do?"

Fischer – Bent Larsen
Fifth game, Candidates Semifinals
Denver 1971
Sicilian Defense,
Sozin Variation (B88)

1	e4	c5
2	♘f3	d6
3	d4	cxd4
4	♘xd4	♘f6
5	♘c3	♘c6

6	♗c4	e6
7	♗b3	♗e7
8	♗e3	0-0
9	0-0	

The position may seem routine yet Fischer had only played it once since Curaçao.

9	...	♗d7
10	f4	♕c8

Larsen prepared this awkward move as a way of discouraging f4-f5. In the third match game he misfired with 10...a6 11 f5 ♕c8? and found himself with a horrible game after 12 fxe6 ♗xe6 (or 12...fxe6 13 ♘f5 ♕c7 14 ♗f4!) 13 ♘xe6 fxe6 14 ♘a4!.

11 f5!?

This tries for more than 11 ♕f3 but should offer no more than equality.

11	...	♘xd4

To win a pawn Black must allow White's bishop a commanding square on d4. The chief alternative, 11...♘a5 12 fxe6 ♗xe6 (not 12...fxe6? 13 ♘f5!) favors White without risk to him.

12	♗xd4	exf5
13	♕d3!	fxe4

There was no reason to incur a kingside weakness with 13...g6?

14 ♖ae1, e.g. 14...♖e8 15 exf5 ♗xf5 16 ♖xf5! ♕xf5 17 ♕xf5 gxf5 18 ♖xe7 or 14...♗d8 15 exf5 ♗xf5 16 ♕g3.

14	♘xe4	♘xe4

Not 14...♗f5? 15 ♖xf5 ♕xf5 16 ♘xf6+.

15	♕xe4	♗e6

16 ♖f3!

The other move that suggests itself is 16 ♖ae1. Then 16...♕c6? is punished by 17 ♕f4! (17...d5 18 ♕e5 ♗f6 19 ♖xf6 and wins, or 17...♗xb3 18 ♖xe7 ♗xc2 19 ♖xf7). However, Black has no major worries after 16..♗xb3! 17 axb3 ♗g5.

16	...	♕c6?

A major aim of White's last move was to discourage 16...♗xb3, which would now be met by 17 ♖g3! g6 18 ♕xe7 with sparkling variations to follow, such as 18...♕e6 19 ♕h4 ♗xc2 20 ♖e3 ♕f5 21 ♕h6! f6 23 ♖e7 or 19...♗d5 20 ♖e3! ♕f5 21 ♖f1 ♕xc2 22 ♕xh7+!. Black should settle for slight inferiority with 17...f6.

Larsen later pointed out 16...d5. Then 17 ♖g3 g6 seemed to leave White scrambling for compensation, e.g. 18 ♕e3 ♖e8 – until 19 ♖xg6+! hxg6 20 ♕h6 and 19...fxg6 20 ♕e5 was pointed out by computers.

Simplest of all is 16...♗d8 and 17 ♗xe6 ♕xe6 18 ♕xb7 ♗b6, approaching equality. But trailing 0-4 Larsen needed more than equality.

17 ♖e1!

Now 17 ♖g3?? is just a blunder because 17...♕xe4 attacks his bishop. Also 17 ♕e3 ♗xb3 18 ♕xe7 ♗xc2 19 ♖g3 is refuted by 19...♗g6.

17 ...   ♕xe4

There was still no time for 17...♗xb3 18 ♕g4! g6? 19 ♖xe7. For example, 19...♗e6 20 ♖xe6! ♕c8 21 ♖e4 f5 22 ♖e7! and wins, or 19...♗d5 20 ♕h5! and mates (21 ♕h6 and 21 ♕xh7+! being the main ideas).

18 ♖xe4   d5

And here 18...♗xb3 19 ♖xb3 leads to a bad ending.

19 ♖g3!   g6

Instant death is 19...dxe4?? 20 ♖xg7+ ♔h8 21 ♖xf7+ ♗f6 22 ♗xf6+ ♔g8 23 ♖g7+ ♔h8 24 ♗c3.

20 ♗xd5!   ♗d6

Black rejects an easy draw (20...♗xd5 22 ♖xe7 ♖fe8) in an effort to save the match.

21 ♖xe6!   ♗xg3

Not 21...fxe6 22 ♗xe6+ ♖f7 23 ♖f3 ♖f8 24 ♗xa7 and wins.

22 ♖e7   ♗d6

23 ♖xb7

Since one Black piece is tied to the defense of f7, White is free to push his c-pawn.

23 ...   ♖ac8?

A final – and this time fatal – error. Better was 23...a5 24 ♖d7 when White has good chances of shepherding the pawns.

For example 24...♖fd8 (not 24...♖ad8? 25 ♗xf7+) 25 ♖xf7 ♗xh2+ 26 ♔xh2 ♖xd5 27 ♖g7+ ♔f8 28 ♖xh7!.

24 c4   a5

25 ♖a7   ♗c7

When he chose his 22nd move Black may have assumed he could put up a good fight with 25...♗c5 26 ♗xc5 ♖xc5 – but now saw that he can't stop the king from reaching d4 after 27 ♔f2. Also lost is 25...♗b4 26 a3 ♗d2 27 ♔f2.

26 g3   ♖fe8

27 ♔f1   ♖e7

28 ♗f6!

A fine move that is too-easily passed over. White avoids 28 ♗c3 ♖ce8! and forces the e7-rook to make a choice.

28 ...   ♖e3

On 28...♖d7 White can win the a-pawn with 29 ♗c3 or bring in the king (♔e2-d3) as reinforcement.

29 ♗c3   h5

30 ♖a6!

Threatening ♖xg6+ and reducing Black's counterplay to a smidgen (compared with 30 ♗xa5 ♗xa5 31 ♖xa5 ♖ce8!, e.g. 32 ♖a7 ♖e1+ 33 ♔g2 ♖8e2+ 34 ♔h3 ♖d2).

30 ...   ♗e5

31 ♗d2!

It's still a fight after 31 ♖xg6+ ♔f8 32 ♖h6 ♗xc3 33 bxc3 ♖ce8.

| 31 | ... | ♖d3 |
| 32 | ♔e2 | ♖d4 |

The rook had no good squares and 32...♖xd2+ 33 ♔xd2 ♗xb2 34 ♖xg6+ ♔f8 35 ♖a6 was lost.

33 ♗c3! ♖cxc4

Virtual concession. Black also loses after 33...♖g4 34 ♗xe5 ♖e8 35 ♖a8, or 33...♖xd5 34 cxd5 ♗xc3 35 bxc3 ♖xc3 36 ♖c6!.

| 34 | ♗xc4 | ♖xc4 |
| 35 | ♔d3! | |

Not 35 ♗xe5 ♖e4+!.

35	...	♖c5
36	♖xa5	♖xa5
37	♗xa5	♗xb2
38	a4	♔f8
39	♗c3!	

White still had chances to go wrong: 39 ♗b6 ♔e7 40 a5 ♔d7 41 a6 ♔c6 42 a7 ♔b7. The text wins control of a7 (39...♗a3 40 a5 ♗c5 41 a6 and ♗d4).

The rest went:

39 ... ♗xc3 40 ♔xc3 ♔e7 41 ♔d4 ♔d6 42 a5 f6 43 a6 ♔c6 44 a7! ♔b7 45 ♔d5 h4 46 ♔e6! Resigns

94

Before the final Candidates match began in September 1971, Petrosian joked about the low expectations for him. "For Fischer to surprise the chess world, he has to beat me 7-0," he said. "But for me to improve on Larsen and Taimanov I need only one draw." In fact, he thought he had good chances of winning the first game.

In preparation for the match, a "council of war" was held among a Soviet analytic team that included Yuri Averbakh and Alexey Suetin. They decided that stopping Fischer's streak was psychologically important – and they had the perfect weapon, an opening idea that would blow up one of Fischer's favonte variations. The debate went back and forth in the council, with Petrosian arguing that Fischer wouldn't walk into such an obvious ambush. "In the end it was decided to 'throw the bomb' at the start," wrote Victor Baturinsky, then a dominant figure in Soviet chess. But the innovation had the same fate as the "fishing trip variation" of Game 10.

Fischer – Tigran Petrosian
First game, Candidates Finals
Buenos Aires 1971
Sicilian Defense (B44)

1	e4	c5
2	♘f3	e6
3	d4	cxd4
4	♘xd4	♘c6
5	♘b5	d6
6	♗f4	e5
7	♗e3	♘f6

8   ♗g5

When Fischer decided to go ahead with the delayed manuscript – tentatively called *My 50 Memorable Games* – he added ten games to make sixty, including one against Najdorf (Game 55 here). In the notes he said Black "could equalize immediately" with 8...♕a5+ 9 ♕d2 ♘xe4 10 ♕xa5 ♘xa5 11 ♗e3 ♔d7 12 ♘xa7 d5.

But when Taimanov followed Fischer's recommendation in their match, Fischer improved with 12 ♘1c3! ♘xc3 13 ♘xc3 ♔d8 14 ♘b5 and won a long endgame after 0-0-0/f2-f4.

Taimanov was in for another surprise after the game when he asked about 12 ♘1c3! and Fischer told him he'd come across the idea in a Russian monograph by Alexander Nikitin, a Soviet trainer (and later Kasparov mentor).

8   ...   ♗e6

Fischer gave this a question mark in annotating the Najdorf game.

9   ♘1c3   a6

10   ♗xf6   gxf6

11   ♘a3

Here he considered only 11...b5, 11...f5 and 11...♗e7, all leading to White's advantage. Clearly Petrosian had a surprise prepared and Fischer should have expected that as early as the sixth move. Then why did he walk into the trap? "I just wanted to see what he had," Fischer explained after the game.

11   ...   d5!!

There are two accounts of how this move was discovered. One that appeared in Russian magazines described the heroic efforts of candidate master Vyacheslav Chebanenko of Kishinev, who had sent a letter addressed "To the winner of the match Petrosian – Korchnoi." The letter was opened by Petrosian right after Korchnoi resigned their semifinals match. Inside was extensive analysis of 11...d5, which Chebanenko had found years before.

But there's another version from Suetin, Petrosian's longtime second, who claimed that he had discovered 11...d5 in 1962 and shared it with Petrosian about the same time that Chebanenko's letter arrived.

12   exd5

Played instantly. On 12 ♘xd5 ♗xa3 13 bxa3 ♕a5+ 14 ♕d2 ♕xd2+ and 15...0-0-0 and ...f5 Black stands excellently.

12   ...   ♗xa3

13   bxa3   ♕a5

14   ♕d2   0-0-0

Only here did Fischer begin to study the position – and the auditorium lights inexplicably failed. He continued to analyze the

268

board on the darkened stage. But Petrosian insisted his clock should be running. Despite his obsession with top quality lighting, Fischer agreed. Eleven minutes later the lights came back on – and Fischer blundered.

15 ♗c4?

After this White walks along a precipice. With 15 ♖d1 he could answer 15...♘d4? with 16 dxe6! and 15...♖hg8 with 16 ♗d3!. Black has to settle for 15...♗xd5 16 ♘xd5 ♖xd5 and a minor endgame edge.

15 ... ♖hg8!
16 ♖d1

Petrosian had been playing instantly but settled down here and after 40 minutes...

16 ... ♗f5?

...he decided against the strong 16...♖xg2!, which he had prepared at home. For example, 17 ♕e3 ♘d4 18 ♔f1 ♗g4! 19 ♔xg2 ♗f3+ 20 ♔h3 ♕c7! 21 ♖xd4 ♕d7+ 22 ♔h4 ♕f5!! and wins (Timman).

Also poor is 17 ♘e4 ♕b6! 18 ♕c3 ♗f5 19 ♗f1 ♗xe4! Or 18 ♕e3 ♕xe3+ 19 fxe3 ♗g4. "Why I didn't play 16...♖xg2 I simply can't answer," Petrosian wrote.

17 ♗d3 ♗xd3?

Black overlooks another golden opportunity, 17...e4!. Taking the pawn loses (18 ♗xe4 ♗xe4 19 ♘xe4 ♖ge8 or 18 ♘xe4 ♗xe4 19 dxc6 ♕e5!) and on 18 ♗e2 ♖xg2 19 ♕e3 ♘e5 20 ♔f1 ♘g4! Black retains a significant edge.

18 ♕xd3

Definitely not 18 dxc6? ♗e4 19 cxb7+ ♗xb7 20 ♕e3 ♖xd1+ 21 ♔xd1 ♖xg2 with advantage.

18 ... ♘d4
19 0-0 ♔b8

20 ♔h1

Black had threatened 20...♕xc3 21 ♕xc3 ♘e2+. But 20 ♘e4 was a promising alternative – 20...f5 21 ♘f6 ♖g6 22 f4! or 20...♕xd5 21 c3 f5 22 ♘g3 f4 23 cxd4 fxg3 24 fxg3.

20 ... ♕xa3

White has a strong ♘e4 and/or f2-f4 after this. Black should have tried 20...f5 21 f4 f6. Then 22 fxe5 fxe5 23 ♖fe1 ♖c8 24 ♖xe5 ♕xc3 25 ♕xd4 ♕xd4 26 ♖xd4 ♖xc2 27 g3 would likely end in a draw.

21 f4

Also good was 21 ♘e4 ♕xa2 22 ♘xf6 ♖g6 23 ♕e4!. Fischer is relying on solid no-risk moves rather than looking for the tactical tricks.

21 ... ♖c8
22 ♘e4 ♕xd3

Black has such a nice position that analysts managed to make 22...♕xa2 work (23 ♘xf6 ♖xg2!). For example, 23 ♖f2 ♖xc2 24 ♖xc2 ♕xc2 25 ♕xc2 ♘xc2 26 ♘xf6 ♖xg2! should draw.

23 cxd3 ♖c2
24 ♖d2 ♖xd2

25 ♘xd2   f5!

"Black has almost completely equalized play and it seems a draw is unavoidable," Suetin wrote. Black would have lost quickly following 25...♖d8 26 fxe5 fxe5 27 ♖xf7 ♖xd5 28 ♖xh7.

26 fxe5   ♖e8
27 ♖e1

The tide shifts quickly after 27 ♘c4? b5.

27 ...   ♘c2
28 ♖e2!

The annotators' preference, 28 ♖c1, wins quickly after 28...♖xe5 29 ♘f3 ♖e2 30 d6! and 28...♘d4 29 ♘c4 b5 30 ♘b6. But not after 28...♘b4 29 d4 ♘xd5 30 g3 f6. Petrosian offered a draw with his next move.

28 ...   ♘d4!
29 ♖e3   ♘c2

30 ♖h3!   ♖xe5
31 ♘f3

The most important factor in a few moves will be...the pawn at h2! For instance. 31...♖e2 32 ♖xh7 ♘d4 33 h4!.

31 ...   ♖xd5
32 ♖xh7   ♖xd3?

Up until this point the annotators agree that Black should draw. But

they disagree about what the losing move – or moves – was. White's win remains problematic after 32...b5 33 h4 b4 34 h5 f4!, e.g. 35 h6 a5 36 ♖xf7 ♖h5+. (But not 34...a5 35 ♖xf7 a4 36 h6 b3 37 axb3 a3 because of 38 ♘e1!! ♘xe1 39 ♖f8+ and 40 h7).

33 h4   ♘e3

A second candidate for losing move. It's true that 33...♘d4 offers more chances, but 34 ♘g5! f6 35 ♘h3 is still difficult for Black.

34 ♖xf7   ♖d1+
35 ♔h2   ♖a1
36 h5   f4?

After 36...♖xa2, Timman's 37 ♘h4, is not entirely convincing (37...♖a5 38 ♔h3 f4 39 h6 ♖h5 40 h7 ♔a7). More testing is Suetin's 37 ♖g7. Then 37...♔a7 38 h6 ♘g4+! 39 ♖xg4 fxg4 40 h7 gxf3 41 h8(♕) ♖xg2+ 42 ♔h3 ♖d2 defends, as does 38 ♔h3 f4 39 h6 ♖a1 40 ♔h4 ♖h1+.

37 ♖xf4   ♖xa2
38 ♖e4!

So that 38...♖xg2+ 39 ♔h3 ♖e2 40 h6 and wins.

38 ...   ♘xg2
39 ♔g3   ♖a5
40 ♘e5   Resigns

95

Fischer admitted he was lucky in the Candidates finals. "Petrosian played very well in the first games," he told Argentine journalists afterwards. "I could have lost all of them." Lev Polugaevsky, writing in *64*, praised Petrosian's ability to steer the first five games into positions in which he was more comfortable, and found it "paradoxical" that in the sixth game, Petrosian was beaten in a closed maneuvering middlegame. The seventh game was quite different.

Fischer – Tigran Petrosian
Seventh game, Candidates Finals
Buenos Aires 1971
Sicilian Defense,
Kan Variation (B42)

1	e4	c5
2	♘f3	e6
3	d4	cxd4
4	♘xd4	a6
5	♗d3	♘c6
6	♘xc6	bxc6
7	0-0	d5
8	c4	♘f6

Trailing by one point, Petrosian decides to take his chances with an isolated d-pawn middlegame rather than a slightly inferior ending (8...dxe4 or 8...dxc4).

9	cxd5	cxd5

10 exd5
Here 10...♘xd5 11 ♗e4! gives White an easy-to-play, hard-to-lose edge (11...♗e7 12 ♘c3 ♗b7 13 ♕a4+

♕d7 14 ♕xd7+ ♔xd7 15 ♖d1 or 11...♖a7 12 ♕d4 ♖d7 13 ♘c3).

10	...	exd5

Petrosian regarded this as better than 10...♕xd5 and it is hard to like Black's position then after 11 ♘c3 ♕d7 12 ♗g5 ♗e7 13 ♕e2 and putting rooks on c1 and d1.

11	♘c3	♗e7

Black hurries to castle and avoids 11...♗e6 12 ♕a4+ ♘d7? 13 ♕c6, e.g. 13...♗e7 14 ♘xd5 ♖c8 15 ♕b7, or 13...d4 14 ♘e2 ♗c5 15 ♘f4.

12 ♕a4+!
A finesse designed to misplace Black's bishop, e.g. 12...♗d7 13 ♕d4 ♗e6 14 ♗f4 0-0 15 ♖fe1 ♕a5 (15...♗d6 16 ♗g5 or 15...♕d7 16 ♘a4!) 16 ♗e5 ♖fc8 17 ♘a4. Then 17...♗b4 is met by 18 ♖ed1 ♕xa4 19 a3 with advantage.

12	...	♕d7?

This offers the Exchange – 13 ♗b5 axb5 14 ♕xa8 0-0 followed by ♗b7 or ...d4, e.g. 15 ♕a5 d4 16 ♘xb5 ♗b7, threatening 17...♗xg2!.

The sacrifice may prove to be unsound – after, say, 17 f3 ♗c6 18 ♘a3 ♖a8 19 ♕d2 d3. But Fischer makes a practical decision to avoid risk or lost clock time.

13 ♖e1! ♕xa4

If Black tries to improve his endgame prospects with 13...♖a7. White can switch directions and stay in a very favorable middlegame with 14 ♕d4 0-0 15 ♖e5!, e.g. 15...♗d6 16 ♖g5 h6? 17 ♖xg7+! ♔xg7 18 ♗xh6+!. And 13...d4 14 ♕xd7+ ♗xd7 15 ♘e2 is an awful ending.

14 ♘xa4 ♗e6
15 ♗e3

This secures c5 since 15...♘d7 would allow 16 f4!, threatening 17 f5. Then 16...g6 17 ♗d4 0-0 18 ♖ac1 is a "serious positional edge" for White, as Polugaevsky put it, and 16..♗b4 17 ♖e2 0-0? is unsound (18 f5 ♘e5 19 fxe6 ♘xd3 20 ♖d1).

15 ... 0-0

16 ♗c5!

There are so many enemy weaknesses that White might have been lured into 16 ♘c5. But 16...a5! 17 ♗d4 ♗xc5 18 ♗xc5 is less advantageous than the game.

Also tempting is 16 ♘b6 ♖ab8 (16...♖a7? 15 ♘xd5) 17 ♗xa6 but Black obtains counterplay with 17...♖fd8 (threat of 18...d4) 18 ♗d4 ♗b4 19 ♖ec1 ♖d6.

16 ... ♖fe8

17 ♗xe7 ♖xe7
18 b4!

After 18 ♘c5 a5 Black solves some of his problems – whereas 18 b4 a5 19 b5 just gives White a strong passed pawn.

18 ... ♔f8

Black opts to defend a6 with his bishop. But 18...♖b8 19 a3 ♖a7 20 ♘c5 ♖b6 at least offers hope of releasing the pressure with ...♗d7-b5.

19 ♘c5 ♗c8
20 f3

20 ... ♖ea7?

As bad as it looks. Petrosian mentioned 20...♖xe1+ as a possible improvement and it certainly would be after 21 ♖xe1 ♘e8 22 ♔f2 ♘c7 23 ♔e3 ♔e7 24 ♔d4+ ♔d6 with a solid position. But White shouldn't let the black king reach the center. A better plan is 22 ♘a4! ♖b8 23 a3 and then 23...♘c7 24 ♖c1, e.g. 24...♘e6 25 ♖c6 or 24...♘b5 25 ♗xb5 axb5 26 ♘c3.

One gets the impression that Petrosian aimed for 21...♗d7, rather than the more logical 21...♘d7!, because it never occurred to him that Fischer would play ♘xd7+.

21 ♖e5! ♗d7

Black prepares 22...♗b5 and would meet 23 a4 with 23...♗c6 and 24...♘d7.

22 ♘xd7+!!

This shocked the grandmasters in the press room and Miguel Najdorf called it much weaker than 22 a4.

But Petrosian and Suetin later awarded it two exclamation points since a white rook must penetrate at c6 or c7 now.

This is perhaps Fischer's most famous and instructive move and is still being cited today. Annotating a Short – Svidler game from the 2002 Russia – World match, the magazine *64* commented that even a superbly placed black knight on an open file will interfere with heavy pieces and therefore should be removed in "the classical example of the seventh game of the Fischer – Petrosian match."

22 ... ♖xd7

23 ♖c1

White threatens both 24 ♖c6 tying Black to the defense of a6, or just 24 ♗xa6 ♖xa6? 25 ♖c8+. He wins on 23...♘e8 24 ♖c6 ♘c7? 25 ♗f5.

23 ... ♖d6

24 ♖c7 ♘d7

Hopeless was 24...♖e8 25 ♖xe8+ ♔xe8 27 ♖a7.

25 ♖e2 g6

26 ♔f2 h5

Botvinnik believed Black needed to pull White's attention to the queenside, e.g. 26...♖b8 27 a3 a5 28 b5 a4 with possibilities such as 29 ♗c2 ♖a8 30 ♖c6 ♖xc6! 31 bxc6 ♘c5 and ...♖c8.

However, White should jump at the chance to create a passed a-pawn. For example, 28 bxa5! ♖b3 29 ♖d2 ♖xa3 30 a6 and 31 a7.

27 f4!

Not 27 ♔e3 ♘e5.

27 ... h4

Afterwards Petrosian agreed with second-guessers who called 27...♘b6 28 ♖ee7 ♖f6 a stauncher defense. After 29 ♔e3 ♖d8 he would threaten ...d4+/...♘d5.

28 ♔f3 f5

29 ♔e3 d4+?

Black loses more slowly with 29...♘f6 30 ♔d4 ♘e4 31 ♖ec2, according to Polugayevsky.

30 ♔d2 ♘b6

Desperation – but 30...♔f7 31 ♖e5! ♔f6 32 ♖a5 or 30...a5 31 bxa5 ♖xa5 32 ♖c8+ ♔g7 33 ♗c4 ♔f6 34 ♖ce8! were also hopeless.

31	♖ee7!	♘d5
32	♖f7+	♔e8
33	♖b7	♘xb4

Black is mated after 33...♘xf4 34 ♗c4 ♘d5 35 ♖h7 and ♖h8, or 34...g5 35 ♖g7 ♖f6 36 ♖g8+ ♖f8 37 ♗f7+.

34	♗c4	**Resigns**

Taimanov had fallen ill after the third match game, Larsen after the fourth – and Petrosian after this game. After the finals became a rout, Fischer said he waited for congratulations from Spassky that never came. But he said he would send him a telegram that read "Congratulations on winning the right to play me for the championship."

96

But nothing in Fischer's past prepared fans for the circus that preceded the 1972 world championship match. Would he go to Reykjavik, or wouldn't he? Did he really offer to play the match for no prize money? And why did he apologize to Spassky as the Russians demanded? When reporters wondered at his behavior, Robert Byrne shrugged it off. "I won't worry until I see him make a crazy move at the board. Then I'll know we've finally lost him." That was before 11...♘h5.

Boris Spassky – Fischer
Third game,
World Championship match
Reykjavik 1972
Modern Benoni Defense (A77)

1	d4	♘f6
2	c4	e6
3	♘f3	c5
4	d5	exd5
5	cxd5	d6
6	♘c3	g6
7	♘d2	♘bd7
8	e4	♗g7
9	♗e2	0-0
10	0-0	♖e8
11	♕c2	

11	...	♘h5!?!

The move left the grandmasters in the press room dumbfounded. "A canvass among the spectators showed a remarkably uniform division of opinion: every average player thought Fischer must have gone a bit mad," said *Chess* magazine. "Every grandmaster (Gligorić, Byrne, Krogius, Geller) considered it fascinatingly interesting." But Ed Edmondson, Fischer's U.S. Chess Federation protector/father-figure, pronounced it the decisive move of the match. "Spassky is already beaten, defeated by the 11th move in the third game."

Actually, the idea of allowing Black's kingside to be wrecked by ...♘h5/♗xh5 occurred in similar form in Timman – Ljubojević from Wijk aan Zee earlier in 1972. But Fischer's version, with 12...f5 in mind, is more dynamic.

In any case, today's grandmasters prefer 12...♘e5 13 a4 a6.

12 ♗xh5

Too dangerous is 12 f4 ♗d4+ 13 ♔h1 ♕h4 14 ♖f3 ♘df6.

12 ... gxh5

13 ♘c4 ♘e5

After a slightly different move order, 11 a4 ♘e5 12 ♕c2 ♘h5 13 ♗xh5 gxh5, the game Gligorić – Kavalek, played a few weeks later, showed the perils Black is accepting. White's 14 ♘d1! enabled him to keep a knight on c4 and he held a substantial edge after 14...♕h4 15 ♘e3 ♘g4 16 ♘xg4 hxg4 17 ♘c4.

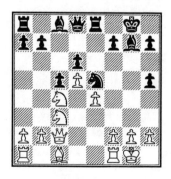

14 ♘e3

This move and the 25 minutes he took to choose 12 ♗xh5 showed that Spassky wasn't mentally prepared

for Fischer. After 14 ♘xe5 ♗xe5, *Shakhmaty v SSSR* recommended 15 f4 ♗d4+ 16 ♔h1 and, if 16...f5, then 17 e5 dxe5 18 fxe5 ♗xe5 19 ♗f4 "with a strong initiative for White." But 16...♗d7 is OK.

Also critical is 15 ♗e3, since 15...f5 16 f4! ♗xc3 17 ♕xc3 ♖xe4 leads to a strong dark-square attack after 18 ♖f3 and ♖g3+, as Euwe and Timman pointed out. This is just the kind of sacrifice that fits into Spassky's style, e.g. 18...h4 19 ♗f2! followed by 20 ♗xh4!. But 19...b5! 20 ♗xh4 ♕xh4 21 ♖h3 b4! barely defends, 22 ♖g3+ ♔f7 23 ♕g7+ ♔e8 24 ♕g8+ ♔d7 25 ♖g7+ ♖e7.

14 ... ♕h4!

15 ♗d2

"Feeble" was one of the most generous adjectives used by annotators. White apparently rejected 15 f4 ♘g4 16 ♘xg4 hxg4 17 f5 because of 17...♗e5 18 ♗f4 g3 19 hxg3 ♗d4+, although he has promising compensation after 20 ♖f2 ♕e7 21 g4.

Also better than the text was 15 ♘e2 (or 15 f3) since 15...♘g4 16 ♘xg4 hxg4 17 ♘g3 ♗e5 18 ♗e3 prepares an active plan of 19 f4, or 19 ♕d2 and ♗g5.

15 ... ♘g4

16 ♘xg4 hxg4

Smyslov believed White's best was to try to set up a good-♘/bad-♗ middlegame with 17 ♘e2! ♗f5 18 ♘g3 ♗g6 19 ♖ae1 h5 20 ♗c3 or 19 ♗c3 ♗xc3 20 bxc3 h5? 21 f4!.

17 ♗f4 ♕f6

18 g3?

White should retreat the bishop to g3 and meet 18...h5 with 19 f3. Or he could play 18 ♕d2 and 19 f3. In either case he has a method of changing the pawn structure that now favors Black.

18	...	♗d7
19	a4	b6

This makes the queenside roller of ...a6/...b5 inevitable and leaves White with only one form of counterplay, e4-e5. But that fails for a tactical reason...

20	♖fe1	a6
21	♖e2	b5!

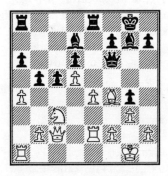

...which was 22 axb5 axb5 23 ♖xa8 ♖xa8 24 e5? ♖a1+ 25 ♔g2 dxe5 and now 26 ♗xe5?? allows mate in one, so White is doomed to play out 26 ♖xe5 b4 27 ♘e4 (and 27 ♘b1) ♕a6! or 27 ♘e2 ♕g6!.

22	♖ae1	♕g6
23	b3	♖e7

Euwe considered this a minor error because it allows White's counterattack. With 23...♖ac8, he said, Black can push either queenside pawn effectively (24 ♕d3 c4!).

24	♕d3	♖b8

The threat is 25...bxa4 26 bxa4 (26 ♘xa4? ♗b5) ♖b4 or 25...c4 26 bxc4 b4. But Krogius said

24...bxa4 25 bxa4 ♖b8 was better and would have stopped Spassky's clever defense.

25	axb5	axb5
26	b4!	

Stopping 26...b4 (with 26...cxb4 27 ♘a2) is a higher priority than granting a passed c-pawn.

26	...	c4
27	♕d2	♖ae8
28	♖e3	h5!
29	♖3e2	♔h7
30	♖e3	♔g8
31	♖3e2	♗xc3
32	♕xc3	♖xe4
33	♖xe4	♖xe4
34	♖xe4	

This actually eases Black's task, compared with 34 ♖a1 ♖e2 35 ♗e3 or 34...♖e8 35 ♕d4.

34	...	♕xe4

Now 35 ♗xd6 allows Black to start threatening mate with 35...♕xd5 and ...♗d7-c6 or ...♕d1+.

The other point is that with the pawn on h7 rather than h5 (as would occur after 28...♗xc3) White could play 35 ♕f6 ♕b1+ 36 ♔g2 ♗f5 37 ♕g5+ ♗g6 38 ♕d8+ ♔g7 39 ♕g5. But with the pawn on h5, Black wins with 38...♔h7! and ...♗e4+.

35	♗h6	♕g6
36	♗c1	♕b1!

Black stops 37 ♗b2 and casts a mating net (37 ♔g2? ♗f5).

37	♔f1	♗f5
38	♔e2	♕e4+
39	♕e3	♕c2+
40	♕d2	♕b3!

Now 41 ♗b2 is *verboten* because of 41...♕f3+ 42 ♔e1 ♕h1+ and 43...♗d3+.

41 ♕d4

Krogius felt 41 ♔e1 and 42 ♗b2 offered chances of resistance (41...c3 42 ♕d4 ♕c2 43 ♗h6). But 42...c2 43 ♗h6 ♕b1+ 44 ♔e2 c1(♘)+! suffices. When play resumed Fischer took several minutes to recheck his analysis of the killer:

41 ... ♗d3+!

White resigns

Decisive: 42 ♔e3 ♕d1! 43 ♕b2 ♕e1+ 44 ♔f4 c3 or 43 ♗b2 ♕f3+.

The alternative, 42 ♔e1 ♕xb4+ 43 ♔d1 ♕b3+ 44 ♔e1 b4 45 ♕e3 ♕b1 and ...c3/...b3-b2 was quite lost.

97

In *Esthetics of Chess*, the Russian chess historian Isaac Linder asked several leading players which game or combination made "a particularly strong impression on you?" Anatoly Karpov said he couldn't name one example but cited these: Legal's mate, Morphy vs. Duke of Brunswick, the "little combinations" of Capablanca, the rook endgame in the last game of the Alekhine vs.

Capablanca match – "and the original plan of attack in the tenth game ... of the Spassky – Fischer match."

Fischer – Boris Spassky
Tenth game,
World Championship match
Reykjavik 1972
Ruy Lopez, Breyer Variation (C95)

1 e4 e5

"In reply to 1 e4 practically any opening can be used against Fischer with the exception of 1...e5," Petrosian wrote to the Soviet Chess Federation in early 1972 when the authorities were canvassing its grandmaster elite for advice.

2	♘f3	♘c6
3	♗b5	a6
4	♗a4	♘f6
5	0-0	♗e7
6	♖e1	b5
7	♗b3	d6
8	c3	0-0
9	h3	♘b8

The Breyer Variation was virtually unknown until Spassky and other members of the Soviet team used it in the 1955 Student Olympiad in Lyons.

10	d4	♘bd7
11	♘bd2	♗b7
12	♗c2	♖e8
13	b4	♗f8
14	a4	♘b6

By 1972 a substantial amount of book was built around the Breyer, and this was the latest finesse. Black had gotten into trouble previously after 14...a5 15 bxa5 ♖xa5 16 ♖b1 or 14...c5 15 bxc5 exd4 16 cxd4.

15 a5   ♘bd7

Now that his b-pawn won't be a target, Black prepares ...d5 or ...c5.

16 ♗b2   ♕b8

Black indirectly protects e5 and eyes ...c5 and even ...♕a7. Later GMs preferred 16...♖b8.

17 ♖b1

Highly praised at the time as a preparation for c3-c4. But the more energetic 17 c4! assures an edge (17...bxc4 18 ♗a4!).

17 ...   c5

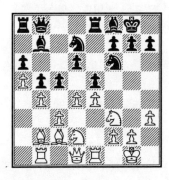

This sets off a chain reaction that both players fight to control. If White closes matters with 18 d5 Black gets typical counterplay with 18...g6 19 ♗a3 c4 and ...♘h5.

18 bxc5!   dxc5

19 dxe5

White would be ditching his middlegame plan with 19 d5? c4.

19 ...   ♘xe5

20 ♘xe5   ♕xe5

21 c4   ♕f4

22 ♗xf6

Euwe recommended 22 e5 ♖ad8 23 exf6! with possibilities such as

23...♖xd2 24 ♕xd2! ♕xd2 25 ♖xe8 ♕xc2 26 fxg7 ♕xb1+ 27 ♔h2 and White wins. However, Black should not lose if he finds 23...♖xe1+ 24 ♕xe1 ♕xd2 and then 25 fxg7 ♕xe1+ 26 ♖xe1 ♗xg7 27 ♗xg7 ♔xg7 and ...♖d2.

22 ...   ♕xf6

Reuben Fine, in one of his last books and certainly his worst claimed 22...gxf6 would favour Black (23 cxb5 ♖ad8 24 ♖e2 axb5 or 24 ♖e3 c4).

White's best, he said, was the "passive defense" of 23 g3 ♕h6 24 h4 ♖ad8 25 ♖e2 b4. But clearly better than that is 24 cxb5 and then 24...♖ad8 25 bxa6 ♗xa6 26 ♕g4+ or 24...♕xh3 25 b6.

23 cxb5   ♖ed8!

There was much second-guessing of the players' moves and second-guessing of the second-guessers. Here, for example, C.H.O'D. Alexander wrote that 23...axb5 was bad because of 24 ♖xb5 ♗c6 25 ♖b6 ♖xa5 26 e5 ♕e6 27 ♘e4 h6 28 ♘d6 and White wins. But 24...♗a6! 25 ♖b6 ♕c3! is much stronger. In fact, White should play 25 ♖b3 c4 with even chances.

24 ♕c1   ♕c3

25 ♘f3   ♕xa5

26 ♗b3!

A dramatic shift to the kingside: 27 ♘g5 ♖d7 28 e5 is threatened.

26 ...   axb5

27 ♕f4   ♖d7

Better was 27...c4 28 ♗xc4 bxc4 29 ♖xb7 f6 and now 30 ♕g4 ♕a6 31 ♖1b1 ♖a7 or 30 e5 ♕d5! are safe.

28 ♘e5   ♕c7

278

29 ♖bd1!

Despite his queen and rook, Black's second-rank is vulnerable: 29...♖xd1?? 30 ♗xf7+ ♔h8 31 ♘g6+! and mates.

29 ... ♖e7

The greatest collective effort of annotators was directed at 29...♖ad8 30 ♗xf7+ ♖xf7 31 ♕xf7+ ♕xf7 32 ♘xf7 ♖xd1 33 ♖xd1. Alexander rejected 33...♗xe4 (33...♔xf7? 34 ♖d7+) 34 ♘g5 ♗c2 35 ♖d8 ♗b3 36 ♘xh7 and wins. But the critical line appears to be 35...b4 after which White's extra rook ultimately beats the connected passed pawns in variations pointed out by Fridrik Olafsson such as 36 ♘e6 ♔f7 37 ♘xf8 b3 38 ♖b8 c4 39 ♘d7 c3 40 ♘e5+. (Timman analyzed it out another 17 moves into a pawn ending.)

However, the last word has yet to be said about this line, and Euwe felt 34...♗f5 35 ♖d5 h6! could save Black. Computers tend to like White's chances after 36 ♖xf5 hxg5 37 ♔f1 (better than 37 ♖xg5 b4!) ♗e7 38 ♔e2 g6 39 ♖e5!.

30 ♗xf7+ ♖xf7
31 ♕xf7+ ♕xf7
32 ♘xf7 ♗xe4!

33 ♖xe4

After 33 ♘h6+ gxh6 34 ♖xe4 c4! Black has real counterplay.

33 ... ♔xf7
34 ♖d7+ ♔f6
35 ♖b7! ♖a1+

Black is not badly off after 35...b4 36 ♔f1 ♖c8! 37 ♖c4 ♖e8! (Gligorić). But 36 ♖b6+! alters the outlook (36...♔f5 37 f3).

36 ♔h2 ♗d6+
37 g3 b4
38 ♔g2 h5
39 ♖b6 ♖d1
40 ♔f3 ♔f7
41 ♔e2 ♖d5
42 f4!

White stops ...♗e5-d4 and prepares the g3-g4 killer.

42 ... g6
43 g4 hxg4
44 hxg4 g5

This makes a horrible impression, creating a connected passed f-pawn in order to get the bishop into play. But Black was in *zugzwang*, e.g. 44...♗c7 45 ♖b7 ♖d7 46 g5 ♔f8 47 ♖e6 ♔f7 48 ♖f6+ ♔g7 49 ♖c6!.

45 f5 ♗e5

46 ♖b5!   ♔f6

After 46...♗d4 White wins with mating threats (47 ♖e6 or 47 ♖b7+).

47 ♖exb4

There was little left:

47 ... ♗d4 48 ♖b6+ ♔e5 49 ♔f3! ♖d8 50 ♖b8 ♖d7 51 ♖4b7 ♖d6 52 ♖b6 ♖d7 53 ♖g6 ♔d5 54 ♖xg5 ♗e5 55 f6 ♔d4 56 ♖b1 Resigns

98

In answer to Linder's question, Mikhail Botvinnik said there was one game in history that made a particularly strong impression on him, the 13th game of the 1972 match. He elaborated on his comments just before he died, calling it "the highest creative achievement of Fischer." To resolve a drawish bishop-of-opposite-color ending he sacrificed his bishop followed by stalemating his rook. "Then five passed pawns struggled with the white rook. Nothing similar had been seen before in chess," he wrote.

Boris Spassky – Fischer
Thirteenth game,
World Championship match,
Reykjavik 1972
Alekhine's Defense (B03)

1	e4	♘f6
2	e5	♘d5
3	d4	d6
4	♘f3	g6
5	♗c4	♘b6
6	♗b3	♗g7
7	♘bd2	

This and White's next move were deservedly hammered by critics as passive. Today 7 ♕e2 or 7 a4 is preferred.

7	...	0-0
8	h3	a5!
9	a4	

White no longer has serious hopes of an advantage (9 a3 a4! 10 ♗a2 dxe5 11 dxe5 ♘c6 11 ♕e2 ♗f5! or 9 c3 dxe5 10 dxe5 ♘c6 11 ♕e2 ♗f5) but this move gets him the worst of it.

9	...	dxe5
10	dxe5	♘a6!

A typical Alekhine's maneuver. White's a-pawn is untenable.

11	0-0	♘c5
12	♕e2	♕e8!

Now 13 ♕b5 ♕xb5 14 axb5 ♗f5! is awful for White.

13	♘e4	♘bxa4
14	♗xa4	♘xa4

White can regain the pawn with 15 ♕c4 but would have the worst of 15...b5 or 15...♗d7 16 ♕xc7 ♗c6 (or 16...♕c8).

15 ♖e1!

It's worth recalling here the comment Fischer made in *Chessworld*, when he named Spassky as one of the ten greatest players in history: When Spassky beat him with the King's Gambit at Mar del Plata 1960, the Russian had "no compensation" when the opening ended. "Then he played as if the pawn he had lost meant nothing." Just as in that game, Fischer now begins to play sloppily (15...♗f5! consolidates quickly).

15	...	♘b6
16	♗d2!	a4
17	♗g5	

One would expect 17 ♗b4. White saves b4 for his queen.

17	...	h6
18	♗h4	♗f5
19	g4	

More promising was 19 ♘d4, since 19...♗xe5 20 ♘xf5 gxf5 allows 21 ♘g3 with excellent compensation. Smyslov noted that White would have better chances than in the game after 19 ♘d4 ♗xe4 20 ♕xe4 c6 21 f4 e6 22 ♘e2! and ♘c3. Better is 20...a3 21 bxa3 ♖a4.

| 19 | ... | ♗e6 |

White is in relatively good shape after 19...♗xe4? 20 ♕xe4 and 21 ♕b4.

| 20 | ♘d4 | ♗c4 |

After 20...♗xe5 21 ♘xe6 fxe6 22 c3 ♖a5 White may have compensation for one pawn but probably not two.

| 21 | ♕d2 | ♕d7 |

The queen doesn't belong here but Black wants to reorganize his pieces with ...♖fe8 and ...♗d5. Here he passes up another chance to take on e5. After 21...♗xe5! 22 ♕xh6 ♗g7 or 22 ♘f6+? exf6 23 ♗xf6 ♗xf6 24 ♖xe8 ♖fxe8 White is losing.

22	♖ad1	♖fe8
23	f4	♗d5
24	♘c5	♕c8

| 25 | ♕c3? | |

White misses his best opportunity in the game: 25 e6! ♘c4 26 ♕e2 and then 26...♘xb2 27 ♘f5!, as pointed out by Smyslov. White's chances are nebulous after 27...♘xd1 28 ♘xg7 ♔xg7 29 ♕e5+ f6 30 ♕xd5 b6 or 30...♘b2 31 ♕d4 g5 but they are at least chances.

25	...	e6
26	♔h2	♘d7
27	♘d3	

Gligorić preferred 27 ♘b5 ♘xc5 28 ♕xc5. But then 28...♖a5! ensures a Black edge, e.g. 29 ♕b4 b6 or 29 c4 ♗c6.

| 27 | ... | c5! |
| 28 | ♘b5 | |

White can resign after 28 ♘e2 b5.

| 28 | ... | ♕c6! |
| 29 | ♘d6 | |

Ditto 29 ♘a3 b5.

29	...	♕xd6!
30	exd6	♗xc3
31	bxc3	f6

Virtually no member of the press room privileged thought this game would last into a second session after this.

32 g5!   hxg5?

Fischer again moves too quickly in a won position. After 32...c4! 33 ♘b4 hxg5 34 fxg5 f5 White lacks the ♘e5! idea that works in the game and is losing after 35 ♘xd5 exd5 (36 ♖xd5 ♖xe1 37 ♗xe1 a3).

33 fxg5   f5

And here 34...fxg5 35 ♗xg5 ♖f8! was winning.

34 ♗g3   ♔f7
35 ♘e5+!   ♘xe5
36 ♗xe5   b5
37 ♖f1!

Suddenly White has a powerful plan: ♖f4-h4-h7+.

37 ...   ♖h8!?!

Alexander called this "a fine reply" and, like Kasparov, awarded it an exclamation point. Byrne gave it a question mark. Euwe called it a "subtle trap" and gave it neither.

The move stops the ♖h7+ plan and invites 38 ♗xh8? ♖xh8, which would doom the d6-pawn and make Black's win fairly direct. But William Lombardy, Fischer's second, argued that 37...♖g8! 38 ♖f4 ♔e8 39 ♖h4 ♖a7 followed by ...♖f7 and a king stroll to c6 was much easier.

38 ♗f6!   a3
39 ♖f4   a2
40 c4!

Spassky gets the maximum out of his bishop, which now controls the queening square. Quite lost was 40 d7? a1(♕) 41 ♖xa1 ♖xa1 42 ♗xh8 ♔e7.

40 ...   ♗xc4
41 d7   ♗d5?

This makes life difficult, compared with 41...e5! 42 ♗xe5 ♖hd8. A key feature is that 43 ♗f6 ♗e2! 44 ♗xd8 ♗xd1 45 ♗f6 is a fairly direct win after 45...a1(♕)! 46 ♗xa1 ♖d8 and ...♖xd7. Or 44 ♖e1 ♖xd7 45 ♖xe2 a1(♕) 46 ♗xa1 ♖xa1.

42 ♔g3!   ♖a3+

Black must avoid the winning threat of 43 ♖h4! and 42...a1(♕) is again premature (43 ♖xa1 ♖xa1 44 ♗xa1 ♖d8 45 ♗f6 ♖xd7 47 ♖h4 etc.). Also unclear is 42...e5 43 ♗xe5 ♔e6 44 ♗xh8 ♖xh8 45 ♖h4 ♖d8 46 ♖h6 ♖xd7 48 ♖xg6+ ♔e5 49 ♖e1+.

43 c3!

The point of Black's check was to close the a1-e5 diagonal and dream of 43 ♔f2 ♖axh3!! 44 d8(♕) ♖xd8 45 ♗xd8 e5! and wins.

43 ...   ♖ha8
44 ♖h4   e5!!

An inspired way of avoiding perpetual check (or loss).

45 ♖h7+   ♔e6
46 ♖e7+   ♔d6
47 ♖xe5   ♖xc3+

Once again it was an error to promote (47...a1(♕)? 48 ♖5xd5+ ♔c6 49 ♖xa1).

48 ♔f2

A dramatic end which might have turned the match around would have been 48 ♔h4?? ♖a4+ and mates.

48	...	♖c2+
49	♔e1	♔xd7
50	♖5xd5+	♔c6
51	♖d6+	♔b7
52	♖d7+	♔a6

Now 53 ♗d8 b4! and the queenside pawns win.

53	♖7d2	♖xd2
54	♔xd2	b4
55	h4!	♔b5
56	h5	c4!

The black pawns are ready to promote, e.g. 57 h6? c3+ 58 ♔d3 a1(♕) 59 ♖xa1 ♖xa1 60 h7 ♖d1+! 61 ♔c2 ♖h1 62 h8(♕) ♖xh8 63 ♗xh8 ♔c4.

57	♖a1!	gxh5
58	g6	

58 ... h4!

Now 59 ♗xh4 ♖g8 60 ♖xa2 ♖xg6 is dead lost.

59	g7!	h3!
60	♗e7	♖g8
61	♗f8	h2

Several analysts tried to prove Black has a forced win after

adjournment, and one focus of their efforts was 61...c3+ 62 ♔d3 h2, so that White doesn't have the saving 67 ♖d1! of the game. After 62...h2 White can do nothing but pass with his rook and king. The outcome then hinges on whether Black's king can penetrate at e4 and f3.

Endgame composer Robert Burger gave 63 ♖f1 f4 64 ♖d1 f3 65 ♔d4 f2 66 ♔d3 ♔c6! since 67 ♔c4 loses to 67...c2 68 ♖c1 ♔d7 69 ♔xb4 ♔e6 70 ♔c3 ♔e5 71 ♔d3 ♔f4.

But 67 ♔c2 a1(♕)! 68 ♖xa1 ♔d5 69 ♔d3 c2! 70 ♔xc2 ♔e4, which Burger said was a win (71 ♔d2 ♔f3), is actually drawn after 71 ♖f1! ♔f3 72 ♗c5 ♖xg7 73 ♖xf2+ ♔g3 74 ♖xh2.

62	♔c2	♔c6
63	♖d1!	b3+
64	♔c3?!	

On 64 ♔b2 the white rook is free to move, e.g. 64...h1(♕) 65 ♖xh1 ♔d5 66 ♖d1+ ♔e4 67 ♖c1! ♔d3 and now even 68 ♖d1+, the move that loses in the game is drawn here after 68...♔e2 69 ♖c1! f4 70 ♖xc4 f3 71 ♖c1 f2 72 ♔xb3.

64 ... h1(♕)!

Only now can the king advance (not 64...f4 65 ♖d6+ ♔c7 66 ♖d1 f3 67 ♔b2 f2 68 ♔c3 ♔c6 68 ♔b2 since there is no *zugzwang*).

65	♖xh1	♔d5
66	♔b2	f4
67	♖d1+!	

Despite his miscue at move 64, this should still draw, as would 67 ♖h3 ♔d4 68 ♔a1! c3 69 ♖f3! c2 70 ♖xf4+ ♔d3 71 ♖f1. But 67 ♖h8 c3+ 68 ♔a1 f3!! 69 ♖xg8 f2 loses.

| 67 ... | ♔e4 |
| 68 ♖c1 | ♔d3 |

69 ♖d1+??

With 69 ♖c3+! ♔d4 70 ♖f3! the rook can shift between the two blockade squares (70...c3+ 71 ♔a1! c2 72 ♖xf4+ ♔c3 73 ♖f3+! ♔d2 74 ♗a3!).

69 ...	♔e2
70 ♖c1	f3
71 ♗c5	

Spassky realized now that 71 ♖xc4 loses to 71...f2.

| 71 ... | ♖xg7 |
| 72 ♖xc4 | ♖d7! |

Black threatens both ...♖d1 and ...♖d2+.

| 73 ♖e4+ | ♔f1 |
| 74 ♗d4 | f2 |

When the spectators saw the two men shake hands, many were unaware Spassky had **resigned**. They thought 75 ♖f4 would draw but it fails to 75...♖xd4! 76 ♖xd4 ♔e2. Also lost is 75 ♗e5 ♖d1 76 ♔xb3 ♖e1.

Before the match Byrne predicted the final score would be Fischer 12½, Spassky 8½. Fischer's victory in the 21st game proved him correct. But Byrne also predicted that Fischer would remain champion for 15 years.

99

The only published games Fischer played in the next 20 years were against an M.l.T. computer in 1977, all won by him. An article in *64*, titled "a Match of Recluses," noted the appropriateness of the matchup of the two – the computer's programmer wouldn't let it play against other computers and Fischer refused to play against other humans.

There were innumerable efforts to get Fischer to play serious chess. Viktor Korchnoi considered a match with him in 1980, under Fischer's 10-wins, draws-not-counting rules, with Fischer guaranteed $3 million.

After the inevitable collapse in negotiations, Korchnoi's confidante, Emanuel Sztein, asked him what the likely outcome would have been. "I would lose approximately by the score of 10-3 or 10-4." Then why would you play such a match, he was asked. "In the match I would draw at least 25 games and who else could make so many draws with Fischer!"

In fact, Fischer didn't play again until September 2, 1992, 20 years and a day after the first match ended. Fischer insisted the event be called a world championship rematch.

Fischer – Boris Spassky
First match game,
Sveti Stefan 1992
Ruy Lopez, Breyer Variation (C95)

1	e4	e5
2	♘f3	♘c6
3	♗b5	a6

This was considered a good-will gesture on Spassky's part, not testing Fischer in the 20 years of Sicilian theory he had missed.

4	♗a4	♘f6
5	0-0	♗e7
6	♖e1	b5
7	♗b3	d6
8	c3	0-0
9	h3	♘b8
10	d4	♘bd7
11	♘bd2	♗b7
12	♗c2	♖e8
13	♘f1	

Varying from 13 b4 as in Game 97.

13	...	♗f8
14	♘g3	g6
15	♗g5	h6

Black gets to use the vacant h7 square but his mix of ...h5 and ...f5 is a bad fit.

| 16 | ♗d2 | ♗g7 |

Book at the time was 16...c5, which was supposed to achieve equality after 17 dxe5? ♘xe5!. But Fischer would likely have replied 17 d5 with the usual slight plus.

Later in the match Spassky tried 16...exd4 17 cxd4 c5 but Fischer got a small edge with 18 d5 ♘b6 19 ♗a5! ♘fd7 20 b3.

| 17 | a4 | c5 |
| 18 | d5 | c4 |

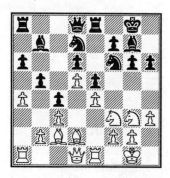

19 b4!

This poses a difficult choice: Should Black abandon queenside play (since 19...a5? 20 axb5 axb4 21 cxb4 fails) and devote his energy to the other wing? Or should he try 19...cxb3 which Karpov endorsed and struggle with his b-pawn, e.g. 20 ♗xb3 ♖c8 21 axb5 axb5 22 ♕e2 and then 22...♕b6 23 ♖eb1 ♖a8 24 ♗a4! ♗a6 25 c4!. Black's best may be 20...♘c5 after which 21 c4 bxa4 22 ♗xa4 ♘xa4 (22...♖e7 23 ♗b4 favors White) 23 ♖xa4 ♘d7 and ...♕c7/...♖eb8.

19	...	♘h7?
20	♗e3	h5
21	♕d2	♖f8
22	♖a3!	♘df6

A King's Indian player might prefer 22...h4 23 ♘f1 f5 24 exf5 gxf5. For example, 25 ♘g5 ♘xg5 26 ♗xg5 ♗f6 27 ♗h6 ♗g7 28 ♗xg7 ♔xg7 29 f4 e4 30 ♘e3 ♕f6 followed by ...♔f7 and ...♖g8.

23	♖ea1	♕d7
24	♖1a2!	♖fc8
25	♕c1	♗f8
26	♕a1	♕e8

"This position, of course, had been evaluated by Spassky when he played his 19th move," Balashov wrote in *Shakhmatny Vestnik*. "It appears completely defensible and solid."

27 ♘f1!

Brilliant partly because of the idea (to attack b5 with a knight on a3 after liquidating along the a-file) and partly because the alternative route, 27 ♘d2 allows Black more counterplay with 27...h4 28 ♘e2 ♔g7 29 ♘b1 ♘xe4! or 28 ♘gf1 ♘h5 29 ♘b1 bxa4! 30 ♖xa4 ♘f4 than in the game.

27	...	♗e7
28	♘1d2	

A bit safer is 28 ♘3d2! and 29 f3, which rules out ...♘xe4.

28	...	♔g7

Duncan Suttles, making a rare return to chess, recommended 28...♔h8 but White's edge would be clear after 29 ♘b1 ♘g8 30 axb5 axb5 31 ♖xa8 ♗xa8 32 ♖a7. For example, 32...f5 33 exf5 g5 34 ♕a6! ♗xd5? 35 ♖xe7! ♘xe7 36 ♕xd6.

29	♘b1	♘xe4!

Perfectly timed, since White left no heavy pieces near the kingside. Black would have been lost soon if he had allowed 30 axb5 axb5 31 ♖xa8 ♖xa8 32 ♖xa8 ♕xa8 33 ♕xa8 ♗xa8 34 ♘a3.

30	♗xe4	f5

Less loosening was 30...♘f6, although 31 ♘bd2 ♘xe4 32 ♘xe4 ♗xd5 favors White solidly after 33 ♘ed2 or even 33 ♘fd2 f5 34 axb5 fxe4 35 bxa6.

31	♗c2	♗xd5
32	axb5	axb5
33	♖a7	♔f6!
34	♘bd2	♖xa7
35	♖xa7	♖a8

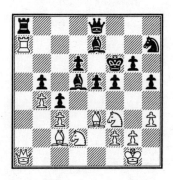

Thanks to Black's centralized king, the endings after 36 ♖xa8 ♕xa8 37 ♕xa8 ♗xa8 38 ♔f1 ♔e6 (not 38...g5 39 g4!) 39 g3 d5 are not at all easy. White's winning task seems suddenly difficult. Yet he took only four minutes for his reply. "When I saw his next move I knew that he was good," Yasser Seirawan wrote in *Inside Chess*. "Bobby was back!"

36	g4!!	hxg4

If Black concedes control of e4 the game is over, e.g. 36...f4 37 ♗b6 and ♘e4+ or 36...hxg4 37 hxg4 fxg4 38 ♘h2.

37 hxg4   ♖xa7

The critical line is 37...f4 38 ♘e4+ ♗xe4 39 ♗xe4 ♖xa7 40 ♗xa7 and 38...♔g7 39 ♗b6 with a likely win.

38 ♕xa7

38 ...   f4?

Again 38...fxg4 39 ♘h2 followed by ♘e4+ and ♘xd6! is bad. But there is also:

(a) 38...♕c6 39 ♘g5! ♘xg5 40 ♗xg5+ ♔xg5 41 ♕xe7+ and wins,

(b) 38...♗c6 39 ♘h4 ♗d7 40 ♗h6 ♗f8 holds out some hope.

(c) 38...♕a8 39 ♕xa8 ♗xa8 40 gxf5 gxf5 41 ♘h4 e4, which Evans claimed was still a fight. But it shouldn't last long after White puts his knights on g3 and f4 and a bishop on d4, and

(d) 38...♗e6 and ...♕d7, which was unclear according to Balashov and Nikitin (39 ♕b7 ♕d7 40 ♕a8 ♕c8).

39 ♗xf4

Kasparov is correct in noting that 39 ♗b6! is cleaner.

39 ...   exf4

After 39...♗xf3 White's best appears to be 40 ♗xe5+ dxe5 41 ♘xf3, for example, 41...♘g5 42 ♘xg5 ♔xg5 43 ♕e3+ ♔f6 44 ♕b6+! and ♕b7.

40 ♘h4!   ♗f7

Also lost was 40...♘f8 41 ♕d4+ ♔e6 42 ♘xg6! ♘xg6 43 ♗f5+ ♔f7 44 ♕xd5+ ♔g7 45 ♕b7.

41 ♕d4+   ♔e6

Mates arise after 41...♔g5 42 ♕g7!, e.g. 42...♘f6 43 ♘df3+ ♔xg4 44 ♗f5+ ♔h5 45 ♘g2!.

42 ♘f5!   ♗f8

Or 42...♕c6 43 ♕xf4 ♔d7 44 ♘xe7 ♔xe7 45 ♕e3+! and ♕h6.

43 ♕xf4   ♔d7

44 ♘d4   ♕e1+?

This ends matters quickly but Black would be out of ammunition after 44...♕e7 45 ♘xb5 ♘g5 46 ♔f1.

45 ♔g2   ♗d5+

46 ♗e4   ♗xe4+

47 ♘xe4   ♗e7

48 ♘xb5   ♘f8

49 ♘bxd6   ♘e6

50 ♕e5   Resigns

100

Fischer's play in that game evoked memories of 1972. In fact, the match games were of a fairly high quality particularly when compared with Kasparov's championship matches of 1993, 1995 and 2000, for example. Yet the games also reminded many fans how out of place Fischer was in 1992. He was still playing the openings of a previous generation. He was, moreover, the only strong player in the world who didn't trust computers and wasn't surrounded by seconds and supplicants. He was a player from the past. But before the match ended in a 17½-12½ Fischer victory he left one more memorable game.

Fischer – Boris Spassky
Eleventh match game,
Sveti Stefan 1992
Sicilian Defense, 3 ♗b5 (B31)

1	e4	c5
2	♘f3	♘c6
3	♗b5	g6

4   ♗xc6!

This had been played before but without Fischer's logic. After the normal 4 0-0 ♗g7 5 ♖e1 Black can continue 5...e5 6 ♗xc6 dxc6! and ...♕e7 with a nice game. Or 5...♘f6 6 ♗xc6 dxc6!.

But after 4 ♗xc6! Black is forced to make his biggest decision of the opening before White is committed to 0-0. After 4...dxc6 5 d3 (or 5 h3) White can castle queenside and attack on the other wing.

4	...	bxc6
5	0-0	♗g7

6   ♖e1   e5

Black avoids 6...♘f6 7 e5 ♘d5 8 c4 and prepares to smooth out his development with ...♘e7. But two games later, Spassky found the superior 6...f6! and ...♘h6-f7.

7   b4!

Fischer thought eight minutes on this gambit, which is similar to but better than one that had appeared in the 1960s – then vanished and suddenly reappeared in the 2018 Carlsen – Caruana world title match (4 0-0 ♗g7 5 ♖e1 e5 6 b4!?).

7   ...   cxb4
8   a3!   c5

White has excellent compensation after 8...bxa3 9 ♗xa3 d6 10 d4 ♗g4 11 ♘bd2 and ♘c4, or 10...exd4 11 e5 dxe5 12 ♘xe5 ♗e6 13 ♘c4 (rather than 13 ♘xc6? ♕d5). Safest is declining the gambit with 8...♘e7 9 axb4 0-0 but White enjoys a quiet superiority after 10 ♗b2.

9   axb4   cxb4
10   d4

10   ...   exd4

Black can keep the e-file closed with 10...d6 since 11 dxe5 dxe5 12 ♕xd8+ ♔xd8 13 ♗d2 isn't a worrisome edge (13...♘e7 14 ♗xb4 ♘c6 15 ♗c5 ♗f8).

If White maintains pressure with 11 ♗b2, Black does best with 11...♘e7 12 dxe5 dxe5 13 ♕xd8+ ♔xd8 14 ♘xe5 ♔c7! 15 ♘d2 ♘c6 16 ♘dc4 ♘xe5.

11 ♗b2   d6

White wins back his material and has a spatial edge after 11...♘e7 12 ♗xd4 ♗xd4 13 ♕xd4 0-0 14 ♕xb4, e.g. 14...d6? 15 ♖d1 or 14...♘c6 15 ♕d6.

12 ♘d4!

White threatens ♘c6 or ♘e6.

12 ...   ♕d7?

"I think that one was a mistake," was Fischer's post-mortem comment. Black's problems are evident after 12...♘f6 13 ♘c6! ♕c7? 14 e5 dxe5 15 ♗xe5 and wins, or 13...♕d7 14 e5 dxe5 15 ♖xe5+ ♔f8 16 ♗d4!.

Garry Kasparov, who ridiculed the quality of play in this match, thought White's gambit was dubious. He claimed Black had good chances after 12...♕b6! and then 13 ♘d2!? ♗xd4 14 ♘c4 ♗xf2+ 15 ♔h1 ♕c5. Black is better after 16 ♘xd6+ ♔e7 17 ♘xc8+ ♖xc8 18 ♗xh8 ♗xe1, he said. Also doubtful is 17 ♕f3 ♗xe1 18 ♕xf7+ ♔xd6 or 17 ♖f1 ♕xd6 18 ♕f3 f6 19 e5 ♕b8 20 ♖xf2.

But more in the gambit spirit is 13 c3 and 14 cxb4 (13...bxc3 14 ♗xc3 ♘e7? 15 ♘f5! ♗xc3 16 ♘xc3! gxf5 17 exf5 with a killing attack).

13 ♘d2   ♗b7

14 ♘c4   ♘h6!

With Black's pieces so loosely connected, tactics are inevitable. For example, 14...♘f6 15 e5 or 15 ♘xd6+ ♕xd6 16 e5. Another minefield is 14...♘e7 15 ♘f5! ♗xb2 16 ♘fxd6+! ♔f8 17 ♘xb2 and ♕d4 (or 15 ♘e6 ♗xb2 16 ♘xd6+ ♕xd6 17 ♕xd6 fxe6 18 ♕xb4).

Black's 14...♘h6 makes 15 ♘e6 impossible because of 15...fxe6 but...

15 ♘f5!!

Fischer took less than seven minutes on this, rejecting 15 ♘b5? ♗xb2! or 15 ♘xd6+? ♕xd6 16 ♘f5 ♕xd1 17 ♘xg7+ ♔e7.

15 ...   ♗xb2!

After 15...♘xf5 16 exf5+ ♔f8 17 f6! White is winning (17...♗h6 18 ♕xd6+ ♕xd6 19 ♘xd6 ♗d5 20 ♖xa7! because 20...♖xa7 allows 21 ♖e8 mate).

16 ♘cxd6+

In contrast with the 14...♘e7 line, here 16 ♘fxd6+ would allow 16...♔e7! and Black wins.

| 16 | ... | ♚f8 |

The ending was lost after 16...♚d8 17 ♘xb7+ ♚c7 18 ♛xd7+, 19 ♜ad1+ and 20 ♘xh6.

| 17 | ♘xh6 |

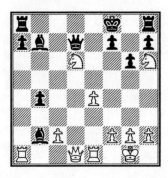

| 17 | ... | f6 |

Another second key test of White's play was 17...♝xa1 18 ♛xa1 ♛xd6! 19 ♛xh8+ ♚e7 and now 20 ♛xh7 ♜f8 21 ♛g7 ♛d2 22 ♜b1 or 20...♛e6? 21 h4 and 22 h5 with a clearer edge.

| 18 | ♘df7! | ♛xd1 |
| 19 | ♜axd1 | ♚e7 |

White wins faster after 19...♜g8 20 ♘xg8 ♚xg8 21 ♜d7 and ♘h6+ On 19...♝c3 White can win with 20 ♘xh8 or 20 ♜e3 ♜g8 21 ♘xg8 ♚xf7 22 ♜d7+.

| 20 | ♘xh8 | ♜xh8 |

| 21 | ♘f5+! | gxf5 |

Or 21...♚e6 22 ♜d6+ ♚e5 23 ♜d7 and Black's new problem is mate (23...♝c6 24 ♜e7+ ♚f4 25 ♘h6 a5? 26 ♜e3!).

| 22 | exf5+ | ♝e5 |
| 23 | f4 | ♜c8 |

Now 23 ♜d2 ♜c5 24 fxe5 ♜xe5 25 ♜xe5+ fxe5 and 26...a5 gives Black more play than he deserves.

| 24 | fxe5! | ♜xc2 |
| 25 | e6! | ♝c6 |

Not 25...♜xg2+ 26 ♚f1 ♝c6 27 ♜d7+! ♚e8 28 ♜c1!.

| 26 | ♜c1 | ♜xc1 |

And here 26...♜xg2+ 27 ♚f1 ♝a8 28 ♜c7+ loses, as does 26...b3 27 ♜xc2 bxc2 28 ♚f2 a5 29 ♜c1 ♝e4 30 g4 and ♚e3.

| 27 | ♜xc1 | ♚d6 |

| 28 | ♜d1+! | ♚e5 |

Or 28...♚e7 29 ♜a1, picking up the a-pawn. Black also loses after 28...♚c5 29 e7 ♝a4 30 ♜d8.

| 29 | e7 |

White has more than one winning line after this, e.g. 29...♚xf5 30 ♜d8 or 30 ♜d6 b3 (30...♝a4 31 ♜a6) 31 ♜xc6 b2 32 ♜c5+ and ♜b5.

| 29 | ... | a5! |

So that 30 e8(♛)+? ♝xe8 31 ♜e1+ ♚d4 32 ♜xe8 b3 33 ♜b8 ♚c3 and both players queen after 34 g4 a4.

30 ♜c1   ♝d7

31 ♜c5+

Now 31...♚d6 32 ♜xa5 ♚xe7 33 ♜a7. Black's only hope lies in the b-pawn.

31 ...   ♚d4

32 ♜xa5   b3

33 ♜a7   ♝e8

34 ♜b7   ♚c3

35 ♚f2   b2

36 ♚e3   ♝f7

On 36...♚c2 White wins as in the game with 37 ♚d4.

37 g4

Here 37...♝e8 38 ♜xb2 is one win (38...♚xb2 39 ♚d4 ♝f7 40 ♚c5 ♚c3 41 ♚d6 ♚d4 42 ♚d7) and 38 ♜b8 ♝f7 39 e8(♛) ♝xe8 40 ♜xe8 b1(♛) 41 ♜c8+ is another.

37 ...   ♚c2

38 ♚d4   b1(♛)

39 ♜xb1   ♚xb1

40 ♚c5   ♚c2

41 ♚d6   Resigns

This was the Fischer that fans remembered. When the world's newest grandmaster, Bu Xiangzi, was interviewed in 2002 he recalled that his favorite book when he was growing up was a Chinese translation of *My 60 Memorable Games*. "His games were fantastic."

Epilogue

Since Fischer died in 2008 there have been at least four film documentaries, one major motion picture and a best-selling biography about him. Yet with each year he has become more and more a mystical figure, separated further from reality. This concerns not just his personality but his chess. For example, in the movie, *Pawn Sacrifice*, Fischer was depicted (by Tobey Maguire) studying an opening at his Brooklyn home: It was 1 h4 and the reply 1...h5.

His games have reached mythic status, often incorrectly. When Arthur Bisguier died in 2017 it was widely reported that Bobby fell asleep against him while playing Game 42. Although Fischer was short of time, Bisguier woke him up. When I read this, it didn't sound entirely right: I witnessed Game 42 being played. I remembered that Fischer was not in time pressure and didn't seem at all tired during the game. Besides, many years ago someone had told me that the game in which Fischer fell asleep was a different one.

The someone who told me that was Arthur Bisguier. I had read about a "sleeping Fischer" game in *Sports Illustrated* and wanted to get Arthur's side of it. So I telephoned him. (That is what people did before texting.) He distinctly remembered

that Bobby was sleepy because he had spent the entire previous night playing high-stakes speed chess. Bisguier could have let Fischer's clock run down "but I didn't want to win that way." And it was definitely a King's Indian Defense they played at the Western Open earlier in 1963, not the Two Knight's Defense that Fischer included in *My 60 Memorable Games*, he said.

There are many other ways I could supplement and correct Bobby's historical record. Instead, I'd like to expand it with games that should have gained attention during his lifetime. Many of his games were overlooked because they were played at fast time controls, at a time when only "classical" chess was respected, or in simuls or training games.

For instance, when Bent Larsen and Fischer arrived in southern California for the Second Piatigorsky Cup in 1966 they played at least one blitz game that has survived:

101

Fischer – Bent Larsen
Speed game, Santa Monica 1966
Alekhine's Defense (B04)

| 1 | e4 | ♘f6 |
| 2 | e5 | ♘d5 |

3	**d4**	**d6**
4	♘**f3**	**dxe5**
5	♘**xe5**	

Larsen had experimented with 4...g6 and 4...♘c6 before. He tried 4...dxe5 in his 1965 Candidates quarterfinals match with Borislav Ivkov.

5	**...**	♘**d7**

He played 5...e6 against Ivkov and was a bit worse after 6 ♕h5 g6 7 ♕f3 ♕e7.

After that game – which he won – it was suggested that Black could try 5...♘d7 and achieve smoother development if he trades knights. But, annotators said, this invites a strong-looking sacrifice on f7.

Nevertheless, Larsen gambled with 5...♘d7 against Mikhail Tal in the Candidates semifinals match that soon followed the Ivkov game. Tal began to calculate 6 ♘xf7 ♔xf7 7 ♕h5+, knowing that Black had to play 7...♔e6 or allow a recapture on d5.

He analyzed further, 8 c4 ♘5f6 9 d5+ ♔d6 10 ♕f7. But the more he calculated, the more he found apparent defenses for Black. In the end he played 6 ♗c4? and only drew.

Tal later tried to prove his intuition was correct. He claimed White could win by force and gave an elaborate analysis that ran 10...♘e5 11 ♗f4 c5 12 ♘c3 a6 13 ♖d1 g6 14 ♗xe5+ ♔xe5 15 d6 g5 16 ♖d2 ♗f5 17 ♖e2+ with mate to follow (17...♔d4 18 ♖e3).

But defenses were found in, for example, 15...♗h6 16 g3 g5. Larsen seemed to be daring Bobby to see who had looked further since the Tal game.

6	♘**xf7**	♔**xf7**
7	♕**h5+**	♔**e6**
8	♕**g4+**	

But maybe it was Fischer who was playing the psychological game. By repeating the position he gave Larsen a way to avoid a draw by repetition – with a blunder.

8	**...**	♔**f7**
9	♕**h5+**	♔**e6**
10	♕**g4+**	♔**d6?**

"Now I play for a win!" Larsen said at this point. But his move loses.

11	**c4**	

11	**...**	♘**7f6**

White regains his piece with a furious attack after 11...♘5f6 12 c5+

because 12...♗d5 or 12...♗c6 allow immediate mate.

The greatest test may be 11...♘7b6 12 ♕g3+ ♔d7. But 13 cxd5 ♘xd5 14 ♘c3 is hardly survivable.

12	♕g3+	♔e6
13	cxd5+	♕xd5?!
14	♘c3	

Morphy chess. Black would be doomed after 14...♕a5 15 ♗c4+ ♔d7 16 0-0, for example. The prettiest finish is 14...♕c6 15 d5+ ♘xd5 16 ♗b5 ♕c5 17 ♕h3+ ♔f7 18 ♕h5+ ♔e6? and now 19 ♗e8! wins.

14	...	♕xd4
15	♗e3	♕b4
16	a3!	♕xb2

Or 16...♕g4 17 ♕xc7 with ♗c4+ to come.

17	♗c4+	♔d7
18	♖d1+	♔e8
19	♘b5!	**Resigns**

After this Larsen switched to 5...g6.

When I included Game 75 in the first edition of this book, few of Fischer's other games from the Herceg-Novi blitz tournament were known. Since then computers have helped us appreciate how dramatic some of those games were. There is no known Fischer game with as many stunning blunders in the finish of this:

102

Mikhail Tal – Fischer
Herceg-Novi blitz tournament 1970

Position after 44 ... a3

Fischer had blundered away a drawable endgame eight moves earlier. Tal's last move, ♔e5, prepared the winning 45 ♔d6!. That would have threatened 46 e7+ and a quick mate.

But with seconds left, Tal didn't see that 45...♖e2! would lose to 46 ♖g4! and the threat of ♖g8 mate.

Then Fischer could have resigned because of 46...♔c8 47 ♖g1 followed by 48 e7 and the unstoppable advance of the h-pawn.

But Tal's **45 d6??** also looked like a winner because 46 e7+ ♔d7 47 ♖c7+! was threatened. The truth emerged after Fischer's **45...♖e2+!**.

White must allow perpetual check, 46 ♔d5 ♖d2+ 47 ♔e5 ♖e2+,

because 47 ♔c6?? would block the c-file and lose to 47...a2!.

Nevertheless, Tal blundered again, **46 ♔f5??**.

Fischer was also close to forfeiting and didn't see that after 46...a2 47 d7 he has the magical move 47...♖e5+!.

Black wins after 48 ♔xe5 a1(♛)+. Or 48 ♔f6! ♖c5! 49 e7+ ♔xd7 50 ♖d4+ ♔c7! 51 e8(♛) a1(♛). Incredibly, White doesn't even have perpetual check in that final position.

In fact, there was a similar win in 47...♔e7! 48 ♖c8 ♖e5+! 49 ♔f4 ♖d5!.

But Fischer played the natural **46...♖f2+??** and Tal responded **47 ♔g4**.

Now 47...♖g2+?? offers to repeat the position (48 ♔f5 ♖f2+). But 48 ♔f3 wins.

The most direct way to draw was 47...♖e2!. Then on 48 e7+ ♔d7 49 ♖c7+ Black must avoid 49...♔e8?? 50 ♖c8+.

He would escape with 49...♔xd6! and 50 ♖xc2 ♖xe7.

But Fischer was not going to give up his last winning chance if one existed. He played **47...a2!**.

This was criticized after the game because White seemed to have winning chances after 48 e7+ ♔d7 49 ♖c7+ ♔xd6 50 e8(♛) ♔xc7. But computers said there was no mixture of queen checks that yield more than a draw.

Fischer's confidence paid off when Tal replied **48 d7?? ♔e7 49 ♖c8.** The former world champion must have expected 49...c1(♛) 50 d8(♛)+ and White wins.

But **49...♖d2!** dashed his hope (50 ♔f5 ♖d5+ 51 ♔-moves ♔xe6). Tal **resigned** after **50 ♖e8+ ♔f6 51 e7 ♖xd7**.

Setting a Bobby Trap

There is only one Fischer – Soltis game in databases. Today it looks like an example of how not to play an opening. The variation I chose was very new. I was hoping to catch Bobby in a new, virtually unknown trap. My thinking was right: Three months later Fischer fell into it against someone else. Here's how:

103

Fischer – Aldo Seidler
Simultaneous exhibition,
Buenos Aires 1971
*Sicilian Defense,
Sveshnikov Variation (B33)*

1	e4	c5
2	♘f3	♘c6
3	d4	

Several months later top Soviet grandmasters studied all of the Fischer games they could find in an effort to prepare Boris Spassky for the upcoming world championship match. They tried to detect subtleties in Fischer's move orders.

One of the GMs, Yuri Averbakh, noticed that Fischer played 3 ♘c3 against me and we transposed after 3...♘f6 4 d4 cxd4 5 ♘xd4. He said Fischer may have rejected 3 d4 because he wanted to avoid 3...cxd4 4 ♘xd4 e5 5 ♘b5 a6 6 ♘d6+ ♗xd6 7 ♕xd6 ♕f6, "of which Soltis has made a good study."

3	...	cxd4
4	♘xd4	♘f6
5	♘c3	e5
6	♘db5	d6
7	♗g5	a6
8	♗xf6	gxf6
9	♘a3	f5

This was how this opening was played before 9...b5! became the main line. Fischer seemed unfamiliar with the position when I played 9...f5. He chose the common sense 10 ♗c4. Instead of 10...♖a7 or 10...♕g5, I ended up with a horrible position after 10...♗g7? 11 ♕h5! 0-0 12 exf5 and got crushed.

The ♕h5 idea looks so good that it apparently made an impression on Fischer.

10	♕h5	d5!

This is what I had hoped to catch Bobby with. Now 11 ♘xd5 ♗xa3 12 bxa3 ♕a5+ 13 c3 ♗e6 is the way I quickly beat a master in 1970.

11	0-0-0!	♗xa3
12	bxa3	fxe4

The more direct 12...♕a5 can lead to 13 ♘xd5 ♗e6 when 14 ♘f6+ offers no more than equality and 14 ♗c4 0-0-0! makes Black's king the safer one.

13	♖xd5	

More of a test is 13 ♘xd5!. Then 13...♗e6 14 ♗c4 is good (14...0-0 15 ♖he1 f5? 16 ♕h6!). White can refute 14...♕a5? with 15 ♘f6+ and 16 ♖d7(+)!.

13	...	♕e7

14 ♘xe4   ♕xa3+

15 ♔d1

Of course, not 15 ♔b1? ♕b4+ and ...♕xe4.

15...♗e6 16 ♘d6+ ♔e7 17 ♕g5+ ♔f8 18 ♕h6+ ♔e7 19 ♕g5+ ♔f8 20 ♕h6+ ♔e7 21 ♕g5+ Draw

My game with Fischer was played in the first double-round of a Manhattan Chess Club speed tournament. This is how Fischer played in the second round.

104

Paul Brandts – Fischer
Speed tournament, New York 1971
King's Indian Defense,
Classical Variation (E98)

1	d4	g6
2	c4	♗g7
3	♘c3	♘f6
4	e4	d6
5	♗e2	0-0
6	♘f3	e5
7	0-0	♘c6
8	d5	♘e7
9	♘e1	♘d7
10	♘d3	f5
11	exf5	

White's 10 ♘d3, instead of 10 ♗e3, was once the main line of the Classical King's Indian Defense.

Fischer had played 11...♘xf5 12 f3 ♘d4 or 12...♘f6 before in this position. Yet he changed his mind when he said retaking with the pawn was "very strong" in *My 60 Memorable Games*.

11	...	gxf5
12	f4	♘g6
13	♗e3	♘f6
14	♕c2	

14 ...   ♖e8

Black usually wants to liquidate the center tension but 14...exf4? 15 ♘xf4 leaves a pawn on f5 that gets in the way of his pieces.

Fischer's 14...♖e8 seems to threaten 15...exf4 16 ♘xf4? ♖xe3. But White can ignore that with 15 ♖ad1 so that 15...exf4 16 ♗c1! and 17 ♘xf4 favors him. A better way to clarify the center was 14...♘e4!.

15	fxe5	dxe5
16	♗g5	h6
17	♗xf6?	♕xf6
18	♕b3?	e4!

Now 19 ♘f2 ♘f4 offers Black a good attack against g2. And 20...♕b6, hoping for an endgame, is also good.

19	♘f4	♘xf4
20	♖xf4	♕g5
21	♖ff1	♕e3+?
22	♔h1	

22 ...   ♕g5

Fischer was stubborn but willing to acknowledge when he made a mistake. He could have ended matters with 21...♗e5 and 22...♕h4 (23 g3 ♗xg3! 24 hxg3 ♕xg3+ 25 ♔h1 ♔h8 and ...♖g8). So, he tried again.

23 c5

White would be back in the game after 23 ♘b5 ♗e5 24 d6!.

23	...	♔h8
24	♖ad1	♗e5
25	g3	♖g8
26	♘b1?	f4!

The outcome would have been in doubt after 26 d6! but now the attack cannot be stopped.

27	♖g1	f3
28	♗c4	♕h5
29	♕e3	

29 ...   ♖xg3

Black's threats included 29...f2. But that still works – 29...f2 30 ♕xf2 ♗g4 and 31...♗xd1 or 31...♗f3+. Fischer's move could have led to a routine finish after 30 ♖xg3 ♗xg3 31 ♖d2 ♗f5.

30 ♕xe4   ♕xh2+!

White Resigns

"Lost" Fischer

When collections claiming to contain all of Bobby's games first appeared, they usually didn't include his simultaneous exhibition games. That meant 1964 was a virtual blank because he entered no tournaments that year. Yet more than 200 Fischer games survived, from his cross-country simul tour. Thanks to John Donaldson and other researchers, these "lost" games can now be enjoyed.

Perhaps Fischer's most impressive simul was in Davis, California in April 1964. Fischer played under tournament conditions – with clocks – against ten opponents. Six of them were rated Experts and most of them soon became strong masters. His opponent in this game won the Northern California Championship that year.

105

Fischer – Roy Hoppe
Clock simultaneous, Davis 1964
French Defense,
Winawer Variation (C16)

1	e4	e6
2	d4	d5

3	♘c3	♗b4
4	e5	♘e7
5	a3	♗xc3+
6	bxc3	b6
7	♕g4	♘g6

In a typical Fischer simul, his weakest opponents replied 1...e5 and were lost after a dozen or so moves of a Two Knights Defense, Evans Gambit or King's Gambit.

Here Black chooses a then-popular line of the Winawer Variation. Fischer's opponent likely knew of Fischer – Ivkov, Santiago 1959, which went 8 ♗g5 ♕d7 9 h4 h6 10 ♗d2 h5 11 ♕f3 ♕a4 and led to a Black edge and victory after 12 ♗d3 ♗a6 13 g4? hxg4 14 ♕xg4 ♗xd3.

8	h4	h5
9	♕g3	

What put the 6...b6 line out of business was the realization that 9 ♕d1! defends White's vulnerable queenside. He would then regain his pawn favorably after 9...♘xh4 10 g3.

9	...	♗a6
10	♗xa6	♘xa6
11	♘e2	c5!

A logical move but there doesn't seem to be a record of it being played before this game. Instead, 11...♘b8 was the main line, followed by the too-slow ...♘c6-a5-c4.

12	♘f4	♘xf4
13	♗xf4	♔f8!
14	♗g5	♕d7
15	0-0	♖c8

Black eyes the win of a c-pawn after ...cxd4. But he has taken so much time that White can ignore Black's plan.

A good idea is 16 a4! followed by ♖fb1 and pressure on the b-file. For example, 16...cxd4 17 cxd4 ♖xc2 18 ♕b3 ♖c4 19 ♕b5!, when Black's failure to castle means his other rook cannot help defend.

16 f4!

Let's add some context: This was *not* the game that Fischer was most concerned with at this point in the simul. He was dead lost on another board. Somehow Fischer managed to win that game, against John Blackstone, who would represent the United States in the World Student Team Championship in 1968. And his game against Ojars Celle was reaching a climax that Fischer was so proud of that he included his victory in *My 60 Memorable Games*.

16	...	♘b8

Fischer's idea was to meet 16...cxd4 17 cxd4 ♖xc2 with 18 f5!.

If Black then allows 19 f6 g6 White can switch to the queenside with ♖fc1. Black's heavy pieces are outgunned because his h8-rook can't play. And 18...exf5? 19 ♛d3 ♛c8 20 ♖xf5 exposes f7.

Black's 16...♘b8 avoids tactics in which ♛d3 attacks the knight. But it allows 17 f5 exf5 18 dxc5! because then 18...♖xc5 19 e6! sets up 20 ♛xb8+. White would also be better after 18...bxc5 19 ♛d3 g6? 20 ♗f6 or 20 ♖ad1. Fischer preferred:

17 ♖ad1!   cxd4

18 cxd4   ♘c6

White's 17th move seemed to be just a way of anticipating an attack on the d4-pawn. But by lining up his rook against the black queen he created tactical chances, even though the d-file was closed.

19 c4

This move reveals a nice idea that could have been improved by 19 f5!. The point is that 19...exf5 20 c4! blows the center open (20...dxc4? 21 d5! ♘d8 22 e6! and wins).

The drawback to 19 c4 is that 19...dxc4 is playable. Then 20 f5 ♔g8 meets the threat of 21 fxe6. White gets nothing visible from 21 ♗f6 ♖h7 or 21 f6 g6 so the game's outcome depends on unclear continuations such as 21 fxe6 fxe6 22 ♛f3.

19 ...   ♘e7?

20 ♗xe7+!   ♔xe7

The center strategy wins after 20...♛xe7 21 cxd5 exd5 22 f5! followed by f5-f6 or an invasion of heavy pieces. For example, 22...♖h6 23 ♖c1! ♖hc6 24 f6! or 23...♛d8 24 ♛g5 is hard to meet.

21 ♛xg7   ♖cg8?!

22 ♛f6+   ♔e8

23 f5!   dxc4

24 d5!

After 24...exf5 Fischer could choose between the winning 25 e6 and 25 d6 followed by 26 e6! fxe6 27 ♖fe1 and ♖xe6+.

24...exd5 25 e6! ♛e7 26 exf7+ ♛xf7 27 ♖de1+ ♔f8 28 ♛d6+ ♔g7 29 ♖e7 ♛xe7 30 ♛xe7+ ♔h6 31 ♖e1 ♖g7 32 ♛f6+ ♔h7 33 ♖e7 Resigns

Fischer won all ten games in the exhibition. The last cache of "lost" games to be found were Bobby's training games with "Gliga" in 1992, when he was preparing for his rematch with Boris Spassky. Perhaps the best of them was this:

106

Fischer – Svetozar Gligorić
Training match, Sveti Stefan 1992
English Opening,
Symmetrical Variation (A30)

	1	c4	c5

Fischer was familiar with this position as he had played the Black side against Tigran Petrosian (twice) and Larsen during 1970-1. They played 2 ♘f3, to which he replied 2...g6.

2	b3	♘c6
3	g3	♘f6
4	♗g2	d5
5	cxd5	♘xd5

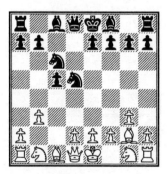

6   f4!

We are in new territory. Black would equalize if he could safely play ...e5. A key game in the 1971 Petrosian – Fischer match had gone 1 ♘f3 c5 2 b3 d5 3 ♗b2? f6! and

Fischer had the superior center after ...e5.

6	...	e6
7	♗b2	

7   ...   h5!

A strong idea. Now 8 ♘f3 h4! 9 ♘xh4? ♖xh4! 10 gxh4 ♕xh4+ 11 ♔f1 ♘xf4 sets up a murderous attack with ...e5 and ...♗h3.

8	♘h3	♘f6
9	♘f2	h4
10	♘c3	

Fischer's friend William Lombardy was very fond of the kingside arrangement of a pawn at f4 and knight at f2. He wrote about this is the April 1969 issue of *Chess Review.*

10	...	hxg3
11	hxg3	♖xh1+
12	♗xh1	♗d7
13	e3	

A good alternative plan for White was ♘a3, at move ten for example, followed by ♘c4. Fischer prefers to expand (g3-g4-g5) on the kingside, which has turned from a Black strength to somewhat of a weakness after the trade of rooks.

13	...	♕a5

14	g4!	0-0-0
15	g5	♘e8
16	♕h5	

| 16 | ... | f5 |

Black had a worthy alternative in 16...♘d6, which stops ♕xf7 while preparing ...c4. Gligoric was likely surprised by Fischer's next move. Or was he used to Bobby's attempts at pawn-grabbing by then?

17	♗xc6!?	♗xc6
18	♕f7	♘c7
19	♘d3	

The threat of ♘e5xc6 is worrisome. Fischer was probably willing to accept a little discomfort (19...♗d6 20 ♕xg7 ♕a6 21 ♘f2 ♗f3) to be up a pawn.

19	...	♖xd3
20	♕xf8+	♘e8
21	♕e7!	

Black has two weak pawns, at e6 and g7. Potential endgames favor White (21...♗d7 22 0-0-0 ♕d8 23 ♕xd8+ and ♖h1-h8.)

| 21 | ... | ♖d6 |
| 22 | 0-0-0 | ♕d8 |

| 23 | ♕xd8+ | |

One of the ideas that's been lurking beneath the surface for some time was ♘b1 followed by ♘a3-c4 and/or ♗e5. Here 23 ♕f8! would make 24 ♘b1! a threat.

| 23 | ... | ♖xd8 |
| 24 | ♘a4 | b6 |

The "Fischer endgame" of rook and bishop versus rook and knight arises after 24...♗xa4 25 bxa4 and could turn into a rout after 25...g6? 26 ♖h1!, e.g. 26...♘d6 27 ♖h7 ♖g8 28 ♗e5 ♘e8 29 ♖e7.

25	♗e5	g6
26	♘b2	♖d7
27	♘c4	♗f3
28	♖f1	♗d5

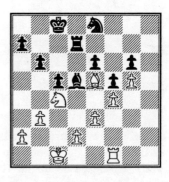

| 29 | ♖d1 | |

White's plan to invade on the h-file has failed (29 ♖f2 ♖h7) and he can switch to a fall-back scheme of 29 a4 followed by ♔c2-c3 and then b3-b4 or d2-d4.

29	...	♖h7
30	a4!	♖h3
31	♔c2	♔b7
32	♔c3	a6

33 b4!

The threat is 34 bxc5 bxc5 35 ♖b1+ ♔c6 36 ♖b6+ or 35...♔a7? 36 ♖b8.

Black could have avoided this with ...♘c7 or ...♗xc4 earlier. For example, 32...♘c7 33 ♗xc7 ♗xc4! (not 33...♔xc7 34 ♘e5) with a likely draw.

33	...	cxb4+
34	♔xb4	♖h2

35 a5! ♗f3

Black's knight is stalemated in key variations and would be lost, for example, after 35...bxa5+ 36 ♘xa5+ ♔b6? 37 ♖c1! and ♖c8.

36	♖c1	b5
37	♘b6	♗c6

38 ♘c8!

Now on 38...♖h7 White continues 39 ♗f6 and ♘e7 as in the game.

38	...	♖xd2
39	♘e7	♗d7

Once again the knight can be lost (39...♗e4 40 ♖c8). But White also wins after ♘xg6 and the advance of the g6-pawn.

40 ♘xg6 ♖a2 41 ♘e7 ♖a4+ 42 ♔b3 ♖e4 43 ♖d1! ♖xe3+ 44 ♔b2 ♖e2+ 45 ♔c1 Resigns

In view of 45...♗c6 46 ♖d8.

Bobby and Magnus

There have been many players so far in the 21st Century who say they were inspired by Fischer. There is one who plays quite a bit like him. Of course, he is a world champion: Magnus Carlsen plays the kind of stamina-driven chess that characterized Bobby at his best. Here is the most Magnus-like example from *My 60 Memorable Games*.

107

Fischer – Vasily Smyslov
Capablanca Memorial, Havana 1965
Ruy Lopez, Steinitz Variation (C77)

1	e4	e5
2	♘f3	♘c6
3	♗b5	a6
4	♗a4	♘f6
5	d3	

The d3 treatment of the Ruy Lopez was considered innocuous in Fischer's day, when 5 0-0 was considered virtually forced.

5	...	d6
6	c3	♗e7

Fischer was a big fan of Wilhelm Steinitz, who explored this system nearly a century before. But this is the only time Fischer played it that we know of. It is *his opponent* who was the world's expert: Vasily Smyslov had played this position eight times as White.

7	♘bd2	0-0
8	♘f1	

Strange? No, this move was a Steinitz idea, to bring the knight to e3 or g3 before castling. A 2010 game saw 6...g6 7 ♘bd2 ♗g7 8 ♘f1. The players were two guys named Carlsen and Caruana.

8	...	b5
9	♗b3	d5
10	♕e2	dxe4
11	dxe4	♗e6

Fischer said he was surprised Smyslov allowed the doubling of his e-pawns. This was 19th century thinking – only to be revived in the 21st century. In Fischer's day, doubled pawns in similar positions were not considered a serious weakness and White often avoided ♗xe6. In this tournament Fischer lost badly in a doubled e-pawn middlegame to Ratmir Kholmov, thanks to pre-game preparation by Smyslov.

12	♗xe6	fxe6
13	♘g3	

13	...	♕d7

Kholmov later claimed that 13...♗d6 14 0-0 ♘e7 is not as bad as Fischer said, after 15 c4 ♕e8 16 a4 ♘g6 17 axb5 axb5 18 ♖xa8 ♕xa8 18 cxb5 ♕a4. But 17 b4 ♗xb4 18 axb5 axb5 19 ♖xa8 ♕xa8 20 cxb5 may be more of a test.

14	0-0	♖ad8
15	a4	♕d3
16	♕xd3	♖xd3
17	axb5	axb5
18	♖a6	♖d6
19	♔h1	

Black threatened to eliminate pressure with 19...♘d4 20 ♖xd6 ♘xf3+. But now he could have approached equality with 19...b4! 20 cxb4 ♘xb4 and 21 ♖a7 ♖c6 22 ♘xe5 ♖c2, with enough compensation for a pawn, as Fischer pointed out.

19	...	♘d7
20	♗e3	♖d8
21	h3	

Fischer repeatedly passes up the thematic b2-b4 and Smyslov rejects the equally thematic ...b4. For example, 21...b4 22 cxb4 ♘xb4 23 ♖a7 ♖c6 looks solid. However, after 22 ♖fa1! bxc3 23 bxc3 and ♖a8 White has the kind of miniscule advantage that Carlsen often exploited in games that lasted more than 60 moves.

21	...	h6
22	♖fa1	♘db8
23	♖a8	♖d1+

24	♔h2	♖xa1
25	♖xa1	♘d7?

26 b4!

Black missed his last opportunity for 25...b4!. Now White makes almost imperceptible progress.

26	...	♔f7
27	♘f1	♗d6
28	g3	♘f6
29	♘1d2	♔e7
30	♖a6	♘b8

Even computers realize how bad Black is after the next move. White's advantage wouldn't be evident for several moves after 30...♔d7 31 ♘e1! followed by ♘d3, f2-f3 and ♘b3-c5+.

31 ♖a5 c6 32 ♔g2 ♘bd7 33 ♔f1 ♖c8 34 ♘e1 ♘e8 35 ♘d3 ♘c7 36 c4 bxc4 37 ♘xc4 ♘b5 38 ♖a6 ♔f6

305

39 ♗c1!

Another Magnus-move. There is no defense to ♗b2 and f2-f4.

39...♗b8 40 ♗b2 c5 41 ♘b6! ♘xb6 42 ♖xb6 c4 43 ♘c5 c3 and Black resigns

Asked to name an ideal player, Magnus Carlsen said in 2015:

"Bobby Fischer ... The precision and energy that he played with is unmatched in the history of chess."

Index of Opponents
(numbers refer to games)

Index of Openings

(numbers refer to games)

ECO Openings Index
(numbers refer to games)

A01	80, 87		B50	60
A02	36		B51	17
A25	73		B53	21, 40
A30	106		B57	11, 12
A35	83		B72	22
A36	88		B77	5, 37
A49	65		B86	49
A50	85		B87	4
A57	59		B88	9, 64, 93
A69	57		B90	32, 39
A71	67		B91	72
A77	96		B92	34
B01	41		B97	29, 51
B03	89, 98		B99	3, 10
B04	101		C00	66, 84
B09	45		C15	77
B10	28, 56, 84		C16	105
B11	13, 69		C19	81, 91
B13	74		C33	47, 71
B23	63		C42	82
B25	48		C43	30
B31	100		C59	43
B32	35		C63	75
B33	103		C69	58, 86
B35	25		C70	46
B41	8		C72	26
B42	95		C77	107
B44	55, 94		C78	2
B45	7		C89	50
B47	24, 78, 90		C92	52, 68

C95	61, 97, 99	D98	38
C96	33	E45	54
C98	6	E51	18
D38	14, 16	E61	70, 79
D41	42	E68	53
D42	27	E70	19, 20
D53	31	E82	76
D79	44	E97	62, 92
D95	15	E98	23, 104
D96	1